managing your **e-commerce business**

second edition

BRENDA KIENAN

PUBLISHED BY
Microsoft Press
A Division of Microsoft Corporation
One Microsoft Way
Redmond, Washington 98052-6399

Library of Congress Cataloging-in-Publication Data
Kienan, Brenda.
    Managing Your E-Commerce Business--2nd ed. / Brenda Kienan.
      p. cm.
    Includes index.
    ISBN 0-7356-1275-7
    1. Electronic commerce.   I. Title.

   HF5548.32 .K538 2001
   658.8'4--dc21   2001016255

Printed and bound in the United States of America.

1 2 3 4 5 6 7 8 9   QWE   6 5 4 3 2 1

Distributed in Canada by Penguin Books Canada Limited.

A CIP catalogue record for this book is available from the British Library.

Figure 7-3: Copyright © 2000 Tauber Kienan Associates. All rights reserved. Reproduced with permission.

Figure 7-8: Copyright © 2000 Aveus. All rights reserved. Reproduced with permission.

An earlier version of this book was published under the title *Small Business Solutions for E-Commerce*, copyright © 2000 by Brenda Kienan.

Microsoft Press books are available through booksellers and distributors worldwide. For further information about international editions, contact your local Microsoft Corporation office or contact Microsoft Press International directly at fax (425) 936-7329. Visit our Web site at mspress.microsoft.com. Send comments to *mspinput@microsoft.com*.

Acquisitions Editor: Alex Blanton
Project Editor: Denise Bankaitis
Manuscript Editor: Ina Chang

Part No. X08-04142

For Dan, who quietly occupies my heart,
And for Claire, who dances there.

Contents at a Glance

Table of Contents

Part 2

Creating Identity and Attracting Customers

Part 3

Building Your E-Commerce Website

Part 4

Maintaining, Promoting, and Succeeding

Acknowledgments

Despite the rolling blackouts, crashing servers, and an earthquake, this project seemed as smooth as lacquer. For making that so, I thank the many fine people mentioned on this page.

Alex Blanton and Christey Bahn, at Microsoft Press, provided opportunity, guidance, and steady encouragement. Anne Hamilton and David Clark have been respected colleagues and pals through many years and several venues. Denise Bankaitis, Ina Chang, Jean Ross, and Julie Xiao kept the language, schedule, screen shots, and facts all on track. Dan Latimer, Jim Kramer, and Joel Panchot transformed text and art into an actual book. Holly Viola copyedited to perfection, and Liz Cunningham painstakingly compiled the index. Kudos to them all.

David and Sherry Rogelberg at Studio B provided their usual fine and wise counsel, for which I am always grateful.

Maureen Nelson researched the first edition—it simply would not have happened without her. Bob Walker, Bruce Molloy, Brian Jeffries, Christina Cheney, Gloria Keene, Leslie Hamilton, Alicia Eckley, Dennis Woo, Barbara Holmes, Kim Albee, Kim Nies, Melissa Rach, and Michael Stein all contributed insight, commentary, or influence; Michael Gross provided invaluable advice regarding the legal chapter; and my students are always inspirational in their inquisitiveness and enthusiasm. Thanks all around.

Nina Duhl somehow creates order in a chaotic existence, while John and Aida Bjorklund, Kent Gerard, Ana Ortiz, and Charlie Wright plain and simply make the daily grind possible; they are also all a pleasure to know.

Special thanks to Dan Tauber, Claire Tauber, Rion Dugan, Lonnie Moseley, and Cordell Sloan, who kept humor and perspective intact while wife, mother, sister, and friend vanished behind a computer screen...*again*.

Also to friends and family who make life the adventure it really ought to be: Joani and Jessi Buehrle; Sharon Crawford and Charlie Russel; the Cunninghams; RD2D; Dames Who Dine; Fred Frumberg; Jessica, Martin, Lori, and Jacob Grant; Mai Le Bazner, Katri Foster, and Peter Bazner; various McArdles and sundry Undercoffers; Carolyn Miller; Wynn Moseley and her family; Margaret Tauber; Ron and Frances Tauber; Judy Tauber; Savitha Varadan; and Robert E. Williams III.

Introduction

The e-commerce industry holds enormous promise. It has been the stuff of dreams and instant fortunes, but it is also business, and anyone who knows beans about business knows that promise and dreams don't automatically lead to success. Launching and managing an e-commerce venture for long-term success takes the same smarts, drive, and follow-through that's required for any other enterprise. It also takes insight into the ways that e-commerce differs from traditional business.

Note

E-commerce isn't just *selling* online—it's any kind of business that's conducted online. So whether your business is consumer-oriented or business-to-business, and no matter what its purpose (sales, service, information, manufacturing, distribution, education, entertainment, or you name it), this book has something to offer you. And even if you plan to continue doing business primarily in the brick-and-mortar world, this book will help you make decisions about your company's online component.

What This Book Can Do for You

Managing Your E-Commerce Business, Second Edition will show you—the e-commerce manager, executive, or entrepreneur—where to start, how to proceed, and which tools and technologies can assist you. This book is a practical guide to e-commerce management. It offers valuable information about everything from developing online strategies to organizing a site plan and overseeing a transaction system. It provides insight into customer relationship management and reaching for profitability. And it covers how to create branding—an instantly recognizable identity for your e-commerce initiative.

This book also reveals what to consider in building a site. It introduces how to maintain freshness and quality, address legal matters, promote the site, and decide whether to house it on your own server or have it hosted elsewhere. Along the way, this book highlights the products and services that make building and maintaining an e-commerce site easier and more manageable.

Because each e-commerce initiative requires solutions tailored to it and to the business goals it serves, this book does not offer one-size-fits-all answers. Rather, it guides you with the means to ask the right questions so you can create strategies that will meet your specific needs. It offers real-world examples and solutions in clear language and provides pointers to additional information available online. It also includes tips and advice gleaned from interviews with people who know e-commerce inside and out.

Note

Many e-commerce principles forged in the big-budget corporate world are applicable to ventures of all sizes, but if you have limited resources, you must deal with special issues ranging from how to keep staff size within reason to knowing how to target and attract users to your website. Throughout this book, you'll find pointers for maximizing resources and facilitating productivity.

Who This Book Is For

You are sharp, resourceful, but perhaps new to e-commerce. You need a clear, practical overview of how business, marketing, content, design, and technology work together in e-commerce. You might be an executive in a large corporation, a manager in a 250-person company who has overall operations and profit and loss responsibility, or the sole operator of a small business. You might envision a quickly expanding digital market for your company's products or perhaps an online venue for tapping a local market for your company's services. In any case, you are responsible for managing the website and for focusing on some or all of its strategy, content, production, and perhaps even technical implementation.

In other words, this book is for any of the various people who will attend to the running of a website, whether the site is an online component of an existing brick-and-mortar operation or an exclusively online venture. This book assumes that readers know how to use a web browser, have used the Internet, and might even have a little background in creating web pages. But this book is not for programmers or would-be programmers. It is for those who need a guide to making business decisions about e-commerce.

What This Book Covers

Written by an Internet professional with years of management, marketing, and content experience, this book covers launching and running an e-commerce website, from a management perspective. It is not a technology book; it's a business book. This book will show you what it takes to succeed in e-commerce and how to assess whether you are succeeding. *Managing Your E-Commerce Business, Second Edition* describes, soup-to-nuts, how to forge a strategy and how to follow through on it. It also describes—from a business strategy perspective—technologies that will help you in your e-commerce endeavors. To use this book, you don't have to be a developer—you don't even have to know one.

The book is organized into four parts that cover how to manage an e-commerce business from planning the site all the way through building it, promoting it, assessing its success, and keeping it fresh.

Part One: Planning for E-Commerce

Part One begins with setting goals because establishing clear and achievable objectives is the foundation of success. (The goals you set also determine how you will measure your success.) Guiding you onward, Part One then delves into identifying your target market, your competitors, and the opportunity before you, as well as writing a business plan or project plan. Pointers for budgeting lead into what it will cost to build large, mid-sized, and smaller websites. Part One ends by introducing you to the new spin e-commerce puts on traditional issues of intellectual property, copyright, trademark, and business law.

Part Two: Creating Identity and Attracting Customers

Part Two is all about customers—establishing an identity they'll recognize, providing excellent customer care, and building a customer base. Here you'll find out how classic branding strategies apply to e-commerce as well as how you can create a clear, consistent, and visible identity for your product, service, or company. You'll discover how you can use e-mail newsletters and discussion groups to establish a one-on-one relationship with your customers. You'll get tips for how to create that powerful but elusive experience called "community" in an online setting, and you'll find out how to transform a community bond among users into long-term customer loyalty to your site and your brand.

Part Three: Building Your E-Commerce Website

Part Three is concerned with planning your website and implementing your plan. It describes the vital-to-your-success preproduction process, including organizing content, creating a site architecture, and working up specifications that will guide the building of your website. Whether you plan to build the site with your own in-house resources or take the project to a designer or developer, you'll find the guidance you need here. You'll gain a general understanding of the technical infrastructure of a website so you can communicate with developers and assess their work. You'll be introduced to HTML, XML, Microsoft FrontPage, working with graphics, and adding interactivity. You'll gain an understanding of basic design issues as well as what can be done with wireless and broadband. You'll also get insight into hiring and managing designers, developers, and other Internet professionals. And finally, you'll learn what you need to know about platforms, servers, hosting, databases, and transaction systems.

Part Four: Maintaining, Promoting, and Succeeding

Part Four reveals methods you can use to promote your e-commerce venture and assess its success based on measures that are appropriate to your goals. As you know, a business does not simply have a grand opening and then achieve success. Daily, ongoing attention is required. E-commerce websites are no exception; for your e-commerce venture to succeed, you'll have to form a plan for marketing the site both online and in traditional media. Whether your promotional budget is large or limited, Part Four will assist you in making the most of it.

Here you'll also discover the ins and outs of listing your site with search engines, directories, and portals (such as AltaVista, Google, MSN Search, and Yahoo!) and how to investigate the number of backlinks leading from other sites to yours. You'll get tips for keeping your website's content and appearance fresh. You'll find out how to measure your site's success based on the goals you set in Chapter 1, but the insight doesn't stop there. Part Four goes where other books don't—it ends by telling you what modifications you can make to improve your site based on the statistics and feedback you gather.

Appendix and Glossary

As a bonus, the Appendix at the end of the book describes how you can augment your e-commerce website with an intranet, which provides internal information to your staff or team, or with an extranet, which provides vital information to vendors, sales reps, or buyers. For your quick reference, a glossary lists various e-commerce and business terms you'll want to be familiar with as you venture into this field.

Contacting the Author

As you meet the challenges inherent in e-commerce, if you'd like to share tips and strategies that you find useful, you can contact the author. Simply send e-mail to the following address:

ecommerce@tauberkienan.com

For e-commerce articles, tools, and strategies, visit the E-Commerce Management Center at the following URL:

www.tauberkienan.com

Contacting Microsoft Press

You can also contact Microsoft Press with any comments or concerns regarding this book. Every effort has been made to ensure the accuracy of this book. Microsoft Press provides corrections for books through the World Wide Web at the following address:

http://mspress.microsoft.com/support/

If you have comments, questions, or ideas regarding this book, please send them to Microsoft Press using either of the following methods:

Postal Mail:

Microsoft Press
Attn: Managing Your E-Commerce Business, Second Edition *Editor*
One Microsoft Way
Redmond, WA 98052-6399

E-mail:

MSPINPUT@MICROSOFT.COM

Please note that Microsoft product support is not offered through the preceding mail addresses. For product support information, visit the Microsoft Product Support Services website at *http://search.support.microsoft.com.*

Chapter 1

Focusing Your E-Commerce Goals

E-commerce is on the rise. Industry analysts and market research firms report that online business trends have far exceeded expectations. According to Giga Information Group, e-commerce revenues could reach between $580 billion and $970 billion in 2002. International Data Corporation (IDC), a research giant, has projected that worldwide e-commerce sales could reach $1.6 trillion by 2003. And these figures don't even account for the cost savings associated with e-commerce ventures such as marketing, procurement, customer service, and improvements in operations. Your first question might well be whether (and how) you can get a piece of this enormous pie. Your second question ought to be how you can manage your e-commerce venture for long-term success.

Whether your e-commerce venture is a new "dot-com" enterprise or an extension of your existing "brick-and-mortar" business, in order to parlay it into consumer-oriented or business-to-business success, you must act with the same keen business savvy you apply to any venture. You must also understand the unique nature of e-commerce and how it differs from traditional business.

Just What Is E-Commerce?

E-commerce is, basically, doing business online. In its most obvious form, e-commerce is selling products online to consumers, but in fact, any business conducted electronically is e-commerce. E-commerce is simply the creating, managing, and extending of commercial relationships online.

Successful e-commerce ventures might involve purchasing, developing and designing products, managing production or manufacturing, marketing and comarketing, sales, service, collaboration among businesses or affiliates, distribution of products, research, dissemination of information, setting up commercial communities, educating, entertaining, and probably all sorts of other business activities that haven't yet been thought up. Here are just a few examples of e-commerce in action:

- Consumers learning about products online before buying at a "real world" (offline) location

- Consumers ordering products online and receiving them either via traditional shipping or via the Internet

- Students participating in online education programs to receive degrees or professional training

- Citizens renewing their drivers' licenses, registering their cars, filing their taxes, applying for building permits, or conducting other business with government agencies online

- Businesses selling products and services online to consumers or to other businesses

- Businesses tracking projects online or transferring electronic files (such as images, database records, or text files) via the Internet

- Businesses providing technical or customer support 24 hours a day, seven days a week

- Entertainment and other venues promoting their events online or even creating online events

- Governments and their agencies receiving and processing requests for proposals and other procurement documents via the Internet

- Educational institutions integrating online components and research techniques into the everyday classroom

Perhaps because it's an emerging industry, e-commerce also spawns a lot of myths. Novices to e-commerce might think that it's all about taking online orders and that once someone sets up shop, scores of customers will immediately buy out warehouses full of widgets. Not so. Running a successful business in the virtual world takes as much savvy as running a successful business in the "real" world. Some people think that because e-commerce is technical, it must be expensive. Also not so. Fantastic e-commerce sites don't always require the services of highly paid programmers, but they aren't built on the cheap by any handy college student, either. And finally, a solid e-commerce venture doesn't have to include all the latest technical marvels—Java applets, Flash, Extensible Markup Language (XML), and whatever's next. None of this is necessary for a winning e-commerce site. What is necessary? Smart planning, implementation, promotion, and maintenance. Read on.

E-Commerce Opportunities Come in All Sizes

At first glance, large companies might appear to dominate e-commerce. Dot-coms and brick-and-mortar companies with booming online divisions appear to be everywhere. But even smaller businesses, according to Giga, can parlay niche specialties and local service into consumer-oriented and business-to-business success.

An online resource devoted to growing businesses, Microsoft bCentral (*www.bcentral.com*), goes beyond the typical information portal model to provide a comprehensive set of integrated services that can help companies improve their business. bCentral delivers real, practical services geared toward getting an e-commerce venture started, building a website, promoting and marketing online, and simply managing a business more effectively.

What It Takes to Win

To win in e-commerce, it is said, you must be first, be the best, or be different. Being first gives you the extra edge of defining a market and setting a benchmark against which others who follow will be measured. But remember this: Even if you're first to offer a product or service and define a market, if your offering is mediocre, someone else can swoop in with a better product. And that someone else will also have the benefit of selling to a defined market—the market you have so graciously identified. You will have mapped out a road others can follow, and if they're smart, they'll look over your target market and come up with ways to serve it better and differently. Your best bet in e-commerce is to be first, of course, but you also want to be extremely adaptable so that, as times and technologies change, you can be the best and be unique.

Tip

Microsoft's websites offer e-commerce insight, tools, events, and information about e-commerce communities; to find out more, start at *www.microsoft.com*. Also, Tauber Kienan Associates provides an E-Commerce Management Center that offers strategy, insight, and tools at *www.tauberkienan.com*.

What E-Commerce Can Do

Forrester Research reports that in the year 2000 alone, 11 million households joined the ranks of online shoppers. When the numbers came in for the year 2000 holiday shopping season, e-commerce sales volume had risen 30 percent over the previous year. And according to the Gartner Group, more than 500,000 companies are expected to use e-marketplaces to buy or sell goods by 2005.

The numbers are just stunning—and so are the various uses of e-commerce. Consider these examples:

- A designer and manufacturer of boutique fashion accessories puts its product catalog online so freelance representatives all over the country can show the new line to buyers. Online customer management tools provide the reps with information on which customers have made repeat purchases of which items and allow the reps to receive inquiries that are routed automatically to e-mail, pagers, or cell phones. This online management system also allows managers to track how responsive reps are to customers and reward reps who achieve the best customer relationships.

- A company that is compelled by business realities to provide only its most popular products in its brick-and-mortar retail stores offers specialty items to consumers via its website, extending the customer base and maximizing revenues for the entire product line.

- An *e-service* (a service that is provided electronically—for example, online tracking of packages that have been shipped) can locate, communicate with, and join forces with another e-service (say, instant messaging to a cell phone or other wireless device) to provide users with a seamless added-value experience.

- A printer accepts a file from a designer via a website, and the printer then tracks the job online so that the designer can see the job's progress and know when to come in for press checks.

- A company that delivers gravel to its construction customers sets up a website that allows foremen to place orders any time, day or night, for next-day delivery. The service is integrated with inventory and shipping systems, contacting the foreman via pager or cell phone to confirm delivery occurs.

- A nonprofit social services agency provides teenagers with a forum in which to ask questions anonymously via e-mail, with responses posted in a searchable database for others to see. The nonprofit agency also conducts both fundraising and social advocacy efforts via e-mail newsletters and direct response e-mail campaigns.

When many people think of e-commerce, they think only of traditional retail sales in an online setting. But consider the California gold rush. In the mid-nineteenth century, scores of people hoping to strike it rich flocked to California, where gold had been discovered in a riverbed. Most people imagined themselves quickly staking a mining claim and easily finding gold. Most didn't find any. But others saw the opportunity created by the sudden influx, and companies such as Levi Strauss & Co. (the jeans maker) and Wells Fargo (the financial institution) got their starts serving the needs of those who headed west to seek their fortunes.

The moral: Think outside the box. Your e-commerce venture might best be developed not to sell to consumers online, but instead to serve others already in e-commerce or brick-and-mortar businesses that hope to get involved. Of course, you probably won't want to change directions altogether if your business already exists and you simply want to extend your offerings to new, online markets. But even so, consider imaginative opportunities for creatively serving your customers. Don't simply sell flowers online; sell fresh flowers direct from the flower market, or track special events for your repeat customers so that you can send them reminders and offer to fill their flower needs. Think about your specific customer base and what would set you apart from your competitors. Give people what they want and need.

Also, keep in mind that although technology is great—without it, there would be no e-commerce—technology is a tool, not a business model. It's easy to be blinded by super-cool bells and whistles, but technology can't guarantee the success of your e-commerce venture. In e-commerce, as in the 3-D world, success comes from smart thinking and a dash of good luck. You'll need a plan for your e-commerce venture, and this plan should be based on a workable strategy.

Note

The consulting arm of Deloitte and Touche, in a published paper on business-to-business e-commerce, points to factors required for the success of any e-commerce venture: sound strategic planning, the necessity of working with existing models and channels (unless they represent major inefficiencies), the retention of customers, and the necessity of optimizing value to the customer.

As innovative business models and solid practices evolve for e-commerce, public acceptance is widening and more and more companies are joining the fray. Before you jump in, ask yourself some key questions.

Will e-commerce improve your business?

You almost certainly would not open additional branches or create a franchise program without solid indications that success would result. Yet it's remarkable how many people launch websites without thinking through what it will take and how the site will impact their business. Before you launch an e-commerce venture, read through this book. Also, take a good look at Microsoft's online e-commerce resources. Consider how you will build and fund your venture, how it will serve your customers, and what return you can expect on your investment.

Do you have what it takes?

Do you have the time and resources required to accomplish your specific e-commerce goals? To answer this question, you must know as much as you can about your goals and what it will take to fulfill them. You need to know what technology, time, funding, and promotional resources you will need to make a go of things.

Creating a business or project plan (as discussed later in this chapter) might not seem like a trip to the beach, but it's essential if you plan to seek funding for your venture. Even if you plan to fund the venture yourself or launch it as an adjunct to your existing business, going through the exercise of thinking through the issues will help you focus on answers to the relevant questions. To start your deliberations, consider what you plan to accomplish by building an e-commerce website.

> ### Not Every E-Commerce Purchase Takes Place Online
>
> What do people shop for online more than anything else? Cars and car parts. Despite the fact that you can't test drive a car online and most actual car purchases take place in traditional dealerships, a CommerceNet/Nielsen Internet Demographic Survey study showed that in one recent year 18.2 million shoppers in the United States and Canada had checked into cars and car parts on the Internet. The numbers for more easily deliverable products, such as books (12.6 million shoppers), computers (12.4 million), clothes (11.6 million), and CDs and videos (11.4 million) lagged behind cars. Online shopping—comparing prices, features, and services—sometimes results in a sale in a traditional store. But this is an e-commerce event, too—the sale was, after all, driven by the convenience of comparison shopping via the World Wide Web. Almost half the respondents in a study by market researchers Roper Starch Worldwide said that they conduct online research as their first step in making a large purchase.

What Do You Intend to Accomplish?

Focusing your e-commerce goals is step one toward creating a successful commercial website. If you think you can zip past this step and move on to building the site, think again. Creating a site is a lot like building a house in that starting without a well-engineered plan will leave you with an unsound structure. If you don't have a good plan, at best you'll only wind up spending time later undoing the unpleasant results of your impatience. At worst, you'll find yourself in a real spot—for example, you might even be several thousand dollars poorer with no viable website to show for it. Without a clear strategy, no amount of technology will produce success.

If your website is an extension of your existing business, you probably have a clear sense of where to begin. Perhaps you have a restaurant where you serve a specialty sauce that you'd like to bottle and sell. That's a no-brainer; all you need is an easy-to-use selling site. Perhaps you have a painting company and you want to attract more upscale clients. In that case, providing general-interest information about your field—such as how to choose a painting contractor or the special preparation that distinguishes a Cadillac paint job from an ordinary paint job—could do the trick.

Choosing a Business Model

Lots of potential business models exist; your task is to identify a model that makes sense for your company. Let's look at some possible paths your e-commerce venture might take.

Tip

Identify between one and three goals for your e-commerce endeavor, and then rank them according to their importance. Keep in mind that although they might change as you go along, focusing on a few goals will prevent you from being spread too thin.

Generating Revenue

Making money through product sales, service charges, subscription sales, and other models is obviously attractive. These methods of conducting e-commerce are perhaps the most apparent routes to take. But not all the business models suggested by these ventures have proven successful. Retail sales—sales of hard deliverables such as books, CDs, and clothing—have worked and worked well when branding and customer service have been good. (See Chapters 4 and 5.)

However, as of this writing, it's been more difficult for pure-play online content-providers (online publications) to persuade the public to pay for information delivered electronically. Although historically people have been quite willing to pay for magazines and other printed sources of information, the Internet's origin as a method for freely disseminating information seems to have inclined the online culture to expect free information. (Perhaps people thought they were paying for the *paper*.)

Some information sites have experienced success by drawing users in with free content and then selling premium content on a per-use basis. Others have been successful mixing revenue streams, which is a wise move for any online venture. One profitable online publication reports that it pools revenue from selling advertising, subscriptions to premium-content e-mail newsletters, and products associated with the topic of the site (including print publications). The same online publication licenses its content for use by others as well. Various aspects of this mix are more successful than others; having a variety of revenue sources, however, prevents the periodic waning of one source from severely undermining the company's overall financial health.

On E-Commerce Sales Cycles and "Back Ends"

In a typical e-commerce retail sale, the customer makes a purchase using a credit card to make a payment. Other methods of payment can be used, but the credit card is the most common. This method has the advantage of being familiar to the customer, so the actual process of the sale is shortened—the customer doesn't have to read an explanation of how the payment method works because it's reassuringly familiar. Behind the scenes (see Figure 1-1), the online merchant and the merchant's bank conduct business pretty much as they do in the brick-and-mortar world.

The big difference between an online retail sale and one that occurs in a traditional setting is that the online transaction occurs over the Internet via computers, modems, and servers—it involves hardware and software that might be unfamiliar to you or your customers. Basically, an e-commerce site includes a *front end* that the users see (the web pages) and a *back end* that's like the behind-the-scenes workings of a retail store in the real world. (The customer never sees the "back end" of a traditional store, but it's there, and the store can't function if the back end doesn't function.) The sales systems, warehousing, delivery systems, and so on that make sales to the customer possible in the brick-and-mortar world are not duplicated exactly in e-commerce, but there are similarities. In a sales website, the back end includes a *database* (which stores information about your products and tracks a customer's purchases while they occur), a *transaction system* (the hardware and software that enables online sales), and some scripts or other programming that make them work together.

You, as the storeowner, also have to have a relationship with the bank in order to make the transaction system work. You'll need an account similar to (but often separate from) the account with the bank that enables credit card sales at a traditional store.

(continued)

On E-Commerce Sales Cycles and "Back Ends" (continued)

What, you might wonder, pushes your operation over a threshold into needing a database and transaction system? The answer is a certain level of complexity of information and function. If your operation is very simple and all you need is a few web pages with basic text and a picture, you don't need a database. The more pages you have on your site and the more complex the material you present on them, the more likely you'll be to need a database. And for simple sales via phone or e-mail, you don't need a transaction system. But to gain credibility and provide your customers with a means of giving you credit card numbers online to close a sale, you do need a transaction system. And to run a transaction system, you again need a database.

Chapter 11 describes transaction systems, but from a business perspective rather than from a programmer's perspective. That ought to help you to understand transaction systems better, but you might also need to help your customers understand what is involved in completing a transaction. Many e-commerce sites offer a page that describes their specific transaction system and its level of security in language the public can understand; this can go a long way toward building customer confidence.

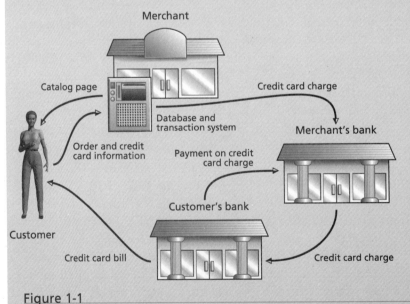

Figure 1-1

An e-commerce site's back end often includes a database and transaction system that enable the sales and payment process.

Revenue-producing e-commerce ventures can include:

- Selling products or services directly online.
- Selling advertising space. (But remember that advertising on your site won't be an attractive proposition unless your traffic is high, and to create a lot of traffic, your content has to be very, very compelling.)
- Selling sponsorships of sites (or of content) to others (much as the Public Broadcasting Service [PBS] does on TV).
- Selling product placements, much like when certain products casually appear in a scene of a movie. (Yes, companies pay for those placements.)
- Selling subscriptions to periodical information, reference information, or site services.
- Licensing content, such as text, information, images, video, or sound, to others.
- Taking commissions on sales, on customer-to-customer or business-to-business auctions, or on aggregate purchases.

Caution

Whatever your planned endeavor, don't expect an overnight windfall. Like every business venture, e-commerce businesses take a while to pay off. More about this as we go along.

Reducing Expenses

Cutting costs is an often overlooked but tangible way for an e-commerce venture to pay for itself. For example, if your product is deliverable over the Internet—meaning that it is digitized, such as software, or it can be digitized, such as images, other printed documents, or music—you can reduce or avoid altogether many costs associated with manufacturing, packaging, and distributing your product. Time-to-market also improves when you don't have to go through traditional manufacturing and distribution channels.

Cost savings can also result from online communication with your sales people; improved document management and workflow processes; project management; and tracking of projects, services, and people. *Intranets* (internal websites available only to staff, not the public) and *extranets* (websites that extend to clients, specific customers, or off-site staff) often come into play for such purposes. (See the Appendix for more information on intranets and extranets.)

Cost savings can also occur through the improved efficiency of your customer care program (see Chapter 5), as well as through the expedited delivery of information directly to customers.

Enhancing Customer Relations

A better relationship with your customers can lead to more revenue or lower costs and is certainly a worthy endeavor on its own. Most successful sites think of the customer first. They make it easy for customers to get the information they need as well as to make purchases. Customer service can be as simple as an e-mail form directed to the site manager or customer service rep. Answers to commonly asked questions might also be listed on a Frequently Asked Questions (FAQ) or Help page to save time and make life easier for you and your customers. More complex customer service initiatives can include tracking customer preferences, suggesting items for purchase related to the customer's interests, and offering special services to repeat customers.

Supporting Your Business

E-commerce initiatives that don't show a direct profit but that enhance or enable your business can include:

- Providing company information and making it easy for customers, clients, job seekers, partners, and others to contact your company.

- Shortening the sales cycle by providing in-depth product information to support purchases that will be made via reps or in a retail setting. You can reach prospects via e-commerce that you might not reach otherwise. To succeed, make getting product information easy and attractive.

- Offering top-notch customer service in an online setting, as described earlier in this section and in more depth in Chapter 5.

- Enhancing connectivity with business associates through strategic partnerships, shared resources, improved systems, and more.

Tip

Keep in mind your long-term goals as you form your strategy, but remember, too, that Internet time is rather like dog years. Things change quickly, and technologies change at the speed of light. The "long term" on the Web is perhaps three years from now, and the "short term" is the immediate future.

Selling via the Internet

How ambitious are your goals? A sales site can range from a simple listing of products with a "call for prices" notice, to a sales site created using Microsoft bCentral services or Microsoft FrontPage, to a full-blown, customized site that offers recommendations to customers based on their previous purchases. (See "On E-Commerce Sales Cycles and 'Back Ends'" earlier in this chapter for more information.) Because sales sites are so commonly of interest to e-commerce entrepreneurs, let's take a closer look at two options: selling to consumers and selling business-to-business.

Note

Creating a site that offers a simple listing of products with the option to send e-mail for more information generally takes fewer resources and less technical skill than creating revenue-producing sites. However, the easier you make it for your customers to buy—and buy now—the more likely they are to bite.

Selling to Consumers

Self-directed consumers come to websites seeking something; they are sales waiting to happen. (If you already sell products to consumers via a catalog, e-commerce is a logical extension to your existing business.) In a traditional setting, most selling occurs when customers (either the public or other businesses) approach a business location with the intent of shopping and perhaps making a purchase. (See Figure 1-2.)

Traditional Sales Model

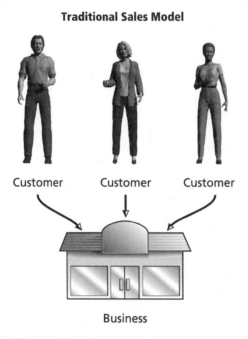

Customer   Customer   Customer

Business

Figure 1-2

Many customers approach one retailer in a traditional model.

E-commerce introduces the possibility of other sales models. For example, a number of businesses might form partnerships or a business cooperative (as shown in Figure 1-3), or various companies might form more extended partnerships to add services, value, and functionality to specialized sites (as shown in Figure 1-4).

Creating a website is only one part of online selling; remember that you must also address order fulfillment, customer and technical service, and so on. Order fulfillment must be quick—it can't depend on someone remembering to check for orders. Also, customer service expectations are high—people expect immediate responses via e-mail or phone. To create an online sales environment that works, you must establish trust and integrity online. Take a look at successful online sales sites, such as Amazon.com (*www.amazon.com*), Lands' End (*www.landsend.com*), Harry and David (*www.harryanddavid.com*), and Barnes & Noble (*www.barnesandnoble.com*) to see what instills confidence in customers.

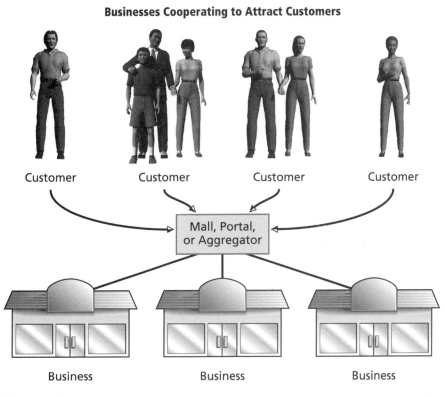

Businesses Cooperating to Attract Customers

Figure 1-3
Many customers approach several online retailers cooperating to attract business.

Obviously, you have to look credible. Create an image for your site that is professional and appropriate to your audience, and use a design that serves your audience and your products. Don't junk up your site with unnecessary clutter such as visitor counters, gratuitous animations, and meaningless links. Have your site edited for typos, confusing grammar, and factual errors, and make your transaction system understandable and convenient to use. Put your site through an all-around quality check, and make sure your users will find your establishment trustworthy.

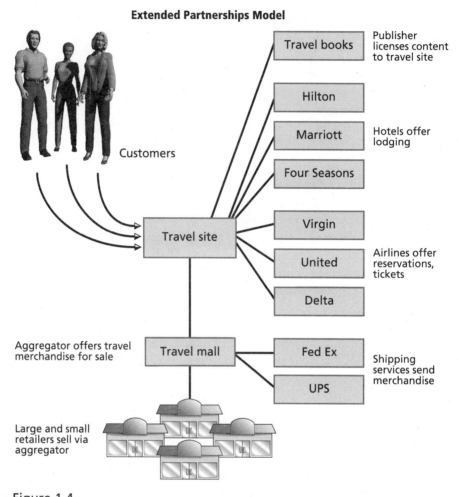

Extended Partnerships Model

Figure 1-4

Businesses form strategic partnerships to leverage assets and offer more value and functionality to customers.

Leverage your assets. If you are locally recognized, play that up. Post reviews of your service or product, testimonials from your business's clients, endorsements by people known in your industry, awards from professional or industry associations, recognition by the Better Business Bureau or the American Academy of Optometry, or whatever says that you are a solid business entity.

Play on what's familiar. Perhaps your company or product is already well-known. Good. Then you might not have to push the issue of establishing identity. But if your endeavor is new and you're going to have to work to make yourself known, you might want to form a strategic partnership with larger, more established companies or solicit testimonials. If nothing else, use established vendors for your site development, hosting, transaction system, and delivery. Creating your site with Microsoft technologies, to use the most convenient example, is an excellent way to gain the credibility that comes with having a back end (the database and transaction system and the programming that makes them function) powered by a company known the world over for its technology solutions.

Give your customers all the information they need to make a purchase. Provide images so customers can view your products. Consider using *thumbnails* (small images the size of postage stamps) so customers can see numerous products on a single page. Link the thumbnails to larger images on a separate page so customers can get a closer look at products that interest them. Place price, size, description, and materials used right where customers can see them. Offer any other information that might entice a sale.

Make buying easy. Never put a barrier in front of a sale. Don't demand marketing information from customers or ask them to fill out a survey or register before they buy. Place Buy buttons where they are most visible, especially on pages that present product information. Remove or edit any language or images that might confuse people. (A confused customer does not ask questions—a confused customer leaves.) Make your forms simple but complete. Walk people through your ordering system quickly (six steps or less is best) and, if possible, provide them with a way to buy with one click.

Offer convenient, known methods of payment. Don't make people send a check by surface mail, then wait for the check to clear, and then wait another four weeks for delivery. Set up a payment system that allows customers to use their credit cards on a *secure server*—a computer that's set up with software that enables the transaction while protecting the customer's credit card number and other personal information. (For more information on secure servers, see Chapter 10.) Consider keeping credit card and delivery information in a database so that customers don't have to enter the information the next time they order, but do this only if you have a secure server that protects confidential data. (Again, see Chapter 10.) Make it easy to buy, and the convenience of your online sales system will become an attractive alternative to getting in the car and shopping around at the local mall.

Let the customer know when the transaction has been processed. Don't make customers wonder whether their orders were successful. Provide them with the opportunity to review their orders, make corrections as needed, and then actually execute their purchases. When their purchases have been processed, say so, and give them unique confirmation numbers that they can use to track their orders during the fulfillment process or if something goes wrong (as it sometimes does).

Explain your delivery system. It's amazing how much more confident people feel when they know what you plan to do to get their purchases to them. Use familiar shipping methods such as the postal service or delivery services such as Federal Express (FedEx) or United Parcel Service (UPS), and tell people how long they might have to wait for delivery.

If something does go wrong, tell your customers that you'll fix any problems. Describe (perhaps by linking to your customer service FAQ) what you'll do if an error occurs with their order. Post your return policy. (For a great example of how returns can be handled well, take a look at how Lands' End does it.) Treat people with respect. Post and stick to your privacy policy, describing how you will (or preferably *won't*) reuse your customers' e-mail addresses and other information and how you will otherwise protect their privacy and security in your online store. Rather than simply including all customers in your mailing list, during the transaction, provide people with a check box labeled "Notify me of future sales, promotions, or specials." They can "opt in" (elect to be included) if they want to get that information.

Caution

However tempting it might be to sell or rent your mailing list as a revenue source, don't sell or give your customers' e-mail addresses to others without offering the customers the option not to be included. Providing your mailing list to others is one sure-fire way to turn off your customers, and you might not survive the onslaught that will result from this faux pas, no matter how innocent your intentions.

Finally, make sure your content is appropriate. For example, lawyer jokes might be appropriate if you are a self-help legal publisher selling books to consumers online, but their irreverence might undermine your credibility if you're a legal firm that handles corporate or criminal law. Running a contest is not the right lure for many sales sites; instead, the products should be the lure. (What's more, the contest will drain valuable resources that should be used to spiff up your customer care program.) If you consider using e-mail messages, chats, or other efforts to create an online community to bring customers in and keep them coming back (see Chapter 6), also consider whether those methods are truly in line with your site's intended purpose. Common wisdom says that each time a user returns, you should show that person something new, but the new feature should be *something that supports your site's mission*. For a sales site, for example, it can be simply a new product or a new idea for using an existing product.

Selling Business-to-Business

Market studies by Forrester Research, Inc. indicate that by 2003, 90 percent of e-commerce will be business-to-business. Business-to-business e-commerce includes ventures in industries such as transportation, electronics, leisure, engineering, and energy; each of these industries is currently worth billions or even trillions of dollars. In a business-to-business setting, you can forget about measuring success by the number of click-throughs or page views (see Chapter 14); getting and keeping customers is what counts. Branding and service make all the difference.

In that sense, business-to-business e-commerce couldn't be more traditional, but its applications can be very innovative. Consider the example of ChemConnect, a portal for the chemical, plastics, and industrial gases industry that enables business-to-business transfers of polymers, petrochemicals, and other commodities. PartMiner, another business-to-business venture, searches for electronic components for its customers. A third example, VerticalNet, reported that in one recent year it generated 47,000 qualified leads for buyers and sellers in vertical markets and auctioned two items worth more than $30 million each via the Internet.

A successful business-to-business e-commerce site can minimize routine sales calls by making ordering quicker and easier via online forms that are available 24 hours a day, seven days a week. It can transfer electronic files to speed up production processes. It can consist of virtual enterprises, virtual cooperatives, virtual markets, or communities of commerce that are combined for mutual benefit. Some of these ideas are not so new in the world of business, but historically they've been considered too expensive to implement. The technology of today's Internet lowers the barriers and makes new models possible.

Note

Remember: Your site's offerings should be driven by your business goals. These goals determine what functionality and features are needed in your website.

Who Is Your Customer?

To serve your customers, you must understand how and why they do business with you. Then you must build your website based on those needs. E-commerce provides a unique opportunity to have a one-on-one relationship with your customers, and you can empower them to control the relationship by providing convenient methods of communicating with you via e-mail and forms on your site.

As you learn more about your target market, it will become easier for others within your market to do business with you. You'll want to find out about your customers' age group, income, education level, gender, desire for accessibility versus sophistication in your products and site design, methods used to access the Internet (using which Internet service providers [ISPs] and which browsers), and more. For more on identifying your market, see Chapter 4, which discusses *branding* (creating a message and image that reaches the market and defines your company and products).

The Internet Is International—Are You?

Your customers in the brick-and-mortar world might be local to your area, but your website might attract a national or international audience. You'll have to make some decisions about selling to this broader market. If your operation is based in Boise, Idaho, will you ship to overseas American military bases? To areas that the U.S. Postal Service treats as domestic (though they are not part of the 50 United States) such as Puerto Rico and Guam? To France? How will you present your content? Will you translate it into other languages so that non-English-speaking customers can read it? Will you accept various currencies? How will you handle sales tax, value-added tax (VAT), and other taxes? Gathering marketing data for other countries requires a different level of respect for privacy than it does in the United States, so you will need to consider cultural differences. For example, in France, asking someone what he or she does for a living is considered very rude. (Supposedly, this knowledge provides you with insight into the person's income level, about which you would certainly never ask.)

Research by IDC indicates that by 2002, Internet users outside the United States will outnumber U.S. users. Western Europe's growth in Internet use is especially strong. It's tempting to try to capitalize on this information, but doing so changes your market and makes e-commerce more complex. People in many countries don't have credit cards, for example. Accepting international orders will bring up numerous issues. Are you prepared to handle them?

Note

You don't have to do business internationally just because the Internet is international. But you should post your policies about international sales on your site. If you accept orders only from within the 50 U.S. states, say so. (And be polite about it.)

Identifying Your Target Market

After launching your website, you'll know your customers through a variety of electronic means. (See Chapter 13.) You might also know your customers through an existing brick-and-mortar business. However, your online customers might differ from your other customers. To find out about Internet users in general and to investigate whatever data might exist about online customers in your industry, seek out statistics via other sources on the Internet. (The statistics presented in this chapter were all obtained via Internet searches.) Good starting places are the usual suspects: Yahoo!, Google, Alta Vista, and other search services. Check the websites of trade associations, industry publications, and professional organizations. You can also contact those groups directly to request information about trends and any resources they might offer, such as, books or reports.

For recent information regarding web usage—including the top 10 most-visited sites each week, how many hours people are spending online each week, and how many sites they visit and for how long—try the Nielsen/NetRatings "Hot Off the Net" feature (*www.nielsen-netratings.com*). You can also try the websites of the various market research companies mentioned in this chapter. Be forewarned: These companies often charge a hefty price for their published reports, which they sell online. But sometimes you'll find sample data on their sites that's actually quite useful and free.

Reaching a Local Market

You need to know where your customers are and how to get to them. If your audience is local, you can list your site with local search services and use a variety of other methods to promote your site locally. (See Chapter 12.) When you create your site, though, remember to include your location *on your home page*. Customers who wander onto your site will need to know that your operation is local, and they'll need to know where "local" is.

Who Is Your Competition?

The good news is that if your competitors are already online, you can check out their sites and conduct a speedy competitive analysis. For that matter, if your operation is local, you can look at the sites of companies that are in your industry but in other towns and cities to get an idea of what's happening in similar companies. You might be able to adapt an idea or two to your own purposes. (Hey, *ideas* aren't copyrighted; it's their expression that is. See Chapter 3.)

The bad news is that if your competitors are already online, they were there first and have defined the market, and now you'll have to be better and different to succeed against them. You'll have to be clever about it. (See Chapter 4 for ideas about how to differentiate your image or brand. See Chapter 5 for ideas about how to set yourself apart with superior customer care.)

If you have an innovative idea for doing business online, you might have no visible competitors. But if the idea is innovative enough, your "competition" might be public perception or public ignorance. Not long ago, I saw a demonstration of a product that had been described to me earlier. The product was nothing like I'd imagined it to be. It was so new and different that the makers had no way of describing it easily. To sell it, they had to demonstrate it in person. Similarly, a few years ago, I cowrote one of the very first books about web browsers. My coauthor and I had to explain in painstaking detail what the Web was, what a browser did, and what an ISP was. Public perception has now caught up with those concepts, but in those days, a web browser's stiffest competition came not from other web browsers but from what the public did not know. Take this into account as you plan your endeavor.

Remember: In an online setting, your competition might become national if not international. (See "The Internet Is International—Are You?"

earlier in this chapter.) It's up to you whether you accept the challenge of a larger sphere of operations; just make sure you've communicated to your customers what the boundaries of your business are.

Caution

The e-commerce industry is highly competitive. If you have an innovative idea, keep it under your hat until you can launch it. Announcing the features of an innovative venture two weeks before launch gives competitors time to upstage you. I've seen it happen.

Aligning Your Resources with Your Goals

Reality check: You might want to build the next eBay, but if you have only one person with little Hypertext Markup Language (HTML) experience to build your site, it isn't going to happen. You'll need to redefine your goals or find and allocate additional resources. On the other hand, you do not need unlimited resources or a $5 million budget to launch an e-commerce site. (See bCentral for solutions to building an economical, easy-to-launch storefront site.)

Note

Keep in mind the ultimate goal: getting your e-commerce endeavor to be profitable or an asset that supports your profitability. It should not be a burden to your core business.

You should think about your resources as you plan your e-commerce endeavor. Think about where funding will come from: Will it come from the profits of your brick-and-mortar business? From investors? Or perhaps from a second mortgage on your house or the liquidation of assets? Think, too, about staff time: What will it take to create your site, launch it, promote it, and maintain it? And what technologies do you anticipate needing? (See Chapter 2 for budget insight; information about technologies appears throughout this book.) Other than your business acumen, what expertise do you have? Will you hire people, outsource, or keep your endeavor scaled back enough to make it manageable without extra staffing? Will your budget allow for equipment? What do you have already? What do you need?

Note
___

Chapter 2 includes a description of what you can expect to build based on your overall budget—for example, what does $500,000 get you that $50,000 doesn't, and what can you do for $10,000, $5,000, or even less than $1,000?

An often-overlooked cost associated with pursuing any venture is the *opportunity cost*. This is the cost of pursuing that venture as opposed to other opportunities that might arise at the same time. Of course, it's common business sense to weigh the relative value and risk of pursuing one opportunity rather than another. However, this weighing process is especially important as you launch your e-commerce venture. Would you be better off opening a second location of your traditional store instead? Only you can make that call.

Building a website includes, at the very least, design, branding, programming, and *hosting* (placing the site on a computer that delivers it to the public). You'll need to weigh the cost of performing these tasks in-house (which has a time cost) versus contracting for outside services (which can have a substantial monetary cost). For the smallest businesses, much of the work will probably fall to unqualified in-house staff. (Again, see bCentral for potential solutions.)

To focus on allocating resources appropriately, ask yourself these questions: What would you spend to grow your business without the e-commerce option? Would you hire a sales rep? Would you spend more on advertising, marketing, or outreach? Would an e-commerce site save some costs? Include both savings and costs in your budget as you plan your site.

Clarifying Your Expectations

Let's talk about return on investment (ROI). Although you might usually judge success by the numbers at the bottom of your Microsoft Excel spreadsheet, some types of web success aren't so apparent. For example, how do you measure the real value of media recognition? Various sites have various purposes, and success has to be measured differently for sites that don't make producing revenue their primary goal. Customer service sites can survey customers to measure success. Business-to-business sites can ask partners about their level of satisfaction.

Caution

In e-commerce, measuring the number of "hits" is almost always irrelevant. A site that is getting millions of hits can nevertheless be a drain on your business resources. How can you consider that a business success?

Long visits might be a measure of the success of a marketing site, where you want customers to spend time viewing information. But the real goal of such a site is probably to create brand awareness or drive purchase decisions. Do lengthy visits prove success? And on a sales site, you want customers to actually make purchases. Too much browsing can distract customers from completing the sales cycle. On such sites, the measures of success are probably concrete: volume of sales, the number of visits that produce purchases, and the profit produced.

Setting Benchmarks for Success

How do you spell success? Traffic, sales, acceptance by the public, savings in cost, media presence? Set benchmarks that are attainable and that correspond to the goals of your site. (See Chapter 13 for more information on measuring success.) Set realistic goals, and err on the conservative side. Give your site time to ramp up to its potential—six months is really inadequate. In many industries, it is believed that it takes at least three to five years to become profitable, which in Internet time translates to a minimum of 18 to 30 months.

Writing a Mission Statement

We've probably all heard the metaphorical thud when someone in some group suggests writing a mission statement and the idea went over like a lead balloon. In truth, a mission statement can be a terrific tool for helping you focus. It's true that a mission statement that uses dull language, includes everything, and offends no one is probably a mission statement that will also inspire no one. Nevertheless, the very process of creating any mission statement will help you achieve clarity.

Ideally, the mission statement offers vision. Visions lead. They drive your endeavor. They provide inspiring focus and help everyone understand how they can contribute. To motivate people to do their best, when you create your mission statement, concentrate not on the creation of the document but on the creation of the vision. The language matters less than the ideas. If you are stuck for ideas about where to begin, ask these questions:

- What service or product does your company provide?
- What are three to five goals that your company wants to achieve? (Rank them in order of importance.)
- What does success look like, given the nature of the company's goals?
- How will the website help achieve the company's goals?
- What are three words that describe the company's image?
- Who is the target market? (Be specific.)
- What content or technology is available?

After you've answered those questions, throw away the answers. (The point of the exercise was to start you thinking.) Most mission statements are overly descriptive. They are written by committees and include everything the company wants to do now and forever. Instead, a mission statement should be very short and should get right to the point. It should prescribe which path, of the many the company might take, the company (or project team) will pursue most vigorously.

Here is an example of a mission statement:

XYZ Unlimited provides the finest experience in extreme sports by creating and building safe, high-performance equipment and by helping sports equipment users find new and better ways to use the equipment XYZ manufactures.

Your mission statement should be specific. Simply saying you'll market your products or services online is much too vague: To whom? How? To what end? Look again at XYZ Unlimited's statement. It really ought to describe results that are defined and measurable:

XYZ Unlimited is the number-one manufacturer of equipment for extreme sports. Quality, the safety of our customers, and providing a fine extreme sports experience are our first concerns.

Note the measurable results: The intention to be *number-one* is measurable through sales figures. The phrases *quality*, *safety*, and *fine experience* are strategic directives. As you shape your mission statement, reach for such measurable goals and defined strategies, but don't overreach. Don't aim for things you can't deliver. Declaring your commitment to 24/7 (24 hours a day, 7 days a week) technical support access is good only if you can keep that promise. Increasing penetration into national or international markets is good only if that's a realistic goal. Can you handle it?

Your mission statement should not be a memorial tacked above your desk. It should be a living document. As your e-commerce venture changes, so should your mission statement. It should be dynamic, growing (or shrinking) with the company. Remember: Your mission statement is a tool to help you focus on your goals and the strategy you will use to accomplish them.

Ten Common E-Commerce Errors

The path to success in e-commerce is full of potholes. To make the journey smoother, here are 10 things to avoid:

- Ignoring your existing business model or sales channels; your marketing, fulfillment, inventory, and accounting procedures; or your customers

- Building a site with bells, whistles, cutting-edge design, or complex navigation that obscures your message

- Creating web pages that download slowly

- Making it hard for users to find your products, product information, service information, and so on

- Confusing customers who are trying to make a purchase—for example, creating a transaction path that isn't brief and orderly, not providing customers with acknowledgment of their purchase or order, or not letting them know if an item is out of stock

- Not giving your customer confidence in the security of the transaction

- Failing to build a back end that's easily managed as well as powerful enough for your current and planned needs

- Charging higher prices for purchases made online than you do for traditional purchases

- Not providing customers with methods for communicating with you

- Building a site that's harder to use than ordering or communicating via phone or fax

Making a Plan of Action

By now, you should have thought through your site's goals and your overall strategy for achieving them. Will your site be built on a cornerstone of community (providing people with like interests a place to gather)? Will it be a portal to information or perhaps to other sites? Will you be selling via secure transactions? A catalog offering purchase support? Taking orders from other businesses? Now that you have in mind what you want to do, what's the next step?

Building a website involves these basic phases:

- Planning
- Design
- Development
- Deployment
- Promotion
- Maintenance

You're ready now to take the next step in the planning phase. Whether you're getting ready to launch an entire online business or simply an online project, you owe it to yourself to write a business plan or project plan.

Creating a Business Plan

Traditionally, every business, large or small, begins with the creation of a business plan that can be presented to bankers or investors. Even if an entrepreneur has no expectation of ever seeking investment capital, a business plan will help him or her focus ideas and form strategies for starting the business. A business plan includes such subplans as a marketing plan, a balance sheet, an income statement, a statement of cash flow (which calculates true expenses against income and then projects that calculation into the future), and so on.

The four major steps in planning a business are:

- Defining the business (mission statement)
- Setting goals, objectives, and milestones (focusing the expectation of return on investment)
- Identifying key staff positions, employees, resources, and associated costs
- Finalizing the plan of action

Writing a mission statement, setting goals, and focusing on expectations of success (return on investment) have been covered earlier in this chapter. As far as resources are concerned, considering key staff or team members, the reasons why they are needed, what other employees might be essential, and what their qualifications and job descriptions will be depends on the scope of your endeavor.

Although the specifics of how to write a detailed business plan and what form it should take are beyond the scope of this book, having read this chapter, you are already well on your way. The remainder of this book will help you define and clarify your plan. Remember to allow for expansion as you outline your plan. Give yourself plenty of time to write everything down—several weeks or more is commonly needed. Time invested here, although it might compete with your day job or existing business, will pay off when you launch your e-commerce endeavor and find that you have all your ducks in a nice, neat row.

Note

Remember: Sales volume alone does not create a successful business. Profits must sustain the necessary staffing, labor, fixed costs, and so on before return on investment occurs. Also, start-ups take work. Two years of 80-hour weeks is common.

Creating a Project Plan

Define your project plan just as you would a business plan. Think about your goals, time lines, budget, technology needs, and who will do what, both before launch and after. How will you build the skills or team you need to carry your project through? Is your endeavor so large or complex that you need some kind of "general contractor" or project manager to keep it coordinated and on track? Will you be that person? Will that job take you away from other, more profitable ventures? Evaluate or define your process for accomplishing tasks. Eliminate unnecessary steps, but focus on your objectives, including quality. Define requirements. Think about staff, technologies, equipment, and the functionality needed to make your project work. How will you select good vendors who will not bleed you over the course of months or years? Above all, understand your goals.

Is Your Plan Really Feasible?

It's important not to fall in love with your e-commerce plan. Instead, be its harshest critic. Show it to your accountant, your lawyer, your spouse. Put it in a drawer for a few days; then take a fresh look, and think hard about any potholes you see along your path. If you know in your gut that you must proceed or live with regret, go forward. If you have doubts, revamp your plan and try again.

Then ask the same questions all over again. Will you kick yourself in years to come if you don't do this? Is the risk worth the return?

Above all, don't be wowed by reports of enormous success. And do think carefully before you jump.

Chapter 2

Setting Up a Budget and Sticking to It

E-commerce is an industry that is still in its youth. As a result, few models exist for creating budgets for e-commerce endeavors. Other industries have formulas that have been tested over many years. For example, the food service industry has its famous ratio of thirds, where one-third of every expense is allocated to each of three categories of cost: food, labor, and other. (This formula, by the way, provides a simple method of dividing costs but doesn't specify a particular profit margin.) Although at least *some* models have evolved for e-commerce budgeting, it will probably be several more years before formulaic budgeting tricks can offer entrepreneurs and managers a leg up in planning their e-commerce ventures.

Budgeting is not the most glamorous aspect of e-commerce. However, it is a vital tool for determining whether your venture is going to be a profit center, a cost center, or an expensive hobby. Let's take a look at the ins and outs of today's e-commerce budgeting.

Where Do You Start?

The specific format for your budget (how it's set up, what categories are included, and so on) often depends on whether your online endeavor is an extension of an existing company or a start-up. It also depends on the size of the project and what components of e-commerce you will include. Different types of e-commerce ventures require different levels and types of funding. For example, a site that publishes information of interest to a trade or professional group will need an editorial budget, while a site that sells hand-knit baby items will need a budget for shooting and processing photographs of the items. Similarly, some sites require a hefty budget for customer care or the technical support of products, and some require a big technology budget for a heavy-duty server that can handle an intense load and for the technical staff to support it.

Follow a Known Format

Your company or your accountant might have a prescribed format for budgeting—one that's easy to understand because it's familiar. If so, you should probably follow that format as best you can. Some tweaking might be necessary to make the format fit a web initiative, but getting in line with the tried and true at this level can help you get budget approval or the kind of advice you need from your accountant before you proceed.

Be aware that a lot of e-commerce lingo is new to executives and accountants. They might not understand, for example, why you need a *staging server* (space on a server where you can post pages for testing before going live; see Chapter 10) or *redundancy in your database* (duplication of the system so that if one part breaks, the system will still function; see Chapter 10). Anticipating potential confusion by providing supporting documentation for any special needs is generally a good idea. (If you need to define terms, check the Glossary at the back of this book.)

If you plan to solicit bids from outside contractors (design firms, back-end developers, content producers, and so on) for your e-commerce project, you will probably want to set up a sample budget first. Doing so offers the following three advantages:

- It allows you to test your plan to see if it's out of whack with your resources.
- It allows you to walk into meetings with an idea of the scope of your project and its general, potential cost.
- It allows you to review bids intelligently.

What's in a Website Budget

What appears in a website budget depends first on the scope of the project. What are your goals for the site? (See Chapter 1.) What resources or personnel are already on hand? Be specific. Will you be building a small, simple site; an e-commerce department; or a standalone e-commerce company? If you will be managing a very small endeavor by yourself, talk to others who've done the same. If you will be building a department within an existing company, talk to people in other departments (especially accounting!) to find out whether you have to figure office space, desks, phones, and equipment into your budget, or whether the company spreads these expenses across all operations without requiring you to specify them for your department.

You simply cannot do too much research. Read everything you can—this book, others, Microsoft's online resources, *everything*. Then branch out from there. The world is full of people who have experience and opinions. Talk to everyone who might help you consider all the angles. If you'll be hiring a team or contracting with a web shop (for design, back-end development, or the whole shebang), pick their brains as you interview them. Ask about projects they've worked on, the scope of those projects, the resources that were available, and what was accomplished with those resources. You probably won't get an answer to a question like "What was your budget?" Answers to such questions are usually squelched in advance by nondisclosure agreements (NDAs). But you can get an idea of the money involved by asking peripheral questions. In the course of all this research, your own budget will begin to gel in your mind.

Tip

During the budgeting process, keep your company's values in mind. A company that employs high-concept branding strategies or believes deeply in sterling customer care will want to budget more for those aspects of its web endeavor than a company that feels research and development are most crucial.

Setting Realistic Expectations

Wondering what your website is actually going to cost? Brace yourself. Building a big, slick, corporate website can easily cost $500,000, and some go upward into the millions. Maintaining such a site (for example, creating fresh content, upgrading functionality, promoting the site, managing the hardware and connection, and so on) commonly costs in excess of $5 million a year. And, interestingly, not all of those sites reap a profit. In fact, many of them are listed by the companies' bean counters as *cost centers*, not profit centers. They might serve the purpose of marketing the company or its products or services, but they are often seen as expensive necessities that don't contribute in any direct way to the company's bottom line. Not all websites are so expensive, and not all are seen as giant holes into which all the money goes. But creating and supporting a working website is not the sort of thing you do with a dab of glue and a shoestring. You have to make some investment to get the benefits of being online; the question is whether the investment you make will produce the return you intend.

Let's take a look at how much bang you can expect for your buck. For the most part, the discussions that follow refer to the cost of creating a site, not promoting it and not updating or maintaining it. Building a site and then not promoting it doesn't make sense because you are unlikely to develop much traffic (or business). And building a site but not maintaining it has about the same effect as building a house and not maintaining it: Things will fall apart. Text will go out of date, links will rot, the site will look old and stale, and functionality will go bad. So as you consider the following budget categories, remember that your budget should also include the ongoing costs of promotion and maintenance. (For more details, see the section titled "Budgeting for Promotion and Maintenance" later in this chapter.)

Note

As mentioned previously, information about the specific costs of websites isn't widely available. However, you can get a credible, ongoing analysis of the median prices of various types of website projects via B2B Online's Price Index at *www.btobonline.com/*.

What Can You Do for $500,000 and Up?

For the really big bucks, you can hire a world-class front-end design shop and back-end developer or the combined talents of a branding consultant, top-notch designer, and seasoned back-end developer. (Big-name advertising agencies usually offer such combos.) If your goal is to sell products or services, you'll also be able to support that by buying the custom development of a slick transaction system and a powerful database to serve your product catalog. If your site is content-rich or slated for frequent updating, you can streamline your ongoing processes by having a fully functional content management system in place. Whatever your goal or offerings, you'll be able to afford a back-end system that can handle a great deal of traffic so that millions of users per month can access your site and use it to its full potential. Your site might incorporate high-end technologies such as Microsoft Commerce Server, Microsoft SQL Server, and Active Server Pages (ASP). You'll be able to employ multiple servers (see Chapter 10 to find out why this might be advantageous) and use lots of custom programming.

Your investment will also allow you to hire professional copywriters, editors, and artists to develop snappy content targeted to your market (as defined by the research your branding consultant has conducted to identify your customers). You will probably have to add more money to your budget if you want to use custom photography (as opposed to stock photographs purchased by your designers from a catalog of images). But hey, when you're in this league, what's a few dollars more?

What Can You Do for $50,000 or $100,000?

For somewhere in the range of $50,000 or $100,000, you can hire a respectable web design shop to create your site. Your site will be professionally designed and will probably have a thoughtful navigational system that enables visitors to get around easily, but it might not be cutting edge in its look or functionality. That's fine; not all sites have to be visually stunning. In many cases, strong content and ease of use are preferable.

Your mid-range investment won't buy a powerful back end that can handle millions of users per month, but it will probably buy one that can handle hundreds of thousands. Commerce Server, SQL Server, and ASP might be at your service, but you might be able to deploy only one or two computers as servers instead of several. Your transaction system won't be as quick to use as the more expensive, highly customized types; customers might have to traverse seven pages instead of three to complete a transaction. You won't be able to afford a branding consultant, but your designers will be able to use the "look-and-feel" elements (colors, fonts, logos, and so on) that define your company's identity. (This assumes, of course, that the elements are translatable into web colors and fonts—not all colors and fonts work on the Web; see Chapters 7, 8, and 9 for more information.)

Remember: Presenting simple text and straightforward content is more economical than offering complex functionality and lots of special effects. As an example, an informational site with approximately 2000 pages of content (which is quite a lot), including regular articles and special reports, can run perhaps $50,000 per year (in ongoing costs). However, the initial design costs for this type of site would be quite low because the design work would involve nothing more than coming up with a handful of fairly simple page templates. A content editor could then paste purchased content into the appropriate template. Keeping the process of creating new pages very simple and providing the editor with a powerful computer would keep time costs as low as possible and would therefore help keep ongoing costs down. Although the site would at first call on the time of at least one staff person, it wouldn't be labor intensive. For a mid-sized organization that presents only information—a trade organization, for example—this type of site could be an excellent e-commerce solution.

What Can You Do for $5,000 to $10,000?

For $5,000, you can create a small site with approximately 10 or 20 pages of professionally designed content—that's *content*, not bells and whistles such as animations of your product in action. You might include, for example, an About the Company page, a small roundup of simple catalog pages (not in a fancy database), a Tech Support or Customer Support page and a FAQ page to support your products, and a form that allows customers to order products or catalogs via e-mail. Your budget can support hiring a designer to apply your company's look to the site, by coming up with a simple page layout that includes your logo, chosen font, and identifying color scheme.

For $5,000, you won't get custom technical development of your back-end system and you can forget about a custom-built database and transaction system. You can consider such technologies as Microsoft Site Server or Internet Information Services (IIS), both of which are excellent off-the-shelf products that are very popular. These products can be customized, but your budget of $5,000 doesn't provide for that, so you'll be using the standard implementations. Your site might also wind up on a shared server (on which you, along with several other sites, rent server space). Again, there's nothing wrong with this; it just isn't the most robust system (meaning that its capacity for traffic isn't what the big sites would demand of their back ends).

At this budget level, you also can't expect the designer to create the company look from scratch or every page to look unique, and you can't expect to include lots of art or nifty effects such as *mouseovers* (text that changes color or form when a mouse pointer passes over it).

For $10,000, you can get all the things a $5,000 budget will buy, plus you can hire a programmer to create a few forms that allow your pages to be updated by someone who has no HTML skills. You won't be able to afford a big, complex database with lots of functionality, but you can add a simple database that is useful nonetheless. You can then store information in the database for efficient presentation on your web pages, and you'll be able to present richer information about your products to your customers. For example, you can offer a larger and more sophisticated product catalog, with photographs and descriptive information.

In addition, with a budget of $10,000, you might even be able to augment your site with a simple *extranet* (a site that is available not to the general public but only to people you designate). Typical uses for an extranet are to support sales by making key information about your products available to your representatives and to allow buyers to enter and track orders. The extranet that you add to your $10,000 website might access the same database that contains the product information you present to the public and present additional data to those who have entered the password required for accessing the extranet. Your extranet can have the same look and feel as your public website, or it can be more utilitarian or more up-scale. (See this book's Appendix for more on extranets.)

What Can You Do with a Minimal Investment?

For less than $1,000 of initial investment, you have three basic options:

- You can hire a designer to create a single, basic page template for a very simple site with perhaps five pages, including a list of your products along with contact information that urges customers to call or send e-mail to find out more. (You or your staff will then pour the content of the five pages into the template.)

- You can use a web authoring program such as Microsoft FrontPage to produce a site with basic functionality yourself. FrontPage allows you to create your own design or use any of a number of predesigned looks called *themes*.

- You can use the services of Microsoft bCentral, which offers the convenience of creating a fully functional e-commerce site even if you don't know anything about HTML, back ends, branding, design, or programming. (For details about how bCentral makes this possible, go to *www.bcentral.com*.)

If you decide to hire a designer, you might want to look around for an entry-level designer who can do HTML coding or who knows enough to work with a novice coder to create the pages. Don't hire a designer who has no web design experience at all. Web pages are simply not the same as printed pages, and the design issues are numerous.

If you decide to go the FrontPage route, you might still want to hire a designer to create the template you'll use when building your pages yourself. (Be sure the designer knows and uses FrontPage.) Before you spring for a designer, though, check out the themes, or predesigned pages, that FrontPage provides.

If you opt to use bCentral's services, you can either use FrontPage to design your site or you can opt to step through a series of wizards (much like those in many Microsoft products) that help you set up your site, choose among the predesigned looks, and enable a transaction system. bCentral's tools for building your website offer looks tailored to specific industries. They let you set up a site with a back end powered by Microsoft server software and a credible transaction system. For smaller businesses, bCentral's services can provide a good deal of cost-effective bang for a minimal investment.

Note

Remember that if you build the site yourself, you'll be investing time in both the learning curve and the actual work of creating the site. You probably need to evaluate the opportunity costs of this time.

No matter how you decide to proceed, keep the number of pages small—fewer than 10, for example—and include no animation, gimmicks, or custom graphics. If you decide to work with a designer, be sure to interview him or her carefully. Read both the chapter of this book on jobbing out work on your site (Chapter 9) and the following section in this chapter, and consider all the angles. A lousy site that costs only $1,000 isn't a bargain; it's a waste of $1,000.

How Can You Keep Costs Down?

To rein in costs and keep them reined in, follow these guidelines:

- **Remember that text costs less.** Text is cheaper to produce than art, video, sound, animation, special visual effects such as mouseovers, and anything that requires programming. It's not that hiring a writer is necessarily cheaper. (According to the B2B Online Price Index, rates for a professional website copy writer can range around $85 per hour or more.) But the cost of producing the pages is less when the pages are all text as opposed to when they include visual and interactive media. Creating the simple HTML code required for text is just not as expensive as art preparation, programming, and the other work required to make more complex pages work.

- **Clarify your goals and stick to them.** Chapter 1 described the process of developing your site's goals. If necessary, go back to that chapter, read it again, and move on from there.

- **Get bids for project costs by the page rather than by the hour.** When a contractor bids by the hour without a cap, you don't know what the site is going to cost until the game's over. Hourly costs can really stack up, and the contractor has no real incentive for keeping the hours (and the cost) to a minimum or for completing the project quickly. Getting fixed-price bidding from contractors or vendors is a more prudent way to go than paying by the hour. Note, however, that it's standard practice for contractors to charge on a per-hour basis for short-term or limited aspects of a project—say, preproduction planning—and then provide a fixed-price bid for the project based on what was specified as the scope of the project during the preproduction planning.

- **Organize and prioritize your content.** Before you speak to designers and before you get bids, gather all the existing content you want to include (company information, product information, customer service documents, contact information, and so on). Then make a list of the new content you plan to create. After that, take a look at Chapter 7. Think carefully about how each piece of information will serve your site's goals, whether it's really needed in an online setting, and how customers will use it. Toss anything that isn't crucial into a folder, and set it aside (just in case you really need it after all). When you talk to designers, having a plan in mind will make it easier to get a real bid, and having a bid will make it easier to monitor costs.

41

- **Avoid gimmicks, bells, and whistles.** The special programming required for nifty effects, such as personalizing web pages with the customer's name, can cost a bundle. What's more, extra effects require a more powerful back end, which can drive up costs. And because effects make the site more complex, they make maintaining it more complex and time-consuming. Think carefully about adding unnecessary thingamabobs. Ask yourself what they contribute to the site. Is it real value and functionality, or are you just draping your store with blinking twinkle lights for no reason?

- **Don't include features you aren't prepared to maintain.** A weekly article about caring for roses might be just the type of content that will keep customers coming back to an online garden store, but are you prepared to take time away from your family or from actually tending your store to write the article every week? Are you prepared to hire a writer, an editor, and an HTML coder to create and post the articles? Will that be cost effective? Will the feature net you the results you hope for, or is your money better spent elsewhere?

- **Keep staffing costs low.** Staffing is a commitment. Hiring people means you will have them, their salaries, their benefits, and their taxes as constant obligations, even when business is slow. While you are ramping up and until you know your e-commerce venture is a go—until you are prepared to commit to payroll, management overhead, human resources staff, and so on—keep your operation lean.

- **Avoid feature creep.** We've all experienced this insidious circumstance. Let's say you're remodeling your kitchen, and the contractor suggests real granite for the counter instead of faux-granite Formica; or you go to a car dealer to buy a basic sedan and wind up with a convertible that has an elaborate stereo system; or you start a programmer on a simple project, and along the way you add features and functionality (chat! interactive puzzles! a weekly contest!) without considering your bottom line. These are all examples of *feature creep*—the creeping in of features that weren't originally in the plan. As you build your site and maintain it, avoid this unfortunate phenomenon. It can swell any budget beyond recognition in no time flat.

Tip

Use Microsoft Project to create your project plan and track your project, and an added bonus will be that you'll be able to see what you've spent at any given time during the project. The same features of Project will show you how spending has deviated from your original project plan's budget. You can then address the situation before it gets out of hand, either by rebudgeting or by modifying your website plan.

Looking at a Sample Spreadsheet

Budgets are often developed in a spreadsheet that includes a line item for each expense. Expenses are logically grouped within the spreadsheet to make reading the budget easier. As mentioned earlier in this chapter, different companies and accountants use varying methods of creating budgets, but no matter what method you use, the spreadsheet should paint a clear picture of the project. Take a look at the sample spreadsheet in Figure 2-1, which might help you in devising your own budget.

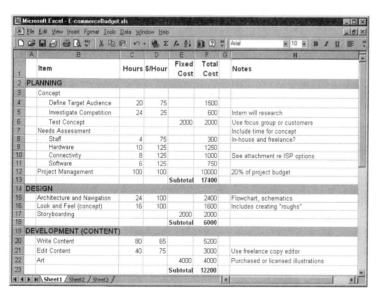

Item	Hours	$/Hour	Fixed Cost	Total Cost	Notes
PLANNING					
Concept					
Define Target Audience	20	75		1500	
Investigate Competition	24	25		600	Intern will research
Test Concept			2000	2000	Use focus group or customers
Needs Assessment					Include time for concept
Staff	4	75		300	In-house and freelance?
Hardware	10	125		1250	
Connectivity	8	125		1000	See attachment re ISP options
Software	6	125		750	
Project Management	100	100		10000	20% of project budget
			Subtotal	17400	
DESIGN					
Architecture and Navigation	24	100		2400	Flowchart, schematics
Look and Feel (concept)	16	100		1600	Includes creating "roughs"
Storyboarding			2000	2000	
			Subtotal	6000	
DEVELOPMENT (CONTENT)					
Write Content	80	65		5200	
Edit Content	40	75		3000	Use freelance copy editor
Art			4000	4000	Purchased or licensed illustrations
			Subtotal	12200	

Figure 2-1

A sample spreadsheet showing the budget for a mid-sized e-commerce site.

**Tip**

No one will ever ding you for coming in _under_ budget. To give yourself some leeway, you might want to boost your estimates by as much as 20 percent. Also, if your budget process involves seeking approval from a higher-up, a review committee, or a board, you might want to include a few line items that you can compromise on or even sacrifice during negotiations.

In the sample spreadsheet, each item is named, its costs are categorized, and categories are summarized as totals. Budget items are also grouped by activity.

General budget categories often include _fixed_ expenses (one-time costs such as a piece of software), _hourly_ expenses (such as the per-hour cost of programmers), and _ongoing_ expenses. (Ongoing expenses are the expenses you will incur regularly. Some examples include rent, utilities, salaries, benefits, and so on. Ongoing costs are so variable by region and industry as well as project that we have not included them in Figure 2-1.)

You'll learn more about the expense categories associated directly with website projects in the section titled "Categorizing Costs by Type" later in this chapter.

**Tip**

For your convenience, the spreadsheet shown in Figure 2-1 is posted in the E-Commerce Management Center at _www.tauberkienan.com._ You are welcome to use it as a model for your own budget spreadsheet.

Grouping Costs by Activity

In Figure 2-1, line items are listed in the column labeled Item and they are grouped in rows according to the activities that are generally involved in building and maintaining a website. (Of course, your line items will be different because they will be based on your site plan and e-commerce goals.) This method of organizing financial information provides a clear picture of what will happen and what each task will cost. It is also an easy way to remember the categories for which you must have a budget.

As mentioned in Chapter 1, building a website involves the following basic steps:

- Planning
- Design

- Development

- Deployment

- Promotion

- Maintenance

Consider the activities involved in each step as you devise your budget. The following sections will help you focus on those activities.

Budgeting for the planning stage

Remember to budget for both needs assessment and project management. Project management can include needs assessment in the sense that you might assign the project manager the task of conducting the needs assessment. But the two activities are actually separate, one being performed before the site is built and the other being an ongoing task performed throughout the project.

The discussion in Chapter 1 of setting goals and writing a business plan or project plan will set you on the road to assessing your needs. Needs assessment includes brainstorming, research, project planning, and perhaps the budgeting process itself. Specifically, it consists of these activities:

- Researching Internet demographics and statistics, industry trends, and information on current Internet marketing and e-commerce strategies

- Identifying target markets (your audience) and ferreting out information about your potential customers, such as the usual demographics (age range, education levels, income levels, location, and so on), how they access the Internet, how they find your existing business, and how they currently buy (offline as well as online)

- Identifying your competitors, the traditional methods they use in business, and the methods they use online, as well as what they offer via their websites and how you might differentiate yourself from your competitors

- Identifying your project's goals, the potential advantages and risks in proceeding, and any advantages and risks in not doing the project

If your endeavor is large enough, you might hire professionals to conduct some of this research for you; otherwise, you'll have to budget your own time or a team member's time to do it. (Note that Chapter 4 includes a series of questions you can use to focus your investigations into identifying and reaching your target audience.)

Project management can eat up as much as 20 percent of the overall time it takes to complete a project. Project management includes managing staff, contractors, schedules, and the budget, but it also involves meetings, phone calls, executive summaries and presentations, and so on. In the course of managing your project, you must create and track the progress of a project plan (which you can do using Microsoft Project). You (or someone on your team) must also write website specifications (specs) and document strategic and tactical decisions that will affect the project as it develops.

During the planning stage, you'll also need to plan and budget for the following:

- Staff and personnel (in-house or contracted)
- Hardware (the computers that act as servers, workstations for your staff, and so on)
- Connectivity (your site's connection to the Internet via an ISP or hosting company, as outlined in Chapter 10)
- Software (HTML editors, graphics programs, word processing software, e-mail systems, traffic analysis systems, transaction and database servers, web servers, and so on)

If the project is being handled in-house, this planning time can be built into the general work schedule. If the project is being handled by freelance contractors or a web shop, the planning time is billable and one way or another you will be billed for it. Some contractors build project management charges into their rates, while others charge separately for it.

Tip

If you are creating a budget for someone else's approval, tie expensive items (such as hardware) to a return on the investment. Point out what specific benefit will result from the expense and what consequences might result if the purchase is not approved. (For example, the server might crash and interrupt service to customers.) Provide detail in an attachment to back up what you predict.

Budgeting for design and development

After you've read Chapter 8 on creating a site, you will find it easier to understand some of the terms used in this section. For now, here is a list of the general activities involved in designing and building a site, all of which have an associated cost in dollars or time:

- Planning the site's size, architecture, and navigation
- Designing the site's look
- Creating a series of *storyboards* (notes and sketches) that mock up each page that composes the site
- Writing (and editing) or licensing the content
- Coding in HTML
- Integrating any graphics and multimedia (and perhaps licensing images, video, or sound)
- Programming scripts (small programs written in languages such as Microsoft Visual Basic, Scripting Edition (VBScript) or JavaScript) to provide some of the site's functionality, such as forms for users to fill out
- Creating interfaces to databases or a transaction system

Tip

Remember that your staff's time isn't free; it has a labor cost *and* an opportunity cost. (While your web team members are building the site, they won't be performing other potentially profitable tasks.) You'll want to think realistically about their time as you develop your budget.

Budgeting for deployment

A number of activities occur just before a site is launched in preparation for "going live." These activities include:

- Testing the site on a staging server, including looking for typos, checking links, verifying that all functionality is in place, and making sure all systems are "go."
- Preparing marketing materials. (This is a deployment activity because it must begin well before the actual launch, but the marketing materials themselves are a line item of the promotion budget.)

After all the preparations have been made, the actual launch includes:

- Placing the site on the live server and checking areas that might have been troublesome in development. (This quality check should turn up no new problems.)
- Announcing that the site is now available to the public.

Caution

After you've made a plan and started to build the site, changing your mind won't be cheap. Feature creep can bloat a budget quickly and horribly, and switching hardware, software, or a database product mid-project can be a setback for both your budget and your timeline. Remember, too, that the farther down the road toward launch you are, the more expensive changing your mind will be. Each decision you make as you go along in building a website affects other decisions, and changing one aspect of the site during implementation will require at least reviewing many other aspects of the site. Reviewing and changing things costs time and money. Again, this is why planning is crucial to the success of your e-commerce venture.

Budgeting for promotion and maintenance

Unfortunately, many people think that after a site is launched, it's "done." Not so. To remain competitive, your website must, at the very least, be maintained with fresh content and attention to technical matters. It must also be promoted. "If you build it, they will come" might work for baseball diamonds in the middle of Iowa cornfields, but it's simply not true for websites.

The hows and whys of maintenance and promotion are discussed throughout this book. Suffice it to say here that, in a recent study by Forrester Research, 54 percent of respondents said they were motivated to frequent sites that are updated often. And how did those people say they found sites? Via search engines (57 percent), e-mail messages (38 percent), links from other sites (35 percent), word of mouth (28 percent), and magazine ads (25 percent)—not, you will notice, by stumbling across them. (By the way, respondents were able to indicate more than one method of finding sites, so these percentages don't tally to 100 percent.)

As you consider the categories involved in your budget, take into account these issues of promotion and maintenance:

- Fixing the bugs and broken or outdated links that inevitably crop up in all websites

- Responding to feedback from customers and website users

- Updating content and adding fresh information about product lines

- Reprinting existing marketing materials to include your web address (known as a *Uniform Resource Locator*, or *URL*) and to promote your e-commerce venture

- Forming partnerships to exchange links with other sites or perhaps to co-develop and co-brand new content or features

- Advertising via traditional media (print advertising, broadcast, or even bus signs) as well as online

- Initiating and monitoring listings in search engines, directories, and portals

Again, remember that staff time will be required to do all these tasks, as well as to monitor server logs (discussed in Chapter 13) and deal with any contractors you retain or hire to do maintenance or upgrades after launch.

Categorizing Costs by Type

In addition to grouping line items by row according to the activities described in the preceding sections, the sample budget shown in Figure 2.1 categorizes costs by column according to the type, or category, of expense. As mentioned earlier, the basic categories include fixed expenses, hourly expenses, and ongoing expenses. The sample spreadsheet includes these column headings:

- **Item** Lists the budget items noted in the preceding sections.

- **Hours** Shows the estimated number of hours needed for in-house staff or contractors to complete a task. The cost of in-house people goes here whether they are paid hourly or on a salary basis; if they get a salary, calculate what that salary breaks down to per hour and enter that number. (The fees you might pay to a web shop are listed in the Fixed Cost column.)

- **$/Hour** Shows the estimated cost per hour for in-house staff or contractors to do the task.

- **Fixed Cost** Shows the cost of an item—for example, computer equipment or software. If you contract with a firm to work for a fixed bid, show that cost here. If both an hourly cost and a fixed cost are associated with a particular item, indicate each cost in its appropriate column and then enter their sum in the Total Cost column.

- **Total Cost** Shows the sum of all the costs listed in the spreadsheet. This number indicates the projected cost of your web endeavor.

- **Notes** Provides additional details about each item.

On E-Commerce Revenue Models

Revenue issues are not addressed in the sample spreadsheet shown in Figure 2-1 because, quite simply, it's impossible to show every revenue model that exists in one example spreadsheet. It is important, of course, to know what revenue model you will be relying on—in other words, how your site will make money. From what source will revenue emerge? Revenue models for online ventures are in a state of flux, with new models falling in and out of favor and even newer ones being invented all the time. Let's take a quick look at a few possibilities.

Product Sales Model

Product sales is the simplest revenue model in town; basically, a merchant sells products and makes a profit by keeping costs lower than the gross income from sales. This model translates nicely to web endeavors, except that, as mentioned at the beginning of this chapter, the standard formulas used in other industries to help entrepreneurs understand and manage their costs simply aren't available yet for e-commerce initiatives. The methods you know and love for keeping costs down in your donut shop won't translate neatly into methods for keeping costs down in your online donut business. Go to Microsoft bCentral (*www.bcentral.com*), Microsoft Business (*www.microsoft.com/business/*), and other online sources for insight into managing costs in specific types of sales sites.

Ad Sales Model

Ad sales as a revenue model seems an obvious option to many who venture into e-commerce. After all, a lot of people are online and they'll see the ads, so advertisers should be willing to pay a pretty penny for ad space, right? The flaws in this reasoning are threefold. First, to attract advertisers who will pay for premium (or even mid-level) ad placement, you need *big* traffic numbers. To get that traffic, you must first invest a lot of capital in building your site, creating compelling content, and promoting your site. Magazines often run on this model. (You don't really think the paltry cost of subscriptions adds up to enough to pay all the expenses of running a magazine, do you? If so, what are all those ads doing there?) And a general rule in launching a new magazine is that it will bleed money for three to five years before the publisher can expect a dime of profit. The road to profitability that relies on ad sales can be long and winding. To reach the necessary traffic levels, you might have to spend a lot of time tuning up your content and operations, measuring the results of your efforts, tuning up again, promoting your refurbished site, measuring again, and so on.

The second challenge to those going after ad sales as a revenue model is that advertisers want outside confirmation of your traffic; your word is fine, but they want an external audit or some other verification to back it up. In the magazine and broadcast world, trusted companies such as ACNielsen Corporation (*www.acnielsen.com*) sell just such a service. In the online world, technologies and standards are emerging to enable the verification that advertisers want. Companies such as Media Metrix (*mediametrix.com*), ACNielsen eRatings.com (*www.eratings.com*), and ABC Interactive (*www.abcinteractiveaudits.com*) provide auditing, but it might be cost-prohibitive for small to mid-sized companies.

The third challenge in ad sales may be based in the fact that the very nature of the Internet, historically, has been to provide information for free. Intrusions into that "free" information (especially commercially-motivated intrusions) are often poorly received by Internet users. Of course, advertising can also be seen as an intrusion into the "user" experience in broadcast and print, but somehow a gauche reminder that this is, after all, a commercial venture is more resented online than elsewhere. In the minds of site designers, ads can also seem intrusive. Usually, the advertiser wants the ad placed at the top of the page, and that's exactly the placement the site's creator wants, too, to establish identity for the site. With time, a solution to all of these challenges will surely come. In the meantime, ad sales are a possible revenue model, but unless you can afford to wait until your traffic ramps up, you might want to look at other options as well.

Paid Sponsorship Model

Paid sponsorship works on a model much like that used by the Public Broadcasting Service (PBS), where a company or individual pays for the privilege of being listed as a sponsor, perhaps in a high profile way. On a website, for example, the sponsor's name might appear in a special font or in a box that highlights the company's (often generous) donation. The prestige of being associated with a certain site might compel an advertiser to sponsor the site; again, the issues of the site's traffic numbers and user perception of the site come into play.

Paid Placement Model

In a *paid placement* scenario, companies pay to have their products or brands actually appear in key places. For example, in a game site, images of certain products—a certain brand of beer, type of car, or name of a hotel—might appear within the game itself. As in the cases of ad sales and paid sponsorship, here the issues of traffic numbers, verification of the numbers, and user perception can arise as drawbacks. An additional drawback is that you have to somehow fit the products into your images. If you can make that a feature of your site instead of an intrusion into your presentation, that's fine, but if products adorning your site as paid placements start to obscure your content or message, users might be repelled.

Subscription Model

At one point, the *subscription* model—in which users pay for information delivered online daily or weekly, for example—seemed to many like an obvious winner. After all, it was reasoned, the Internet was a fast medium for delivering information and people were already used to paying for journalism and reference materials. So what went wrong? Again, the inherent nature of the Internet as a source of *free* information might have disinclined users to pay for the very same information they'd be willing to pay for if it were printed on paper. Some sites have gotten around this by offering premium information—newer, larger, or more recent versions of reports or newsletters, for example—to paying subscribers while offering smaller samplings to those who have not paid a subscription fee.

Fee for Services Model

Fee for services is a model that works perfectly well for transactions such as registering a car, and it shows a lot of promise in the area of online education and training. In this scenario, the customer generally knows what will be delivered: a tangible item or product. However, it's a bit trickier in cases such as offering consulting services online for a fee. (The clients of consultants seem to prefer to see the consultant in person; perhaps this is because they want an in-person assessment or because the generally high cost of consulting suggests in-person service.)

Licensing Model

Licensing is an interesting option for people or companies who have something of such interest that others are willing to pay to use it. Content can be licensed—so can software, code, services, images, music, video, and so on. Licensing can be for a specified length of time, specified venues, specified uses, and so on. The keys to making licensing work are having offerings others want, having licensing models that work, and having a solid contract. If you don't have any licensing experience, it's best to get professionals involved. A lot of blues singers licensed all rights to their work in the '50s, for example, only to find in the '70s that others had gotten rich on their talent while they were still scraping by. This experience would give anyone the blues.

Affiliate or Affinity Program Model

Affiliate, affinity, and associate programs involve one company setting up a system to sell their products through other companies (usually by linking to the first company's sales site). The seller often gets a small royalty, bounty, or commission for each sale that comes from the seller's site. Examples of this arrangement include the programs set up by big online booksellers to encourage other, smaller sites to sell books through them. The larger bookseller is able to extend its reach enormously via its affiliates, in effect creating many sales outlets without incurring the expense of creating many sites. bCentral offers tools and services for making administration of an affiliate program easier; see *www.bcentral.com*. Also see Chapter 12 for more explanation of how affiliate programs work.

Commission Model

Commission models have proved strikingly successful. In one example, on auction websites (such as those where items are sold by one consumer to another consumer) the company hosting the website receives a percentage of the sales price. In another scenario, several smaller companies might pool their purchasing power to get discounts by purchasing supplies in volume via a website. Again, the website rakes in a commission on the pooled sale, and in a real way, everyone wins—the website gets the commission, the companies making the purchase get better prices, and the companies selling the products get access to markets they might not have reached so easily in the past.

Cost-Savings Model

Cost savings via online ventures can be very compelling. Anything that can be digitized (such as software, music, and art) can be distributed over the Internet, saving manufacturing and packaging costs as well as improving time to market (because the manufacturing, packaging, and distribution cycles effectively vanish). But other cost savings can also occur. One company that used to print a customer service registration card to include in its product packaging found that enormous savings were realized when the registration card was posted online instead. The company still had to package and distribute its products, but moving the product registration system to the company website involved very little set-up expense and was a great success. What's more, the customer data that was obtained via online product registrations could be automatically routed into a database and compiled into usable reports that informed the company's marketing and product development groups and helped them to better reach and serve the company's customers.

Whatever your site's goal, your revenue model must line up with the type of site you are creating. You'll want to play with spreadsheets that consider various what-if scenarios to determine which revenue model or combination of models will result in a reasonable return on your investment.

Tip

It's generally wise to maximize your opportunities to bring in revenue. Given the wild ride that e-commerce promises until the industry matures, you'd be especially smart to develop multiple revenue streams. Diversify your revenue sources, but base them all on leveraging your core offerings. One content-driven website venture reports that it pulls in revenue from selling advertising space, selling subscriptions to premium content both online and in print newsletters, selling products related to the topic of the website's content, licensing content to other sites, and even offering special in-person conferences that feature the experts who write for the site.

Considering the Return on Your Investment

Every e-commerce website must return *something* on the investment that was made in order to create it. If there is no return, financial support for the website will evaporate. Profit is an obvious return, and sites that sell products or services are generally intended to return a profit. Increased branding, retail sales, maintenance of wholesale accounts, and public relations—also legitimate reasons for building a website—also all demand a return, although the return might not be as clearly delineated as a direct profit.

Your venture's primary goal might not be to turn a profit. The goals of many sites don't include profit. Some are cost centers whose purpose is to make a product or a company's identity (its brand) known to a wider market, to gather research data that will be analyzed and published as a report, or to allow a city's citizens to easily obtain information or such items as business licenses or building permits. Whatever your site's purpose or offerings, in the course of developing your budget, you must account not only for costs but also for revenue or some other return. For the site to survive, you must be able to show that it brings value to the company and that value must be clearly justified by an understanding of the site's goals, the site's costs, and the company's standards for measuring the site's success. (See Chapter 13.) Remember: An e-commerce venture that does not realize a return on its investment is nothing but a hobby.

In a typical budgeting or business plan situation, a manager calculates return on investment by comparing the actual or predicted costs of a project (both the dollars spent and the "soft costs" of time spent) with the anticipated gain. Generally, you can figure the expected return on investment (ROI) for your specific project by using a formula such as this one:

```
(Net revenue + hard savings + soft savings - Total investment)/
(Total investment) x 100 = ROI
```

Note that the result of the formula is a *percentage*; typically, return on investment is described as a percentage of the investment that was (or will be) made. In a best-case scenario, the percentage is a positive number (for example, 4 percent, 28 percent, or 136 percent) showing that the project will be profitable. In your budget or project plan, tie the factors (revenue, cost savings, and so on) to explanations that detail the source of the revenue or savings you expect.

Even if the project isn't expected to turn a profit for some time, you can use a spreadsheet to facilitate more complex calculations that analyze ongoing costs and track (hopefully) increasing revenues until the balance of costs against revenues becomes favorable. When the return cannot be directly tied to hard numbers (as is the case with a promotional site, for example), the whole matter gets fuzzier. Chapter 13 describes various metrics you can use to assess the success of websites based on their actual business goals. Again, setting up a spreadsheet that tracks the achievements of the site and the success of whatever it promotes, provides, or offers in relation to the investment made in the site can help you put together hard numbers to underscore the site's real business value.

Using Microsoft Excel

Microsoft Excel offers a comprehensive set of tools for creating spreadsheets and analyzing business scenarios. You can convert a spreadsheet to HTML via a simple menu choice and then post it on a website—for example, on an extranet that provides sales representatives or buyers with information, or on an intranet that keeps web team members up-to-date as they build or maintain your site. When data has to be changed, a nifty feature of newer versions of Excel allows you to make the change on your spreadsheet and have the change appear automatically on your website. (Conversely, you can also easily import data from a website into an Excel spreadsheet.)

Building an Excel spreadsheet involves labeling the columns and rows (as shown in Figure 2.1 on page 43), then entering the appropriate numbers into *cells* (the junctions of columns and rows), and finally writing formulas that use the numbers to perform calculations. You can manipulate the *data* (the numbers in the cells) in all sorts of ways—for example, by running what-if scenarios such as: "What if the website gets 200,000 visitors a month; how much revenue can I then expect from ad sales?" or "If costs exceed revenue by 20 percent, how much of a cushion will I need to keep things going for a year?"

To find out more about using Excel, see Microsoft's website (*www.microsoft.com*) or one of the Microsoft Press books devoted exclusively to using Excel.

Note

Microsoft's website also offers tools and products that help businesses use Microsoft Office (and Excel) effectively. You'll find information on how to run what-if scenarios and how to do the kind of financial modeling that large corporations do.

Using Microsoft bCentral's Management Tools

Smaller businesses can use Microsoft bCentral's Finance Manager to manage business finances and accounting. Finance Manager offers (via any Web-connected personal computer) a host of features for managing receivables, payables, general ledgers, inventory, and financial reporting. Finance

Manager makes monitoring business vital statistics easy. Because this tool is offered as an online service, you can even specify that your CPA can securely access your important business information and consult with you about it.

You can use Finance Manager in conjunction with an integrated set of services bCentral offers (Commerce Manager and Customer Manager) to automate the receivables process. Using these tools together, you can manage information about your customers and their orders effectively. You can track their payments and your inventory. Finance Manager offers easy-to-use tools for automatically compiling financial information, enabling you to make sound business decisions without investing in your own in-house network or an expensive IT department. With Finance Manager, you can always have your eye on the bottom line without taking it off serving your customers.

Chapter 3

Knowing the Legal Issues

You might not own what you think you own, even if you've paid for it. Further, not everything that is easy to take and use can be taken and used legally. And yet, your ideas and the tangible assets that make up your website can often be taken and used by others quite easily—sometimes without repercussions.

These seemingly paranoid realities are at the core of a set of issues you must understand and deal with in order to protect your investment in your e-commerce venture. However large, small, or even altruistic your venture might be, if you don't know and attend to legal matters, you might open yourself up to a world of legal trouble.

As a businessperson, you've probably dealt with the laws that govern setting up or running a business. If your company is of the brick-and-mortar variety, you're probably well aware of the ongoing legal issues that affect your business. For example, it's only common sense that you cannot defraud your customers, that you must honor your guarantees, and so on. You also know that to protect your company and your merchandise, you have to lock the door and provide security systems. In e-commerce, a new twist is added to these familiar business practices—e-commerce involves *publishing* (when you make your website public, you are publishing it), so some issues arise that might be less familiar to you than standard business practices. This chapter introduces the general legal issues involved in launching and maintaining an e-commerce website.

Note

I'm no lawyer, and what you read here is not meant as legal advice. For legal advice pertaining to your particular situation, consult an attorney who practices Internet or e-commerce law. Developments occur rapidly, so it's especially important to stay on top of the issues. For general legal information, one great online source is FindLaw at _www.findlaw.com_. But again, the best resource is an attorney who is versed in Internet and e-commerce law.

What Is Intellectual Property?

Intellectual property is, quite simply, something that is owned (at least at first) by the person who thought it up (its creator). From the content that attracts traffic to your website to the code that drives the back end, someone owns every bit of everything that composes the site, and it isn't always clear who owns what. For example, at one level the creator of a page "owns" that page, but the page might include a licensed image, a piece of public domain text, or a bit of code that was created by a programmer who assigned the rights to use it in a limited way. (Whoever creates a piece of code or text owns it, though the creator can transfer ownership to another person or other people.) You want to be sure that you have legally created, bought, or licensed all the components of your website, and you want to be sure that no one is going to steal them from you.

Intellectual property is a business asset. But unlike "tangible" property, such as inventory or real estate, intellectual property is not something you can necessarily hold in your hand, walk on, or point to, though you can usually document it or capture it in an art form. Intellectual property can be the plans for a specific kind of computer, the operating system running on a computer, or a specific piece of the code that makes up that operating system. It can also be a piece of art, music, or writing—say, the verses a poet types using a word processor (a piece of software that is, of course, another type of intellectual property).

Note

Unlike tangible property, intellectual property is infinitely reproducible; it can be consumed by one user and still be available for use by any number of other users.

In contracts, a creation that is intellectual property is often called *the Work* (with a capital *W*), and the Work is owned by its creator. (For the rest of this chapter, the term *Work* will have this connotation.) Essentially, intellectual property laws address ownership and control over the *representation* and implementation of ideas (not the ideas themselves—read on). As the owner or manager of an e-commerce website, you should be aware of five areas of intellectual property law:

- **Trademark law** Protects identifying symbols, words, and names of businesses, products, and services.
- **Trade dress law** Protects how a product or its packaging or presentation looks. (In e-commerce, the product might actually be the website itself; its design or look might be thought of as its trade dress.)
- **Trade secret law** Protects information of value kept secret by a company, such as the exact formulation of the Colonel's 11 herbs and spices in Kentucky Fried Chicken, or a proprietary, internal process for managing specialized website content.
- **Copyright law** Protects original Works created by an author or artist, such as written material, illustrations, music, or videos. Note that copyrights are more commonly licensed or sold than some other intellectual property; we'll get into that later in this chapter.
- **Patent law** Protects inventions and processes. Patents, too, are commonly licensed or sold.

Caution

To play it safe, assume that everything on the Internet is owned by someone. That someone, however, might be willing to grant you permission to use his or her property or might agree to a licensing contract (perhaps with fees).

Who Owns What on a Website?

A website is made up of a lot of bits and pieces. The most obvious components are the art, text, and page layout that users see. Behind the scenes is a lot of code—usually HTML and other code—that makes the page layout work. Behind that is often a database (holding the pieces that make up a catalog of products, or even holding some of the content of the site) and a transaction system. More code and a variety of tools (software, forms, and other stuff) make the database and transaction system work. What seems simple and easy to use on the surface is actually a complex system of components, all working together. Any of these pieces—and the bits that make up these pieces—can be owned. And the various bits that make up a single, larger piece are not necessarily owned by the same person.

Here's what it all boils down to: When you purchase a piece of "original" commercial art from a designer, the designer might use as a departure point or as an integral part of the final image any combination of "stock" photography, clip art, or original images. Different *fonts* (styles of type) might also be used to incorporate text into the piece. The designer has to pay a fee for the use of stock photography and might have to pay to use other types of images or some fonts. If an original photograph is taken, a fee might also have to be paid to the photographer and to anyone who appears in the photo. Each of these fees might be for one-time use in a limited venue (for example, in a print brochure to be distributed only in the United States) or for unlimited use.

Along the same lines, when a designer creates a web page, it might include text that was purchased for one kind of use, a piece of art that was purchased for another kind of use, yet another piece of art that was purchased for a more narrow use, and so on. In fact, a single piece of art could contain several small images, each licensed for a different kind of use!

Similarly, a developer hired to create your site's back end (see Chapters 1 and 10) might use *proprietary* code or tools. (Proprietary means privately owned and controlled.) The developer might, for example, use code or tools that are owned by his or her own company. In a worst-case scenario, you might find after you've paid for your site that pieces of it are not actually yours. In fact, various pieces might belong to an assortment of different entities and might be licensed to you for only limited uses. These uses might not all match up with each other or with your plans.

Regardless of who actually creates your website, you need to know what you can and can't legally use and whether you have to pay fees for the use. You don't want to get an unpleasant letter from a lawyer demanding that you either dismantle your site or pay for the unwitting use of material that belongs to someone else.

Caution

Whether you hire a firm to create your website or you create it yourself, it's imperative that you know the details about what makes up your site and what legal rights you have to use or reuse text, images, code, and tools. An attorney can help you sort this out by reviewing any contracts you set up with developers or designers.

You Can View the Source, But Don't Use It

Unlike the specifications for a computer or a building, you can easily see a web page's specifications. (You can view the workings of the page itself but not those of the back end.) Simply choose Source (or a similar command) from your browser's View menu to display the source code that makes up the current web page. Technically, you could simply cut and paste that code into a new document and use it yourself. In fact, in days gone by, some web design students were told by naïve instructors to do exactly that. But the code was created by someone else—not you—and if you use it, in general, you are stealing.

An exception to this principle is that some people—including "open source" proponents—do allow others to use their code, but they usually post a notice offering permission on their web pages or in the underlying code.

Most people, however (and particularly their lawyers), believe that stealing and reusing their code, content, or even the "look" of their pages is a violation of intellectual property rights. So remember: You can look, but unless you've been given permission, you cannot touch.

Ownership of Look and Feel

In the e-commerce industry, the public face of a website, including both its design and functionality, is often called its *look and feel*. Look and feel are closely tied to branding. (See Chapter 5.) The elements that make up look and feel (colors, graphics, navigation tools, layout, typeface, and anything that visually distinguishes one site from another) are often referred to in legal documents as *trade dress*. The 11th Circuit Court of Appeals defines trade dress as the "total image of a product [, which] may include features such as size, shape, color or color combinations, texture, [or] graphics."

To understand this, think about the differences between an online gaming site and a site devoted to working moms. One wants to convey excitement, competition, speed, power, and hyperreality. The other wants to present itself as a resource for overextended women who are trying to juggle career and family and still somehow find time for refreshment and renewal. Both sets of concepts can be telegraphed to the user by the purposeful choice of colors and graphics. A company that realizes that the look of its website is part of its branding devotes attention and resources to defining and refining that look. The company then pumps even more resources into keeping the look consistent and extending it into the world. The company is not about to let anyone muscle in on that look and feel because it's part of the company's intellectual property.

Ownership of Back-End Systems

As mentioned in Chapter 1, *back end* is a catchall term for the technical underpinnings of a website. A back end can be as simple as a few *scripts* (simple programs) that enable a customer to add her name to a mailing list via a form, or it can be as complex as a large catalog database and transaction system that facilitates credit card purchases and electronic interactions with suppliers and distributors, along with a sophisticated content management system that enables workflow among multiple content creators and editors as well as distribution of content among licensees.

When you hire a web shop or individual programmer to create a back end or modify an existing back end, either of them might use pieces of code or tools that they own or that are owned by someone else. You must know who owns what, including what pieces of code the web shop or programmer has developed and licensed to you for a specific purpose or a specific time and what tools they have licensed on your behalf for your use. How can you acquire this information? You have to ask. Ask during the initial interview, before the contract is written. Ask a lot of questions, and then make sure your understanding is clearly spelled out in the contract. (See Chapter 9 for more about hiring a web shop or programmer and about what you should ask before entering into a contract.)

Note

If you use an off-the-shelf back-end product, such as Microsoft SQL Server, you are *licensing* the technology. The manufacturer still owns it; you have simply paid for the privilege of using it (probably within specified limitations).

Ownership of Content

Content is, to many people, a nebulous term. Legally speaking, it refers to the images, text, video, and sound on a page, but it also refers to the *expression* of ideas those elements contain. Note that no one can own an idea. It is the expression of the idea that is owned, and the expression becomes owned the moment it is fixed in tangible form. (See the section titled "Can Copyright Laws Protect You?" later in this chapter.) An artist, musician, or writer owns any original Work he or she creates. Technically, any individual who writes an original sentence (even in the form of an e-mail) owns his or her "Work" (the sentence). In traditional media—books, maps, lyrics, poetry, screenplays, images, written instructions, and others—a Work is owned by its creator until and unless the creator assigns, sells, or licenses rights to the Work to another entity. Most employment contracts require employees to assign the company the rights to any Works they create on the job. Similarly, some publishing contracts assign rights to a written Work to the publisher.

Note

If a person writes e-mail at work, the terms of his or her employment agreement might specify that the e-mail, like other Works created on the job, is the property of the company.

Ownership of Ideas

As stated in the previous section, in legal terms, no one can own an idea. Only the expression of the idea can be owned and protected. You cannot protect a claim to ownership of the idea of a story about star-crossed lovers on a sinking ship, but you can protect a claim to ownership of the movie *Titanic*. (Don't you wish!) The tangible form, expression, or implementation of an idea can be owned and protected but not the idea itself. Even when an invention is patented, it is not the idea that is protected by the patent; it is the tangible implementation of the idea. To obtain a patent, you must have fixed the idea in the tangible form of a drawn or written plan for a process. Likewise, to hold a copyright, you must have expressed the idea in a tangible form.

Can Copyright Laws Protect You?

Although you might not think of yourself as a publisher, copyright laws figure strongly into your e-commerce site. Generally, intellectual property is divided into two types: industrial property, such as inventions, industrial designs, trademarks, trade dress, and trade names; and copyright, which protects a variety of creations, such as plays, music, books, poems, photographs, movies, maps, and more. Copyright laws don't protect your inventions, processes, back-end systems, and look and feel. Copyright does address the *content* of your website. To hold the copyright to that content, you must be its creator or you must have been assigned rights to it by the content's creator or creators. Before you assign rights or have them assigned to you, however, make sure you understand what copyright is, what you are protecting when you hold copyright, and how the law protects copyright. Above all, when rights are being assigned, be sure that the party assigning them actually owns the rights being assigned.

What Is a Copyright?

A *copyright* is a right of intellectual property that, for a limited time, provides the creator of a Work (or someone to whom the creator assigns rights) specific, exclusive rights to the Work. Copyright does not cover ideas, facts, blank forms, specific words, titles, or names. It also does not cover existing material the creator of the Work incorporated into the Work. It covers only the *original expression of an idea* (a creation), and only once it is *in tangible form* (a Work).

Caution

Simply placing a copyright notice on your website does not mean you own everything on the site. You cannot protect your rights to something you don't actually own. Ownership must exist first; copyright notices simply signal the intention to protect ownership.

Originally, the term *copyright* meant the right to make copies—to produce or reproduce a Work. Copyright law came into being with the invention of the printing press and was created to sort out who had the right to make, and profit from, copies of Works that could be printed. In today's world, a Work is owned by its creator, who holds the copyright as soon as the Work is created and fixed in *any* tangible form. For example, a piece of writing does not have to be printed in ink to be in tangible form. If it's written on a word processor and exists only on a hard drive, it is still considered "fixed in tangible form." Similarly, digital art or music that is distributed over the Internet—Works that exist only in digital form—are considered fixed in tangible form and are owned by someone.

Works in new media—websites, for example—present new twists in the copyright story. One dilemma, as described earlier in this chapter, is that each page is created from a number of other elements—text, images, other media, code—that might each be a Work in and of itself. Another problem is that a web page viewed in one browser might look different when it is viewed in another browser. Can this "changing" web page be considered an original Work fixed in tangible form? The consensus has been that it can because the web page is fundamentally a fixed arrangement of elements, laid out by a creator as an original Work and fixed in a tangible (if digital) form. Websites, like printed Works, are covered by copyright.

Copyright law recognizes the following rights:

- The right to reproduce the Work by any means and in all media
- The right to prepare derivative Works based on the copyrighted Work
- The right to distribute copies of the Work
- The right to perform the Work in public
- The right to display the Work in public
- The right to claim authorship and to prevent use of the author's name on a Work that he or she did not create
- The right to prevent distortion of the protected Work

Tip

The U.S. Copyright Office is part of the Library of Congress; you can find it at *www.lcweb.loc.gov/copyright*. Also, attorney Ivan Hoffman maintains a website full of useful articles on copyright and other intellectual property issues at *www.ivanhoffman.com*.

How Does Copyright Law Work?

In the United States, which (like most countries) supports the Berne Copyright Convention, almost all Works created after March 1, 1989, are protected by copyright, whether or not they are marked with a copyright notice. (Placing a copyright notice on a Work does, however, make it easier to defend the copyright. More on this in a moment.) Copyright is a federal law. It is also a civil law rather than a criminal law, so those accused of violating copyright law might be sued but do not face potential jail time (although criminal charges can be filed in cases of commercial counterfeiting, such as when someone prints counterfeit CDs).

The term of a copyright is, as of this writing, the life of the creator of the Work (or his or her heirs) plus 70 years. (The term was 50 years until a change was signed into law in 1998.) Copyright is transferable to heirs or others and can be sold or licensed. Rights to a good deal of the Works created by the Beatles were sold decades ago when the lads were young. The rights to some of their Works later became the property of pop icon Michael Jackson, for example.

In some special cases, such as when an independent contractor is hired to create a Work, the terms of copyright can differ. If you are an independent contractor or are hiring one, you can find out more by consulting online resources or, preferably, an attorney.

Marking Your Site with a Copyright Notice

To notify visitors to your site of your copyright, it is advisable to place a copyright notice on the site. A typical copyright notice looks like this: *Copyright © [date] [author or owner's name]*. (Replace *[date]* with the date the Work was created and *[author or owner's name]* with the name of the person or company that holds the copyright.) Whether you need the © symbol varies from country to country, but it isn't a problem to have it, and it can help. Also, in the United States, you don't have to use the phrase *All rights reserved*, but in some other countries it is required, and it doesn't hurt to include it, especially because the Web knows no boundaries. You might also want to include more lengthy and specific legalese; your attorney can advise you on what's best for your situation.

Note

HTML does not include a code for the © symbol. You can produce the symbol in many browsers using the code *&#169* or, better yet, *&copy*. However, because not all browsers recognize those codes, the safest route is to use the word *copyright* in your website's copyright notice as well as the symbol.

You can register a Work with the U.S. Copyright Office (*www. lcweb.loc.gov/copyright/*). Doing so provides extra proof that you are the creator of the Work and, more importantly, is necessary to protect your Work in court. In fact, before you file suit for infringement, you must have your copyright registered. Registering a Work also brings additional rights, which you can investigate via the Copyright Website (*www.benedict.com*) or other resources.

What About Copyright Infringement?

Copyright infringement is like poaching; it's taking something you don't own. The best way to avoid infringing a copyright is to create something new. Don't cut and paste someone else's code, don't nab someone else's image files and use them, and don't copy someone else's text. As you are putting together your web pages, keep in mind these points:

- Don't delude yourself into thinking that the owner of the Work you copied will be flattered that you took it. More likely, he or she will be peeved.

- Don't lull yourself into thinking that because you altered the Work a tad, you're not stealing. You can paint that blue Buick red, but it's still stolen.

- Don't think that merely giving credit (or *attribution*) for the Work on your site is good enough. For one reason or another, the owner of the copyright might not want to be associated with your site.

Admittedly, it's tough to be original. Even George Harrison might have said, "Oh, was *that* the song I was humming?" when he was accused of plagiarism. In that case, Bright Tunes Music Corp., copyright owner of the Chiffons' song "He's So Fine," sued and won against Harrisongs Music for lifting harmonies and using them in "My Sweet Lord." The plaintiffs did not have to prove the infringement was purposeful; the ruling was based on unintentional infringement.

And don't think that the Web is so big that no one will know you took and used something. Copyright owners frequently search the Web for their own names and sometimes for key phrases from their Works. What seems like a tiny needle in the huge World Wide Web haystack can come right to the top of a list of search results. Your best bet, if you're enamored of some content and want to use it, is to e-mail the Work's owner and *ask* if you can use it. (Of course, you'll probably want to document all permissions granted and store that information among your files.)

Legal matters get worked out in the courts, and lawyers turn to precedents set in the courts for guidance in interpreting the laws. Because the advent of the Internet—and the Web in particular—brought about situations no one had considered before, the application of copyright law to the Internet has had to be tested in the courts. Cases have addressed such questions as whether an ISP is responsible or liable for infringement on the part of its subscribers. How all this unfolds will be up to the courts.

Note

The development of a new technology, for example, could bring up the question of whether a website's visitors can embed notes on a site's pages for others to view. If the notes are displayed in such a way that they appear to be part of the pages' content but they were not put there by the pages' creator or creators, visitors probably can't embed the notes.

Can you ever use someone else's Work without first getting formal permission? Under some circumstances, it is permissible. When the use of a portion of a Work is what's known as *fair use*, the portion of the Work can be used without first getting permission. When the Work is in the public domain, anyone can use it.

What About Fair Use and the Public Domain?

Fair use refers to the granting of the privilege (not the right) to use a small portion of a copyrighted Work for the purpose of reviewing the Work, teaching, reporting events, or creating a parody. While reviewing a book, a reviewer can quote a brief passage. She cannot reproduce the whole Work, but a few lines from a poem or story might be acceptable. Although a person cannot photocopy another person's poems and sell them, an instructor can reproduce a few lines for the purpose of teaching about that poem. To report on the news, a journalist can quote a brief passage from another Work. (Again, the whole Work cannot be reproduced.)

Under fair use, you cannot copy a passage from someone else's Work and simply put it on your e-commerce site because you like it. To recap why:

- You cannot copy someone else's Work without their permission.

- You cannot profit from someone else's Work without their permission.

In fair use cases, the portion of the material you use in relation to the size of the whole Work is generally important, as is the actual use to which you put the quoted Work. Anything that could be construed as decreasing the income of the Work's creator is unacceptable. Here is an example: In the book you hold in your hands, screen shots appear as illustrations. Within the book, they are generally considered to fall under the fair use umbrella because the book is instructive and because it reports on or reviews web pages. However, printing any of the same screen shots on the book's cover would not be fair use because the purpose of the cover is not to instruct or review but rather to sell the book.

Caution

It's quite difficult to know when fair use is applicable. The privilege grants limited use in limited ways of limited amounts of material, but the specifics of each case vary and judgment calls are not easy. It has been said that copyright is the one branch of the law you really know you're violating only when a judge tells you so.

Some Works are in the public domain. These Works can be used by anyone for any purpose. A Work can enter the public domain in any of several ways, including:

- The copyright was defective. (For example, the owner might not have followed the copyright laws in effect at the time and so might not really own the copyright.)

- The copyright might have been granted before 1909 and not renewed.

- The copyright expired without being transferred to heirs or sold.

Very old Works (for example, the Bible and the plays of Shakespeare) are generally in the public domain, but the Works of Ernest Hemingway (and indeed his personal letters) are not. Publications of the U.S. Government are in the public domain, but only because the U.S. Government said they would be.

Caution

The laws of public domain vary from country to country and can be very complex. As always, seek professional legal advice to be safe.

You can publish public domain Works on your website without repercussions. But exercise caution: Don't simply assume that a Work is in the public domain; make sure of it. For example, clip art sites have cropped up all over the Web. They offer snippets of art that you are told you can use without paying a fee or for a very small fee. Be very careful. In some cases, a practiced eye can see that what is presented as clip art is actually a photo scanned from a national magazine. True clip art is public domain because its creator put it in the public domain; photos scanned from magazines are not clip art.

Can You Use People's Images?

Can you use someone else's image on your website? This is a stickier question than it might at first seem. Perhaps obviously, using a picture of Tom Cruise or some other celebrity to sell cars on your site is likely to bring lawyers to your door. Celebrities profit from their images and protect them as a business asset. In fact, the heirs of deceased celebrities do the same, so don't imagine you can simply substitute James Dean for Tom Cruise. In some states and countries, people also have a *right of privacy,* which prevents disclosure of embarrassing private facts, casting someone in a false light, intrusion, and (of most interest here) misappropriation, which is also known as the *right of publicity*. According to the right of publicity, each person has a right to control the use of his or her name, likeness, voice, biography, and overall persona such that others cannot use them for commercial purposes. This means that you should probably get permission from your Aunt Matilda before you use *her* image to sell your products on your website.

Why Does Licensing Matter?

You might be the owner of a Work that someone else wants to use, or you might want to use a Work owned by someone else. In either case, a written agreement, however simple, keeps the lines of the deal clear. It does not always involve payment, but it does always involve rights.

When you want to use a Work that someone else owns, you can simply request permission, which is easy enough to do and often results in success. Sometimes the granting of the permission will involve restrictions on the use.

If the owner of a Work prefers to *license* its use rather than simply grant permission to use it, the licensed use can involve special restrictions or require payment. Generally, licensing specifies length of time, types of use, geographic location of the use, and so on. It does not transfer ownership. The owner can license as many uses to as many people or entities as he or she likes, and several licensees can license similar or identical uses.

Typical licenses provide for any of the following types of rights:

- **Nonexclusive rights** grant permission to one of perhaps many licensees the right to use the Work in certain specified ways. Restrictions might include such items as length of time, type of use (for example, print or electronic), use within a geographic area, or a specific venue (for example, only a particular brochure or print ad).

- **Exclusive rights** grant permission to one licensee, who has exclusive use of the Work for the time and perhaps the use specified in the agreement.

Note

Assigning copyright is not licensing; it is transferring the copyright itself, usually for a one-time payment or royalties or other payment based on income the Work produces. Note that when a copyright is transferred, the entity to whom it's transferred can actually assign (or transfer) it to others unless the written agreement says otherwise. When you "sell" your copyright, you are actually assigning it.

Licensing, then, provides a way for the creator of a Work to allow others to use it without giving up ownership rights to it. To the owner of a Work, licensing provides a method for gaining profit from it; to the licensee, it provides an opportunity to gain use of the Work without having to pay a larger sum to own it. Many companies choose to acquire the use of Works, such as graphics, text, video, and audio, by licensing them instead of buying them. Licensing is cheaper than outright buying and is the sort of deal that results in your favorite rock songs showing up in car, footwear, and jeans ads. Most licenses include lots of legalese; you will almost certainly want to consult with an attorney before entering into a licensing agreement.

Note

Debate rages about whether license agreements like those you "accept" when you click on a dialog box in a piece of downloaded software are actually enforceable. Some people contend that because there is no piece of paper with a signature on it, an actual agreement hasn't been signed. However, as a user, you probably don't want to test this matter in the courts yourself, so it might be wise to treat these licenses as real agreements.

About "Work for Hire"

In one distinct situation, a Work is not owned by its creator. According to the Copyright Act, a *Work made for hire* is "a Work prepared by an employee within the scope of his or her employment." It can also be "a Work specially ordered or commissioned for use as a contribution to a collective Work, as a part of a motion picture or other audio-visual Work, as a translation, as a supplementary Work, as a compilation, as an instructional text, as a test, as answer material for a test, or as an atlas, if the parties expressly agree in a written instrument signed by them that the Work shall be considered a Work made for hire." You can hire someone to create a Work and specify in the contract that it is a "Work for hire." In that case, you (the employer or commissioning party) will hold the copyright to the Work just as if you were its creator.

What Does Trademarking Mean to You?

A *trademark* is a right of ownership protecting a word, phrase, or symbol that represents a product or company in the marketplace. Examples might include the red-ring Lucent Technologies logo or the *It's the real thing* tagline of Coca-Cola. McDonald's has trademarked everything from its golden arches to its clown spokesman to the prefix *Mc*. The title of a specific book cannot be copyrighted or trademarked, but the title of a series of books can be. And of most interest to you, a domain name can be trademarked. The U.S. Patent and Trademark Office attempts to apply to domain names the same standards it applies to other trademarks.

Caution

Domain name conflicts are among the most common Internet-related lawsuits. Knowing and respecting the rights of other companies and people is your best bet for avoiding trouble in this area.

Trademark rights become important and valuable when the trademark gains commercial worth. *It's the real thing* was worth nothing until it became a company asset. The Coca-Cola Company invested huge amounts of money to make that asset a commercially successful brand identifier, and then it gained value. The asset issue has bearing on the trademarking of domain names because the courts have ruled that if a private person registers a domain name that includes a trademarked term, the holder of the trademarked term can basically demand the right to use the domain name.

Note

Related to the trademark is the *servicemark* (SM), which protects the representation of a service instead of a product.

If you use an image, logo, tagline, or other identifying element on your website, you might well want to trademark it. Downloading just about anything from your site is easy for others to do, and once you've made the investment in an identifier, it might be worth going to the extra trouble of protecting your investment as best you can.

Consider this example of trademarking: A few years ago, two industry leaders merged. Company A and Company B were distinguished by different looks; a new brand with yet a different look was created to signal a merged identity to their customers. The new brand's look consisted of specific colors, with the name of the merged company and a logo of curved stripes or *arcs*. "The arc," as the logo became known to the marketing team, became a defining element of the look of all printed pieces produced by the company, and eventually, of the look of the company's website. Even the company's intranet sites were redesigned to include the arc, so that all employees would have a consistent user experience. The arc became the company's identifying symbol; it was part of the company's identity.

If you were to use *an* arc on your site or in your logo, you probably would not bring the wrath of this company down on you. But if you were to use *the* arc, or any arc accompanied by the company's color scheme, font, layout, and other elements in such a way as to duplicate the company's look or user experience, you would probably be told to "cease and desist" or explain yourself in front of a judge.

What Can You Trademark?

You can trademark a word, phrase, symbol, or design, or a combination of those elements that distinguishes your products from the products of other companies. A trademark must, however, distinguish and identify rather than simply describe. You cannot protect a trademark for banana chips, but you can trademark and protect DynoChips (assuming someone else hasn't gotten to it first). You can also protect dynochips.com. Your trademark (and *trade dress*, or look and feel) must be clearly distinguishable from those of others, especially others in your line of business. Domino Sugar is trademarked; Domino's Pizza is as well, although it is also a company with a food product. But other companies could not trademark the too-similar names Domino's Sugar or Domino Pizza. You cannot register or protect a trademark that causes confusion to consumers.

In addition to preventing consumer confusion, the purpose of a trademark is to protect commercial identity, including goodwill, reputation, and marketing investments, by ensuring your exclusive right to use the trademarked item to identify your goods and services. An infringement of trademark occurs when a trademark is used or copied in a way that causes consumer confusion. An infringer can be sued to stop the infringement, and if the trademark holder prevails, the infringer might have to pay both costs and damages.

Tip

The Nolo Press Self-Help Law Center, at *www.nolo.com*, discusses trademark, copyright, patent, and other issues and provides resources and forms for setting up businesses.

Deciphering Trademarks: ™ and ®

What's the difference between ™ and ®? The ™ symbol can be used before a trademark has been registered with the U.S. Patent and Trademark Office. You can replace the ™ with the ® symbol when the registration process is complete. Companies that have registration pending will use a ™ until they can legally use the ®.

Registering Trademarks

To register a trademark, you can simply file an application for registration with the Patent and Trademark Office in Washington, D.C., and pay the requisite fee. You can file for a trademark before you start using it. Because paperwork seldom moves quickly, you might want to file early. Searching the database of existing trademarks to determine whether yours is unique might save you time and money in the long run. You might need the help of a legal professional for the process, but it does provide the strongest possibility for protecting your asset.

How Does the Law Affect Linking?

The Web is, by its very nature, a set of linked documents. In days gone by, it was widely believed that anyone could link anywhere. Linking was the way of the Web. Many thought that the mere act of publishing a website implied permission to link to it. But it turns out that in some situations, links are not welcome. For example, if your site is concerned with family values or presenting material of interest to children, you probably don't want links to your site on pornography sites. If you're trying to establish an environmentally conscious business, you might not want links to your site on the website of the local toxic dumping kings. Similarly, if you are a chemical company, you might not want environmentalists intent on debunking you to be able to link to your site to illustrate their points. An irony of the Internet is that the larger the Web gets, the smaller the world gets—and the faster word can travel about a product's defects, a company's practices, or an executive's foibles.

Here's yet another twist on the issue: Although some sites encourage others to link to specific "buy" pages in their online catalogs, thinking that these links encourage sales, other companies feel quite differently. Why would a company discourage others from linking to its site's internal pages? Perhaps because part of the company's revenue comes from the advertising it sells on its home page, or because the company delivers an important part of its overall marketing message on its home page.

Tip

You can find out about backlinks to your site quite easily. See Chapter 12 to learn how.

If unwelcome links are leading visitors to your site, a simple e-mail message requesting unlinking might do the trick. Remember: It's often best to make your first request polite and even friendly. There's no point in offending the linking party, and alienating them might result in a more unpleasant link before you can finally resolve the issue.

And if you are considering linking to someone else's site, it doesn't hurt to ask permission. You might find, in fact, that asking permission results in a link back to you.

Where Does Business Liability Begin and End?

Like brick-and-mortar stores, your online business must be concerned with *liability*. Liability is essentially *accountability*. You are accountable to customers, co-owners, business affiliates, the government, and the public. If you violate agreements, break laws, cause damage, deceive, or engage in other poor business practices, you might be liable. At best, you might lose customers or have to pay fines; at worst, depending on the infraction and your degree of liability, you could lose your business or be jailed. Doing business on the Internet has opened many new legal questions with which you must be concerned, some of which have been described in this chapter. To protect yourself and your investment, a consultation with an attorney might be a wise investment indeed.

Should You Worry About Slander and Libel?

Slander and *libel* are, respectively, spoken or written messages that reflect on someone negatively or falsely. (TV and radio are technically "spoken," but defamation that occurs via TV or radio is considered libel.) To prove defamation, the offended party has to prove that what was said was damaging. If someone insults you in a forest with no one else there to hear, has defamation occurred? Probably not. Defamation laws specify that the disparagement must be revealed to a third party.

Defamation is a matter of serious concern in the publishing industry, and journalists are trained carefully to avoid it. Given that your website is a publishing venture (you are "publishing" electronic material when you make your website public), the prudent move for you is to avoid defamation, too. If you get into trouble, most states have retraction statutes. If you are accused successfully, you can be forced to retract what you said and even to post an apology on your website or elsewhere. In some cases, a retraction might spare you punitive damages but not compensatory damages. Consider this: The Web is a community of 40 to 90 million users, depending on whose estimate you believe. If a lawyer asks for damages of even 50 cents for every person who might have seen your libelous remark, the bill for the remark can get very expensive very fast.

Avoiding Trouble

With most legal matters, it is usually fairly clear under which set of laws and in which court of which state or country any particular matter falls. But by its very nature, the Web is without boundaries. An e-commerce company can be in one state, the server or servers hosting its website can be in several others, fulfillment of orders for its products can occur in another, and the customer can be, quite literally, anywhere in the world. As a result, it is unclear where a single transaction has occurred, and that in turn makes it difficult to know just whose laws govern the transaction. This does not mean that *no* laws govern the transaction. It does mean that you, as a businessperson, might be subject to laws you are unaware of. It is always best, in this context, to err on the side of caution. Follow the industry's best standards and practices, and watch for overall developments in the regulation of e-commerce.

All this legal talk might seem daunting. Keep in mind that as a businessperson, part of what you do is assess risk. The laws are there to be used and interpreted; that very fact drives the entire legal profession and the court system. You have to make judgments about whether a given situation is worth the business risk. The more you know about the law, however, the more informed your assessment of risk will be and the more likely you will be to stay out of trouble. It is always easiest and cheapest to simply avoid trouble to begin with, rather than step in it and have to deal with the consequences.

Part 2

Creating Identity and Attracting Customers

Chapter 4

Establishing Online Branding

When a product, company, or service is immediately recognized by customers and potential customers, its identity has been successfully established through a process known as *branding*. Branding has a direct effect on a website's traffic and on whether customers make a purchase.

To understand the effect of branding on consumers, imagine that you need to buy laundry detergent. You'll probably go to a store you know. In a new town, especially, you'll most likely head for a store that's part of a familiar chain. When you get there, you'll probably select a product you recognize—one that looks familiar and whose name rings a bell for you. Branding will make this sale because it has created an immediately recognizable identity for a particular store and a certain type of detergent, to such an extent that you choose that store and that brand instead of an unknown store and brand X.

Consider these statistics:

- Forty-two percent of online buyers say that they plan their purchases in advance and that they know ahead of time what brand they want and from which merchant they'll buy (Graphics, Visualization, & Usability Center [GVU] 10th WWW User Survey).

- Eighty-two percent of online buyers indicate that recognizing a product's brand name is an important factor in making their buying decision (Ernst & Young).

To create a brand presence, you must differentiate your website, your product, and your service. You must also create an identity that your customers can and will remember. Admittedly, a corporation with a big budget has an advantage when it comes to creating slick ads and buying media space. But with ingenuity and the pointers in this chapter, you can create effective branding for your e-commerce endeavor. The bottom line is that you must be creative, consistent, and aggressive. And remember: Your competitors will be doing the same thing, so go as many extra yards as it takes.

Tip

Microsoft FrontPage and Microsoft bCentral (*www.bcentral.com*) both offer ways to quickly and easily create a consistent look and feel throughout a website. You can find out more about using either FrontPage or bCentral to build your site in Chapter 8.

The Case of Martha Stewart

Martha Stewart is not just a person; she's a brand. As recognizable now as Betty Crocker was in the 1950s, Martha can put her stamp on anything related to fine homemaking or living a comfortable, pleasant life in town or country. For a lesson in online branding (and branding in general), look at MarthaStewart.com's Martha By Mail (at *www.marthabymail.com*). On this site, products are easy to find, the information customers need is right there, the product photos are clear (users can see a larger photo quite easily), and the transaction system runs like clockwork. When a customer makes a purchase, he or she receives an immediate e-mail confirmation, a follow-up surface mail postcard, and quick delivery. If shipment will be delayed for any reason, the customer finds out about it quickly via both e-mail and surface mail. Martha's smiling (and highly recognizable) face, the user's experience, and the design all establish and support Martha Stewart's branding message. And Martha extends her brand relentlessly through appearances, books, her magazine, and other means. Now that's branding.

The Elements of Successful Online Branding

In the brick-and-mortar world, branding includes *differentiation* (making your product stand out from the crowd), recognizable packaging, and a relentless releasing of messages (TV and print ads, media announcements, and so on) to make sure that the name and appearance of your product are firmly rooted in the minds of the buying public. (Can you sing the Oscar Mayer hot dog jingle?) It's no accident that UPS trucks and FedEx trucks look completely different from each other. Each company—UPS with its brown trucks and staid look, and FedEx with its white trucks and bright colors—is trying to distinguish itself from the other. One look might seem to say "Reliability"; the other "Energy." Each company, through its look, advertising, and messages about its service, underscores those themes at every opportunity. Creating those opportunities and taking advantage of them is known as *extending the brand.*

In an online setting, branding includes:

- Identifying the *goal* of your e-commerce endeavor and making sure that the identity you're creating furthers the goal without muddying the image

- Selecting an appropriate, easy-to-remember *domain name* and making your site's URL a snap to find

- Creating a *look and feel* that is appealing to your target audience, is recognizable, is differentiated from your competitors, and, again, furthers your goal

- Providing your customers with the right *quality of experience*— in other words, making sure they have a positive experience when they enter your place of business (your website)

- Building a website with fine *usability*, which includes smooth, logical navigation; clear organization; general ease of use; appropriate placement of images and media; and smooth readability

- Offering features and content (as well as products and services) that are of *interest and consequence* to the people in your target market or audience

- Maintaining *integrity of service* by seeing to it that your business practices are up to par with your customers' expectations, that your systems and products deliver, and that your customer service is solid

- Putting forth the *relentless message* that your product is good, your service is good, and your company has its customers in mind

Christina Cheney, President and CEO of Simmedia (*www.simmedia.com*), says of online branding, "First impressions are critical and so is the ease of use of navigation and information design. Every aspect of a site, from the functionality to the logo placement, communicates your brand."

Banner Ads Can Boost Visibility

Banner ads can be an effective tool for getting your message out to the public. (See Chapter 12.) Don't expect a lot of people to click those ads to get to your site, however. A "click-through" rate of *half a percent* is considered more than decent. (That's half a person (!) for each 100 people who view the ad.) Think of banner ads—along with print ads and, if your budget allows it, radio and even TV ads—as a method of putting forth your image. A joint study by Stanford University and the Poynter Institute (*www.poynter.org*) showed that even if they don't click, users opening and glancing at a web page do focus on the banner ad on that page for perhaps one second. That one second, according to the study, was determined to be long enough to get a branding message across. For tips on using banner ads effectively, see Chapter 12 in this book as well as ClickZ (*www.clickz.com*) and ICONOCAST (*www.iconocast.com*). For a focus on smaller businesses and on swapping ad space with other sites, visit Microsoft bCentral at *www.bcentral.com.*

Do you need a "hook"? Well, you do need a targeted message. A recognizable tag line and a certain attitude that is communicated in your text, color scheme, and product and domain names can set your brand apart. Whether you expect your ad to result primarily in click-throughs or in delivering a branding message, your ad will be clickable. When a user chooses to click, he or she should arrive at a page on your site that delivers on the "promise" made in your ad. Appropriately applied site features, product demos, key information, or downloadable freebies can work. In your ad, animations can add pizzazz to your identity and attract attention, but as always, don't junk up your image. Make sure that whatever you use is appropriate and not distracting. After all, you want *positive* attention. Don't festoon your ad or your site with gimmicks. One striking image or animation is an accent. Too many is just...too much.

Tip

Associate your site with an attitude or point of view. Stand for something. Just make sure it's an attitude or point of view your target audience will find appealing. Having some people disagree with you is not so bad. You can't be all things to all people, and trying to do so leaves you *un*differentiated.

Naming Companies, Products, and Domains

When people think of your website (and therefore your e-commerce venture), one of the first things that will pop into their heads is the site's domain name. Choosing and registering a good domain name might be the most fundamental thing you can do to brand your site and make it easy to find. Your domain name might be based on your existing company's name, or you might prefer that your website have a different name. If your site sells a single product, you might want to use that product's name as the site's domain name. (But if you have more than one product or you'll be expanding your product line, consider the implications of having a domain name for each product. Supporting a website for each of your products can be unwieldy, expensive, and labor-intensive.)

Note

Internet domain names are not at all related to Microsoft Windows or to Microsoft Windows NT or Windows 2000 network domains. Network domains provide a method for organizing groups of networked users, whereas Internet domains describe the location of a network or server that's attached to the Internet.

Do You Need a Domain Name?

Your domain name will be your online address and will provide you with a business location as well as credibility and an opportunity to create branding. So for the highest level of e-commerce positioning, yes, you need a domain name that fully distinguishes your site.

However, not everyone who wants to engage in e-commerce should feel compelled to set up and maintain a website. (See Chapter 1.) If you plan to sell only a few hand-loomed scarves, you probably won't want to spend much for site setup and maintenance, and the relatively small fee required to register a domain name might actually be too big a bite out of your budget. You'd be better off selling your product via a page on a site that aggregates craftspeople into an online mall. You would then use the mall's domain name and would have no need for your own.

Let's say you are planning to launch a site, but you aren't quite ready yet. You might be concerned that someone else will nab your chosen domain name before you get around to building your site. The dictionary, after all, has only so many words in it, and many of them are already registered as domain names. So are a lot of people's names. There is simply no time like the present when it comes to nailing down a good domain name. Register your chosen domain name now, and you can let it sit like a piece of real estate on which you plan to build someday.

Note

You can "reserve" a domain name for a limited time; this is not the same as registering a domain name. Reserving a domain name is a bit like reserving a hotel room; you have a reservation but you actually register at the hotel when you take possession of the room. To actually use the domain to launch your site, you must have server space lined up to host your site.

Choosing Memorable, Meaningful Names

Whether you are building your site now or next year, you need to consider the issue of your domain name carefully and make sure the name represents your business well. Your company and product names should convey what you're all about. So should the name of your site and your domain name.

In some cases, using generic words as a name is a great way to instantly communicate what your company does. But many people have used that method already; you might have difficulty finding a generic word that both describes your business and is available.

In another twist on the concept, generic words can be used within the domain name. For example, 1-800-Flowers is clearly the name of a flower company that you can reach by phone. It contains a generic word that describes the company's primary product, but notice this: The company name implies using the phone to order, not the Internet. Still, translating that name into 1800flowers.com for the company's e-commerce incarnation can work mainly because the brand is already so well established. If you provide a product or service and your name is already known and trusted, you might want to capitalize on that fact when naming your e-commerce venture.

**Tip**

These days, Internet users often dispense with search engines and simply guess at a domain name. If you want your customers to have a reasonable chance of getting your name right, choose a name that is logical and easy to remember.

Tips for successful naming

In devising the perfect name for your e-commerce venture, keep in mind the following guidelines for naming domains and e-commerce products:

- **Make it memorable.** Your domain name can be your company name, a brand name, or a word that describes your product or service. But make it something people don't have to write down.

- **Make it easy to spell.** Keep the name's spelling simple and easy. If your product is commonly spelled two ways (for example, _donuts_ and _doughnuts_), consider registering a separate domain name for each spelling, along with domain names for any common misspellings. Avoid domain names that include hyphens (such as coffee-express.com) to separate words.

- **Keep it short.** The perfect domain name is less than six letters long, followed by .com or some other suffix. Short domain names are easier to remember and type. However, let's be realistic: Fewer and fewer one-word domain names are left with each passing hour. So...

- **Be flexible.** If your perfect domain name is taken, dream up alternatives. Consider concepts and creative variations. If your company name is Southridge Video, it's a virtual certainty that southridge.com, video.com, and movies.com are all taken. Instead, you might be forced to break some rules and go with southridgevideo.com or southridge-video.com (shudder). You might also consider a solution such as the one that Ryder (the truck rental company) came up with when it named its domain yellowtruck.com after the distinctive coloring of its vehicles. You might even score with a clever domain name that reflects what you do—for example, an earthquake retrofitting company might decide to go with something like stopquake.com, if it's available.

- **Think about the future.** You don't want your name to be too limiting. What once was called Software.net is now called Beyond.com because the company envisioned selling more than just software (and, perhaps secondarily, because it wanted a more memorable and more standard *dot-com* name instead of a *dot-net* name).

- **Give products their own names.** Your website can have the same name as your company, or it can have the same name as your product (if the website is about that product alone). But give your company and your product distinct names. Giving them the same moniker makes it difficult to distinguish the two, and if and when you have more than one product, you'll have a hard time associating your company with the new products. For example, Netscape the company originally marketed only Netscape the web browser. When the company introduced other products, it renamed the browser Navigator, but many people continued to call the browser "Netscape."

- **Investigate the competition.** To succeed in business, you must have one eye on the competition. Take a look at their domain names. If a rival grocer has registered bobsgroceries.com, you might have an opportunity to grab perfectproduce.com.

- **Avoid trademarked names.** Single words cannot be copyrighted, but they can be trademarked. (See Chapter 3.) Phrases and domain names can also be trademarked. What's more, *styles* of naming can be more or less trademarked (at least enough to defend in court). For example, it's best to stay away from Mc-anything or Gadgets R Us to avoid the unwelcome interest of lawyers representing McDonalds and Toys "R" Us. Note, too, that even if a big company hasn't yet registered its trademarked name as a domain, that company will defend its right to do so with great legal vigor. (See Chapter 3 for more information about trademarks and intellectual property.)

Caution

Do your homework. Research a potential domain name. Investigate whether the name is taken (via bCentral.com or at NetworkSolutions.com), whether it's the name of a corporation that might legally take the domain away from you, and whether it infringes on trademarks or copyrights. Conducting a trademark search might involve a lawyer but can be worth the savings in anxiety and lawsuits.

- **Consider registering more than one name.** Registering variations of your chosen name will help guide users who might otherwise accidentally stray to sites with similar domain names. If your domain is propertymgt.com, you might want to register propertymanagement.com and property-management.com as well. (You don't have to actually post your site at all the different domain names; talk to your hosting company about *redirecting* traffic from the variations to the main domain name.) Registering a lot of domain names gets expensive (discussed in the section titled "Registering Your Domain Name" later in this chapter), but it might be worthwhile to also register negative versions of your domain name. The online publication Slate (*www.slate.com*), if it had also registered stale.com, might have stopped a scathing parody in its tracks. Disgruntled consumers have expressed their hostility by registering company or product names in unflattering variations; you might or might not want to go to the trouble and expense of preempting that kind of registration.

To dot com or not to dot com

Whether your company already exists and has a name or you are starting and naming a new company, product, and website, you must think carefully about your domain name. It's your primary identifier on the Internet. You might wonder why some companies use *.com* in their URLs and others use *.net, .org,* or even *.pro*. The next section explains what the different suffixes mean. Suffice it to say here that most users in the United States assume that URLs end in *.com*. Some organizations (and individuals) that are not at all commercial (*com* stands for *commercial*) use the *.com* designation simply to make it easier for users who make that common assumption when they look for a site. You certainly have alternatives, and some alternatives might suit you better than *.com*, especially if your perfect domain name is taken in its *.com* form. To get a grip on how domain names actually work, read on.

Understanding the Domain Name System

A *domain* is a network or single computer that's represented as a *server* on the Internet. (For more about servers, see Chapter 10.) The system that keeps all of the domains distinct from each other is the *Domain Name System* (DNS).

To see how the DNS works, look at this URL:

http://www.microsoft.com/catalog/product/superstuff.html

URLs go from the specific (a document, which is shown on the rightmost end of the URL) to the general (the protocol used to access the document on the Internet, shown at the leftmost end of the URL). The document is in a subdirectory, which is in a directory, which is on a computer, which is part of the network of computers that make up the Web. The fictitious URL in our example shows the document *superstuff.html* within the subdirectory *product* within the directory *catalog* on the server *microsoft.com*, which is a web server (*www*) accessed by using Hypertext Transfer Protocol (*http://*). The *www.microsoft.com* portion also indicates that, in this case, the web server is in the domain *microsoft.com*. The domain name shows who "owns" the URL, but it can also be used for other purposes. For example, in the e-mail address *someone@microsoft.com*, the user *someone* receives his or her messages on the e-mail server whose domain name is *microsoft.com*.

The suffix *.com* in the URL example indicates that this domain is commercial and presumably, but not necessarily, located in the United States. (Because a *.com* suffix is expected by so many users, many European, Asian, and other companies now use it.) Domains that use *.com* are very common, but other suffixes do exist. For example, most countries have a suffix that can be used by the domains registered within that country. Here are a few examples:

.de	Domains registered in Germany
.jp	Domains registered in Japan
.ru	Domains registered in Russia
.uk	Domains registered in United Kingdom

You can find out more about domain suffixes on the Internet Corporation for Assigned Names and Numbers (ICANN) website at *www.icann.org*.

Domains originating in the United States are so numerous that the *.us* country suffix is rarely used. Many U.S. domain types are instead identified by the following suffixes:

.com	Commercial (profit-making) domains
.gov	U.S. government domains
.edu	Educational institution domains
.mil	U.S. military domains
.org	Not-for-profit organization domains
.net	Network provider domains

Other domain name suffixes that describe more specific types of entities (such as museums (*.museum*), co-ops (*.coop*), and professional people (*.pro*) have also been approved for use; however, as of this writing, they have not yet been widely adopted. See the ICANN website at *www.icann.org* for developments.

Note

As mentioned earlier, some European, Asian, and other companies register their sites with the *.com* suffix. Nothing prevents them from using this or any of the other suffixes commonly presumed to be for U.S. sites. For example, *paris.net* is as likely to be in Paris, France, as in Paris, Texas.

Domains are assigned names because names are easy for humans to remember. The domain name must be unique among all domain names so that the computer or computers it represents is not confused with other computers on the Internet. However, computers are machines, and machines understand numbers better than names. For this reason, in the DNS, each domain name corresponds to a unique numeric address—called an *Internet Protocol (IP) address*—that specifically identifies each computer to all the others. In other words, a domain name is a kind of pseudonym for an IP address. As an example, *www.microsoft.com* is a pseudonym for the computer known to other computers as 131.107.1.240, which lives in the domain *microsoft.com*.

Is Your Prospective Name Taken?

One simple (but not foolproof) way to check whether a domain name has already been registered by someone else is to open up your web browser, enter the name as a URL (preceded by *www.* and followed by *.com*), press Enter, and see if your browser locates a website. This method isn't completely accurate because not every domain has a currently operating website, but it is quick and easy.

A far better way to check whether a prospective domain is available is to use a domain lookup service such as those provided by all the standard domain registrars. Microsoft's bCentral website offers such a service, as does Network Solutions (*www.networksolutions.com*). Verio Domain Name Registration (*home.verio.com*) also offers domain name lookup. Usually, looking up a domain name to verify its availability is a quick matter of typing the domain name of interest into a simple online form, clicking a Submit button, and getting an immediate report showing whether the domain is taken.

If your prospective domain name is available, scoop it up immediately. If you don't, you can be assured that someone else will.

Registering Your Domain Name

After you've determined that your prospective domain name is available, registering it is a simple matter. You can usually do it through the hosting company that will house your site. (See Chapter 10.) The hosting company will provide the appropriate form or forms and might charge you a small service fee for getting your domain set up. It will also provide the DNS with all the information (the IP address and so on) that's needed.

Tip

You can also use the service at bCentral to register your domain name.

No matter who registers your domain name, you will receive a bill. To finalize your registration, you'll have to make payment. You'll renew your registration by paying annually thereafter.

Note

The process for registering a domain name might have changed by the time you read this book. Check *www.icann.org* to find out more.

If you prefer to register your domain yourself (for example, if you're hosting the site on your own server at your own location, rather than through an ISP), you can do it through any of the domain registrars, such as Network Solutions or bCentral. The forms on those websites will step you through the process. You'll need information about your IP address and other items, so check what's needed and gather that information before you start.

So now you know what your e-commerce venture is trying to achieve, and you know what you are going to call it. The next question is: What will your site look like?

Establishing Your Site's Brand Identity

The look and feel of your site starts with the *palette* (selection of colors) you use. Web design books are full of information about selecting a palette. For a calm, soothing look, the experts suggest choosing cool blues, greens, and grays. These are classic, corporate colors. (Think IBM.) For a hipper, more modern look, choose the colors in the current week's ads on MTV. Also consider a general look that conveys the image you want to present: If your site is chock full of stuff, go for a busy look; to convey that your site is backed by a stable, trustworthy company, go for an uncluttered look.

Use Browser-Safe Colors

Some computers "recognize" and can display only a certain range of colors—216 of them, to be exact. That range, known as *browser-safe colors*, includes yellows, blues, purples, and so on. It even includes ranges of fuchsias, magentas, and the like. But it does not include all tints or hues of all colors. Yellow, for example, is a notorious problem. There are only a handful of browser-safe yellows, and they are not all terribly attractive. When you select your site's palette and the colors of logos and other identifying elements on your site, your best bet is to stick with browser-safe colors. (See Chapter 8.) You might even want to check out these colors before selecting colors for your signage and print materials. More than one large company has found that its signature color simply cannot be reproduced on the Web, causing no end of dismay for their marketing staffs.

Identifying Your Audience and What They Want

Go back to what you know about your target audience. (See Chapter 1.) Select a visual style that appeals to that audience. Set aside your personal preferences in favor of what works for that audience. If you hate purple but your site sells herbal products and the color lavender will work for your target market, so be it. If you love chartreuse but your target audience is not that adventurous, you might have to go with cobalt. Presumably, your e-commerce site is not a vanity site. It's there to serve your customers. Know your customers, and meet their needs. Think about the following questions:

- What is your product?
- Who is the audience?
- How and why does the product appeal to this audience?
- Are you already reaching an audience you'd like to retain?
- What new audience do you want to reach?

- Does most of your audience already know you?

- How do they see your company or product?

- How do you want them to see your company or product?

- Do they have any general or specific attitudes you ought to take into consideration?

- Where are the greatest opportunities for growth, given your current or projected audience?

- What is the risk that you might lose your audience?

The answers to these questions will help you form a basis for thinking about the development of your website from a branding perspective.

As your business grows, stay close to your customers. FedEx changed its name (and branding) from *Federal Express* to *FedEx* at about the time its customers were starting to refer to it as *FedEx* and even coin the verb "to FedEx" meaning to send an express parcel.

Tip

Brand messages (ads, for instance) take two general forms: those that tell you about a company and those that tell you about its product. Company messages might mention the products ("the makers of WingTips Toys") if they are well known, and product messages might mention the company name ("brought to you by Contoso Pharmaceuticals") if the name will help sell the product. But seldom does one brand message try to do all things. Consider this separation as you create your online brand messages.

What Does Your Logo Say About You?

Your logo (visual identifier) is the stamp you place on all your products, including your website, to identify them as yours. For online purposes, your logo must be available in a horizontal form (to fit pages, banners, and ads more conveniently). It can also be in a vertical form, but that can't be the only form available. Think about how it will work in postage-stamp-size ads. (See Chapter 12 for more about advertising.) Also think about how it will look with a tag line attached to tell people who you are or what you do. Try out different versions of your logo so that you have flexibility in advertising and page design.

Consider the logos of two online brokerage sites, Charles Schwab (*www.schwab.com*) and E*Trade (*www.etrade.com*). The logo for Charles Schwab, the more traditional company of the two, uses a font with *serifs* (those little dangly things hanging off the corners of each letter), which is a more traditional style. The logo itself is in one color on a navy blue, pinstriped background. The E*Trade logo is in a more modern *sans serif* font (one without serifs) and uses three colors (one of which is lime green!), and although navy blue does appear on the site, most of the page backgrounds are black or white, heightening the contrast of the lime green accent color. The differences between these two companies seem obvious from their logos. Both deal with people's money, so they have to inspire trust. But E*Trade, the purely electronic brokerage firm, seems a tad more modern than Charles Schwab, the more traditional, click-and-mortar company.

Defining Your Website's Look and Feel

The design of your site's pages should be consistent with your logo's look. Remember: The key to branding is to be relentless in conveying the branding message. If your site is company-oriented, carry over the look of the company's logo to the site. Repeat the color scheme, the design elements, the fonts, and so on. If your site is product-oriented, repeat that product's look in the site design. It's all about identity.

Go back once more to what you know about your target audience, and ask yourself the following additional questions as you consider how to create your site's look and feel. (If you are using a web shop, you might also want to provide this information to the designers before they begin the project.)

- What is most distinctive about your company or product? What are its strengths and weaknesses?

- Who are your competitors? What are their strengths and weakness?

- What products or services do you offer? Do you plan additions? (If so, describe what and when.)

- Where are you located? Do you prefer to market and sell locally, nationally, or internationally?

- What is the main purpose of your website? Does it have a secondary purpose?

- What image do you want to convey to your audience? Which of these words describe it most closely: conservative, contemporary, modern, creative, elegant, innovative, exciting, earthy, calm, warm, casual, witty, personal, confident, formal, sophisticated, serious, professional, educational, technical, artistic, smooth, dramatic, sympathetic, fun, energetic, or easy? Can you think of any other words to describe the image you want to convey?

- Is there a general image to be avoided?

- What photographs or illustrations will convey the site's message? Are any types of photographs or illustrations to be avoided?

- In order to convey its message, should the site include the company's history or philosophy? What about staff biographies?

- Will case studies, testimonials, or other evidence of customer satisfaction help convey the site's message?

- How long do you plan to keep the site running after launch? Do you plan to minimize maintenance or add fresh content frequently? What sort of content, and how often?

- Will the site need to be tied in to other branding efforts, such as print brochures, the look of your real-world location, or the look of other sites?

- What are your overall marketing objectives?

Sound and Video as Part of Your Branding Message

Identifiers certainly can be audio or even video, as evidenced by the Oscar Mayer hot dog jingle and those computerized tones that identify the Intel Pentium processor. But don't use bells and whistles you don't need. Sound and video might be appropriate for high-tech sites, especially if bells and whistles are the product, and you might want to use them to deliver a message that adds a personal note to your site. Excellent use has been made of animation, sound, and video, but usually as an accent. And accents, by definition, are sparsely applied.

For an example of an e-commerce site with a strong branding that extends into the topics it covers, its general angle on offering branded e-commerce information, and even the tone of its text, take a look at ClickZ (*www.clickz.com*). And to see a cleanly designed and highly functional site that was created for a nonprofit organization, look at the Redland Baptist Church site (*www.redlandbaptist.org*).

So What Works?

As you define your branding message, take a look at what works for other companies. Consider what you might learn from the campaigns of companies that hire high-priced branding consultants. Along with what has already been described in this chapter, your research will tell you:

- **Trade on what you have.** If you are number one in your industry, say so. If you are not, you might be able to turn a seeming disadvantage into a source of inspiration. Remember the Avis campaign from years gone by? Avis was number two (behind Hertz) in the rental car industry, and it very cleverly made a whole campaign out of "trying harder."

- **Get there first to own the space.** It's always easier to stake a new claim than to take one from someone else. Yahoo!, Amazon, and eBay are all examples of companies that were first to market and defined the playing field for others.

- **Market your brand offline.** Use your signage and any print advertising to further your online brand. If your company isn't in a position to launch a print campaign, consider partnering with a company whose brand is already known or a company that is also putting in the effort to get known.

- **Be relentless about getting out there.** Make friends, affiliates, and linking partners. It's the Web, so use links, get reciprocal links, share content, barter for ad space, and build some co-marketing agreements. Work with suppliers to co-market. Create your own affiliate programs. Curry favor with the press. Offer freebies to users who will display your logo or text link on their sites, and never give up the cause.

- **Be consistent.** Maintain a consistent look and message among your packaging, products, ads, and site design. Within the site, don't confuse people by switching the design and color scheme from page to page or from area to area. Make your site's style of writing consistent with its look and feel. A conservative site should have a formal look and more formal writing; a site with a cutting-edge attitude should have an intrusive look and in-your-face writing. Be sure your transaction pages follow through with whatever style you choose for the rest of your site.

- **Actually deliver value to your customer.** Now there's a concept! Make your product or products strong, your service impeccable, and your site's operation smooth. Nothing does more for branding than being the best.

Note

Chapter 12 discusses techniques for promoting your site both online and using traditional promotional methods.

Providing a Quality User Experience

In the world of e-commerce, the customer's experience is a major component of branding. You need to create a positive experience by making sales easy and service solid. Take a look at successful mail-order companies such as Lands' End, and then consider these guidelines:

- **Don't keep people waiting.** Pages should load quickly. Don't assume that customers will have the fastest connections. Unless your audience is primarily high-end techies, design for the lowest common denominator among the target audience you have specifically identified. You don't have to take into account every browser that ever existed and modem speeds that went out with the last century, but do figure out (as best you can) the likely *range* of browsers and modem speeds members of your audience might have and design for the slowest systems among them.

- **Put the goods out in the open.** Make it easy to find what you're promoting or selling. Put links to sales pages in prominent places (such as your home page). Present pertinent information clearly. A confused customer is a customer who will simply walk away. Don't let that happen.

- **Create multiple ways to search your online catalog.** Make it easy to find items based on the price, size, color, brand name, year, topic, and so on.

- **Don't place barriers between the customer and a sale.** Make it easy to pay in as few steps as possible. Don't require registration (the providing of e-mail addresses and survey information) before the customer can make a purchase. Reduce the number of hoops that a customer must jump through to a bare minimum.

- **Build trust.** Online shoppers are a skeptical bunch, and rightfully so. Like all customers, they want to know what they're getting, when, and how it will be delivered. They want to know how you're protecting their credit card information. They also want to know to whom you're selling their name and e-mail address (which they'd prefer you didn't do, by the way) and what you're doing with any marketing data you might have gleaned from them. According to a survey by IntelliQuest, an Internet research company, people who do not buy online cite the following reasons for their reluctance:

  - Concern about fly-by-night retailers (81 percent)

  - Don't want to deal with returns (72 percent)

  - Concern about using their credit card online (69 percent)

  - Concern about getting a lot of junk e-mail (63 percent)

  - Prefer to see and touch what they buy (62 percent)

Given that data, it seems evident that the e-commerce industry as a whole must provide reasons for Internet users to become Internet customers. And that means that e-commerce businesspeople have to instill trust in their customers.

Establishing Integrity and Trust

People want to know what they're getting. In an online setting, the most tangible way to convey what you are going to deliver is via pictures and words. There are, however, other methods for gaining the sort of trust that inspires people to do business online.

First and foremost, be predictable. Follow through on your promises, and deliver what you said you would on time, without fuss. According to online branding pro Christina Cheney, "The most common mistake people make is to overhype and overpromise. Don't launch too fast—make sure you're ready. And don't offer anything you cannot deliver. Of course, time to market is incredibly crucial to an online brand, but follow-through is even more important."

In general, make sure yours is a quality operation. Show your merchandise in detail. (Provide thumbnail-size photos as links to larger images if necessary.) If you are a retailer, feature name-brand products the customer will recognize. Make communication with you or your staff easy by making an e-mail address obvious and including both a surface mail address and a customer service phone number on your site. Display testimonials from satisfied customers. Publish your privacy policy, telling customers what you will and won't do with their e-mail address and any personal information they have provided by registering on your site or making a purchase. (bCentral offers resources for creating a privacy policy.) Assure customers that if they are victimized by fraud while shopping at your site (an unlikely event if you've addressed security issues; see Chapter 10), you'll cover any charges. Create, stand behind, and publish a *no-hassle* return policy that allows customers to send back merchandise for a refund or exchange. If possible, affiliate yourself with a respected association or a large, known, and trusted company.

Here's a thought: Use a face—a well-known spokesperson or, if not the face of a celebrity, then your own. Consider the example of a website for a real estate consultant. His smiling face appears beside a brief description of his credentials and the various associations he belongs to. A navigation bar provides links to standards of practice and other information that can inspire trust in potential clients. If you're shy, perhaps a cartooned likeness can step in for you. But don't use Mickey Mouse, Ronald McDonald, or any other trademarked image. They are part of someone else's brand, and using them will both muddy up your brand and cause the company that owns those images to defend their brands by coming after you. (For information about trademarking, see Chapter 3.)

One final tip: When you use technology to bolster your branding by providing a strong user experience, you have to constantly look ahead. Don't rely on whatever created last year's buzz. And don't just toss in the latest bells and whistles for the sake of bells and whistles. Make sure they count for something, that they further the brand message, and, most important, that they add quality to the customer's experience.

Chapter 5

Enhancing Customer Relationships

Whatever your business, if you are *in* business, you have customers. How you treat them has a profound, immediate, and lasting impact on whether your business thrives. If your business involves e-commerce, you have a notable opportunity to identify, track, target, and stay close to your customers. And, quite significantly, you can interact directly with your customers rather than communicate with them via buyers from your distribution channels, who might be filtering or interpreting your customers' feedback.

Online shoppers are an attractively affluent market. In the United States, they control more than 50 percent of household income. They are also becoming more savvy every day. Because of these factors, you might do well to focus less on *customer service* (a fallback measure for when things go wrong) and more on building customer relationships through service and the savvy use of technology. A *customer care* program tends to the needs of customers from the moment they approach your site until they buy, receive, and use your product or services. Customer care extends beyond the sales cycle to include the entire customer relationship and can include these possible goals:

- Expanding and retaining customer loyalty
- Boosting profit by increasing sales and decreasing costs
- Minimizing the time it takes to get a product or service to market
- Improving products and services in step with what the customer needs and wants

Let's consider for a moment what *service* really means. Whatever your e-commerce website's purpose, when a customer approaches the site, service should be the goal. Naturally, for a sales site, having service as a goal means making your products easy to see, experience, and buy. But suppose your company sells, installs, and services heaters. You might think that all your website has to do is list your company contact information and describe your services. If so, you are missing an opportunity to provide service, attract traffic, and telegraph to potential customers that your company is service-oriented. On your website, you can post seasonal reminders of the services a homeowner or company might need, provide a scheduling service via a simple online form, and offer tips about keeping heating costs in line by regularly maintaining heating systems. You can also display the products you use so that customers don't have to wait for you to mail or drop off a brochure. (And you don't have to check your supply of brochures, either.) In short, you can market your service and products much more effectively.

Here are some other examples of service at work in the overall strategy of a website:

- A health insurer's website can provide listings of doctors who accept the insurance plan. Similarly, a pediatrician's office can provide a list of the insurance plans it accepts, along with immunization schedules and other information of interest to the parents of its patients.

- A local utility company or an electrician can describe how businesses, homeowners, and renters can arrange for electrical service after a move.

- A small company can do without a sales force by posting product or service information online and then sending out direct mail postcards to potential customers, guiding them to the website.

Doing as little as using your website for standard customer service can cut your costs. Forrester Research reports that online customer service efforts can cut overall customer service costs by 43 percent. The savings result primarily from reductions in staffing and phone-service costs. But other, less obvious savings can result from offering extended customer care via a website. In the case of the health insurer in the list of examples just presented, you can see that providing an online list of doctors associated with the insurance plan can save on the cost of printing pamphlets and distributing them. Posting the list online also allows the insurer to update the list more frequently and less expensively, and it gives clients multiple ways to search the list (by ZIP code, medical specialty, or other criteria). Now that's service!

Your website might have building customer relationships through sterling customer care as its central goal rather than simply providing customer service as part of its offerings. Websites oriented toward customer care can effectively communicate with existing customers and prospective customers, provide service and support, augment traditional customer service communications, and offer internal communications about customer service or other topics. But remember: A customer who wants information is likely to use an online option for getting it, while a customer who wants to discuss a bill or invoice will invariably want to talk to a human being. Placing service options before a customer via websites should be part of your customer care program, but it should not be the only avenue your customers have to gaining satisfaction.

Why Service Matters— Especially in E-Commerce

E-commerce is still a new industry, and the public has been somewhat skeptical about embracing it. Who wouldn't be? Aren't we all reluctant to do business with companies we don't know? It just makes sense that we want assurances before we entrust our credit card numbers and purchasing power to an entire industry that's less than familiar. Individual companies engaged in e-commerce are up against the same challenges that face the industry as a whole: How do you build trust? The public is flocking to the Internet and has enormous purchasing power, but how do you sell to it effectively?

You Are Your Website

Your online customers experience your website as if they are walking into your place of business. In fact, to them that's exactly what it is; your website might be their only experience of you and your business. Like customers in the brick-and-mortar world, online customers decide to buy based on their impression of your products and services, your pricing, and how all of that compares with what your competitors offer. But customers also decide whether to buy based on the experience they have while they're at your website.

Chapter 4 discussed the importance of making your site functional, persuasive, easy to use, and easy to navigate. These points also come to bear here, as aspects of establishing and maintaining customer relationships. Just as a "real-world" storefront and the merchandising within can either persuade customers to come in and make purchases or drive them away, so can a website and its "merchandising." If the site's pages are geared to its audience, its information is easy to find, and the catalog of products or services is easy to use and attractive, online customers are more likely to stick around and buy. For pointers on attracting traffic and creating a striking identity for your site, see Chapter 4. For more information about serving your customers effectively, read on in this chapter.

First Impressions Are Lasting

Perhaps you've had the experience of walking into a store, glancing around, not seeing what you want (either the actual product or the level of merchandising and store maintenance you expect), and walking right back out again. If you're like most people, you probably won't give that store another chance. Similarly, you might have had the experience of trying a new restaurant, thinking it was OK but not great, and without being able to put your finger on just why, knowing you aren't interested in trying it again.

Note

The first impression you make is both a lasting one and the easiest one to get right. If a first impression is good, customers will come back. If it's bad, you might not get another chance. Even if you do, you'll be fighting that first failure. It's a lot easier to get it right the first time than to correct a mistaken or disappointing first impression later.

The bottom line here is that if customers doubt your integrity, can't find what they want, or feel misunderstood or confused, they won't stay and they won't buy. Make your website look inviting and trustworthy. Make it function well, not just look good. And make sure that a customer who goes to your site sees what he or she wants—the style, information, products and services, and benefit of being there—immediately. That's the way to keep customers clicking in and keep them from clicking right back out again.

In Customer Relationships, Credibility Counts

No one wants to buy from hucksters. If the e-commerce industry doesn't adhere to solid business standards, including providing first-rate customer care, the industry as a whole will suffer, as will each e-commerce endeavor. Because e-commerce is such a new industry, not only is every e-commerce endeavor creating a first impression, but also the industry as a whole. As more and more well-known companies have started doing business online (bringing with them their reputations for integrity), and as more people have had positive experiences with online business in general, the credibility of the industry as a whole has risen, which in turn has led to more business being conducted online. To continue this trend and enhance the e-commerce industry as a whole, each e-commerce venture must conduct itself with integrity and treat each customer with respect. What else but that, after all, is customer care?

The National Association of Consumer Agency Administrators reports that the top consumer complaints about e-commerce have been that the customer:

- Did not receive the goods or services ordered
- Received damaged merchandise
- Experienced problems getting a refund on returned goods
- Was overcharged
- Believed advertising was false or misleading

Perhaps the truest test of customer service is how returns are handled. A post-holiday survey by Jupiter Communications showed that 42 percent of e-commerce sites never responded to customer inquiries about returns, took more than five days to reply, or didn't offer to respond by e-mail to reported problems. Of course, your employees will occasionally make mistakes. Customer service is about addressing those errors, but it's also about preventing them from happening.

Remember: Bolstering customer care on your website—taking care of each customer from the moment he or she enters your front door (your home page) until well after he or she has received your product or service—will benefit both your business and the entire e-commerce industry. "Making up for it later" gets expensive.

Consider the case of a neighborhood restaurant. This restaurant does no advertising but draws customers from a 50-mile radius. How do people learn about the place? It's simple: word of mouth. The owner of the restaurant feels strongly that his best shot at building a strong customer base is to provide good food and good service, pouring the money that might have been used for advertising into the product. And if something goes wrong— for example, if a cook misreads an order and prepares the wrong entrée and the waiter doesn't notice the mistake but the customer does—the restaurant's policy is not only to correct the error but also to offer dessert on the house. That's great customer service. But is it great *customer care*?

From the customer's viewpoint, the restaurant has made amends for its error. It would have been better if the error had not occurred, but hey, people make mistakes. It's better to acknowledge mistakes, correct them, and learn from them. From the viewpoint of the restaurant, the customer service gesture has preserved the customer's loyalty, but at the cost of the profit margin on the meal.

You're always better off providing good customer care and getting things right the first time than having to pay for customer service after a poorly executed transaction. Bruce Molloy of Brigade (*www.brigade.com*), a provider of outsourced electronic customer service solutions, says, "In the case of low-profit-margin items like a $75 piece of software, many companies find that responding to just two or three customer service calls can kill the profit margin on a specific sale." Molloy goes on to suggest that providing customer service response via e-mail can cut costs dramatically. However, industry experts, including Molloy, agree that the best way to keep overall customer service costs down is to provide good customer care in the course of everyday business rather than in response to a mistake.

Building Customer Loyalty

A good start in providing excellent customer care is to offer customers the options and quality they expect. Make sure you and your product are actually available. You or your staff must be "in the store," items must be in stock, and your products and services must be deliverable. That might seem obvious, but it's remarkable how often the simple issue of order fulfillment trips up a business plan. (See Chapter 1.) Make sure you can service all of your accounts, and make sure your products are usable. Pour resources into making your product or service the best. And above all, understand what your customers want and what will bring them back for more.

E-commerce provides a unique opportunity to stay close to customers. Bruce Molloy suggests, "Focus on customer care, on problems and inquiries, but also on getting a base of information about the customer—how happy are they, and what other services or features might they want?"

You might think you know your customers very well indeed. But asking them what they want can yield surprising results. You might find, for example, that customers want phone support for your high-tech product when you thought they preferred online support. Build simple forms into your website to conduct online surveys, and you'll find out more about your customers as the results roll in. Whether you choose to find out about your customers through surveys, it's a good idea to offer customers an easy way to send e-mail inquiries to you. (Again, you can use Microsoft FrontPage to create an online form that lets customers send e-mail directly from your site to you in a snap.) You can even send customers e-mail responses with small surveys embedded in them. (For more about customer surveys and e-mail feedback, see the section titled "Ask Your Customers—and Listen!" later in this chapter.)

It goes almost without saying that your decisions have a profound effect on your product, your company, and your customers. Remember: It's how well you fulfill your customers' needs that will make or break your business, not how well you satisfy your personal beliefs about what your customers *might* need.

Establish Rapport

Every customer is a good customer; each one spends good money at your business. To keep customers coming back, treat each one as your most important, most valued customer. It's common wisdom in customer service circles that customers respond well to key phrases such as these:

- **Welcome.** You need not say this literally, as in "Welcome to our website"; you can *be* welcoming without actually saying "welcome." Use whatever form of welcoming the target market expects.

- **How can I help?** Let people talk to you!

- **I understand.** Again, you need not say this literally, but do offer messages that reach out and establish rapport.

- **Is this what you had in mind?** If not, find ways to improve it.

- **Is there anything else I can help you with?** This signals an end to the overall communication without alienating the customer.

- **Has this transaction met your expectations?** Using some phrasing that asks how the customer perceives the success of the interaction will communicate that your goal is to serve the customer's needs.

To each customer, his or her own needs matter most. Your goal in providing excellent customer care is to show the customer, via your website's design, its functionality, and its content, as well as through the quality of your communications, that his or her needs matter most to you, also.

Breaches in Privacy Cost Sales

Rushing to get online at the expense of protecting your customers' privacy simply does not pay. Take the time to make sure your systems are secure. Give any programmers you hire the time and resources needed to build and test your transaction system and to address all security issues before you go live. Inadvertently leaving holes in your systems can allow unscrupulous hackers to get to names, addresses, phone numbers, credit card numbers, and other purchasing information. A breach of security such as this is the kiss of death in e-commerce

> ***Breaches in Privacy Cost Sales*** *(continued)*
>
> customer care. And it doesn't even take a knowledgeable hacker to break into a system—innocent users can sometimes get to sensitive information accidentally by, for example, using certain keywords in searches.
>
> Large businesses tend to be more aware of these issues and often spend more money to make systems secure; smaller businesses must make the same conscious effort. The U.S. Department of Commerce and the Federal Trade Commission are discussing how to encourage privacy protection. If the e-commerce industry does not set its own standards and provide the public with good security, these governmental bodies might step in more strongly to enforce privacy standards. At the TRUSTe website (*www.truste.com*), you can find a great deal of information about how to address consumer privacy issues on your website.
>
> If you hire programmers to build your transaction system, verify their credentials and get references. If you hire friends or an untested agency to create your site, be aware of the pitfalls. For example, nonprofessionals might not know the intricacies of security well enough to provide you with the means to protect the privacy of your customers. If you are building the site yourself, be sure to use only those products and turnkey solutions that can back up their security claims with experience and proof. Not protecting the security of your customers is the surest way to lose them. Your customers must trust you in order to do business with you.

Communicate Positively

On your e-commerce website and in customer service e-mails, phrase communications positively to get the best results. Consider the difference between the more reassuring "We'll have it in stock on Tuesday" and the more abrupt "That item is out of stock." In the first case, the customer knows he is being taken care of and will get what he wants; in the latter case, the customer has to fend for himself by asking further questions or just forgetting the whole matter. Consider, too, the difference between "No smoking" and "Thank you for not smoking" (or, better yet, "Smoking is permitted in the outdoor courtyard").

Compare the following examples:

Negative Version	Positive Version
Our product isn't for everyone.	Our product appeals to connoisseurs.
We don't accept American Express.	We accept Visa and MasterCard.
No, we can't walk it down to the mailroom to shave a day off shipping.	Expedited shipping is available for a small fee.

What's an example of the worst kind of customer service failure? Blaming the customer. Here's a true story: A customer ordered a pizza for delivery, and it didn't arrive. The customer called to inquire about the order, and the dispatcher insisted that the delivery person had arrived and knocked, and that the customer "hid" behind the door. The customer replied that no one had knocked on his door. The dispatcher said he was lying. The customer asked to speak to a manager. The dispatcher said he was the manager. The customer pleaded, "All I want is my pizza." The dispatcher (who later turned out not to be a manager at all) answered, "Then you should have answered the door." In this outrageous example, the dispatcher had several opportunities—missed at every turn—to right the situation. It's remarkable that this customer remained calm and that his reaction was only that he vowed never to call or recommend this pizza chain again.

Be Easy to Reach

In many ways, the Internet is all about communication. In traditional sales, communication tends to flow in one direction, from company to customer, and getting feedback from the customer often involves convening expensive focus groups or waiting for communication in the form of complaints or sales figures. In e-commerce, not only can communication flow easily in both directions, but the channels can be more open and immediate. Your website should provide customers with several methods of contacting you. Online forms, e-mail addresses, phone numbers, postal addresses—each has its place in customer interaction, and offering customers a variety of methods to contact you empowers them to communicate effectively and appropriately. The faster, more convenient, and more complete your service is, the more likely casual browsers are to turn into loyal, returning customers. Even more important, providing the means for easy communication instills in customers the sense that their input is valued. In many cases, simply having a way to contact you is so reassuring that a customer's actual need to contact you is diminished. Just as offering a money-back guarantee persuades many people of your good intentions but is an option that few will take advantage of, offering easy communication telegraphs your accessibility to many more people than you will ever hear from.

Handling the Disgruntled Customer

Things sometimes go wrong, and at times even the most service-oriented company finds itself facing an angry customer. Perhaps the customer had a lousy experience with the company, or perhaps the customer is simply an angry, unhappy person. In either case, the customer service representative must handle both the complaint and the customer's outrage.

Responding to an angry customer effectively is an art. Start by listening. Look for an opportunity to tell them they're right—about something. You obviously don't want to tell them that they're right about something that isn't true or that opens the company to legal liability, but find something, even if it's just to say, "I'm glad you're calling this to my attention." At the very least, don't disagree. Instead, ask for details. Getting an angry customer to talk about the situation shifts him or her out of yelling and into problem solving. Next commit to solving the problem. Instead of saying "We'll see about it," say something that starts with "I will...." Something as simple as "I will make a note of that" can help. Ask for the customer's input in coming up with a solution. "How would you like this resolved?" goes a long way toward allowing someone to let off steam and move the conversation forward. Finally, if this is an urgent issue or an especially loyal customer, drop everything and deal with it right away, perhaps by phone or even face-to-face. Keep in mind that only one thing matters to the customer: that the problem be solved.

There are, of course, situations where personal interaction is most effective and even quite necessary. Complex negotiations, the resolving of complicated problems, and addressing concerns about bills are all best done by phone or in person. Further, though the purchase of big-ticket items such as cars and capital equipment can be supported via online information, closing the sale of large, pricey goods or expensive services generally requires personal contact. A survey of online shoppers by NFO Interactive revealed that about 50 percent of those surveyed preferred to shop for cars online but to buy at a dealer. They liked to gather dealer invoicing information from the Web, get the inside scoop, and avoid the stereotypical sales hype, but only 11 percent would actually buy the car online without visiting a dealer. (Of course, the key attraction of the dealer might simply be the opportunity to take a test drive.)

Another survey of online shoppers by NFO Interactive found that some retail customers shopping for items much smaller than cars simply want someone to talk to. Nearly 35 percent of those surveyed said they would buy more if they could interact in real time with an e-commerce salesperson. Of those who had not yet purchased anything online, almost 14 percent said they would if they could speak directly to a customer service representative. Online chat, direct phone contact (as in conventional catalog sales), and e-mail are all options for providing personal interaction.

Caution

Keep in mind that real-time, interactive support can be very labor intensive and, by extension, very costly. It's a great option for some e-commerce businesses, but it's not for everyone.

One option for providing interaction with service and sales representatives can be found in Microsoft NetMeeting, a product that offers online conferencing (via text, audio, or video), an online whiteboard, software sharing, desktop sharing, and file transfer, as well as point-to-point audio and video. Software companies (such as Baan Company) routinely use NetMeeting to remotely train value-added resellers (VARs) by introducing and demonstrating new products over the Internet. Companies can also provide real-time training and support to in-house and freelance team members (including customer service staff). Customer service representatives can provide interactive support to customers via chat sessions and, if necessary, can draw on an online whiteboard that customers can view via their web browsers.

Respond Promptly

Customers see response time as an indication of what it will be like to do business with your company, and the overall promise of the Internet is speed and convenience. Make that the promise of your company, also. When customers contact you, they expect you to answer right away. Confirm orders and answer e-mail immediately. Remember: Big-ticket items demand the quickest response. The more someone spends, the more service they expect. But in general, your goal should be to respond before your customer logs off.

Not too long ago, I ordered a couple of items from a big-name retail sales site. Before I had time to switch to my e-mail window, I'd received a message confirming my order. A follow-up e-mail told me when to expect delivery, and a postcard arrived a few days later reiterating the same information. One item was on back order and had to be delivered later. I received an e-mail to that effect, with the same type of follow-up generated by my initial order. By contrast, that same week I ordered a digital music player from a major distributor of hardware and software. They sent no confirmation e-mail and no notice that the item was out of stock. When it didn't arrive, I called to follow up. They insisted that they'd sent out a letter via the postal service, but over a week had passed and the letter had not yet arrived. I canceled the order.

Caution

The urgency of generating an e-mail confirmation should not inspire you to disregard quality. Incorrect information creates a poor impression, as do poor spelling and grammar.

As you plan your communications strategy, remember to account for possible spikes in traffic. For example, anyone who's bought a house will tell you that the last few days of closing the deal are a frantic time of papers moving back and forth among many players, including the mortgage lender. And any mortgage lender can tell you that the most popular time to close deals is the end of the month. There is always a surge in business then. Using electronic methods to move communications around during the home-buying process can be a real boon, but for mortgage lenders, the end-of-the month spike can still be a problem. Suppose responses at the end of the month take 24 hours. The deals on dozens of houses might be closing in that 24-hour period. To manage this issue, one lender installed a smart system that "understands" customers' e-mail questions and automates responses. That lending company can now answer many routine e-mails within a minute. More complex inquiries are directed to a customer service center that handles questions by personal e-mail or by phone.

Note

In addition to offering e-mail support for their products, more and more companies are staffing chat rooms with technical support staff. Be aware, though, that this can be an expensive solution—staff time costs money, and a real-time conversation can get stretched out with unnecessary back-and-forth chatter.

Offer Customer Service via E-Mail

E-mail is far and away the most-used Internet application. The number of e-mail users eclipses the number of Web users, and many new users cite wanting e-mail as their reason for going online. The popularity of e-mail does not mean that e-mail is the best solution for initial contact with customers or even for presenting or selling your products or services. For one thing, users deeply hate *spam* (unsolicited commercial e-mail); for another, e-mail is often text-based and allows for little or no visual presentation of what you are selling.

The popularity of e-mail does, however, mean that e-mail is a communications tool with profound possibilities. Some businesses already use e-mail as their customer service communications medium. They might use e-mail instead of telephone call centers or in addition to them. E-mail customer service can be more cost-effective than telephone call centers because long-distance phone charges are not typically associated with e-mail. Furthermore, because e-mail responses can be automated or stored in a database and then mixed and matched by representatives, staff time is reduced. "Phone support typically costs three to five times as much as e-mail support," says Brigade's Bruce Molloy. Others agree that costs can drop 50 percent or more when e-mail support is implemented.

Here are some typical uses of e-mail in customer care scenarios:

- A maker of extracts used in cooking and sold via retail channels and catalog sales creates an e-mail service center staffed with customer care representatives to augment its phone call center.

- A local realtor that offers the usual listings of homes for sale and interior and exterior views of the homes via the company website also hosts a live chat area where home buyers can ask questions and get quick answers from the realtor's staff.

- A car dealer follows up with customers who have bought cars by sending service reminders and special offers via e-mail rather than postal mail.

You have many options when organizing the flow of customer care information via e-mail. You can hold e-mail messages overnight and send them in the morning, automate responses to go out instantly, and prepare stock responses for the issues customers raise frequently. You can also cross-sell via customer care e-mail. As long as your style suggests that you are performing another service (instead of pushing another product), you can, for example, suggest another product if one hasn't met the customer's expectations.

Tip

E-mail newsletters can be a very effective tool for reaching customers to notify them of changes on your site, new products, sales, trends in your industry, and so on. See Chapter 6 to find out more about staying in touch with customers via e-mail newsletters.

Customers who send you e-mail are giving you an opportunity to talk to them. Grab it. Offer special deals to those who sign up for e-mail newsletters, or point to an online survey that customers can fill out via a simple form. Take care, however, to avoid offending your customers or intruding on their privacy. Remind people of how you got their e-mail addresses, and don't send out e-mail unless you're asked to. As mentioned, spam is universally disliked, and far from helping your cause, its use will backfire on you. You'll find more on this in Chapter 6, but for now, keep in mind that the customers who opt in to e-mail offers are the most receptive to receiving them. You'll get more response from sending 1000 e-mails to people who want to hear what you have to say than from sending 10,000 e-mails to people who are annoyed to find your message in their inboxes.

Caution

If you begin to depend heavily on e-mail for your customer service program, you'll want to know that if technical trouble waylays your e-mail server or your Internet connection goes down, your e-mail will still come in and go out. Find out what your ISP or the company serving your e-mail has in place in the way of backup systems.

The big-ticket solution

To understand the potential of e-mail customer service, consider the big-league case of a large auction site that receives anywhere from 40,000 to 75,000 customer e-mails per week. Its customer service staff numbers more than 200 people, including 60 independent contractors across 27 states. Its systems include a central database of scripted and semi-scripted replies. It also has a public message board where customers can post questions to service representatives; answers appear within minutes. This use of e-mail and message board communication has improved support staff productivity by as much as 50 percent. It's also had an impact on business: Happier customers return to the site more frequently, and they buy more, too.

Tip

If you get more than 100 e-mail inquiries per day, you might want to consider automating or outsourcing responses.

What does all this technology and people power cost? Big software solutions that provide an automated e-mail response system can cost between $100,000 and $250,000 to buy and install. The price of outsourced e-mail customer service varies according to the level of service you want and often involves a setup charge as well as monthly fees. Both are probably beyond the budget of many smaller companies but can be tremendously cost-effective for larger companies dealing with high-volume customer support e-mail.

A mid-level solution

If either your in-house network or your ISP uses Microsoft Exchange Server as its mail server software, you can use the AutoReply feature in Microsoft Outlook to automate responses to customers who send you e-mail. (Many ISPs, including MSN, use Exchange Server as their mail server software, but check with yours to find out if it does.) Setting up AutoReply is simple, and the one-two power combo of Outlook and Exchange Server offers a number of features that automatically monitor, organize, and process e-mail. For example, via a series of simple check box "rules and actions," you can specify that when certain words or phrases appear within the To or From boxes in an incoming e-mail or within the Subject line or the text of the message, a certain response will be sent. You can even monitor the date and time that the e-mail was received and have responding messages sent out at certain intervals after that time. This can be very useful when, for example, you want to acknowledge an order, get a confirmation of some aspect of the order from your customer, and nudge your customer gently until you receive that confirmation.

You can also create personalized, prewritten e-mail responses to various customer questions or requests. The incoming e-mail will be searched for a designated word or phrase, and based on that word or phrase ("send me a catalog," for example), an outgoing message will be sent automatically.

In addition, you can include value-added attachments to your automated responses. When customers make requests for certain kinds of information, you can send them images, spreadsheets, documents, or slide presentations, all without any human intervention.

Mail often, with ease   Gathering customer information is tedious for some retail businesses but essential for e-commerce companies. Again, Exchange Server makes this easy. You can specify that when a customer sends e-mail, the e-mail address will be stored, and you can even indicate that certain addresses be stored in one or more distribution lists. This allows you to send out information to those lists on specific dates or at regular intervals. Before you know it, you'll have a newsletter mailing list. And to make this very nifty, you can specify that not every name and address on the list appear on every message, so that each message can seem to be directed only to each individual customer who receives it.

A few things Microsoft Outlook can do without Microsoft Exchange Server   Most of the features described here require both Outlook and Exchange Server in order to work properly, but you can also use Outlook to create distribution mailing lists without Exchange Server. Outlook's distribution list feature lets you quickly create and name distribution lists, and then as an incoming e-mail arrives, you can assign it to one or more distribution lists.

Using the contact list capability in Outlook in conjunction with Microsoft Word offers another cool option: You can store names and addresses using Outlook and then do a mail merge in Word to send out printed mailings the old-fashioned way, via surface mail. Alternatively, you can first export your list of names and addresses to a Microsoft Access database, sort and analyze the information as you like, and then export only a certain type of address (such as all international addresses) to Word for your print mailing.

A low-cost solution

You can look into Microsoft bCentral (*www.bcentral.com*) for low-cost solutions. For example, Traffic Builder, a tool provided by bCentral, helps keep e-mail efforts manageable by automatically collecting visitor e-mail addresses and managing existing mailing lists. It allows you to send e-mail messages to multiple addresses with one click and conveniently stores your messages for reuse later. So even if your operation is very small, you can manage your e-mail and send mail to a targeted list regularly, quickly, and with professional grace.

The New Customer Service Employee

E-mail changes the customer service job description. A pleasant voice and unflappability have been the traditional hallmarks of excellence in customer service employees, but in an e-mail setting, these qualities make way for good writing, spelling, and grammar. As you hire and train your customer service staff, ask how they've handled situations in past—not just on the phone but in writing. Ask for writing samples, and look at the samples for both content (what did they say?) and quality (how did their use of language represent the company? Is the message clear and spelled correctly?). You might find that salaries are higher for those with solid communication skills but that those people are faster and more productive at answering e-mail.

Once you've hired good customer service employees, provide them with written guidelines, but don't overscript—that is, don't prescribe every word and insist that overly specified, "boilerplate" sentences be included in every message. Give them the authority they need to actually solve problems. Above all, listen to your customer service employees—they're often your front-line personal contact with your customers. Despite the contention that every customer is a good

The New Customer Service Employee (*continued*)

customer, some people simply aren't worth the trouble they cause. Your customer service people will tell you when a customer is truly impossible to please. The customer who consistently wastes time with nuisance complaints or who abuses employees with foul language isn't likely to be worth the time and hassle in the long run.

Use a Customer Relationship Management Solution

Customer relationship management (CRM) is a business strategy that is used to understand, respond to, and even anticipate the needs of both current and potential customers. Customer relationship management solutions offer tools for effectively following up on contacts, tracking interactions, and providing the kind of service that closes sales. CRM solutions also aid in retaining customers, converting them into loyal, repeat customers. High-end CRM solutions are generally built from several components that might be licensed from or developed by various vendors. This makes them customizable, and, of course, they can be very expensive.

If you don't have the resources to set up a large-scale IT infrastructure, Microsoft bCentral (*www.bcentral.com*) offers a cost-effective suite of services that still allows you to streamline, simplify, and integrate core business processes.

Among these services is Customer Manager, a set of tools that lets you manage your customer information and communications from an easy online interface. With Customer Manager, you can streamline the sales process. Leads will come in via e-mail, pager, or cell phone; those contacts can then be forwarded or escalated to a colleague or manager. You can track and follow up on sales as they occur. You can also automate e-mail responses and use customizable e-mail templates to personalize your messages.

Note

Visitors to your website are sales waiting to happen. Typically, an e-commerce customer is well-informed, and often—having done their comparison shopping online—they're ready to buy. Following up on your first contact with an e-commerce customer is crucial. From one location, using Customer Manager, you and your team can manage contacts, communications (e-mails, phone calls, and faxes), tasks, documents, and the purchases that come with personalized service.

Let's say your company distributes bicycles. You, knowing that a key customer has purchased 10 top-of-the-line bikes, want to cultivate that relationship. You might want to follow up with suggestions for accessories or see how the bikes are selling and find out whether the customer has interest in additional models. Using Customer Manager, you can easily touch base via a personalized e-mail message. The communication and any response will be logged and tracked. You can then automate the delivery of another follow-up (specifying that it occur at a certain date and time) or a "thank you" message after the sale is closed.

Further, your whole team can have access to information about the customer as well as how the sale is progressing. You can track the status of follow-ups from your office or on the road. A small architectural firm, for example, might consist of only the architect and an office manager, who handles incoming sales calls. Both can have access to the customer information tracked by Customer Manager—the office manager can enter information about leads from the office, and the architect can follow up from the road.

Personalized service supports long-lasting customer relationships. Tools such as Customer Manager can make the difference in responding quickly to your customers and providing terrific customer care. Customer Manager integrates well with bCentral Commerce Manager, an online service that allows you to sell your products and services on popular Internet marketplaces with or without your own website. Commerce Manager provides online catalog, ordering, and channel management services. Customer Manager also integrates with Finance Manager, the bCentral online accounting and finance management software. Together, these services provide powerful tools for managing your e-commerce business, extending your business reach, and optimizing customer relations.

Whatever the size or complexity of your endeavor, your e-mail customer care program can be a proactive effort for gaining customer loyalty and cross-selling products and services. You can also take the responses to the questions asked most often and build them into a FAQ page that your customers can access via your website. Read on.

Offer an Easy-to-Use FAQ or Help Page

Giving your customers answers to their questions up front saves time and money. It also makes them happy. Including a FAQ or Help page on your website solves a basic customer service problem. It relieves you (or your staff) of the burden of answering the same questions over and over, and it gives your customers quick, hassle-free answers.

Tip

A FAQ list or Help page does not have to be organized in the traditional question-followed-by-answer format. You can simply provide answers or solutions; many Help pages are not devised as Q & A sessions. Look around at various websites, find several Help pages you admire for their ease and simplicity, and model yours after the best options you see.

Savvy e-commerce sites use FAQ pages or Help pages as their first line of defense in customer service. This just makes sense. Many people prefer not to have to ask someone for help, and most people prefer quick answers. If the answer to a customer's question is easy to find and understand, that person won't call you or send e-mail, and you'll have one less thing to do today. You might also stop a wondering customer from turning into a wandering customer.

Given that a customer who can find a quick answer on a FAQ or Help page won't have to contact you, it's probably obvious that providing a FAQ page will save money. But a well-constructed FAQ or Help page can also increase sales by providing more information about your products and services. It can't close a sale, and it can't answer every potential question a customer might have, but it can be a very important tool for customer service and sales.

A typical FAQ is a simple list of questions, with each question followed immediately by an answer. (See the MSN FAQ in Figure 5-1.) A FAQ can include information about your company such as who you are, where you are, how to contact you, how you process orders, what shipping methods you use, how you handle returns, what your privacy policies are, how you maintain the security of your transaction system, and so on. It might also include answers to often-asked questions about specific products—for example, how to launder the linen/rayon blend garments you sell, or why your painting company prefers to use premium products despite their extra cost.

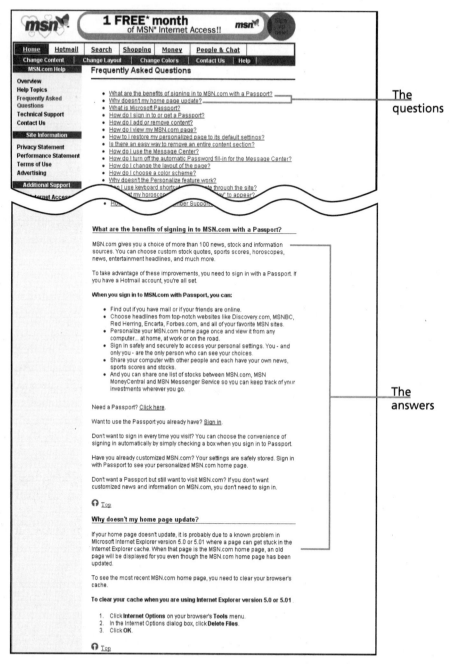

The questions

The answers

Figure 5-1

A FAQ page such as this can be the customer's first resource for quick answers.

A typical Help page can cover a lot of ground, but it should make clear to users whether it offers help with using the website, help with using the company's products or services, or both. Figure 5-2 shows a well-organized, easily navigated Help page from MSN that offers links to a variety of on-site resources.

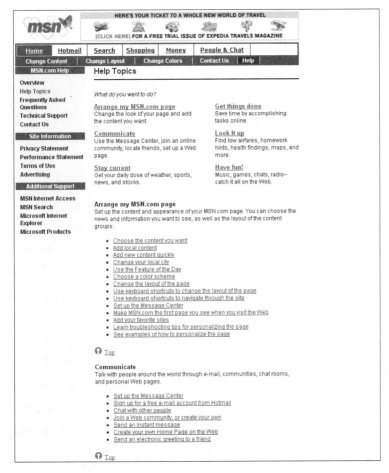

Figure 5-2

A well-organized Help page enables users to help themselves.

As you build your FAQ or Help page, keep in mind the following pointers:

- **Make it easy to find.** Don't bury your FAQ or Help page in a section titled "About the Company." Instead, place it in an obvious location—for example, as a link from your home page and from your storefront page. At the very least, provide a distinct customer service page or area with a link to the FAQ or Help page. A FAQ or Help page should certainly never be more than three clicks away from your home page.

- **Make it quick to access.** Don't gunk it up with art, animations, and gimmicks. This page is meant to offer fast answers. It should load quickly. To make this so, stick to simple text with just enough look and feel to establish your company identity. If you find you have so many questions and answers on your FAQ list that the page gets long, break it into several pages and provide an index page that shows only the questions—as links your customers can click on to find instant answers.

- **Make its organization obvious.** For a FAQ, list the questions at the top of the page with links to the actual question-and-answer entry. For either a FAQ or a Help page, group questions or links according to their subject, with brief headings. Keep similar questions or links together so they flow naturally—for example, go from buying figs to eating figs to removing fig stains from carpets. Don't group questions in a FAQ list according to how often they're asked. Although this might seem to make sense, it will make finding answers to other, less often posed but equally important questions quite a bit harder. If you can't come up with a natural flow, organize alphabetically or according to some other easy-to-see system.

- **Focus on the customer.** Write answers and helpful information from the user's point of view, not that of the sales representatives, the engineer, or the programmer. Start with what customers want to do, and tell them how to do it, rather than start with how your system works and describe its components and processes.

- **Tailor the FAQs and Help to segments of users.** Prospective customers will want different information from customers who have already had experience with your product or service and might have seen its flaws. Channel buyers or sales representatives might want the same information as customers, but you'll want to use different language and terminology when you're talking to them than you do with end customers. If you need to offer FAQs or Help to more than one audience, place the FAQ list or Help page for each audience on its own page and perhaps even in a different area of your site.

- **Provide brief, to-the-point answers and solutions.** If the answer to a question stretches beyond a few short sentences, break it down. Create subquestions, and answer them separately, below the original question. (You can either indent the subquestions so that they appear to be part of the primary question and answer, or you can somehow make them distinct from the original.)

- **Be clear, be honest, and be complete.** Your FAQ or Help page isn't doing its job if, after reading it, customers are still confused or doubtful and they have to call you (or worse yet, they leave). If your product has a bug or includes an error, give them a workaround. Product weaknesses don't have to be the first thing a customer sees on your FAQ page, but the answers customers need should be there.

- **Keep it fresh.** Maintain your FAQ or Help page by adding current information. As customers ask new questions and you or your customer service staff answers them, add the questions and answers to your FAQ (not every question, but those you find to be truly FAQs). Take a tip from local fire departments who, when the twice-yearly time change occurs, remind the public to change the batteries in their smoke alarms. Tie major overhauls of your FAQ or Help page to some twice-yearly event to make sure they happen.

- **Link, link, link.** There is simply no point in rewriting existing text, especially on the Web. Link to other areas of your site that offer the information customers need. Answer the question "How can I contact your company?" by linking to the Contact Us page. And if your customers frequently ask questions for which you don't have answers or that you don't want to answer, consider linking to other sites that do have answers or that are in the business of answering that type of question.

In the end, though, remember that your FAQ or Help page is not meant to be documentation. It doesn't have to answer every question anyone might ask, and it doesn't have to tell your customers everything they ever wanted to know about you and your company. Whether it is in question-and-answer format, the help you offer need only cover the FAQs. For deeper insights, specific how-to information, and predictions of industry trends, you can direct users to manuals, books, or oracles.

Set Up Your Systems So Service Is Easy

Rule number one for selling anything (and by extension, for customer care) is to never, ever, put a barrier in the way of a sale. In e-commerce, that principle translates into making transactions quick, easy, and painless. To address this point, e-commerce ventures have created systems that take advantage of their technological underpinnings. For example, storing the password and account information customers provide with their first purchase means that, on return visits, the customers don't have to enter that information again. They can purchase by clicking a single button. Making buying easy includes making the forms customers fill out in the course of a transaction simple to use and uncluttered so that they are a snap to read. It also includes keeping customers informed—for example, by telling them how shipping occurs and letting them track where their purchases are in the fulfillment process. ("It's been shipped. It will be delivered in two days. It will be delivered in one day. It's arrived!") As mentioned, telling people how to make returns is crucial to good service.

To prevent customer service snafus, integrate your e-commerce systems smoothly with your supply chain. Carefully plan and execute your venture so that all systems flow together to avoid mixed-up orders, late deliveries, and damaged goods. If your operation has several departments, each with a profile of the same individual customers, build yourself a nice central database so that all customer data is stored in one location. This will prevent conflicting or erroneous data from creeping into your systems. (For example, three departments storing varying information about the same customer under the names *bkienan*, *brenda kienan*, and *brenda keinan*.) It will also prevent your employees from acting on different data and either giving different responses one day and the next or—gasp!—revealing that your operation is badly organized. Integrating all of your back-end systems, including tracking customers for customer service, shipping, order taking, and marketing, will make your whole operation smoother and allow you to provide far better customer care throughout your business cycle.

When a Problem Occurs, Make Good

A dollar spent on correcting an error today can retain a customer who might spend 10 dollars next week. Moreover, that customer will probably tell a friend that at the end of the day, yours is a very good company. The dollar you spend might also forestall the spending of 10 more dollars on damage control.

Everyone makes an occasional mistake. A wrong item might be shipped, a piece of a ceramic candelabra might arrive broken, or a misunderstanding might result in the wrong type of service being provided. ("Oh! You wanted our one-hour consultation? We thought you wanted our three-hour assessment.") Be prepared to make amends. What exactly those "amends" are will vary from business to business, but you must have policies and procedures in place for correcting errors, responding to the customer's annoyance, and addressing any inconvenience you have caused.

In brick-and-mortar retail, 10 percent of what's sold during the December holidays is returned as soon as the holidays are over. If your e-commerce venture is a shopping site, make sure you are prepared for similar return rates. If you don't have a smooth method for handling those returns and processing customer credits, 10 percent of your customers are going to be very annoyed indeed.

Whenever possible, use existing systems. Companies that sell via traditional print catalogs are famous for good return policies and systems, and that makes all the difference in customer confidence. Include return information with every shipped item on the back of the shipping form, as Lands' End does. On that form, ask why the customer is returning the item. Provide options for getting the correct size, color, or product, as well as the option to simply get the money back. If you have to require that customers call before they return a purchase, or if you have to keep systems to a minimum and can't offer online management of returns, provide a toll-free phone number and have staff available to respond. For damaged products, arrange for pickup and pay for it. Customers who have to pay to return something that was damaged through no fault of theirs will be turned off to buying from you again.

Note

In some cases, taking returns isn't cost effective. For example, what's the point of getting back a dead or dying plant or melted chocolate? The cost of having the customer return such items exceeds the cost of simply replacing them. Some online retailers simply accept their customers' word that an item arrived damaged. They then replace the item without asking for the return of the damaged one. Of course, those companies also keep track of returns so that if a customer starts to report a suspicious number of "broken" items, the matter can be investigated.

Everyone does things a little differently, and there is no "right" way to handle returns. One retailer has a nifty system set up so that customer service staff need only press a button to process a refund, another to process an exchange, or another to arrange for company credit for broken or returned items. Another retailer allows returns of online purchases only to the website's distribution center, not to a local brick-and-mortar store. Yet another retailer allows returns only to a store and not to the website distribution center. You can tailor your policy to suit both your customers' needs and your own needs, but be sure you've told your customers what your return policy is and how returns are processed.

Tip

Remember: You can turn a problem into a sale. When an item is returned because it doesn't meet the customer's needs, you or a customer service representative have the opportunity to offer an appropriate upgrade as a replacement. You can also suggest an upgrade or an add-on to replace or augment a product that's old or has finally broken down. Just be sure these options are presented as a service and not as a hard sell.

Ask Your Customers—and Listen!

Part of the beauty of e-commerce is that you can build systems that help you to know—and tailor your site to—your customers' patterns and preferences. Of course, the first time you launch a site, you probably won't know everything about your online customers, but if you include opportunities for customers to contact you and provide you with feedback, you'll soon find out what gets people to click. Pay careful attention to patterns in your customers' feedback. Not doing so risks building a site that customers will visit only once—and no repeat business means diminished returns.

Track E-Mail Feedback

What are you going to do with all that great feedback you'll receive from customers who will e-mail you about this or that? Don't just toss those messages—file them. You might find that numerous people are asking the same question repeatedly, perhaps in different ways. If that's the case, you can add that information to your FAQ or Help page. You might find that many people are requesting a new flavor in your gourmet coffee line, or a change in your method of offering accounting services, or a better explanation of how to make payment in your online transaction system. To track comments, you can file paper copies of customer e-mails or you can sort them into Outlook folders. Whatever your method, don't toss aside that valuable information.

Conduct Surveys

If you collect and analyze customer information as it comes in, you will be able to personalize sales, marketing, and distribution strategies in ways that add value and inspire customer loyalty. Because of the immediacy and convenience of online communication, surveys are often easier to conduct in e-commerce than in the brick-and-mortar world.

Options for building online survey forms range from off-the-shelf software and simple tools to big-ticket software to outsourced solutions. At the low end (if you expect fewer than, say, a dozen responses per day), you can use a program such as Microsoft FrontPage to build the form, have the results from each form e-mailed to you, and save the results in a file. (Figure 5-3 shows a survey form created with FrontPage.) If you expect dozens, hundreds, or thousands of responses per day, you ought to have the results automatically routed into a database that's set up to store the data and facilitate tracking trends. You can use Microsoft Access and Microsoft Excel to track and analyze the information compiled from your survey, whatever its scope and size.

It can be tricky, though, to get a random sampling of people. Surveys are often skewed, for example, because they indicate the preferences of the people who have the time or inclination to fill out the survey form. The value of a survey depends on the quality of both the questions and the sampling, and in many cases you want the most random sampling possible. Site-based surveys of customers and visitors can be as skewed as any other surveys, but they can be a good tool for getting feedback and are relatively easy and inexpensive to conduct compared to focus groups or offline surveys.

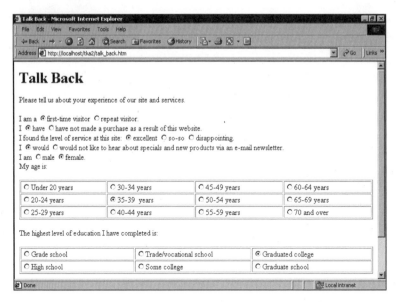

Figure 5-3

An online survey for getting feedback from customers.

One clever method for gathering more representative information might be to conduct surveys by intercepting every twentieth or so online visitor and asking that person to complete a quick survey form. In one case, two-thirds of the intercepted visitors agreed to participate in a survey just because they were asked. Alternatively, you can offer an incentive such as a small gift or token for participation, but keep in mind the costs of fulfilling that obligation. (See the sidebar "Car Talk: A Case Study in Cleverness" for an example of how to get around the costs of sending out such incentives.)

In addition, be aware that participants who seek gimmicks or give-aways will respond, skewing results. You might get some "participants" who are there only to collect the prize and a few who enter repeatedly under different names to get more prizes. These are probably not people who are offering quality feedback.

Asking visitors to "Leave your comments" is a fine technique for making people think you're listening, but be aware that it often draws few responses and sometimes draws responses only from those with axes to grind. This feedback won't be representative of all your users—at least you hope not!

Keep any requests for feedback very short—keep the survey to under 10 questions or five minutes of a customer's time. Include multiple-choice questions in your survey, but also include open-ended questions.

(For example: How can we improve our product or service?) And if you're a car dealer asking whether visitors to your site would buy a car online, remember to ask, "If you wouldn't buy online, is it because you want a test drive? What other reasons do you have?"

Tip

You might want to embed a few survey questions in your outgoing customer service e-mail. For example, you can ask customers about the quality of your service or for feedback about your site. For the best response, though, keep your questions especially short or consider providing a URL or link to a survey page on your site.

Car Talk: A Case Study in Cleverness

Speaking of cars, a popular radio show, Car Talk, has used an interesting method for surveying customers on its website (*www.cartalk.com*). On the surface, the feature is presented as an amusing service to users of the site. "Car-O-Scope," says the site, "is here to help you determine if you're driving a car that fits your psychographic profile." The user is promised a personalized e-mail telling her whether the car she is currently driving suits her personality and suggesting alternatives if it doesn't. To participate, the user fills out an online survey form that includes questions about how well various statements apply to her—statements such as "If there were only two jobs in the world—accountants and social workers—I'd want to be an accountant." Like any good survey, this one includes questions about how much money the user makes and what car she currently drives, but rather than ask away, it offers such an enticing incentive that the user might not even realize she is actually being surveyed. The website managers get a great deal of demographic and "psychographic" information about the site's audience (its "customers"), which allows them to tailor their site's offerings. It also allows them to provide a remarkable amount of information about the audience to companies interested in purchasing ad space. And, as a special bonus, they get an enormously long list of e-mail addresses that might be of use (depending on how it fits in with their privacy policy) in other ways.

Try to get feedback from repeat customers; their viewpoint will be very different from that of first-timers. Repeat customers have had experience with you, and they know your warts. Analyze the data you receive from repeat customers and first-timers separately. And get viewers to look at the site before responding—you want feedback based on an actual impression of the site, not just on someone's general beliefs or preconceived notions.

And finally, remember that your competitors can respond to your survey, and they might well do so. This might sound like a sitcom plot, but an unscrupulous competitor can easily seed your survey with multiple responses, throwing you off track about what your customers want or need. To prevent such distortion, weed out responses that come from competitors' domains and any multiple responses from a single address or computer.

Keep Things in Perspective

In the end, many customers will tell you many things. One might want your site to be blue; another might prefer green. You simply cannot be all things to all people, and part of being in business is determining which of the many paths you could take is your best bet. Providing excellent customer care involves not only listening and responding to your customers, but also setting clear guidelines—creating policies and procedures that will work for most of your customers. You can then bend your policies for special cases, and you can build triage systems to handle any errors that crop up. As mentioned at the beginning of this chapter, whatever your site's business purpose, service should be its goal. To be successful, you must serve as many of your target customers as well as you can.

Chapter 6

Leveraging Community to Boost Traffic

There's been a lot of talk about *community* in online circles. It's a terrifically compelling concept, but "community" is also a buzzword that's frequently tossed around in conversations, meetings, and even business plans without much thought to what community actually is and how it is created or supported.

Community, when it thrives, is a powerful force for building traffic and retaining the loyalty of a target audience. CNET's Builder.com site (*www.builder.com*) has reported that while the Web itself has been growing at 50 percent per year, online communities have been expanding at 20 percent *per month*. The potential that growth represents is very attractive to the managers of e-commerce ventures.

The very history of the Internet is one of community. Long before web browsers debuted and the first e-commerce sites opened shop, bulletin board services (BBSs)—networked communities with shared interests—pulled together groups of people with common interests who talked online in text-based messaging systems. Usenet newsgroups, another type of online discussion system, were also very popular on the Internet before the advent of the web browser.

135

Note

You know, of course, that the Internet is actually more than 25 years old. Its popularity with the general public boomed when the first web browser made it possible to see pictures and nicely laid-out type rather than just plain text in documents that were difficult to navigate.

As online tools became more sophisticated, audiences came together and new online alliances formed in new venues. Communities formed in e-mail discussion groups, in discussions on web pages, in chat areas, and so on.

It's not too surprising that community is of such interest to users. However, as mentioned, many website managers, business owners, and corporate executives talk about building community on their sites without a clear understanding of what the word means. A *community* is a group of people who interact online. But community is more than just clusters of people. Communities don't form just because you put out chips and salsa and throw open your door. Communities need a reason for being—a common interest or purpose that draws an audience. For the community to thrive, frequent interaction among its members must occur and participants must identify with the community. Let's look at the issues surrounding building online communities more closely.

Building Focused Community

Community requires interaction among a group of people who share a common interest or purpose. Perhaps the most important key to building community is to provide an environment or forum that encourages a reciprocal exchange of information, ideas, conversation, or even goods. Users who get involved in online communities might want to meet people, exchange knowledge on a given topic, argue, or even seek out romance. In general, they want electronic interaction with other people with whom they share *affinity*. In this context, affinity can be thought of as a bond or alliance forged of common interest and often a drive toward achieving some common purpose.

As examples, let's consider two very powerful online communities: a community of open-source software developers and a global community of expectant mothers all due to deliver their babies in the same month. In both cases, the groups have formed around a common interest and members have plenty to talk about—participants in the developer community share information about the software they're creating and pass code back and forth, while the expectant mothers share insights about the symptoms, hopes, and fears they are experiencing on the same pregnancy timeline. In both cases, individual members also experience a powerful identification with the group. The developer group sees itself as building something valuable and important; each member is proud to be a contributor to the effort. The expectant mothers become so attached to each other that they create a virtual baby shower, set up regional and national in-person meetings, help each other through personal crises, and sustain their community well into the toddler years.

Commonality of interest and frequent interaction, then, are clearly crucial for bonding to occur. An individual can be an ex-Marine, but if he hasn't had contact with other ex-Marines lately, he might not feel strongly about the community of ex-Marines. True identification with the group must also occur for a community to form. For example, a woman isn't a feminist unless she says so. Other people might think she walks and talks like a feminist, but if she doesn't identify with the group, she isn't part of that community.

To create an online community, you must start by targeting specific groups based on their affinities. Affinities can include interests; gender, age, or other demographics; shared experiences in the past, present, or future; or social groups that people identify with or join. Commercial communities are as viable as noncommercial communities. Consider the possibilities of a community of physicians sharing information about their specialties (with behind-the-scenes talk about unusual patients and cases) or of a community based on a professional association. The Association of Internet Professionals (*www.association.org*) is such a community. Women who work on websites have formed a strong national community in the form of Webgrrls at *www.webgrrls.com* and strong regional communities such as San Francisco Women on the Web (SFWoW) at *www.sfwow.org*. These women share not only technical and career development information but also "off-topic" tips for finding housing, painless dentists, and alluring vacation spots.

Auction sites such as ChemConnect (*www.chemconnect.com*) and eBay (*www.ebay.com*) represent another type of community—a community of buyers and sellers. In fact, eBay turned the entire notion of community on its ear when it opened shop with the model of bringing together buyers and sellers of all sorts of goods in a commercial community where they could transact sales of individual items. In yet another take on community,

VerticalNet (*www.vertical.net*) creates commercial communities that target specific, narrow markets (vertical markets) such as bakeries, environmental engineers, nurses, laboratory scientists, solid waste utilities, tool shops, and so on.

Choosing a Technology

Much of this chapter addresses how to build, leverage, and serve a community. Let's start by describing the gathering places where communities grow—the types of technologies on which they exist. Large sites such as eBay, ChemConnect, and VerticalNet use technologies that might not be within reach of smaller e-commerce sites, but many options exist for creating community on sites of all sizes.

E-mail newsletters: From one to many

E-mail newsletters are pretty much what they sound like—outgoing messages. The industry term "one-to-many" describes newsletters well; they are broadcast from one computer to many recipients. Newsletters can contain news or announcements, but they don't have to. Some companies have built their entire businesses around sending subscribers brief (usually one-paragraph) tips on a variety of topics.

The defining characteristic of an e-mail newsletter is that communication is one-way at regular, stated intervals, from sender to recipients. No discussion takes place among the recipients. In the most sophisticated cases, mailing list software is used to send the newsletters; the To line of the e-mail message usually includes the e-mail address of only one recipient because the mailing list software takes care of obscuring the addresses of other recipients who've subscribed to the list. How do you, the sender, get addresses for the mailing list? Usually, you offer the opportunity to get something of value and interest to potential subscribers. On the web page that introduces the option to subscribe, you can place a small sign-up box such as the one shown here:

In addition, you can provide details about the benefits of signing up, a link for getting help, and instructions for unsubscribing.

To persuade people to sign up for your mailing list, you have to offer something of value *to them*. Getting your product information into the inboxes of a group of subscribers might be very valuable *to you*, but is it really attractive to them, or will the information just seem like more junk e-mail? Here's the trick: A newsletter that blares a hard pitch on gourmet cooking equipment is less compelling than a rhapsodizing newsletter that offers a recipe, a tip about using a specific piece of equipment, and a special on, say, mandoline slicers.

It's important to allow people to sign up for your newsletter (to *opt in*) rather than automatically include everyone who makes a purchase from your site and expect those who don't want your wonderful newsletter to cancel (or *opt out*). Later in this chapter, you'll learn more about these issues; for the moment, keep in mind that your customers will appreciate and respond better to opting in as well as to the publication of your privacy policy (the promise you make to them about how private information such as their e-mail address will be used).

Tip

You can learn more about privacy policies and even write your own using online resources; see TRUSTe, a nonprofit organization that addresses such matters, at *www.truste.com*. Or look into the Privacy Wizard on Microsoft bCentral at *www.bcentral.com*.

E-mail discussion groups: From many to many

In e-mail discussion groups, one person (or a company) sets up a mailing list of subscribers (or "members"), but any member can send a message that will be received by all other members. Any member can then respond with comments or questions, and that response will also go to all other members. Voilà! It's a discussion.

Note

Some of the terminology here might be a little confusing. People use the term "mailing list" to describe a list of addresses to which they send out e-mail newsletters (described in the preceding section). However, the same term can also mean an online discussion group that takes place in the form of e-mail. In both cases, a list of "subscribers" has signed up to receive the e-mail. To better distinguish between e-mail newsletters and e-mail discussion groups, this chapter uses the term *mailing list* to refer only to a *list* of e-mail addresses.

The discussions that take place are often dynamic, even if they don't take place in real time. Messages appear in a member's inbox and can be read and responded to at the member's convenience. The discussions themselves can be *moderated*, meaning that someone sees to it that the "conversation" sticks to the stated topic, that administrative issues are handled, and even that disputes are resolved. Or they can be *unmoderated*, meaning that members regulate themselves. (To find out more about the implications of moderating or not moderating a discussion group, see the section titled "To Moderate or Not to Moderate" later in this chapter.)

Usually, subscribers join an e-mail discussion group by signing up (opting in) just as they sign up for a newsletter. Again, enabling people to opt in is a much more effective strategy than signing them up automatically and allowing them to opt out. Presuming that people will want to join your e-mail discussion group is a fatal faux pas. As with a newsletter, you must offer value. "Join my discussion group" isn't very compelling. To make a discussion group work, you must provide a forum in which a specific niche of people can discuss a powerful shared interest. The discussion topic must be focused, and ideally it should remain focused. Discussion groups often get sidetracked into off-topic sub-discussions; it's up to the group (or its moderator) whether to allow these tangents.

As the "host" of a discussion group, you should be sure to provide members with a list of ground rules as well as a clearly stated privacy policy. (Sharing the e-mail addresses of the people who subscribe to your discussion group is frowned upon, and few people will subscribe if they think that's what you intend to do.)

A compelling e-mail discussion group can work very well as a way to attract traffic to a low-volume site. In fact, more than one business that started with a simple e-mail discussion group has grown into a powerhouse in its industry. But building traffic is only one of the advantages of hosting a community. You can also use the material obtained from the group in a variety of ways, such as in the development of site content. For information about transforming e-mail discussions into site content, see the section titled "Leveraging Archived E-Mail as Valuable Content" later in this chapter.

Message boards: Threaded and serial discussions

Message boards differ from e-mail discussion groups in that the discussion takes place not in e-mail messages but in an electronic forum contained within a web page. Users typically don't have to subscribe to join a discussion; they can simply post messages and respond to the messages of others.

Unlike chat sessions, these discussions do not take place in real time; users read, post, and respond at their convenience.

Typical formats include *threaded* discussions (where messages are grouped according to subject and users can click a subject to read all the messages pertaining to that topic) and *serial* discussions (where all of the messages appear in a single, unindexed list). Threaded discussions generally work best when users want to follow a "conversation" about a particular topic—for example, when users are interested in discussions about particular aspects of a topic or are likely to want to search the talk for answers to specific questions. Serial discussions have more appeal in cases where the talk is less focused and is perhaps more social.

Getting a threaded or serial discussion off the ground is easier on a site where many users with an interest in the discussion topics are already passing through than on a site that is still trying to attract its base audience. If you're thinking of offering threaded or serial discussions, be sure you have the audience, traffic, and compelling topics you'll need to launch and sustain discussions. According to Forrester Research, if you don't have a powerful draw, such as a celebrity or a well-publicized niche topic, you need to have "foot traffic" of at least 2500 daily visitors to your site to support a *message board* (a threaded or serial discussion area). Note that if you set up a message board and no one shows up, the lack of traffic will be clearly visible to anyone who stops by. And a deserted forum will hold little appeal for the people who happen upon it.

Chat areas: Real-time interaction among users

In a chat session, users join an electronic discussion that takes place in the form of typed communication. Participants can see and respond to the discussion in real time by typing comments and responses that appear on the participants' screens as they are typed. In addition, many users can chat simultaneously.

Chat can be effective in the right circumstances, but as in threaded and serial discussions, if no one shows up, the silence is deafening. Chat areas work well when a session has a *big draw*—someone or something that attracts participants. A celebrity name is a big draw. ("Chat about ice skating with Brian Boitano!") If you don't have a celebrity name to tout, you must market your chat sessions aggressively to a motivated niche audience (for example, seniors looking for retirement-related tax tips) or find an underrepresented, compelling topic (bird watching, perhaps) and target the audience that cares deeply about that topic.

Another option for building community via a successful chat area is to place the area on a site or part of a site where traffic is already extremely heavy. Forrester Research says that supporting a chat area requires foot traffic of 25,000 individual, daily visitors to the website that's sponsoring the chat. (That's not hits; it's visitors.)

Caution

Chats can degenerate quickly into flame wars or other unsavory dialogues if they aren't moderated. For commercial ventures, it's probably best to moderate to avoid both getting too far off topic and potential liability.

Chat is an alluring technology, but implementing it successfully can be time consuming and is probably not cost effective for smaller sites with less traffic. The costs associated with chat don't revolve around simply implementing the technology; chat technology isn't all that expensive. The real cost of chat is in generating user interest; scheduling, rescheduling, organizing, and managing the chats; managing the vendor relationship if you outsource the running of chat technology; transcribing and archiving chat discussions for reading by website users; and so on.

Chat can be effective for distance learning sites, for providing real-time technical support, and for the press conferences of famous people. Chat sessions are also well-known gathering places for electronic social communities. Let's face it: Chat is fun.

Guest books: Simple sign-in for others to see

Yet another type of community forms when users enter informational blurbs about themselves into an electronic guest book. Guest books are simple to set up and are often offered as an option by ISPs and other companies that provide tools for easy web page setup. But guest books provide minimal interactivity for users and little opportunity for leveraging community to build traffic. Although they often appear on personal pages and amateur sites, guest books are rarely employed in professional websites, so they are not discussed further in this chapter.

Identifying a Community of Shared Interests

Simply placing a "Community" button on your site does not result in the formation of a community. In order for a community to form, you must give users a reason to join it. As described earlier, you must offer users value as well as provide a service in the form of a place to gather.

Although community can form around such affinities as gender, age, and shared experiences, shared interests are generally the most powerful affinity. Consider this: Why would you feel compelled to join your immediate neighbors in an electronic forum? You probably would find online discussions with them compelling only if you shared a purpose, intent, or interest with them. For example, a neighborhood in Oakland, California, used e-mail newsletters and online discussion to implement an emergency preparedness effort based on immediate concerns about the Y2K bug and on general concerns about earthquakes and other potential disasters. The effort was a success: A small neighborhood initiative turned into a larger citywide drive toward emergency preparedness, with Y2K as the catalyst. This example demonstrates that shared interests are as powerful—or more powerful—than geography. Its success was the result of a shared intent among a geographic community, not the opportunity to have an "online block party."

To build a successful community, find an underserved niche and fill it. Going deep (rather than broad) is an accessible option for many online enterprises. Creating a broad community takes deep pockets—the kind of budget some e-commerce ventures don't have. (America Online is an example of a broad-based venture; we can assume that its budget for community features is huge.)

How do you find the right niche? Think about your audience and its communities of shared interests. From among those potential communities, choose those that really, really care. Pregnant women who share the same due date really care; open source software developers really care; birdwatchers really care; sales reps and buyers might really care. The question to ask is, "In my industry, who really cares?"

Caution

If someone else has beaten you to the punch by creating a popular community for the niche you would otherwise go for, forget about it. They got there first, and unless the current community is deeply flawed in some way that you can improve on, you're better off trying another avenue. (Remember: To win in e-commerce, you have to be first, be the best, and be different. But being first gives you the real jump.)

What Are Your Community Goals?

Defining your goals is crucial to building a successful community. You might want to create an entire site around a particular community, or you might want to leverage community discussions as free content for your site by archiving it into a searchable database. (See the section titled "Leveraging Archived E-Mail as Valuable Content" later in this chapter.) You might have a more altruistic purpose. Think about whether any of the following are your true motives:

- Building a subscription base so that you can sell advertising that will appear within the community's discussion

- Building traffic to your website so that you can sell advertising, content, or your products or services

- Building a commercial community that supports or sells your products or services

- Building a *destination website*, which is one that users seek out because of its appeal to a particular community

- Building an audience for your views, opinions, or beliefs

- Building a forum for promoting yourself as a consultant or personality

Note

Remember that not all groups can be reached electronically. Luddites (people who oppose or fear technology), the Amish community, and healthcare workers in underdeveloped countries would probably be better reached by other means.

For more information about setting goals for your e-commerce venture, see Chapter 1. For more information on defining your audience and tailoring your offerings to that target audience, see Chapter 2.

Inviting People to Join the Community

Once you have set your goals and defined your audience and your community offerings, it's time to invite people to join your community. The invitation you present to your potential community might be a simple button on your home page that offers the opportunity to join. Right there, beside that button, you should provide users with a quick, clear sense of the benefits of membership. In general, it's best to stick to a few words that specify the value. (For example, "Free! Tips! Daily! Straight to your inbox!" But don't use all those exclamation marks; they lose their punch when they're bunched up.)

Alternatively, you might want to notify potential participants via e-mail. But remember: If you have a list of addresses you've gleaned from another source, use that list to announce your new community and invite participation if, and only if, those users have explicitly indicated their willingness to receive unsolicited e-mail. Even if the message is an invitation, unsolicited commercial e-mail is unpopular at best, and sending it out can do more harm than good.

Welcoming New Participants

Greet people as they join your community. Tell them how the community works, what its guidelines are, and how you deal with privacy issues. (Do you or don't you offer your mailing list to others for their use? Can users opt out? How?) Let people know how problem users will be handled; that might not seem very welcoming, but it can prevent some problems and will signal to everyone that your community is a safe place.

To have a workable, thriving discussion group requires between 3 and 200 subscribers or users. A good 85 or 90 percent of those people will be *lurkers* (who will read but not write). Perhaps 10 percent will participate from time to time; a smaller percentage will form the active core of the community. You might think your goal is to bring out the wallflowers and persuade the 85 or 90 percent to participate more, but it isn't. Focus instead on the 2 percent or so who are core participants. They generate the richest content, they are committed, and by giving the lurkers something to read, they provide the show. They also attract additional lurkers through the liveliness and interest of their interaction. You might consider offering these core people some reward—perhaps a title and responsibility for moderating a group, or a community-within-the-community for moderators, or even special discounts on your products.

As discussions take place and digress into new topics, subgroups of the original community will spawn. Spin them off to create additional communities if needed and if multiple communities fit your business goals. Communities tend to fail when they get too big and lose their focus or sense of purpose; active participants get bored or annoyed, spam starts to fly, and things can get ugly.

Finally, provide a method for users to send you feedback, and listen to it. Remember: These people are the community you sought and built so carefully. Although you might not react to every whim of every individual participant, you will surely want to keep the group as a whole happy and thriving. Keep them busy, let them interact, give them a way to offer feedback, and they'll reward you with rich content and a lively community.

Providing Stability

As you sort through your options for setting up a community, make it a high priority to choose a stable, reliable technology or hosting service. Users prefer stable communities; they also feel more confident about telling like-minded associates about the community if it isn't a moving target. What's more, communities don't just up and move with ease. So before you make your final selection of technology or hosting options, be sure the service or software you're planning to use can handle the traffic load you anticipate and offers the features your users will expect.

Of course, every vendor claims to have the most reliable, stable, full-featured product available. So how can you find out who are among the more stable and reliable community technology providers? Ask around. Ask users of community software; ask community managers and moderators, also. You might have to join a community or two to do this research, but checking references now can save you valuable time in the long run.

Caution

Community software, like all software, sometimes crashes. Users don't enjoy the thought that their carefully crafted messages could vanish into the ether, and that's exactly what can happen if your community software goes down and you don't have a good backup system. Just as you would with any other important business software, make sure your community software is capable of making backups and then back up everything regularly.

Offering Value

Specifically, what does your target community value? This is a strategic question you'll have to answer in order to build compelling community. For example, pictures of the heaters your company sells are compelling only to a target community of heating system sales reps (who, even then, probably look only when they have to, to make a sale). Tips for troubleshooting heaters or for seasonally maintaining heating systems are more likely to be compelling to heating contractors and the general public—especially as winter months approach.

Other uses of discussion groups and chat that can offer value include delivering training, news, or analyses of relevant issues. Communities can be formed around information libraries, searchable directories, virtual trade shows, or job fairs. Event calendars and event registration can punch up the offerings. Some communities might also be interested in editorial content such as career or commerce features, but that content can be expensive to create and keep fresh; so before you go for it, plan your budget carefully. Although classifieds and advertising might seem more like revenue options than community-oriented features, to a community of job seekers they can be very compelling. Similarly, for a community of association or trade organization members, attractive content can include special benefits, member signup, and a description of the advantages of joining the association.

As always, start your search for content of value by carefully considering what your specific audience wants, and continue your strategizing by thinking "outside the box" of what's been done and overdone. Beyond being true to your audience, freshness is your main goal.

Sending E-Mail Newsletters

Sending out e-mail newsletters with compelling content that reminds readers at regular intervals to visit your site can be a powerful method for building traffic. A Forrester Research study of 8600 Internet-enabled households showed that 38 percent found websites through e-mail. (The only more common method for finding sites, through search engines, was cited by 57 percent of respondents.) However, nobody likes spam, so in your e-mail newsletters you must offer value. You're also better off allowing people to opt in to receiving your newsletter. And you should provide brief instructions for unsubscribing in every issue.

E-mail newsletters fall into the following two basic types:

- **Announcement newsletters.** This is the more traditional type. They generally include product or service information or some other sort of promotional material. They can also include a teaser that entices users to click to a site. Announcement e-mails are far more effective, however, if they are written so that they don't appear to be blatantly self-serving. Offer subscribers something of value in each newsletter—specials, news, tips, or some other content that is related to the product or service. Otherwise, your carefully crafted newsletter will go into the recycling bin as quickly as last week's grocery store flyer.

- **Value-added or content-driven newsletters.** These primarily provide users with free information, tips, news, or some other valuable content. They often include brief ads as a revenue producer, but they can also include teasers that drive traffic to the newsletter producer's website. For example, one newsletter producer with 70,000 unique users offers top news stories, technical advice, how-to news, and fun feature articles. Half of the newsletter traffic clicks through to the associated website within 16 hours of newsletter delivery.

Tip

For best response, send out your newsletters on Monday or Tuesday, early in the day. Make sure the subject lines are intriguing and that they indicate the benefit of the content—how and why this material will be of use. Keep the subject lines short, and use an appropriate tone. Verbs work well for how-to material, while adjectives spice up food writing and evoke far-away places in travel information. If you send out several newsletters, differentiate them by topic or some other system.

Tracking Down Content

Are you stumped about where to find valuable content for your newsletters? You can use one of the many free press release services, such as PR Newswire (*www.prnewswire.com*), PR Web (*www.prweb.com*), Web Wire (*www.webwire.com*), Internet News Bureau (*www.internetnewsbureau.com*), or Internet Wire (*www.internetwire.com*). Just visit these sites or subscribe to their services, and sift out newsworthy items of interest to your audience. You can also sign up for push news sources or other free e-mail tip newsletters—not to nab their material but to get inspiration from the topics they cover. A third alternative is to ask your audience to send in ideas and even stories and tips. People love the validation and thrill of seeing their own writing published; why not give them the chance to send you material that you might use?

Note
Of course, you should attribute any material you use to its creator. Doing so will inspire yet another bit of loyalty in your audience. What's more, writers whose work you publish in your e-mail newsletter might well be inclined to send the newsletter around to friends and family to show off the accomplishment, widening your circulation base.

Formatting for Effect

E-mail newsletters can have the usual text-based e-mail look (as shown in Figure 6-1), or they can have an attractive HTML-formatted look such as the one BabyCenter (*www.babycenter.com*) uses for its newsletter. (See Figure 6-2.) The HTML-formatted look is available for viewing only by recipients whose e-mail programs are HTML-enabled, such as Microsoft Outlook. It's unlikely (though possible) that your entire audience is able to view HTML-formatted mail, so generally speaking, you'll want to offer people the option of receiving your newsletter in the format that works best for them.

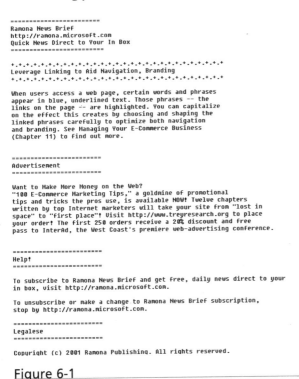

Figure 6-1

Text-based e-mail can include limited formatting.

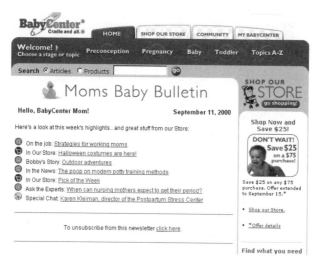

Figure 6-2

HTML-formatted e-mail such as this newsletter from BabyCenter looks great.

You can do various types of formatting in text-based e-mail. Figure 6-1 shows a variety of vertical lines made with equal signs (= = =), plus signs and periods (+.+.+.+), and simple hyphens (- - -). Be careful not to junk up the message—readability is most important. But you can make the message more readable with judicious use of vertical lines. Note that, to avoid looking funny in some e-mail programs, the lines should be no more than 65 characters long.

Offering the Opt-In Opportunity

It can certainly be tempting to think that every customer who makes a purchase or an inquiry on your e-commerce website is "obviously interested" in your product and will welcome a newsletter. But this just isn't so. Take it from the pros who've researched this point: You'll get far better response from newsletter recipients who opt in than from those who are automatically included in your mailing list and have to opt out if they prefer not to be bothered. Click-through rates actually double or even triple when people opt in to newsletters.

To encourage people to subscribe and to willingly supply their e-mail addresses, offer them something of value in exchange for their interest, as mentioned earlier. You then have real permission to follow up with that person, and you have the opportunity to turn that person's interest into loyalty. No stigma of spam will be associated with your opt-in e-mail newsletter, so you can send it out with a clear conscience and heightened optimism.

Providing a Way to Unsubscribe

It's best to make it relatively easy for subscribers to your newsletter to unsubscribe. Clearly, you don't want to make that option the most prominent item in your newsletter, but do make it possible to find the information. Giving people an easy way to unsubscribe increases credibility; it also decreases management overhead. Even those who remain subscribers will appreciate you making the unsubscribing process easy for them; they'll appreciate knowing that if and when they want to unsubscribe, they can.

Typically, subscription management information appears at the bottom of an e-mail newsletter; it describes how to subscribe, unsubscribe, and change the subscription (for example, if the subscriber changes e-mail addresses). You can also provide a link to a support area on your site (such as a FAQ or Help page) where subscribers will find all the assistance they need.

Maintaining Subscribers' Privacy

In your wildest dreams, you'll wind up with a long list of interested, motivated, targeted subscribers to your newsletter. Sooner or later it will occur to you that the list is a gold mine. You will probably consider either trading lists with a non-competitor or selling the list. Trading your list can get you more addresses, and selling your list can be a revenue producer, but either option can also irritate customers and drive them away, especially if your action comes as a surprise.

Perhaps in the future, Internet users will look on unsolicited commercial e-mail the same way as printed junk mail—as a mild nuisance that comes with having a post box. At this time, however, Internet users are highly incensed by spam. In fact, sending out spam will probably alienate more people than it will ever persuade to take an interest in your product, service, or site.

Tools for Creating and Managing Newsletters

Microsoft offers several tools you can use to create and send e-mail newsletters. For example, you can compose a newsletter in Microsoft Word without any fancy formatting, cut and paste a simple version into your e-mail software, and then send out the text-based e-mail newsletter to the subscribers who can read that format. You can then format the newsletter as HTML mail and send that version to the subscribers who can read that format.

Creating Simple Mailing Lists with Outlook and Exchange

The combination of Microsoft Exchange Server as mail server software and Microsoft Outlook as e-mail software allows you to set up outgoing e-mail newsletters to be delivered at regular intervals. You have to check with your ISP or hosting company (or, if you have an in-house network, your network administrator) to make sure you have Exchange Server working in conjunction with Outlook; if you do, you can take advantage of features that automatically monitor, organize, and process e-mail. For example, you can use a series of simple check box "rules and actions" to specify when mail should go out; you can even create newsletters that will be delivered with personalized greetings. You can also attach value-added documents such as spreadsheets, images, or slide presentations to your newsletters, expanding your options for providing subscribers with rich content.

Tip

You can send e-mail newsletters using Outlook simply by placing your own address in the To line and the list of all other addresses in the Bcc (blind courtesy copy) line. Recipients will see only their own addresses when they receive your newsletter. They won't see the addresses of the other recipients on the Bcc list.

Using Exchange Server, you can also store e-mail addresses in one or more distribution lists, making it possible to send information out to those lists at regular intervals. You can even specify that recipients should see only their own names and addresses and not those of everyone on the list, making the presentation clean and professional.

Even without Exchange Server, you can use Outlook to create distribution mailing lists. As incoming e-mail arrives (say, from someone requesting a subscription to your newsletter), you can assign the sender's address to one or more distribution lists.

Managing mailing lists with List Builder

One simple and effective method of managing e-mail mailing lists and newsletters (as well as e-mail discussion groups) is to use List Builder, which is available through bCentral. List Builder is a component of Microsoft Traffic Builder, which is a bundle of promotional services that comes in two versions: standard Traffic Builder, which addresses the needs of smaller operations, and Traffic Builder Pro, which offers additional promotional power and has special appeal for those who are managing larger sites or multiple sites.

List Builder is full-featured in both versions of the bundle. It collects e-mail addresses automatically and allows you to import existing mailing lists. Through an easy web page interface, it allows you to store outgoing messages (your newsletters, for example) and send them with one click. You can send messages in either text formatting or rich HTML formatting. List Builder also collects demographic information from your subscribers for you and archives past messages. List Builder is a very credible product that you can use to manage your mailing lists and send out newsletters effectively.

Offering Discussion Groups

Discussion groups as a broad category can take the specific form of e-mail discussion groups, message boards or forums, or chat sessions. For details about the distinctions, see the section titled "Choosing a Technology" earlier in this chapter.

One e-commerce website that offers discussion groups reports that more than 20 percent of its traffic is on the pages associated with the groups. The site offers between four and eight new discussion topics per week, rotating out those that aren't on fire. Each discussion is hosted by a staff member or a contributing editor, who is actually chosen from among discussion participants for his or her lively and knowledgeable postings. Hosts are paid a minimal fee if they have true expertise, and they sign a contract for a specified period of time. No registration is required of participants as they join in; they don't provide any demographic data. The discussion groups are heavily promoted on the site's home page with teasers that describe the current discussion topics.

In another example, a software maker that used to go to the trouble and expense of researching, writing, editing, and posting online tutorials for its products now provides discussion groups for each product. Users can log in to the discussion to trade tips, get advice, and find friendly mentors. The users get quick, easy access to real-world solutions, and the software maker gains immediate knowledge of how users are making the most of its products, what tips they've developed, which features are more (and less) popular, and what users want to see in the next version. This two-way communication enables the software maker to save the cost of creating tutorials and running focus groups, and it serves the users more effectively than tutorials do.

In the course of setting up a discussion group, you must consider some of the same issues you'd consider in setting up a newsletter. For example, your privacy policy will be of concern to many of your discussion group's users, and you should provide easy instructions for getting in and out of the discussion, as well as links to a clear, well organized FAQ or Help page that answers specific technical support and customer service questions.

Gathering demographic data from participants as they join the discussion is alluring to many e-commerce managers. You can gather the data by requiring participants to fill out what amounts to a survey on their way into the discussion; doing so offers a valuable tool for understanding your audience and valuable demographic data that you can offer to potential advertisers. The downside, though, is that you make participants jump through a hoop before joining the discussion. This isn't always wise, and it can drive traffic away from your group. Generally, only the most compelling discussions will inspire users to answer questions before they join in the talk. But because demographic data is so appealing to potential advertisers, you'll have to decide which is more valuable—the extra traffic or the extra data.

To Moderate or Not to Moderate?

The advantages of having a moderator in a discussion group are that the moderator can keep the discussion on topic, monitor the discussion to avoid potential liability issues (slander, for example, as described in Chapter 3), and generally troubleshoot the discussion as well as the participants' experience. The disadvantage is that someone has to spend time moderating.

In some cases, having a moderator is necessary. For example, you wouldn't want an unmoderated discussion group for minors because there is simply too much room for trouble to occur and too much likelihood that liability issues will arise if trouble does occur. On the other hand, some unmoderated discussion groups for adults have managed to stay generally on topic and avoid devastating conflict among the group members for years.

Discussion groups have distinct cultures—so much so that newbies are often advised to lurk for a while to get to know the group before joining in the discussion. Many discussion groups develop their own shorthand for frequently used phrases. (The expectant mothers described earlier in this chapter often refer to their "DHs," for *darling husbands*.) The culture of a discussion group can shift like the weather; in fact, small or even large shifts occur with each posting. Discussions taking place in these groups are, after all, occurring within a community, which by definition is a group of people with relationships to each other. As any psychologist or human resources manager will tell you, group dynamics are deep, complex, and ever-changing, and although people generally prefer to get along, there is almost always one rabble-rouser and a loose cannon or two in every crowd.

Moderators should be polite and appropriate; they also should have good written communication skills and knowledge of the discussion topic. Handling difficult community members can be the most challenging aspect of moderating a discussion; remember that although familiarity can breed comfort and ease at first, later the fabled contempt is likely to erupt between at least some community members. A loose cannon might go off, a rabble-rouser might see flames and fan them, and someone else might misunderstand what is happening and jump to the undeserved defense of the loose cannon. The moderator's job in the midst of all this turmoil is to remain calm and smooth things out.

A moderator might have the option of subscribing or unsubscribing members manually as needed and is usually responsible for troubleshooting subscription problems. The moderator might also be responsible for approving postings according to the discussion group's guidelines, which preferably will be written and posted as part of the FAQ or Help page. A moderator can (figuratively) slap the hands of those who post inappropriately, send out periodic reminders or notices, do outreach for the group, and even facilitate discussions by bringing up relevant or slightly provocative points. In groups of less technical people, there are always some who don't know how to use their own e-mail software; the moderator might wind up troubleshooting even at that level. Depending on the breadth of responsibility, the culture of the discussion group, and phases of the moon, moderating can take very little time or as much as two or three hours a day.

Tip

One moderator reports success in handling flame wars by creating a board that includes a balance of types of people to dilute the effect of interest blocs. The board has a prewritten reprimand for unruly members, which reduces the likelihood that a reprimandee will take the notice personally.

Options for Hosting

When it comes to actually building your discussion group, you have the usual options. You can outsource it or do it yourself, and you can select among BMW, Chevy, and Hyundai tiers.

Outsourcing offers the advantages of ease and expertise. If you outsource, you'll sign a contract with a hosting service that (presumably) has experience and knowledge you might not have. You'll have to sort out your business relationship with the hosting service, and you'll have to manage the service as well as prepare a strategy for how to end your business relationship with the service when the time comes. But you won't have to guess what your budget will have to be, you won't have to learn the necessary software and technology, and above all, you won't have to struggle with the community-building learning curve.

Hosting service options range from those that are free but offer limited functionality and no expert staff, to those that cost in excess of $1,000 per month and come with friendly, experienced community development people to assist you in your endeavor. Some charge setup fees as well as monthly service fees. Features vary; in general, as you assess your options, you'll also want to look into how friendly the interface is.

Note

The free services almost always tack their own third-party ads onto your discussion group's messages; that's how they make revenue.

One option for outsourcing e-mail discussion group hosting is to sign up with any of the sites that provide free or inexpensive hosting of discussion groups. Services such as these are available through Yahoo! Groups (*groups.yahoo.com*), Topica (*www.topica.com*), and other sources.

Note

If you aren't in a position to create a community but have some other offering that might be of value to a successful community developer, consider partnering. Strategic partnerships allow both companies to co-brand offerings so that they can each concentrate on their core business while broadening their online offerings.

If you prefer to run the whole shebang yourself, you can expect to have total control over the look and feel of your discussion group's interface, and you can avoid managing an outside vendor. But you'll be swapping those advantages for the complexities of staffing, writing workable usage and privacy policies, and keeping the software up and running. Unless your operation is fairly large or you have technical staff with time on their hands, a hosting service might be a better option.

Leveraging Archived E-Mail as Valuable Content

Let's say you run a lively, focused discussion group and have a core group of subscribers posting quality comments regularly. Your discussion group software is storing all that e-mail, and pretty soon you have gigabytes of it lying around and (metaphorically) collecting dust. Isn't it a shame to not use all that valuable content? (All that *free* valuable content?) Why not archive it, make it searchable, and leverage it as yet another reason for users to come to your site?

You can accomplish this in a number of ways, ranging from do-it-yourself methods to more sophisticated options. Using Microsoft FrontPage, you can add a full-text search option to a site with archived content. (You post the e-mail as web pages on your site, and then allow users to search the content. This is time consuming, but it is possible.) If you use the List Builder service, you're home free. List Builder automatically archives the messages posted to your discussion group and allows you to provide group members with access to the archive. A third option is (with some custom programming and database development) to use Microsoft SQL Server for your database and Microsoft Index Server to make the database searchable. The SQL Server option isn't a do-it-yourself project. Because you'd need developers to work with SQL Server and Index Server, it would take some investment. But after you've set up an archiving system, the strong, value-added content generated by your discussion group essentially provides your site with free, continually updated content that can increase interest in your site, involvement in your community, and your business credibility.

Community-Based Websites

It is, of course, quite possible to build an entire website around community. Successful examples of community-based websites include eBay, where the community focus is collaborating on the buying and selling of individual items, and SFWoW, where an association of women who work on the Web meets the needs of its members. Other collaborative communities are now fulfilling some of the Web's promise of innovation by creating electronic communities that have no parallel in the brick-and-mortar world. Examples of these types of communities are listed on the following page.

- Users get help planning social events, inviting guests, and recording events in photo albums and on web pages.

- Users buy and sell expertise and experience in an auction model.

- Customers pool their purchases to get volume discounts on products or supplies.

- Users make predictions on sports and finance outcomes and find out later how their predictions compare to those of other users.

Integrating Community into a Sales Site

The oft-repeated mantra that in order to succeed, an e-commerce website must include "content, community, and commerce" is wise, but all too often it's taken too literally. In a typical misapplication of this concept, a website is planned with articles (content), chat (community), and shopping (commerce), each segregated into its own area of the website. This is neither the most sophisticated mapping of a website nor the most effective interpretation of content, community, and commerce.

A far, far better way is to clearly delineate your target audience (see Chapter 1) and in every area of your site—on every page, in fact—seek opportunities to offer appropriate content, community, and commerce that addresses the real needs of your audience. Amazon (*www.amazon.com*) is a brilliant example of a site that leverages community on each of its sales pages by offering users the chance to review books, comment on each other's reviews (by rating their value), and so on. On Amazon, community isn't a "chat" area off to one side of the sales area of the site; it's a fully integrated feature that helps to sell books. On Amazon's sales pages, commerce, content, and community are seamlessly integrated into a compelling user experience. They aren't separate sections of the site; they are integral components of the shopping experience, and they fully support a user's purchase decision. Other bookseller sites offer similar features; many integrate content and community neatly into the site's commerce offerings.

Other examples include sites that empower users to create content. Users read content created by other users; submit their own comments, articles, reviews, and so on; receive acknowledgment for their contributions, which might then be put through an editorial cycle; and might later see their own contributions included as part of the site's content. In some cases, contributors receive special recognition or rewards; in other cases, publication on the site is apparently reward enough to win user loyalty. About.com (*www.about.com*) works on the model of making its audience into contributors and elevating some participants to a status known as "guides."

Measuring Community Success

Success can and should be measured differently for different types of websites. Gone (happily) are the days when all sites measured success in terms of "hits." *Hits* (actually a count of the number of files served when a user accesses a page) were a poor and primitive measurement. Because every image, piece of text, and so on, on a web page is a file and one page can consist of many files, some designs generate more hits than others.

How a given site's success should be measured depends a great deal on the site's goals. Measuring success is the subject of Chapter 13 and not a subject to dwell on here, but a few words on the specific measurement of success for online community endeavors are in order.

The most relevant measures for online communities might include such factors as the number of unique visitors to the site per month, week, or day; the number of *impressions* or *page views* that occur (meaning the number of pages that are seen by a pair of eyes in the course of a given time frame); the number of registered members (or subscribers) that exist; how many postings occur per month, week, or day (this measurement clearly does not work for chat); the length of time the average user spends in a session; the *posting ratio* (the number of posts that occur compared to the number of page views); or *audience penetration* (the percentage of the potential audience that the site or service has actually reached).

As of this writing, measurements for the success of online community ventures have not been standardized or accepted. In order for online communities to become as attractive to advertisers, sponsors, and others as they promise, such measures will have to become more generalized. Audit systems are also needed. The online community world needs a system such as that used in broadcast or print, where third-party companies verify (by audit) the measurement of success for a given site, discussion group, or newsletter. (See Chapter 13 for a description of auditing traffic numbers.)

In the meantime, owners, producers, and managers of online community ventures must define for themselves what success means in the context of their particular endeavors. As always, go back to the goal you set for your venture. Which of the possible measurements of success corresponds to that goal? Has another success unexpectedly arisen from the venture? Which measure of success corresponds to that piece of serendipity? At this point, the question is open-ended: What is success to your venture?

Chapter 7

Organizing Your Site Plan

You've focused your goals, created a budget, and set strategies for branding and service. Now it's time to create a viable site plan. Just as building a house without an architectural blueprint is sure to produce an unsound, unlivable structure, building a website without a plan—on paper, in writing, with notes and sketches that spell out the details—will produce an unsound, unnavigable website. And a confusing website is a website that customers won't visit.

If you follow the steps laid out in this chapter, you'll have a general plan for your website's structure that you, your in-house website team, or a web shop can then implement. In any case, you'll be far better off than if you try to make decisions on the fly. There is simply no substitute for preproduction planning.

An Overview of Site Planning Steps

When people read a book, a magazine, or other printed material, they generally read linearly. In English, for example, we read from top to bottom and from front to back. (See Figure 7-1.) But a visitor to a website might jump from one page to another, following links in intuitive yet nonlinear ways. (See Figure 7-2.) That doesn't mean the organization of your site doesn't matter. In fact, it matters a lot. A website's *architecture*—its overall organizational structure—has a profound impact on navigational paths and the overall user experience. Without an organizational framework, a website becomes a maze of links and illogical clickpaths.

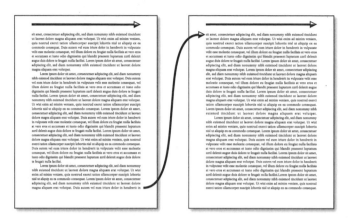

Figure 7-1
Printed material is usually read linearly.

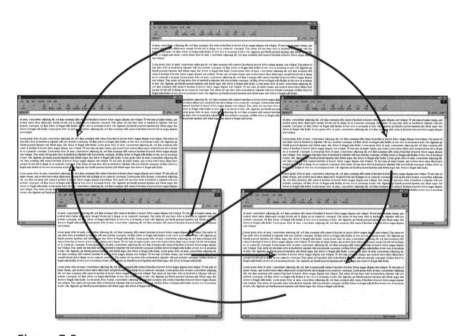

Figure 7-2
Website material is usually read nonlinearly.

Just as a good filing system in your office or a good directory structure on your desktop computer makes life easier, a clear, functional, behind-the-scenes structure for your website will also make maintaining the site and adapting it to changing markets far less daunting and difficult. If you have a good site plan, it'll be a snap to identify and remove outdated content or link new web pages to existing content, images, and other items.

Keeping Your E-Commerce Goals in Mind

Before you roll up your sleeves and begin creating a site plan, take a few moments to review your e-commerce strategy. Take another look at the goals you set and the mission statement you wrote, review your budget, and go over the decisions you made about branding and customer care. These considerations—as they affect both the business goals and user goals you've specified—drive everything. Also, as you sort through your ideas for the website's topics, features, and content, consider any legal issues that might arise from the use of such items as licensed articles, photos of people, downloadable software, or even user comments.

If you plan to build the site yourself or lead an in-house team, your business goals and your customers will obviously be in the forefront of your mind as you proceed. If you hire a web shop, bear in mind that although they might know more about building an e-commerce site than you do, you are the expert on your business and your e-commerce strategy. You also know where your venture will be headed in the future—it's up to you to communicate that knowledge to those who work on your website. Doing so will enable those who do the hands-on building to fulfill your expectations.

Most people who are new to planning websites approach the task by thinking about what should be on the home page and moving deeper into the site they're planning from there. This is a big mistake. It's like finalizing the façade and front door of a house before you complete the interior floor plan—you could easily wind up with the front door leading directly into a bathroom! Start your website plan by figuring out in some detail what's going to be contained in the site and how the site will be structured. After you plan the content and structure of the site, you'll probably find that "what goes on the home page" will actually become evident more easily than if you did things the other way around.

Large-scale websites are generally planned and developed by armies of people, all of whom usually have some area of specialty. (These areas of specialty are discussed in Chapter 9.) The process of planning and building a large-scale website is very complex. Figure 7-3 illustrates one company's take on the various stages involved. Other companies do things differently, but in all cases stages such as defining, strategizing, and organizing must precede designing, building, and launching.

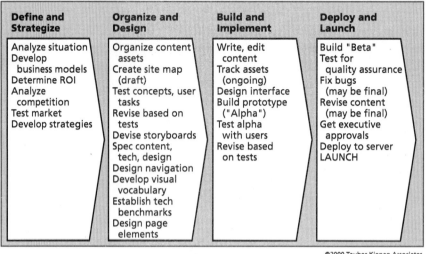

©2000 Tauber Kienan Associates
www.tauberkeinan.com
infor@tauberkienan.com

Figure 7-3

Stages in planning and building a large website.

This chapter covers the typical, most basic and necessary steps for organizing a website's architectural plan. The steps are as follows:

1. Identify the general topics you expect the site to cover. Remember to include such essential categories as About Us, Contact Us, and Customer Service as well as topics that relate specifically to your site's offerings (features, content, community, shopping, and so on).

2. Sketch a hierarchical site map, which will function as a blueprint of the pages on your site and how they relate to one another. (This site map won't be seen by the public; it's for internal use during the building of your site. If you keep it up to date after you launch and modify the site, it will also aid the maintenance of your site.)

3. Create a storyboard (a set of notes and sketches) for each page on the site, indicating as precisely as possible what the page's message or purpose will be; what language, art, or media will support that message or purpose; and how the page will be linked to other pages.

Note

Your website's site map and storyboards will provide a clear picture of the site's organization and what content (text, images, downloadable files, and so on) you'll need. They'll assist you in identifying specifically which content you can repurpose from existing documents (such as marketing materials) and which must be created for the website. But perhaps most importantly, these organizational tools will enable you to verify that each page on the site is appropriately and optimally achieving the goals you've set for the site.

Whether you're turning over the building of the site to an in-house team, hiring a web shop, or building a smaller site yourself, the site map and storyboards will be part of a larger package of information about your site known as the specifications, or *specs*, which will provide a clear picture of your project. (Specs will be discussed in greater detail later in the chapter.) The site map is also often the basis of your website server's *directory structure*. (The electronic files that make up your website will be stored in that directory structure; this is also described later in the chapter.)

Organizing the Content

What you offer in terms of topics, content, features, and functionality on your website depends on what sort of site you're creating. A basic sales site, for example, might include descriptions of specials or innovative uses of a product, a product catalog, a customer or product support FAQ, and a few pages that describe the company and how to contact key people. It's also usually wise to offer search capabilities so users can search the catalog or even the whole site. A payment system of some sort is *de rigueur*. And if you want to use an e-mail newsletter to stay in touch with customers, you'll need sign-up and subscription management pages. Other kinds of sites, such as auction sites, distance learning sites, or information provider sites, will have very different content and features, depending, as always, on what the site is intended to accomplish and how it can most powerfully deliver its message to its target audience.

As you focus on possible content and features, review the websites of your competitors. Don't just copy them or try to one-up them. You must improve on their sites and ideas by focusing on your own audience and their needs. What can you offer that will intrigue your audience more or serve them better? What do your competitors do that seems off track? Do you have to keep up with them even if what they're doing seems off track? If so, how can you refocus their misguided efforts or change direction altogether so you can better address your target market's needs or interests?

Tip

You can create a competitive analysis matrix (using a Microsoft Excel spreadsheet, for example) showing how each aspect of what you plan to offer compares with what your competitors offer. Having that information in an easy-to-scan column-and-row format will enable you to focus your ideas.

To get the planning process going, identify and make notes about the content and features you might present on your site. Don't be concerned yet about how to organize everything; for now, just compile a list. When you get to the site map and storyboarding phases, you can get more specific about what each item of content (also known as your *content assets*) will be.

Where Does Content Come From?

Some of your content can come from existing documents. For example, the material for an About Us section might be pulled from company brochures or press releases. Details about your products are probably also available in printed or electronic form. A customer support FAQ can be adapted from existing customer support documents or from the scripts customer service staff use when they take phone calls. A Jobs Available section will list openings, but it can also support recruiting efforts with information drawn from existing material about the company's benefits program. It can even include material drawn from community sources (such as the Chamber of Commerce) to describe the local culture and the benefits of living and working in the area.

Where Does Content Come From *(continued)*

Some content will have to be created specifically for your site. You can produce it yourself, hire a writer to produce it, license it (see Chapter 3 for a discussion of the legal issues), have your company marketing or public relations group create it, or, if your budget allows, have an ad agency, web shop, or professional content developer create it.

Note

As you plan your content, consider carefully whether each piece furthers your site's goals and adds value to your customers' experience. Also consider whether each piece will justify the effort and expense of implementing or maintaining it, as well as whether it will work within the technical, navigational, and legal parameters of e-commerce.

Typically, the pages on your site will fall into the following types:

- **Home page**   This page, also known as the *default page*, the *index page*, or the *front door*, provides the first navigational entry into the site, establishing its purpose and personality (including its branding message). It often displays links to the site's offerings and in that sense it functions like a cross between a book's cover and its table of contents. Some home pages offer actual content—if you choose to offer content on your home page, it should clearly convey the site's branding and should not obscure navigation into deeper levels of the site. The most compelling and essential items in the site should be easily accessible from the home page; less important pages can be linked to from other parts of the site. Note that subsections of the site often have index pages as well. For example, a software distribution site might include index pages that act as entryways to areas for major categories of products or to the technical support sections.

- **Content pages**   These pages hold the main content of the site, whatever that content might be. Content pages might be product pages, promotional pages, informational pages, or some other type of page, depending on the site's purpose. Content should be well organized, and all content pages should have a similar look in order to promote branding. (The simplest way to achieve a consistent look is to repeat design elements such as the color scheme, logo, and the overall layout on every page.)

- **Navigational pages**   These pages help users navigate around the site. They should be easy to use and have the sole purpose of facilitating navigation. A site map page or a site guide are typical navigational pages. The site map page (which is different from the site map mentioned earlier, which is for internal use only) can act as a large, linked table of contents that includes every significant page on the site and is much more comprehensive than the site's home page. A site guide might also include links to topics that help visitors use the site.

Note

The navigation bar—a list of links that often appears along the left side or the top of web pages—is obviously not a navigation page, although it is a navigational device.

- **Help pages**   A help page (which can take the form of a FAQ list or some other style, as discussed in Chapter 5) helps visitors use your site. Help pages are most useful for educating users about how to navigate your site, use your transaction system, use the site search engine, and find out about your products or services. It's wise to provide links to Help (or Support or whatever you decide to call it) on your home page as well as on every page where a user might have questions. Also place a Help or Support link on your navigation bar.

- **Search pages**   These pages enable users to find items of interest on the site efficiently and offer them a direct path to those items. Setting up a site search option might involve creating a dedicated search page or simply placing a search box directly on your home page or on other types of pages. It also requires a page that displays the results of the search. Offering an additional page that provides tips for carrying out a search correctly and for using advanced search techniques helps users to make the most of the search system. You'll also need a page that lets users know when a search has been unsuccessful (and perhaps why and what to do about it). Microsoft Windows 2000 Indexing Service provides search capabilities for web pages,

Microsoft Office documents, and Multipurpose Internet Mail Extension (MIME) content. Chapter 10 offers additional information about search systems.

Tip

Much of the search engine software that's available to enable search functionality on individual websites (as opposed to search engines such as Alta Vista, MSN Search, Google, and Yahoo! that search the entire Web) includes sample query and results pages that your developer can customize. If you use such a search engine, be sure to modify those pages so that another company's logo doesn't litter your site, misidentifying your pages to your customers.

- **Company pages**   These pages (often found in an About Us or an About the Company area) offer company background, provide location and contact information, describe the company values, list key personnel, provide job descriptions and listings, and display other company information. Unless you're building a corporate image site, put all company information in one area where interested users can find it and where it won't trip up those who have some other agenda—such as making a purchase. Press releases and a list of awards can fit in About Us, or they can go into a Press Room that is either a category unto itself or a subsection of About Us.

- **Transaction pages**   These pages lead the user through the steps in a financial transaction. A financial transaction might include purchasing a single item or a shopping cart full of items, transferring cash from one bank account to another, or buying an item from a third-party seller at an auction site. Navigation of transaction pages should be a breeze; you don't want the user to encounter any speed bumps or barriers along the way. As you sketch out and oversee the design of these pages, job one will be to make the flow simple and the process clear. The number of pages it takes to get from selecting a product to completing the purchase should be six or (preferably) fewer. At the end of the process, a page should notify the user that the transaction is complete. Additional pages might be necessary for error messages, help, and other functional information that will assist the user in completing the transaction.

Creating Categories and Subcategories

After you compile a list of possible content and features for your site and think about the types of pages you'll need, the next step is to sort the items into categories and subcategories. A process for doing this is described in this section. As you go along, you can set aside or toss out whatever doesn't make sense or doesn't fit, move items around, or add pieces. You should wind up in the end with a set of logical, refined categories that will help you as you go on to determine what areas the site should have, how they will relate to one another, and how users will navigate through the site to get its message and accomplish certain tasks (such as subscribing to your newsletter, signing up for your online classes, or making a purchase).

To create your categories and subcategories, look at the types of content you've identified and your notes, and ask yourself which items are logically similar to others. You'll probably see that your material naturally falls into groups according to the subject or according to the task it allows a user to accomplish. For example, if your site sells gourmet foods, you might be able to group material into the big-picture subjects of products and cooking. Within the cooking category, you might subcategorize material into appetizers, entrees, and desserts. And within the category of entrees, you might even subcategorize entrees into meat, fish, and vegetarian. If you were to group the material by task instead, you might consider whether a user will be looking for information about gourmet foods in general, looking for a specific product, looking for information about your company, or making a purchase.

Grouping by utility—a third option—involves considering what you or the developers will do with the content or especially with items that support the text. It's common practice to put the art or images that will appear on a site into one location, for example, so they can be stored and linked to efficiently. In our gourmet foods example, you might place photographs of various dishes (Ricotta Pancakes, Baked Alaska, Lemon Sorbet) together so you can later use those images in multiple areas of the site.

How you group your material depends a great deal on what it is, what your industry is, and what will best serve the needs of you and your audience. As you refine the organization of your material, jot down the various big-picture subjects, tasks, and utilities the material might fall into. Then create appropriate headings that describe those subjects, tasks, or utilities. You can do this by physically spreading the material out as pieces of paper on a large surface and shuffling the paper around, by drawing on a whiteboard, or by sketching electronically using your drawing software. You can do it by creating an outline in Microsoft Word. Or you can use Microsoft Excel to create a list of material that you can then sort and shuffle electronically. (If you use Excel, you can take advantage of its comment feature to take notes and then use functions such as SUM, COUNT, and some statistics features to estimate and tally page counts.)

If you find that some material doesn't fit in anywhere, you might have to rethink your headings. You also might find yourself adding, changing, or deleting headings as you go. If so, don't worry—refining is the goal of this exercise. If and when the whole thing is finally working out, you will have categorized all of your material. You need not have sophisticated relationships among the groupings worked out—that's a later step. The example in Figure 7-4 shows material for a sample website grouped into categories under appropriate headings.

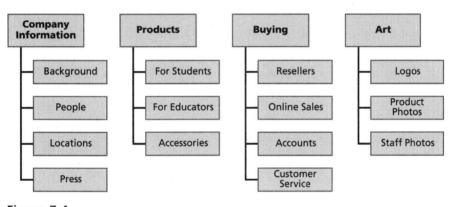

Figure 7-4

Material grouped into categories.

Note

You'll want to avoid duplicating material in your site. For example, if you plan to talk about the company in an About Us section, you won't repeat that text as supporting material in your product catalog or FAQ; you'll simply link to it. During the early organizational stage, if you find that a piece of material might fit nicely in more than one place, select the most logical placement for it and make a note of the need to link to it from elsewhere.

Mapping Out a Hierarchy

Next you'll take the categories and subcategories you've identified and establish a more specific hierarchical structure for your material. A hierarchy is a system that goes from the top, or more general, down to the more specific. (See Figure 7-5.) If you've created appropriate categories and subcategories, establishing a hierarchy will be a simple matter of drawing up a hierarchical structure that recreates and formalizes those categories and subcategories in relation to one another. The hierarchical structure for your website—also known as the site's content architecture—will be the basis of your site map. It will also provide a foundation for creating URLs, in that the levels of the hierarchy will usually translate later into a directory structure, and the directories and subdirectories contained in that structure will become segments of your site's web addresses—its URLs. (How URLs are constructed was explained in Chapter 4 in the discussion of the Domain Name System.)

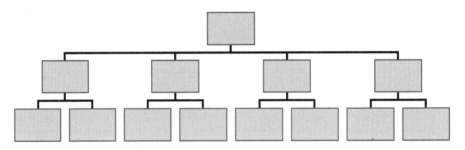

Figure 7-5
A basic hierarchy.

At the top of your hierarchy will be a box that should be empty now but eventually will become your home page. The next level down will be big-picture topics based on the broad categories of material you identified. Within each of these might be third-level subcategories. (In some cases, there might not be a third level; in others, there might be a fourth level.) Shuffle and shift the categories and subcategories you defined earlier until they fit into a true hierarchy.

Tip

Organize the hierarchical structure so that it makes sense and is appealing from your customer's viewpoint, not your company's. Rather than creating a Products area, for example, think about what categories of products users will want and organize the structure on that basis.

As you shape your hierarchy, bear in mind that this process is an art, not a science. Guidelines exist, but not firm rules. In general, don't make your hierarchical structure too wide (with many second-level categories and fewer third-level subcategories) or too deep (with few second-level categories and lots of third-level and even fourth-level subcategories). But if you must err, lean toward a wider rather than a deeper hierarchy, creating perhaps as many as seven large categories under which you create subcategories. That will make organizing links to your home page easier later. Also, note that because important content should be no more than three clicks from your home page, any important material in your hierarchy should be no more than three levels down from the top of the structure.

All of the material and content assets you will use must go someplace in the hierarchy. If something doesn't fit, temporarily place it in a "miscellaneous" category. Later, look through that category for like items and group them together. In rare cases, a miscellaneous item might need its own stand-alone category.

Note

If a clear hierarchy for your material just doesn't gel, you might need to revisit your categorized list of materials and content assets. Review the categories you considered earlier, and think about whether the amount or type of content you project for the site is actually appropriate.

Keeping Pages Short

You can determine how long your web pages should be by following this simple guideline: A single page should address one point or one issue and be less than 500 words long (preferably much less—in fact, 250 words or less is optimal). Use as few words as you can while still making your point. A page should optimally fit within one "screen" without requiring the user to scroll down.

If you get stuck trying to organize lengthy pages, look for where material can be broken down. Shorter pages make for more interactivity, suit the dynamic nature of web content, and can easily be linked, leading the user along a suitable clickpath. Don't just slap "continued" links on at the bottom of each page, however—instead, write a phrase or sentence that tells the user what benefit he or she will get from following the link and reading on. Chapter 13 describes effective techniques for linking and otherwise making content more usable.

Creating a Site Map

Once you're satisfied that your hierarchical structure makes sense, to create an actual blueprint for your website, you can convert the hierarchy you've created into a more formal site map. Choose a drawing surface: You can continue with that big piece of paper, use a whiteboard, or take advantage of software such as Microsoft Visio (which is optimized for drawings such as site maps and integrates nicely with Office and other Microsoft products). At the upper center of the page, draw a box and label it "Home Page." Under that box, draw more boxes along a horizontal line to represent the major content groupings you determined for your material. Label each of those boxes with an appropriate name, and draw a connecting line from each of these second-level boxes to the Home Page box.

As you do this, note that each line between the Home Page and the other boxes on the map now represents a link from your home page to a second-level page in the site. Now work down to the third (and, if necessary, fourth) levels. Again, each box is a page, and each line leading to it from a box that's higher up is a link. Figure 7-6 shows what the resulting drawing might look like. Keep going, naming the pages as you go.

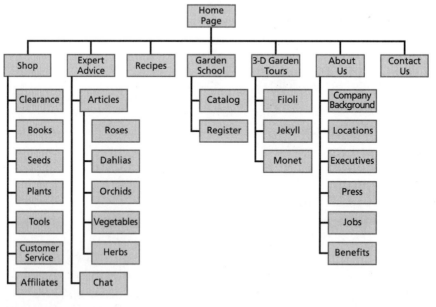

Figure 7-6

A site map beginning to form.

Understanding the Front End and Back End

From a user's viewpoint, a website looks like images and text on designed pages, some of it featuring clickable buttons and links. That's the *front end*, also known as the *interface*—it's the face of the site with which the user interacts. The site also has a *back end*, which is the technical infrastructure—the behind-the-scenes computers, software, databases, and code that make up the site and ensure its functionality. As a clarifying analogy, think about a theater production. A website's front end is comparable to what the audience sees (a stage, action, lights, and smoothly working scenery), and the back end is comparable to what the stagehands see (the scaffolding that holds up the scenery, the tables with props lined up for actors to use, the switches that the lighting technicians throw, and so on).

A site map is analogous to a plan for what the audience will experience, which also tells the designers and stagehands what needs to be done backstage. It provides an overview of the site. You (or the web shop or developers you hire) can work from it to create content and design pages as well as to create directories on your server to hold the material for your site. Note that the directories you create might not exactly match the site map you create during preproduction planning because as the site is built you'll probably encounter and sort through some unexpected technical, content, and other issues. But the site map is the basic plan from which both the user's experience and the technical underpinnings are ultimately created.

Note

If you use Microsoft FrontPage to create your site (see Chapter 8), you'll have the option to see a site map as you build. Keep in mind, though, that while FrontPage is a powerful, easy-to-use option for creating and managing a site yourself without knowing HTML, its capabilities are no substitute for solid preproduction planning.

As you work through your site map, also clarify for yourself what each page will contain. What will its main message or offering be? If it will introduce another page, is it really necessary or can the job be done by a page that's higher up in the hierarchy?

Consider, also, what promise each page will make to the user. What will he or she expect to find here? Will the offerings on that page fulfill that expectation? How? Will some secondary message or piece of content, art, or media support the main offering? Where will users go from here? What will the promise be there, and how will it be fulfilled? Again, you might have to make adjustments in various places on the site map to accommodate decisions you make elsewhere as you go along.

Linking and Navigation

Now is a good time to start thinking about linking strategies for your site. You might want to limit the number of links going to or coming from certain pages on your site, for example. You certainly don't want to interrupt a sales transaction by placing ads on your transaction pages that link away from the sale (especially ones that link to another site!). On some types of pages, such as in promotional sites or purchase-support sites, you'll want the user to follow a specific path through the material. In other areas of the site, you might want users to experience your content as a clickpath free-for-all. You can influence the user's experience on your site by carefully planning how, where, and when to link.

After you've mapped out what you can, look for the paths users might take in browsing between the sections of the site or in completing tasks. To navigate from the home page to a page that allows the user to download a particular piece of software or a document, what route would you expect the user to take? Draw dotted lines to show how navigation through the most important tasks would occur. Figure 7-7 shows a site map at this stage.

As you chart potential paths, you might discover that the map isn't working quite as you'd imagined. That's fine—the point of all this planning is to iron out the kinks. As always, make adjustments as needed and move forward. If the plan or some aspect of it is just plain not working and you have to go back several steps to make a fix, remember that uncovering a major flaw now is better than encountering it just before the launch of your site, when you have too much invested to pause or reconsider. You're still in the preproduction phase at this point, and the purpose of preproduction planning is to create a workable plan that will see you through implementation.

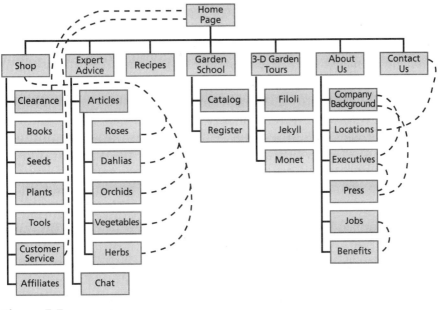

Figure 7-7

The site map with some linking paths shown.

Storyboarding the Site

Storyboards are sketches (either visual representations or written notes that appear in worksheet-type forms) that describe the content, features, navigation, and other items that will go on each page of the website. The process of storyboarding each page will allow you to make increasingly specific decisions "on paper" (either literally or in electronic form), which is far less expensive than making decisions on the fly during production. It also allows you to focus and optimize the message or offerings on each page so that you are promoting your business goals and enabling users to get what you want them to get from the page. Using storyboards, you can address many issues while there's still time to make clarifications or change your mind—you won't be boxed in on one page by a decision you made on another.

Visio is an excellent tool for storyboarding your entire site. You can use Word or any of a number of other tools, but with Visio you can create both the site map and the storyboards and then embed clickable links in the site map leading to each page's storyboard. Figure 7-8 shows a particularly well thought out storyboard form that was created by Melissa Rach at Aveus (*www.aveus.com*). You'll almost certainly want to develop your own based on your needs.

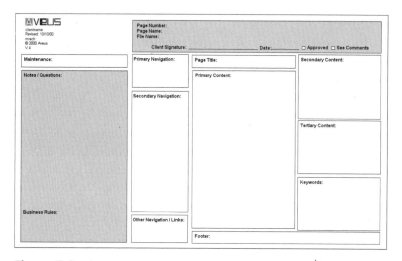

Figure 7-8

A very effective storyboard form.

On each of your storyboards, you can create fields (specific areas) that show items such as:

- The page's name (which should match the name shown on the site map)

- The most important links or buttons that will appear on the navigation bar

- The primary message or offering on the page

- The secondary message or offering on the page (such as a special promotion on an otherwise purely content page or the "cross-sell" of a related product on a product page)

- The tertiary message or offering (perhaps a testimonial or a poll—something that supports the main purpose of the page but doesn't warrant prominent display)

- The *footer* (the text that appears at the bottom of every page, which might include, for example, a copyright notice and a link to the "terms of use" information)

Tip

If you create a template (one storyboard that contains the standard information that will appear on all pages, such as the footer), you can use that template as the basis for each storyboard. Also, if you number each page in addition to naming it, you'll have an easier time keeping track of the pages.

Content That Plays a Supporting Role

Each page on your site will have a main purpose—a message or offering that is the page's reason for being. If you also include secondary and even tertiary content, it should support or harmonize with the primary content of the page. For example, on a site that sells gardening supplies, a page that sells bare-root Princess Diana roses will have specific information about that product (price, hardiness of the plant, scent, color, and so on) as its primary content. The secondary content might be an offer for rose food or aphid spray—something that can be purchased to be used with whatever's presented in the primary content. The tertiary content might be an expert tip about pruning roses or when to apply rose food or aphid spray.

Appropriate secondary and tertiary content might include:

- **Cross-sell** Offering of products or services related to the main offering, such as accessories
- **Upsell** Offering of an alternative, upgraded version of the main offering
- **Promotion** Offering of a special, a rebate, a discount, or marketing copy that promotes the product or service that's the primary content; on a community page, promotional content might be a snippet of community interaction intended to entice users to join
- **Counterpoint** A tidbit of content, an animation, or some other feature that comments on or adds interest to the main content
- **Comment** A remark, testimonial, interpretive comment, or quote
- **Guidance** Links that lead to a related area of the site or a related external page (on another site)

Work your way through your site map page by page, creating a storyboard for each page and filling in notes about what will go on each page, where the links will lead, and so on. As you do this exercise, imagine yourself as a user navigating through the site. As a decision you make on one page affects another page, make changes—as usual, that's the point of this exercise. Make ever more detailed notes, but don't feel compelled to write the actual content. That will come later. For now, your goal is to translate your strategies into notes and to uncover places where you are forced to make choices you didn't anticipate.

Note

You might wind up altering your site map based on what you learn from the storyboarding process. Again, that's far better than finding yourself painted into a corner while you're actually building the site.

Creating a Directory Structure

Having a general site plan will allow you (if you're building the site yourself) or the developers you work with to create a directory structure for the site. The directory structure is a plan for how the site will be stored on a server. It differs from the site map in that the site map describes an abstract concept—the website's organization—while the directory structure describes the actual organization of files on a server.

If you hire a web shop to create your site, the team that's assigned to your project will create a directory structure for you and pour the necessary files into it before completing your site and delivering it. If your in-house team creates the site, they'll do the same. In any case, it helps to understand enough about what the developers are doing so that you can tell whether they're doing it properly. (If you use FrontPage or Microsoft bCentral to create your site, the software will create a directory structure for you.)

Tip

An excellent directory structure includes directory names that are short, easy to remember, and descriptive. Because the directory structure will help those who work on your site find and maintain the site's files, and because the directory structure forms the basis of your site's URLs, a good directory structure leads to easier maintenance and easy-to-use URLs.

The "root" of your directory structure (the top of the hierarchy of directories and subdirectories) will correspond to a directory on your server called the *document root directory*. You might notice a correspondence between the root and the home page. The root is not the home page itself; it is a directory that contains the file or files that make up the home page. Exactly where the root directory exists on a server depends on the server software that's running; for example, Microsoft Internet Information Service (IIS) handles things differently than other kinds of server software do. But in the hierarchical chart of directories and subdirectories that's called a directory structure, the root is at the top of the hierarchy.

Understanding the Index File

When a user accesses a URL such as *http://www.microsoft.com*, the server at that location serves an index file (or *default file*) that exists in the server's document root directory. The index file is served when no other document is specified in the URL. In other words, at *www.microsoft.com*, the server's document root directory actually has a file with a name such as index.html or default.htm that is the site's home page file. When a user visits *www.microsoft.com*, the web browser at the user's end and the server at the other end "assume" the correct filename and don't require the user to type in a full URL such as *www.microsoft.com/default.htm*.

For the most part, the structure will be suggested by the flow of the site and by the structure of the site map—this is a practice that has become customary. Other practices have also become fairly standard—for example, special directories are often used to hold art, images, or graphics; these are often named (cleverly enough) *images* directories. Still other special directories can hold scripts (pieces of programming code) or media (sound and video files); these are named, accordingly, *scripts* and *media*.

Tip

If an image or graphic (your logo, for example) is to appear in several places on the site, you can place it in the *images* directory. You can then link to that image or graphic from various locations around the site.

Again, the simplest way to structure a directory is to mirror the site map you created earlier. You can use the same groupings and simply plot out a structure in which the server's document root directory holds the files from the home page, the directories under it hold the major sections of the site, and the subdirectories under those directories hold the files for the third level down. Ignore any lines in your site map that indicate linking; linking comes later. Figure 7-9 shows a directory structure for the site you saw mapped out earlier.

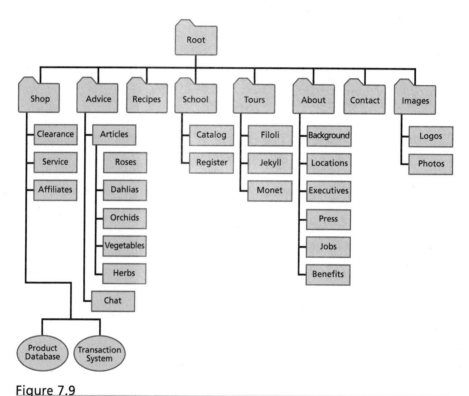

Figure 7.9

A directory structure emerges.

Do You Need a Database?

Many sites have one or more databases as a major part of their back ends. If you're creating a sales site with a catalog of products and a transaction system, for example, your product catalog will be organized in a database, along with a list of resellers that's searchable by ZIP code. But many other kinds of content can also be stored in a database. Chapter 10 discusses databases in more detail, but let's briefly consider the overall issue of whether your site will need a database. You'll need a database if any of these circumstances applies to you:

- You plan to sell products through an online catalog. (You might actually need multiple databases—say, one for customer information and another to track sales.)

- You plan to use the same content on multiple sites.

- You plan to have pages that will change based on user input. (For instance, on a page that displays search results, you might want to let users specify how many items returned from the search will display on a page.)

- You plan a site that is complex or whose content is updated so frequently that an automated content management system is warranted. (Chapter 11 describes how to choose a content management system.)

You also might find a database handy if you plan a large site with many pages that will use common elements, such as repeated product specifications, weather data, or stock quotes. Storing certain types of content in a database makes life a lot easier because making changes in multiple places can be a one-step process. For example, if you keep product specifications in a database, you can simply link to the information in the database every time the specs are referenced. If something changes in the specs (for example, if the product is improved), you can simply make the change in the database and all the pages that show the specs will show that change. You won't have to make the change on each page and then check each change for typos; you also won't have to hope you didn't miss a page. At this juncture, in fact, the only e-commerce sites that can operate without a database are small ones that are not at all labor intensive.

How deeply you need to dig into the building of a database is another question. If you use bCentral as your solution for selling online, you pretty much don't have to attend to the database question; bCentral offers turnkey products that don't require you to plan a database in order to create a catalog and a transaction system or sell to various types of electronic marketplaces. Of course, if you need more functionality than bCentral provides, you need a more powerful database, such as a higher-end Microsoft SQL Server solution.

Chapter 10 goes into more detail about databases; if you need a database, you'll have to plan its basic functionality. For now, review your site plan and directory structure and think about whether anything you're planning suggests a need for a database.

Building It Yourself vs. Hiring a Web Shop

Whether you or your team should build the site or you should job it out is an important consideration. The site plan you've developed will help you predict how big and complex (or small and manageable) the project of building your site will be. At this point, you can address what level of skill and expertise will be necessary to implement your plan. You can assess whether you're prepared to take on the task in-house by answering the following questions:

- Do you or your team have the expertise? This question really gets to the heart of things. Are you or your team already proficient with HTML or the other necessary technologies? Will your site require database development, and if so, do you have those skills? Do you or your staff know what practices lead to the building of successful transaction systems?

- Do you or your staff have the time? Can you take time away from your core business? If you need to learn HTML or become familiar with any other required technologies, can you afford the time it will take?

- How does your budget look? If you have a budget for development but can't take valuable time away from your core business, you might be better off hiring a web shop. If you have more time than money and your site isn't too ambitious, you might be in a position to build it yourself.

- How complex is the project? Is it a few dozen basic HTML pages, hundreds of pages plus a catalog, or thousands of pages with sophisticated registration required or community technologies included? Does it require a database and a transaction system? Do those have to be custom-developed or are they pretty basic?

If you or your team don't have the right technical expertise and you or they can't afford to take time away from your existing, core business to embark on a steep learning curve, you should probably hire a web shop. (See Chapter 9.) In any case, you must spec out the project before you proceed further.

Writing Specs and a Request for Proposal

Whether you're jobbing out the building of your site either in whole or in part, turning over pieces of the project to your in-house staff, or embarking on the adventure of creating the site yourself, you must document all your planning in what's known as the project specifications, or *specs*. Doing so will provide anyone involved in the project with a plan they can follow. It will also help those who maintain the site after it is launched to stick with the design as they create, modify, and improve the site.

Specs also form the basis of a *request for proposal* (RFP), which is a document you can send out to prospective vendors to inform them of the scope of the project. This aids in getting apples-to-apples bids, which will enable you to assess the bids and choose among them appropriately. (What goes in an RFP is described in Chapter 9.)

Note

Even if you have sole responsibility for your site, rest assured that a few weeks or months from now you will have forgotten some of what you decided in the course of planning and building. Notes and documentation (starting with specs) will help you recall your decisions and how implementation occurred.

A typical set of specs includes the following:

- A description of the key goals and general scope of the project (revamping of an existing site or creation of a new site; front-end design only or both front-end and back-end development)

- The site's mission statement

- The site's branding guidelines

- The site plan, consisting of the site map and storyboards for all pages

- Lists of the text elements your pages might use, including titles and headings, lists (multi-column, bulleted, numbered, and simple), text set off as special notes, special fonts or formatting of special text (bold, italic, or a font used for programming code on a software site), tabular information, "back to" links, linked headings, and so on

- Lists of the visual elements your pages are likely to use, including logos, product photos, and other images

- A directory structure, if one is available

- Sketches showing your ideas for how pages will look or a list of sites that are comparable to the one you plan to build

- A list of the deliverables (if you're hiring a web shop) and a timeline for the project

The specs can also include the following technical information (which you'll find explained further in later chapters and which is usually defined by the technical developers):

- The server platform you plan to use (This is the operating system for the computer that will serve the website; examples of appropriate operating systems are Windows 2000 Server or Windows NT Server.)

- The server software you plan to use (This is the software that enables a computer to serve the website to users who request access to the site's pages or features.)

- Any database requirements, including as many specifics as possible

- Any information about the transaction system you want to use, or what you want a transaction system to do for you

- Any information about special content management, customer relationship management, or special applications you plan to run (such as e-mail for newsletters)

- Any programming requirements you know about (although they might be few at this early stage)

Note that your specs are no more etched in granite than any other aspect of your website; you can make changes later. However, the more solid the plan, the better off you'll be; making major changes will certainly slow the project and probably increase your expenses, so try to settle as much as possible at this stage.

Tip

If you're working with a team, place your spec sheet online where everyone can access it. If you make changes to it, notify team members that they should look at the latest version.

In addition to using the specs as the basis of your RFP, share them with everyone who designs, implements, or posts content on your site so they'll know how things should be and where new content should go. It will make the process of working with a team run more smoothly. The specs can also form the basis of a style guide (explained in detail in Chapter 11), which is essential for keeping your site consistent and credible.

With your site plan and specs complete, you're ready to tackle building the site. For information about design considerations and the technologies you or your team can use to build the site's front end (HTML, XML, and all the rest), read Chapter 8. For insight into hiring and working with a web shop, developers, or an in-house team, see Chapter 9. And for the low down on back end technologies, see Chapter 10.

Tackling Basic Front-End Technologies

Each of the topics covered in this chapter could be a book unto itself. In fact, many hefty books have been written on every single subject covered here. This chapter offers you brief overviews that will help you make site-related business decisions. It will also help you understand some of the basics of what can and can't be done in building a website so that you can deal effectively with designers and developers.

Note

If you want to understand or tackle basic HTML, graphics, and other front-end technologies that are the building blocks of websites; if you want a quick introduction to Extensible Markup Language (XML), wireless, broadband, and interactivity; or if you want to find out how to use Microsoft tools to get a site up and running with no knowledge of HTML or web technology, this chapter will help you.

HTML 101

Basic HTML is easy—really. HTML (which, you might recall, stands for Hypertext Markup Language) is not programming, and it doesn't require a special college degree. HTML is simply a *markup language*, which means that it's a codified method for marking certain items (mainly the elements on a page, such as headings, body text, captions, and so on) so that a web browser knows how to display them to the user. (Markup languages were first used long ago to tell typesetters how to place type on the page.) HTML is based on another markup language, Standard Generalized Markup Language (SGML). SGML allows content to be marked up for display in any of a wide variety of media (print, electronic, and otherwise); HTML's strength is that it enables billions of documents (web pages) to be linked to each other. HTML makes the Web—and web browsers—possible.

Note

Yet another markup language, XML, is also based on SGML; XML allows content to be marked up so that it can be used in a variety of electronic and print media. XML offers additional advantages over SGML and HTML, but as of this writing, HTML remains the standard markup language for creating websites. See the section titled "Introducing XML" later in this chapter for an introduction to XML.

Many people think that nothing jazzy can be done using only basic HTML. It's true that to create the most sophisticated page layouts, complex coding and tricks of the trade are used, and to create interactivity that is more involved than simple linking, at least simple programming skills are required. Still, truly beautiful web pages can be created using basic HTML, and to understand how web pages work and what can and can't be done, you must start by understanding HTML.

Note

Most professional website designers and production people "hard code" in HTML rather than use WYSIWYG (what-you-see-is-what-you-get, pronounced *wizzywig*) tools that make creating web pages a snap. Hard coding offers much more control than do WYSIWYG tools.

How HTML Works

A web page is actually a text document. It contains instructions (code) that tell web browsers how to display the content in a format that is conventional and easy to read. HTML uses *tags* (individual pieces of code) to code documents. Tags appear in *angle brackets* (< >), often in opening and closing pairs. For example, <HTML> is a code that signals the beginning of a web page, and </HTML> (notice the addition of the slash) signals the end of the page. If tags are used correctly, they aren't visible to the user who is viewing the page.

A very simple document with HTML coding looks like this:

```
<HTML>
<HEAD>
<TITLE>The Page's Title Goes Here</TITLE>
</HEAD>
<BODY>
The page's "body" text (its main text) goes here. It can be short or
long, but it must appear within tags that indicate that it is the
body text.
</BODY>
</HTML>
```

To a web browser, any piece of text that is surrounded by brackets is a tag. In our example, the title of the page, *The Page's Title Goes Here*, is preceded by an opening tag (<TITLE>) indicating that it should be displayed as the page's title (in the browser window's title bar, as shown in Figure 8-1). Various other tags can indicate that an item is art, how that art should appear (at what relative size, for example), what page layout conventions are being used for that particular page, which phrases are linked, where the links "go," and so on. Because the tags themselves do not appear on the web page, you can even include comments to yourself or to others within special tags.

Tip

As you or your team go along, document the decisions you make about how to use HTML. This will help you and others who work on your site to create a consistent look. It will also save time because you won't have to create a new solution every time you encounter a challenge. See Chapter 11 for tips about creating and using a style guide.

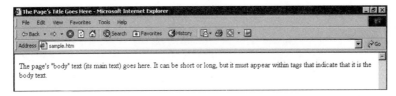

Figure 8-1

Very simple HTML appearing as a web page.

Note

In this book, tags appear in uppercase letters to make them easier to see. Many people also do that when they code web pages, simply to make the tags more visible within the text. But HTML is not case sensitive; if in your code the tags are lowercase, the coding will still work.

To create a web page, you or your team can write the content and the tags in simple-to-use software such as Notepad or in word-processing software such as Microsoft Word. You also have the option to bypass the basic HTML markup step altogether by creating documents in Microsoft Office applications, such as Word or Microsoft Excel, and then simply saving them as HTML files. Or, you can create entire sites or individual pages using Microsoft FrontPage. (More on the Office and FrontPage options will be presented later in this chapter; other special HTML authoring or editing software is also available. Simply search on *html editor* or *html tool* in any popular search engine to find a wide variety of options.) To make more informed assumptions about what can and cannot be done on a website, to do the actual markup (the HTML coding), or to modify a site, you'll have to know a bit more about HTML. Read on.

Required Tags and Their Order

Certain tags are required in an HTML document. For example, the <HTML> tag indicates that the document is an HTML document. That tag must always appear at the beginning of the document. Some HTML authoring tools automatically place it and other tags in their correct locations. If you create an HTML document using Notepad or using Word as a simple text editor (as opposed to creating a document in Word and saving it as HTML), you must add the <HTML> tag yourself.

The <HEAD> tag typically follows <HTML> to indicate to web browsers that some code invisible to the user—a title for the page and related information—will follow.

Within the <HEAD> tag, you can also place two types of META tags. The first is for specifying keywords that search engines can use when indexing your site. The second is for a description that might be displayed in the search engine if your site is "found." (See Chapter 12 for specifics about using META tags.)

The <BODY> tag is also essential. It identifies the main text on the page, as mentioned earlier. To get a sense of how tags look, open any web page using your web browser, and from the View menu, choose Source. (Your browser might use different names for this feature.) You'll be able to see the HTML coding that makes up the page. Although other tags will usually appear as well, you'll see that the required tags are always there, always in the same order. If you scroll down, you'll see that a closing version of each of the essential tags also appears.

Opening and Closing Tags

Most tags come in pairs. An opening tag (such as <HTML>) indicates the beginning of the particular element, and a closing tag (a tag with a slash, such as </HTML>) indicates the end of the element.

Certain tags don't require closing tags. These include <P> (which indicates where a new paragraph should begin),
 (which indicates where a line break should occur), and <IMG> (which indicates an image).

Note

Tags are often nested between other tags. For example, among the essential tags described in the earlier example, <HTML> and </HTML> enclose the other tags. And to make the word *ponchos* both bold (<B>) and italic (<I>), the markup would be <B><I>ponchos</I></B>. For more information on nesting tags, see the note on page197.

Tags That Do Special Jobs

Some tags, such as anchor tags, "mail to" tags, tags for fonts and colors, and comment tags, perform special tasks. The tag that indicates a link (confusingly enough) is the <A> (or anchor) tag. To specify a link, you must add an *attribute* (special descriptive information) to the tag, which, in the case of an <A> tag, points to the destination of the link (the item to which the link leads). In this example

```
<A href="http://www.tauberkienan.com">Tauber Kienan Associates</A>
```

the opening anchor tag contains the following attribute, which specifies the destination of the link:

```
href="http://www.tauberkienan.com"
```

The linked phrase *Tauber Kienan Associates* is enclosed by the entire opening anchor tag:

```
<A href="http://www.tauberkienan.com">
```

and the closing anchor tag:

```
</A>
```

"Mail to" links open the user's e-mail software with a specified address prewritten within the To line. They are similar to the anchor tags, except that instead of the target being followed by a website URL, MAILTO: appears followed by an e-mail address.

Here, the user is being encouraged to send me e-mail:

```
Send comments to <A href="mailto:ecommerce@tauberkienan.com">
Brenda Kienan</A>
```

Fonts and colors are indicated by attributes within tags. Fonts have names such as Times New Roman and Helvetica; colors are indicated by alphanumeric codes. More on the use of colors and where you can get those alphanumeric codes in a moment; for now let's look at how the numbers work. To indicate that a piece of text should be in the font Arial and in a certain shade of green (indicated by the number assigned to that color), the coding would look like this:

```
<FONT FACE="Arial" COLOR="#336600">Tauber Kienan Associates</FONT>
```

Note

The nesting of tags can get quite complex. To specify a certain font for the word *ponchos* and to format it as bold and italic, the markup would be <FONT FACE="Arial"><B><I>ponchos</I></B></FONT> Note the "first-in, last-out" order of the tags; when the font is specified first, the bold tag second, and the italics tag third, all of those tags must be closed in the reverse order.

You can use comment tags to make notes within HTML. For example, you can include a tag such as <!-- Updated 11/30/02 CET --> to indicate that the page was updated on a certain date. (The initials *CET* indicate who made the update.) When a web browser encounters a tag that begins with <!-- and ends with -->, it simply ignores whatever is enclosed within the tag.

Tip

Even veteran HTML coders sometimes have to look up a tag. For a comprehensive online reference to HTML, including browser-specific extensions and information about cascading style sheets, see the HTML reference at *www.htmlreference.com*. Also, Lynda Weinman's website (*www.lynda.com*) is a terrific resource for learning more about color and graphics. You'll find the alphanumeric codes you need among the resources at that site.

Limitations of HTML (and a Few Workarounds)

Because HTML was created for marking up text (research results) to be shared internationally by scientists and not as a tool for sophisticated layout design, it has some basic limitations. In the early days, for example, only two fonts (Courier and Times, which is like Times New Roman) were available. As web browsers became popular and public interest in the Internet took off, the capabilities of HTML expanded and web designers came up with clever workarounds. The options have widened, but the limitations of HTML are still notable.

- A relatively narrow range of fonts is available to HTML, and you can't know exactly which fonts are installed on a user's computer. You can specify a font in your page design, but if it's not available to a certain user, that user's browser will substitute another. (You can provide in your coding a list of fonts to be used as alternatives, using the <FONT> tag.)

- You can't specify the exact size of type because different browsers interpret type sizes differently. For example, you cannot specify 12 points (a typical type size used by print designers). You can choose among a range of sizes, however; 1 is the smallest and 7 is the largest. (See Figure 8-2.) Size 3 is fairly standard for web page text. Any given user's browser will translate the size you've chosen into a size it can display. But exactly how large the type is when it appears in a user's browser window can vary.

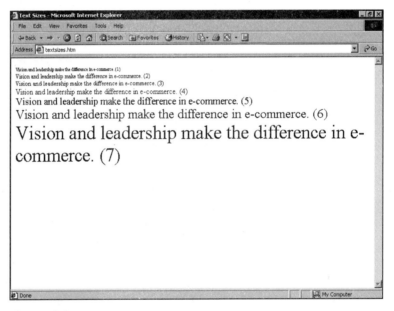

Figure 8-2

The relative sizes of text.

- Specifications for headings also cannot be exact. You can specify one of the six heading levels (ranging from 1, the largest, through 6, the smallest, as shown in Figure 8-3). But this determines only the relative size of the heading compared to other headings; it doesn't specify an exact size.

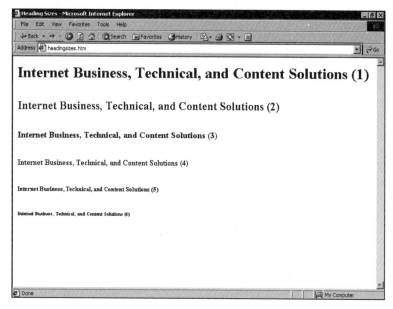

Figure 8-3

The relative sizes of headings.

Note

You can specify font and color for headings, but the coding can become cumbersome and the advantages of using headings can be lost. (Some search engines' crawlers, or robots, take headings into account as they index sites, and some automated document maintenance processes rely on the appearance of headings.)

- You can use either of two methods to create emphasis—which one to use is a matter of some controversy. Some people prefer to emphasize text by making it bold (<B>) or italic (<I>), but many designers prefer to let the user's web browser determine how the emphasis will occur. They use the <STRONG> tag (which usually renders text in bold) and the <EM> tag (which generally renders text in italics).

- Some characters aren't readily available. You can use special characters such as ™, ©, and ®, but they require special coding made up of an ampersand (&) and an *alphanumeric code* (which consists of a blend of numbers, letters, and sometimes other symbols) followed by a semicolon. (To find out your options for handling special characters, see *www.webmonkey.com*.) Other characters, such as *em dashes* (—) and *en dashes* (–), can be coded, but the code isn't recognized by all browsers. If those browsers are used by your audience, as a workaround, you can use two hyphens to represent an em dash and one for an en dash.

- Specifying colors for web pages is an inexact science. Until recently, most computer systems were able to display only 216 colors. The upshot was that website designers had to design using only colors that were part of this "web-safe palette" or "browser-safe palette." This limited what you could do with color. Now many computer systems are capable of displaying 16 million colors or even more, so some designers are abandoning the browser-safe palette. But (and this is a big but) not all machines and not all browsers recognize all colors, and what a color actually looks like on one computer screen compared to another can vary tremendously. You simply cannot be certain that the colors you or your designers choose (especially if you are attempting to match colors chosen for brochures, business cards, and other printed items) will always appear exactly as you want them to. That soft, earthy tan might in fact look like a mossy green to half your audience. Remember that each web-safe color is assigned an identifying alphanumeric code. When you specify a background color or any other color, you'll provide the code. Lynda Weinman's website (*www.lynda.com*) includes an easy-to-use tool for identifying browser-safe colors and their alphanumeric codes.

Tip

Despite the apparent broader range of available colors, in most cases you should stick to the 216-color browser-safe palette in designing your site. If possible, choose the colors for your logo, letterhead, and print publications from the browser-safe palette rather than choose print colors first and try to match your site to them; that will make translating your company look to a website much easier. Also, keep in mind that the browser-safe palette includes very few yellows. If yellow is among your preferred colors, be especially careful to choose one that will work for your website.

Page Layout Tricks

In the world of print, designers and typesetters have a great deal of control over page layout. This is not so in HTML. HTML's beauty is its simplicity, but that simplicity comes at a price, and the price to web page designers is a distinct inability to control exactly how a page will look. What looks like terrific page layout when viewed in Internet Explorer 5 on a Microsoft Windows PC might look quite different when viewed with another browser on a Mac, for example. Clever people have come up with some techniques for getting around this; notably, the use of HTML tables, single-pixel GIFs, frames, and cascading style sheets.

HTML tables

In HTML, there's no "absolute positioning." You can't specify that an element on the page should appear a specific distance from the left margin, for example. You also can't specify how much space will appear between one line of text and another. To get around these limitations, most web designers use *tables* to lay out pages. These are not informational tables; rather, they invisibly stake out areas of the page (cells) within which text, images, and other elements can appear. (See Figure 8-4.)

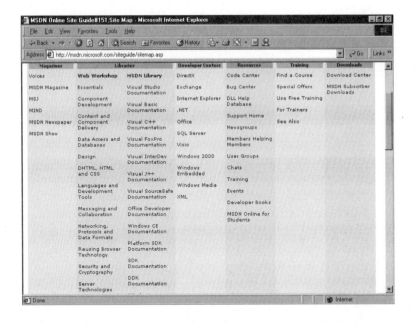

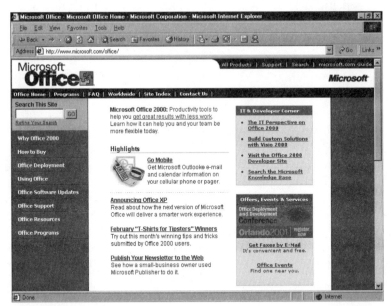

Figure 8-4

An informational table (top) and a web page created using a layout table (bottom).

The single-pixel GIF trick

To create some control over spacing, many designers use the *single-pixel GIF trick*. The designer creates a small GIF file (an image file) that is actually an image of nothing—it either matches the page's background color or is transparent—and places it where a bit of space is needed.

Tip

To minimize design time and maintenance overhead, you can create a *template* (a prototype layout) and then drop your text and images into the template to create new pages instead of having to create them from scratch. You can also save time by keeping a copy of the template among your archived files so that you'll always have a clean page to start with.

Frames

The use of *frames* ("panes" within the larger browser window, as shown in Figure 8-5) also offers some control over page layout. However, using frames on your site can make your pages ineligible for indexing by search engines. (See Chapter 12.) This is because a page created using frames is actually the sum of several pages of HTML coding. Each frame is coded as a separate page; a *frame set* (yet another page of coding) holds instructions for how the frames should appear and function as a whole.

Caution

The inclusion of frames in a website tends to make the site more difficult to use in several ways; for example, pages created with frames are tougher to bookmark and trickier to print. Also, the web browser's Back button doesn't navigate frames very well. For these reasons and others, the use of frames is universally frowned upon by usability experts.

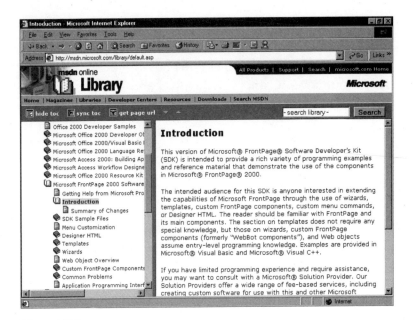

Figure 8-5

Frames offer layout control but come with important disadvantages.

Cascading Style Sheets

Cascading style sheets offer yet another option for gaining control over page layout. Using cascading style sheets, you can store specific formatting information (including fonts, sizes, colors, and other attributes as well as the exact location of text and images on the page) in the form of electronic data. You can then embed the style sheet in the HTML code for a single page or document (using the <STYLE> tag) or store it in a separate file. When the style sheet is within a single document, it defines how that document will look. When the style sheet is stored in a separate file, many web pages on a site can refer to it for instructions that automatically define the visual look of those pages. This simplifies the process of applying a consistent look across many web pages and makes it easier to change the look of those pages. For example, if you want to change the background color for all the pages, you have to change the color only once, in the style sheet. The change will occur automatically on all of the web pages that the style sheet affects.

Note that cascading style sheets are recognized only by newer browsers (Microsoft Internet Explorer 3 or later and Netscape Navigator 4 or later), so if part of your audience is using older browsers, this option might not be viable. Also, Internet Explorer and Netscape Navigator interpret style sheets differently (as do various versions of each), so style sheets don't actually offer as much control as one would hope. Even with these disadvantages, style sheets are becoming a standard method for web designers to exercise greater control over the look of web pages.

Naming Files

As you save the files that make up your website, keep in mind a few tips that will make life easier:

- Filenames should be meaningful so they're easy to remember and easy to identify when you're looking through a list of files. (For example, classlist.html is better than cl.html or newpage7.html.)

- Keep filenames short so that they are easier to type. (The name augclasslist.html is better than augustclasslist.html, for example.)

- Filenames should not include blank spaces, underscoring, punctuation, or special characters such as ampersands, exclamation points, or vertical lines because those symbols have special meanings to some operating systems.

These tips also apply to naming directories (or folders). The discussion of directories in Chapter 7 includes additional information about organizing directories logically.

HTML files, by the way, always end with the extension .htm or .html. Be sure your web page files are saved with one of those extensions.

Dynamic HTML

Dynamic HTML (DHTML) allows elements on a web page to respond to a user's actions. It is what's often working behind the scenes when you move your cursor over text and the text brightens up or changes color, when site navigation includes cute or useful pop-up windows, or when a new page opens in response to a selection from a drop-down list.

DHTML can look a little like magic compared to HTML. In fact, DHTML actually isn't a kind of HTML at all—it's really a clever combination of JavaScript and cascading style sheets. Creating DHTML by hand requires programming ability and is best left to advanced HTML coders or programmers. But many WYSIWYG tools such as FrontPage allow those with less expertise to incorporate DHTML elements into web pages.

Posting Your HTML Pages

If you or your team are creating web pages using HTML, you or they will probably use File Transfer Protocol (FTP) to transfer the files to the live server. You might create the files on your desktop computer and then assemble them on a staging server for testing, or if the site is very small, you might do all the work on your computer and simply upload the files from there. Windows comes with a basic text-only FTP program that you can use; most recent web browsers also provide a graphical FTP tool that allows you to upload files simply by dragging them from your desktop and dropping them into another window. A user name and password are necessary when you send content via FTP. You can get these from your ISP or IS department or from whomever is hosting the site. (See Chapter 10 for more on hosting, servers, and ISPs.)

Using Images

Placing art and images on a website isn't difficult, but you have to know the ins and outs. Properly prepared images can look stunning, while sloppily prepared images will slow the site down as well as look bad. Knowing the basics will get you started in handling images more adeptly and in understanding what your team means when they talk about "preparing" art for the website.

The Basics of Image Files and Formats

Two types of images generally appear on websites: true graphics (images that are composed of pieces of relatively solid colors—illustrations, clip art, and text, for example) and photographs (black-and-white or color). To appear in an electronic medium such as a website, an image has to be translated into digital form—little dots of color. (This is true even of black-and-white images.) More complex images—mainly those that have many colors or many gradations of colors or those images that are more realistic looking—require more complexity in the dots. The more complex the dots, the bigger the size of the file—and therein lies the problem.

Because larger files take longer to download, and because you want your web pages to load in your users' browsers quickly, it's best to avoid large files. A web page generally should not be larger than 50 KB in size—that is, the sum size of all the files that make up the page should not exceed 50 KB. A photographic image, for example, can easily be 12 KB or more, and the average banner ad is 10 KB.

Page Size and Download Times

You've probably encountered web pages that take just about forever to arrive on your screen. This usually happens because the page is designed and implemented in such a way that the file sizes have become bloated. The following table indicates in seconds how long pages of varying sizes take to load with the typical types of connections.

How Connection Speed Affects Download Time

Page Size	14.4K Modem	56K Modem	One ISDN B Channel	Two ISDN B Channels	DSL	Cable Modem
25 KB	13.89	3.57	3.13	1.56	0.52	0.03
50 KB	27.78	7.14	6.25	3.13	1.04	0.07
100 KB	55.56	14.29	12.50	6.25	2.08	0.13
200 KB	111.11	28.57	25.00	12.50	4.17	0.26

Each element on a page is an electronic file, as you'll recall, and the size of each file contributes to the overall size of the page. To a user with a 56K modem experiencing optimal conditions (no network delays, for example), a 50 KB page would appear in 7.14 seconds.

Various file formats (methods for saving files) are used for various purposes; the two most commonly used for images on websites are GIF and JPEG. Both formats translate images into files by compressing them. GIF compresses some image files more, making them smaller; it is best used for true graphics. JPEG allows for much more complexity and is best used for photographs.

Is It Text or Is It Art?

Not every graphic on the Web looks like art. Some *text* is actually a graphic rather than straight HTML. For example, in Figure 8-6, some of the text is straight HTML; some is actually a graphic. Because specifying fonts, sizes, colors, and placement is so difficult in HTML, sometimes it's best to create the text in a drawing program and place it on the page as a graphic to get exactly what you want.

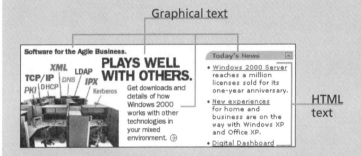

Figure 8-6

Text as straight HTML and as a graphic on the Microsoft website.

How can you tell which text is HTML and which is a graphic? Watch as a web page is loading, and you can see the graphics appearing first as lightly drawn boxes within which the images then appear. Any text that appears in this way is a graphic. You'll soon get a feel for this and know immediately when you look at text whether it was created as straight HTML or as a graphic. Buttons, some headlines, and almost all ads (even if they contain only text) are graphics. Navigation bars are often built with buttons that are graphics.

Remember as you plan and create your site that text created with straight HTML is much easier to alter than text that's really a graphic. If, for example, you build your navigation bar with linked buttons rather than HTML links, you might have to get an artist to create the buttons the first time and then create them again any time you want to make a change. Microsoft PhotoDraw provides tools for creating buttons, so you can easily create them yourself, but it's still more time-consuming than simply altering the HTML.

Preparing Images: A Word on Dithering

Placing images on web pages isn't a matter of simply slapping them into place. They must be properly prepared. You start by creating the image using drawing software or by translating it into digital format (by scanning it, for example), and then saving it in the appropriate file format (GIF or JPEG, essentially). In working with GIFs, avoid *dithering* (which occurs when dots of color appear next to each other to produce a third color) by making sure the files use only the browser-safe palette. (Most current software can deal with this.) In working with JPEGs, avoiding dithering is neither necessary nor advisable because JPEGs achieve the visual gradations required by photographs through their own processes, and sometimes dithering is part of those processes.

Other Image Types

While true graphics formatted as simple GIFs and photographs formatted as basic JPEGs are commonly used, website designers employ a number of variations, tricks, and conventions to achieve greater range in their work. You'll frequently run across these other methods of handling images:

- **Animated GIFs** Small animations that you can create by drawing a series of GIFs (using drawing software or a special utility) that appear in succession, flipbook-style.

- **Transparency** A graphics technique that allows a background color or image to shine through the area surrounding a logo or other image. When you save a file as a GIF, you usually have the option to create a transparency.

- **Interlaced GIFs** GIF files that load in several passes. The first pass loads more quickly than a whole GIF would; this means that an image begins to appear on the user's screen more quickly. In subsequent passes, the image is clarified. Again, when you save a file as a GIF, you usually have the option to make the file interlaced.

- **Thumbnails** Small versions of larger images that are usually linked to the larger image on a separate page. Most drawing software offers the option to shrink images into thumbnails.

- **Image maps**   Large illustrations or other images, portions of which are clickable as links. A classic example is a geographic map (such as the state of Pennsylvania); users can click a spot on the map and jump to a page related to that region. Image maps are usually created through the use of an HTML editor (such as FrontPage) or a special utility.

Tip

You can use the <IMG> tag's ALT attribute to identify your images. This attribute lets you specify a text description of an image that will appear before the image does or when a user moves the mouse over the image. If a user has turned off graphics, the description will appear instead of the image.

Designing for Wireless and Handheld Devices

The fastest growing method of web browsing is through wireless and handheld devices (cell phones, hand-held computers, and PDAs [Personal Digital Assistants]). Designing pages for viewing on these devices involves very different challenges than designing for web browsers as they appear on users' desktop or laptop computers.

Some of the issues you'll have to address include: very small screen sizes, limited input ability, slow download speeds, lack of graphics, and limited or no color support. What makes the task even more difficult is that different wireless devices (which range from cell phones to small, handheld computers) impose different combinations of these restrictions. Web-enabled cell phones as they appeared in their first generation (in say, 2000 or 2001), for example, were highly restrictive—providing no graphics, miniscule text-only display areas, and only telephone keypads for user input. At the same time, some handheld computers running Microsoft Windows CE provided larger color displays, miniaturized desktop-style keyboards for input, and stripped down versions of Internet Explorer (rather than the text-only browsers available with cell phones).

Because of the special limitations inherent in serving content to cell phones and handheld computers, companies that target these markets often produce specialized content just for viewing via these types of devices. You must identify the precise range and types of wireless devices you are targeting and follow specific development guidelines for those devices. If you're serving content to a variety of wireless devices, you might have to build various versions of your content in order to optimize it for each type of device. Some other basic rules to follow include:

- **Keep text brief.** Make page length as short as possible. Offering a quick summary followed by many short pages is far better than offering only a single long page of content.

- **Offer a menu of topics and subtopics.** Let users drill down (not more than three levels) through a series of headings to find what they seek. Make each set of topics or subtopics no more than six options long, and keep the headings for the topics and subtopics very brief. More than a few words per heading is going to be too much, so make those words count.

- **Use graphics sparingly if at all.** Keep image sizes very small, don't count on color being available on the display device, and don't make graphics crucial to the user's understanding of the content.

- **Minimize what users have to type.** Typing is inconvenient at best on small devices, and can be downright dangerous on an in-transit cell phone! On forms, as an example, don't make users type their names into empty boxes. Instead, have those boxes pre-filled with the user's name at the moment he or she accesses the page. This shouldn't be difficult if your back-end systems store people's names.

Tip

Many people who use handheld computers that lack wireless Internet access nonetheless find ways to access the Web via those devices. They use special software that actually copies web pages from their desktop computers to their handheld devices. To do this, they have to go through some hoops to "synchronize" the two systems. AvantGo (*avantgo.com*) provides user-friendly software that does this job nicely.

As wireless access comes into its own, we're likely to see increasingly innovative uses of this new medium. Drill-down menus of text-only content are likely to give way to more exciting possibilities. Remember that wireless means on-the-go. Those little handheld devices are very mobile—the applications that become possible for wireless content should be equally mobile. Among the more interesting options for developing wireless content might be to have cell phones ring to alert users if, say, a dip occurs in a stock that interests them, or a sudden traffic jam occurs on their commute route. Audio files seem a good bet for wireless—movie reviews delivered via cell phones could include sound clips, for example.

Mobile devices also seem likely candidates for community-driven applications. In fact, as of this writing, people in some countries are already using wireless access to register their interests with an online service. The service tracks the whereabouts of its subscriber, and when two people with like interests are near each other, both of their cell phones ring, allowing them to contact each other for a quick round of golf, bowling, coffee klatching, or whatever they like.

Just as the Web was once young and all websites were once uniformly gray with simple text and kludgy "What's New" areas, wireless is now in its infancy. As it matures, smart developers of content and technology are bound to come up with services, content, and tools that make the most of this burgeoning medium.

What About Broadband?

The advent of broadband access (fast connections with lots of bandwidth) has been heralded for years. These days, many users do have Internet access connections such as DSL and cable modems, and those connections are pretty fast compared to the only options that were available not too long ago. But the excitement about broadband is that it allows widespread delivery of very sophisticated media such as seamless streaming video and audio to millions and millions of users. As of this writing, we just aren't quite there yet.

It's been predicted by Forrester Research that by the year 2003, 27 million users will have broadband access. When broadband becomes ubiquitous, video shopping, games, movies, and live entertainment are all likely to be launched. Many other business, research, educational, and engineering applications are likely. Surgical procedures might be demonstrated or taught through broadband media. That's a fine use of the medium, and not to be sneezed at.

But the big question is how broadband applications will really differ from television. Television is a passive medium, whereas the Internet has always had interactivity at its heart. Like wireless content, broadband content should be developed to make the most of what differentiates the Internet (over which broadband content will be delivered) from television. Online conferencing could easily boom with broadband. Video conferencing; shared applications (such as shared software, online whiteboards, and other work environments); and online presentations are already in play, but with broadband widely available these technologies seem likely to push telecommuting and virtual workgroups into new dimensions.

The potential is enormous. Broadband, when it is a reality, is likely to change the way we do business. But potential and practical use that results in profitability are not one and the same. How broadband will actually shake out remains to be seen.

Introducing XML

Among the many limitations of HTML is that although it defines the way electronically delivered files look, it defines those files only as web pages. This might not seem like much of a problem, but imagine the possibilities if electronic files were defined in such a way that they could be repurposed smoothly in a variety of media without having to be marked up, typeset, or otherwise redefined based on which media were used. You could take one set of information (your catalog or product specifications, for example) and package it easily and efficiently in a print version, a website version, a wireless version, and a CD version, all without having to re-code the text to make it work on each of those electronic media. You could also distribute that information to resellers, licensees, or other partners, and they could publish it in various media again without having to re-code it.

This is the beauty of XML: It separates content from design completely. Using XML, you can code items of information according to what they are instead of how they should look. As an example, you can code all the prices in your catalog simply to indicate that they are prices. Compare the following example of information coded in HTML to the same information coded in XML.

The HTML version:

```
<P><B><I>Conseco Alcohol Swabs</I></B>
<P><FONT SIZE="-1"><I>$2.79</I></FONT>
<P><FONT SIZE="-1">High-quality swabs from Conseco Pharmaceuticals
</FONT>
```

The XML version:

```
<Product>
<Name>Conseco Alcohol Swabs</Name>
<Price>$2.79</Price>
<Description> High-quality swabs from Conseco Pharmaceuticals
</Description>
</Product>
```

In the XML version, prices, product names, and descriptions are marked up to identify what they are (such as Name) rather than how they should look (such as bold and italic, in the case of the product names). When the information is to appear in a print catalog, a brief set of coded instructions will indicate how the product names and other items of information should look in that catalog; when it is to appear on a web page, another set of brief instructions will indicate how the items of information should look there. This, again, enables the information to be distributed and repurposed more efficiently.

What's more, XML allows the creation of specialized or customized tags. The retail industry might want one set of tags (for prices, and so on), the chemical industry might want other tags (for chemical compounds and their components), and banking might want still others (for various types of transactions). Within each industry, individual companies can have their own tags, but the real power of XML lies in having industry-wide standards.

Once standards are set—in other words, once members of a given industry agree on which tags are most useful to it—information can be shared freely among entities and organizations in that industry. In e-commerce, websites and transaction systems have to shuffle about quite a bit of information (as described in Chapters 1 and 10). An e-commerce site's shopping system might need to get a credit card authorization from a bank, get product catalog information from another website, or get package tracking information from yet another source. XML allows all that data to be exchanged smoothly.

If your information is marked up in XML, you can participate in many online marketplaces, provide your product catalog to many potential retailers, or provide customer records to your customers; to do those tasks and more, your programmers won't have to work out the differences in standards for each type of communication or transaction. Microsoft is leading an initiative for speeding up the adoption of XML standards for all the information interchange required to run a business. To find out more, see *www.biztalk.org*.

Creating and Managing Your Site with FrontPage

Using FrontPage, you can build and maintain a website without having to know HTML. FrontPage includes a set of tools for creating and managing websites. The FrontPage interface is the same as the interface for other Office applications (such as Word or Excel), so if you're already an Office user, the learning curve for FrontPage will be minimal. You can use FrontPage to build your site from the ground up, to create individual pages, or to edit HTML that's been written using an application such as Notepad or Word. Using FrontPage, you can create a website that has a consistent look and feel across all its pages, and you can monitor, manage, and update your site. One person can work on the site individually, or a team can work together using the FrontPage management tools.

A full discussion of FrontPage is beyond the scope of this chapter, but the following sections provide an overview.

FrontPage Conventions

Before you start, you need to know about some conventions and terms that are unique to FrontPage. First, FrontPage uses the term *Web* to mean a website or an area of a website. A FrontPage Web is made up of web pages and is created in HTML (although FrontPage lifts the burden of HTML coding from your shoulders). In addition to HTML files, a FrontPage Web can contain image files, animations, Office files, audio and video files, and whatever else might make up a website. You can import into FrontPage websites or areas of sites that were created without FrontPage; if you do, FrontPage calls the imported material a Web as well.

FrontPage also comes with special web-server software that you'll need for creating your FrontPage website. This software is different, however, from the web-server software you need to make your site go live to the public. The FrontPage web-server software is there only to allow you to build a site and view it as you build.

Creating a Site or a Page

To create a website in FrontPage, you begin by using a wizard that steps you through the process of adding content to a set of pages based on a template—a page with a preformatted layout and design. You can create a whole site based on this template or use it for only one page.

You can then change the look if you like, by selecting any of a number of *themes*. Themes include such details as background and other colors; heading size and formatting; and the look of bulleted lists, links, and other elements. Alternatively, you can customize pages to give them a look that you prefer; you can even give them a look that's been professionally designed.

As you work, FrontPage does the HTML coding for you behind the scenes. You can see the pages you're working on in a WYSIWYG view that looks like a web page, shows your changes as you make them, and allows you to edit them. You also have the option of seeing the HTML source code as it develops or by previewing the pages in Internet Explorer. You can add images, links, video, and audio as well as alter the formatting of the pages.

Mapping the Site and Its Navigation

Using the FrontPage navigation tools and features, you can chart how users will make their way around your website. You can make choices about how the navigation will work and whether the navigation links will be buttons or text, among other options. FrontPage will then generate navigation bars automatically based on your choices. As you add new pages to your site, you can add them to the navigation structure with ease.

FrontPage also offers a mapping feature that shows how the links on the site interconnect the site's pages. As you link to newly created pages, these links will be added to the hyperlinks view of the site. This view helps you to identify any content that should be linked but isn't. You can also see the potential clickpaths that a user might have to travel to get from one area of the site to another. You can use what you learn to both modify the site and make decisions about the site's navigation.

Adding a Catalog, Transaction System, and Shopping Cart

You can easily use FrontPage to create product pages that describe your wares, or you can use FrontPage to design the look of your catalog pages and call up the product information from a database back end. (See Chapter 10.) As of this writing, you cannot design a shopping cart or transaction system using FrontPage alone, but you can create your site and catalog using FrontPage and create the shopping portion of your site using a tool such as Microsoft bCentral Business Web (available through bCentral at *www.bcentral.com*). You can then link the shopping portion to your site seamlessly.

Working with FrontPage and HTML

You can import pages that were created using hard-coded HTML into your FrontPage Web. The HTML in those pages will not be altered. You can then edit the pages using the FrontPage WYSIWYG tools and other features to integrate the pages smoothly into the site's overall look and navigation.

Caution

Not all HTML authoring and editing tools are compatible. Some versions of some tools add their own codes to the HTML code; these special codes are unrecognizable to other tools. It's generally best, if you're working with a team or otherwise passing files around, to stick to one tool.

You can also edit pages using HTML (as opposed to using the FrontPage WYSIWYG editor), which gives you finer control over the page layout and general look. For example, you can apply your company's colors to the background and text (within the limits of the browser-safe palette) and even create a look that matches your print material's look and feel.

Managing Your FrontPage Website

FrontPage automatically generates a series of reports that outline and describe your website's status, making site management more efficient. You can easily find out about *orphan files* (those that are not reachable through any path of links starting from the home page) as well as files that load too slowly, files that are growing stale and need updating, files that have been recently modified, links that are no longer viable, and tasks that have yet to be completed.

The tasks feature in FrontPage allows you to note specific items to be done, mark them off as they are completed, and even assign them to various team members, who can then mark them as "completed" for you to see. Use this tasks feature to plot out for yourself or team members what needs to be done in as much detail as possible. Content management consultant Alicia Eckley advises that "people often look at big pictures and tend not to think about the details. The only way you can get everything done in the time you've usually got with a quality outcome is to think through, detail by detail, the elements of the site and the processes involved. Content has to be created, revised, coded, tested, and proofread. Scrambling at the end never gets the best result." (See Chapter 11 for further information about content management processes.)

Tip

You can put the directory structure you planned in Chapter 7 directly into action as you create your FrontPage Web, using a feature that allows you to view, create, and rearrange the folders that make up your Web.

You can create a site map in FrontPage, print it exactly as it appears in the navigation view, and use it in meetings or in printed documentation or reports. Other FrontPage features automatically fix links when the files they lead to are renamed or moved, check spelling in the background as the site is created, and track revisions so that team members don't mix up versions of a single page as they make changes to it.

Making the Site Live

When your FrontPage Web is set to go, making it live is a simple operation: You move the site from the desktop computer on which it was created to the server that will host it. (See Chapter 10 for information about server and hosting options.) A series of dialog boxes steps you through the procedure easily.

Note

For a FrontPage-created website to work as a live site, you'll have to verify that the server hosting it has FrontPage Server Extensions (a set of special scripts that enables FrontPage to work) installed. Ask your ISP (if it is hosting the site) or your tech people (if the site is on an in-house server). You'll find a list of ISPs that host FrontPage websites at *www.microsoftwpp.com*.

Designing for Multiple Browsers

Regardless of how you or your team create your site, in the design stage you must consider which browsers your audience is using. Various browsers recognize different tags. Even among the tags they all recognize, not everything will look the same on every computer. A simple example is that any given font appears two to three times larger on a PC than it does on a Macintosh. Further, different browsers support different technologies. Internet Explorer, for example, supports Visual Basic, Scripting Edition (VBScript), but not all browsers do.

Identify the browsers and operating systems you anticipate your audience will be using before you design your site. As you design, look at the pages you are creating in various browsers on various computers, matching as closely as possible the range of systems (computers and browsers) you think your audience will be using. You needn't have every browser on every computer in your office; if you were to test all of the most commonly used browsers and software versions, you'd have to test at least 18! Instead, ask associates and friends to view the pages from their computers and report what they see and what operating system and browser they are using. Then make adjustments and ask them to look again.

You can create multiple versions of your site (or individual pages within it) that are tailored to the operating systems and browsers you expect your audience to use. However, this option increases maintenance overhead quite a bit. Each change you make to any given web page will have to be replicated on all the versions of that page, and all the versions of the pages will also have to be tested and maintained. Only the most mission-critical sites with the biggest budgets are likely to go this route.

General Design Rules

Following these general guidelines will help you create an attractive and functional website:

- **Choose colors that complement each other.** Backgrounds, links, and visited links must not clash. Dark text on a white or neutral color background is the easiest to read.

- **Make your site's purpose, navigation, and personality clear.** From the moment a user accesses your home page, the page's main message or reason for being, its primary navigational options, and its overall personality should be obvious.

- **Place the most important items near the top of the page.** Don't expect users to scroll to see what you want them to see. Break pages that extend longer than two screens into separate pages, with a link leading from one to the next.

- **Make whatever looks like a button behave like a button.** Don't get tricky about this. If a user clicks something that looks like a button and it turns out not to be, the user will either be confused or think your site is broken. Either way, it gives a bad impression.

- **Write or edit links so they make the destination and its benefit attractive.** Avoid generic phrases for links, such as *click here*. "Click here" tells the user nothing about why she should care to follow the link or what she will get if she does.

- **Avoid duplicate links.** They startle and annoy users. Be sure that no two links placed near each other on the same page go to the same destination. Also, two links with the same name (wherever they're located) should always have the same destination.

- **Keep maintenance in mind.** For easier maintenance of items that have to be updated (including navigation bars), use HTML text rather than images. Also, write text with an eye toward minimizing maintenance; Chapter 11 describes how.

General Design Rules *(continued)*

- **Avoid the gratuitous.** Wild animation, excessive art, blinking text, and anything that diverts the eye will distract users from your main message. Too many fonts on a single page will just look like a mishmash; too many colors can look like fruit salad. Balance large and small art and long and short blocks of text to achieve balance and draw the eye to your main offerings.

- **Banish horizontal ruled lines.** They're usually unnecessary. They act as a speed bump, tripping up the user's eye as it travels down the page. Paragraph breaks and other less obvious devices will accomplish the job and be less visually intrusive.

More tips on making your website usable are throughout this book; in particular, see the site architecture and content tips in Chapters 7 and 11.

Tip

To get a clear picture of what does and doesn't work in website design, see Jakob Nielsen's site (*www.useit.com*), Builder.com's tutorials and critiques of websites (*www.builder.com*), and Web Pages That Suck's reviews of lousy sites and counterproductive navigation (*www.webpagesthatsuck.com*).

Jazzing Things Up with Interactivity

Interactivity on websites takes many forms and can add plenty of pizzazz. Interactive elements can include:

- Navigational features such as mouseovers or clickable buttons that glow or change shape

- Entertaining components such as puzzles, games, and electronic postcards

- Value-added interactive tools such as calendars and mortgage calculators (Figure 8-7)

- Forms that gather data (online surveys) or allow users to self-assess (instant-response quizzes)

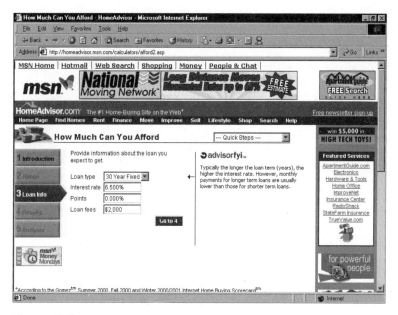

Figure 8-7

An interactive mortgage calculator

If interactive elements are overused or done poorly, they can seem gratuitous or even silly. Use interactive elements only to further your cause. If a specific activity or gadget will enhance your audience's experience or support the goals and branding message of your site, fine. But be judicious.

Many of the nifty effects mentioned require programming skills beyond the grasp of those without real experience. However, nonprogrammers still have options for adding some interactivity to their sites. FrontPage offers several such options, such as components for mouseovers and discussion boards and ways to create interactive forms for surveys, quizzes, or other purposes.

You can also download some cool interactive components (for a fee) from websites such as *www.webmonkey.com* and *javascripts.earthweb.com* and incorporate them into your site. (Instructions are usually included with the download.)

Including Office Documents

You can easily save documents created using Office as HTML documents and then upload them to your website, just as you would any other HTML document. You can edit these documents using Notepad, Word, or FrontPage (or any other HTML editing tool). For example, you can tinker with Web pages that were first created as Word documents in order to add imagery and interactivity.

Another option is to upload to your site the document file in its original format (.doc, .xls, or .ppt, for example). If you embed a link to the document in your HTML, users who have Office will be able to access the file in its Word, Excel, or Microsoft PowerPoint format and use it. (This is how the spreadsheet mentioned in Chapter 2 was made available at the E-Commerce Management Center at *www.tauberkienan.com*.) The code for creating such a link is similar to the code for creating other links; it looks like this:

```
<A href="http://www.tauberkienan.com/ecommerce/ecommercebudget.xls">
Sample Budget</A>
```

Most Office applications allow you to save files directly to a web server (instead of your local computer) using either FTP or FrontPage Server Extensions. This can be handy for quickly updating Office documents stored on your web server. But be sure that copies of all of the Office documents that are on your web server are also stored on your desktop computer.

FrontPage includes additional tools for publishing Microsoft Access databases online. Users can query the database using a FrontPage-generated form; the results appear as a new web page. Using this technique, you can create a product catalog, a customer support knowledge base, or a retail outlet locator.

Building an E-Commerce Site with bCentral

bCentral (*www.bcentral.com*) offers an integrated set of tools and services you can use to create a website tailored to your industry and manage your business online. For example, with bCentral Site Manager (a tool included in the Business Web services), you can have a functional, attractive catalog, shopping cart, and transaction system up and running quickly without needing any programming skills and without hiring developers. (You also won't have to install any special software on your computer.) You can include pages for customer support, for technical help, and for contacting your company in your bCentral-built website. You can use other features of bCentral to extend your business reach into broader business-to-consumer (b2c) and business-to-business (b2b) marketplaces as well.

Creating a Shopping System with Business Web

To create a website using bCentral Business Web, you pull together and organize your content just as you would if you were hiring designers and developers. Then, with your content in hand, you sign up for the service.

Business Web steps you through the process of creating your site using wizards. You simply answer the questions asked and choose the look you like. As you set up the site, you can preview the pages as they'll appear on the Internet.

Tip

You can customize your Business Web website using FrontPage. You'll find a quick and easy tutorial at bCentral.

You can set up your own business rules and specify tax tables for your Business Web website. You can also indicate the shipping methods you will provide and rate information. While you must make arrangements with your own bank to handle your merchant account (see Chapter 10), your Business Web service can include credit card processing capabilities.

Site hosting, server maintenance, and order summarizing are included among Business Web services. Tools for accounting and the tracking of fulfillment are also available through bCentral.

Extending Marketplace Reach with Commerce Manager

Most businesses want to sell their goods in as many markets as possible. Of course, a particular company might have reasons to focus its business plan on a narrower market, but in general, the more markets the merrier. Commerce Manager, one of the many services available through bCentral (*www.bcentral.com*), allows you to extend your reach into multiple online marketplaces, including auctions and fixed-price channels. Using Commerce Manager, you can focus on selling b2c, b2b, or both. You need not create separate sales sites or separate product listings for each channel or marketplace; you can catalog what is for sale in a single location and then select which of the supported marketplaces will carry which products. Your products will get maximum exposure at minimal investment in site development and business administration.

When you sign up for Commerce Manager, a wizard will lead you through the process of setting up a catalog of products. After you set up your catalog, you can select marketplaces supported by Commerce Manager that seem right for your products. Once the sales activity starts, you can review and manage sales activity on all those marketplaces from a single Commerce Manager administrative page. Commerce Manager can be a fast and easy method for boosting overall sales by extending your reach into new and expanded markets. Commerce Manager also integrates well with other bCentral online business services, notably, Finance Manager and Customer Manager (described in Chapters 2 and 5), enabling smoother, more efficient, and more customer-centric e-commerce operations.

Small businesses and e-commerce managers who have almost no technical skills can launch and run a functional e-commerce website with a back end powered by Microsoft. The bCentral solution is easy and economical. Hiring a web shop, designer, or developer to build your website is a much higher-end solution (and is the subject of the next chapter).

Chapter 9

Working with Web Shops, Developers, and Teams

If you're considering jobbing out the building and maintenance of your e-commerce website, you must decide whether to job out the whole project or just parts of it (and, if so, which parts). You must also decide whether to use vendors or in-house resources.

Working with a vendor in the e-commerce industry has its ins and outs, and knowing how to find and work with good companies is essential. You need to know how to present your needs so you'll get good proposals from vendor candidates, how to assess vendor experience, and how to build good relationships so that the project goes smoothly. Maintaining good vendor relations is also important if you want a vendor to maintain your site or support you when you're ready to bring maintenance tasks in-house.

Note

Even if you assign the job of running your site to one or more departments within your own company, knowing how to assess the experience of people in those departments is important. Read through this chapter to understand what skills and experience the in-house team should have.

Assessing Your Needs

The type of shop you need (or whether you need one at all) depends on factors such as:

- The scope of the project—whether it's the soup-to-nuts building of an entire site or just a bit of sprucing up (some modifications, functionality improvements, or fresh graphics)

- The size of your budget and how it compares to the scope of your project

- The level of expertise you or your team can bring to the project

Another factor might be how much hand-holding you need during the project. If you or your in-house team don't have much experience planning or building e-commerce websites and need a web shop to lead you through the process step by step, guiding you as you make decisions, you can expect the shop to take that into account when it formulates a bid.

Consider Assembling an In-House Website Team

Hiring, training, and keeping on even a minimal in-house website team requires significant investment in salaries, benefits, management, and infrastructure (including equipment, work areas, technical support, and more). Salaries are notoriously high, although after the "dot-com crash" that started in 2000, they leveled off from the booming ascent that occurred in 1999. See the salary wizard at Salary.com (*www.salary.com*) to find good job descriptions and discover what compensation people on e-commerce web teams expect to receive.

Note

The first person you hire for your website team should be a sharp, web-savvy site manager who can see to it that your e-commerce projects address your interests. Face facts: That person cannot be all things. Depending on the nature of your site and the type of expertise it most requires, the site manager might be primarily a programmer, designer, marketing whiz, or content creator, but it's highly unlikely that you will find all those skills in one person.

To get a keen sense of the various roles a web team fulfills, you can read through the sections of this chapter that describe web shops of assorted types. Generally speaking, you might want to make a commitment to hiring a full-time, in-house team only after you've concluded that the viability of your e-commerce venture warrants that step. During the start-up phase of your operation, you might instead consider the short-term solutions of outsourcing (contracting jobs to outside resources), insourcing (assigning employees borrowed from other departments to handle website responsibilities), or even outtasking (jobbing out small jobs on a contract basis).

Consider Outsourcing and Insourcing

If you aren't prepared to invest in an in-house team, in addition to the option of *outsourcing*, you have the option of *insourcing*. You might, for example, have your in-house graphics department do the graphics and your tech department do the programming.

Note

Companies often see insourcing as a logical way to avoid redundant functions within the company—for example, two different art departments (one devoted to print and one to the web initiative) or two different tech groups (one for the company network and one for the website).

Tips for Effective Insourcing

When a team is pulled together from different departments to work on the e-commerce initiative, the politics can be difficult to navigate. The following pointers can help smooth the way:

- **Evangelize.** Send out e-mail now and then to let everyone in the company know what the web team has been up to and what results were achieved. This will help ensure that future web projects are taken seriously. When it's necessary to borrow employees to participate in a web project, that project won't seem expendable if the overall e-commerce initiative is seen as successful.

- **Don't poach.** Talk to the managers of any employees you want to borrow before you talk to the employees themselves.

- **Look in unlikely places for insourcing candidates.** Is there an administrative assistant or programmer who is a writer in disguise? Is there a page layout person in corporate communications who is eager to learn HTML? Look past job titles and "hire" for potential.

- **Ask HR which departments are ramping down.** If you can absorb one department's downsizing casualties onto your roster, you might get some grateful employees who will attack their new assignments with enthusiasm.

- **Cross-train by empowering other departments to post on the company intranet.** Orient staff in various departments in HTML and web processes, and you'll have a pool of trained insourcing candidates from which to draw as needed.

- **Give generous credit where credit is due.** Remember to thank employees *and their managers* at every milestone and as publicly as possible. Send an e-mail message up and down the ranks mentioning that without the support of those talented people and the generous managers (name them) who lent them, the work might never have gotten done.

- **Buy pizza.** Or take the gang out to lunch, the beach, or laser tag. Do something social that gives them time to gel as a team, and as the project progresses and important milestones are achieved, reward their extra efforts.

However, insourcing can create some challenges for the main web team. People from other departments assigned to the web initiative sometimes consider that assignment a lower priority than their usual work. Their ongoing tasks are generally more crucial to supporting the company's core business than the web endeavor; that can leave the insourced tasks at the bottom of the "borrowed" employee's priority list. In such a scenario, the web team leader is left with insufficient authority and resources to get the job done. Further, if the borrowed staff is not web-savvy, the required training can be time consuming for all involved. Nonetheless, in some cases, especially when the need is short-term and limited in scope, or when the borrowed staff is actually web-savvy, insourcing might be the best solution available.

Consider the Outtasking Alternative

Outtasking is yet another option. This is simply a matter of hiring freelancers or contract workers to complete a specific, definable, deliverable portion of the overall job. You can outtask a piece of the programming, writing, design, or some other part of the project. The difference between outsourcing and outtasking is in the size of what's jobbed out; jobbing out all of the database development, the look-and-feel design work, or even all of the human resources functions would be considered outsourcing, while jobbing out a portion of one of those jobs would be considered outtasking.

Microsoft Products That Facilitate Collaboration

Microsoft offers a number of solutions for keeping both vendor and in-house workgroups on track and in communication. Microsoft Exchange Server provides a platform for business communications and offers inexpensive administration while enabling collaborative features. Microsoft Office, Microsoft Project, and Microsoft NetMeeting offer online access to shared calendars, contact lists, and project responsibilities. Project's project management features help you track tasks and projects, and team members or officemates can easily share calendars, software, information, and documents across a corporate LAN or the Internet. Microsoft Outlook—part of Office—offers everyday scheduling features that can be viewed via your intranet. (See the Appendix to find out more about intranets.) NetMeeting offers the additional advantage of facilitating collaboration among team members in various geographic locations. It allows for voice communication and video conferencing; it also offers a virtual whiteboard on which various team members can interactively draw or write.

Microsoft SharePoint provides new capabilities for team collaboration via workgroup websites. Essentially, it offers options for file sharing, calendaring, discussion groups, polling (to reach group consensus, for example), and other workgroup-enabling tools.

At the higher end, Microsoft Visual SourceSafe provides collaboration tools for team members to use during development. Version control is a key issue in team collaboration; team members working on the same document or file need to know they aren't mixing up the changes they're making as they go along. Visual SourceSafe provides easy-to-use version control capabilities, and it generates site maps and tests links automatically. Using Visual SourceSafe, team members can develop web content, code, and supporting files in the same environment. They can then deploy the files directly to the website. Visual SourceSafe offers a very capable collaboration and management environment for working on websites.

Who's Who Among Shops and Developers

Whether you're seeking a building contractor to remodel your home or a web contractor to build your website, you'll find that companies range in size from large to small. They all offer varying degrees of service, skill, and experience. Each company approaches the building process from its own unique angle and will have its own recommendations about what you ought to do with your site. Let's take a quick look at the general categories of web shops and contractors.

ISPs and Hosting Companies

You probably already have an ISP. Your ISP is the company that provides you, personally, access to the Internet. It also offers access to software that you can use for e-mail or web browsing and perhaps other services. You might recognize the names of larger ISPs, such as MSN, MindSpring, and America Online; smaller regional ISPs also exist in many areas. Most ISPs offer customers the option to create a free website that is hosted on the ISP's server. This is an attractive option for personal websites, but for creating and hosting a fully-featured, viable website or storefront for a mid-sized or large e-commerce venture, hosting at an ISP is simply not an option. The server space an ISP offers is inadequate for a large site, and usually the ISP does not allow its clients to implement websites that include the kind of programming and front-end features required for selling and other types of e-commerce.

Note

Typically, the account you have for hosting your e-commerce website will be of a different type and will have more robust capabilities and higher-end options than the account you use for your personal Internet service. For more on choosing the right company to host your e-commerce site, see Chapter 10.

Internet presence providers (IPPs) offer clients a wider range of services and higher-end options than ISPs typically do; they differ from hosting companies in that they provide some combination of design, implementation, and even consulting services as well as hosting. An IPP, then, provides a *presence* on the Internet—but what *presence* means varies from company to company. Sometimes a company that calls itself an IPP provides more robust hosting options with a bit of design but no development or implementation. Sometimes the service is complete and might even include some after-launch maintenance.

If you are considering using a full-service IPP to do development, design, and implementation, ask the company whether it has a design team (and perhaps a content team) that works independently of the technical implementation and hosting team. A techie is not a designer, and asking a programmer who "does design" to lay out your website is unlikely to result in a professional look.

Some key questions to ask an IPP include:

- What services are available? What percentage of the time spent on a given project is devoted to which services?

- How many staff members are devoted to creative services such as content or design? Who are they, and what is the scope of their responsibility in a project? What skills and experience do they bring to the table?

- To get the benefit of creative services, is it necessary to contract for hosting services? Are any package deals available for both or for each?

If you find that an IPP is an excellent company and offers some services you need but not full service, you can contract with other companies for those additional services or you can have your own staff do those tasks.

Ad Agencies and Marketing Firms

Advertising and marketing agencies often have "creative" departments that forge words and pictures into full-blown campaigns to sell anything from diapers to political candidates. (Sometimes they subcontract the hands-on work to design agencies and simply provide the strategy.)

Because they see the Web as yet another medium (augmenting TV, print, or radio) with a large audience available to be marketed to, most large ad agencies now have departments or subcontractors that specialize in creating Internet presences. Hiring ad or marketing agencies to create the e-commerce branding message holds some advantage for companies that have the budget for it. If you've worked with an agency before and it has creative, talented people on hand, it probably knows your message and style. But if you're considering having the agency actually implement the site, find out what its background in e-commerce is. There's a big difference between creating ads or brochures and producing a compelling website that functions smoothly. Many designers who have been designing for print for years look at websites and think, "I can do that," but the Web is a whole different animal, with particular limitations and challenges. Question closely any agencies and designers you are considering; later in this chapter, you'll learn more about the questions you should ask in assessing anyone's suitability for your endeavor.

Tip

One option for working with an ad or marketing agency is to retain the agency as your branding or creative consultant but assign the actual implementation to a company that has the experience you need. This strategy adds to your management overhead, but it does net you the sum of two companies' best expertise. Just remember to decide who is top dog.

If the ad agency you already work with is genuinely web-savvy, hiring it to create your site might be a good way to achieve an overall branding presence with just the right message for all media.

Design Shops Large and Small

Some companies specialize in designing, developing, or building websites (without offering hosting or providing overall ad or marketing campaigns). These companies come in various configurations and range from large, renowned web shops that work for large clients to smaller outfits and even independent operators. Some smaller companies and independent operators are backed up by "virtual" organizations in the sense that they pull together freelancers or other small companies based on the needs of a given project. Choosing among these firms requires looking at your budget, how much time you have for managing outsourced services, and, as always, your site's goals.

Large, full-service design firms

Innovative, exclusive web design firms (such as Organic Online and Razorfish) include talented, skilled staff who know many cutting edge tricks for creating websites. They also are in high demand, they are expensive, and they can afford to turn away work that won't enhance their portfolio of clients.

If you hire such a firm, you will presumably be hiring a cadre of experienced, skilled specialists who know how to plan and execute a working website. When you contract with a shop such as this, it will form a team assigned to produce your site. This team might include any combination of the following specialists necessary to get the job done:

- An account manager to handle the agency's business relationship with you, the client

- A producer or project manager to manage the process of creating and implementing the site and to track the achievement of benchmarks

- A content strategist, content manager, or content developer along with writers and editors to plan, track, create, and shape the site's content

- An information architect, usability engineer, or both to organize the site and create navigational paths

- A designer or creative director to create the look and feel

- Artists to create or edit graphics for the site (with direction from the designer)

- A technical lead or senior developer to make technical decisions and coordinate the programmers
- Programmers to code the scripts needed to make forms, applets, message boards, chat areas, and other specialized applications run on the site
- Production staff, or HTML coders, to convert into HTML the work of the content developer, designer, and artists

The team might also include an extended, behind-the-scenes army of specialists in marketing, branding, typography, video and sound production, database development, security, integration of back-end components, testing, and so on. Your primary contacts, however, will be the account manager and producer (or project manager).

Note

Job titles for web team members differ from company to company. Minimally, you ought to be introduced to a producer or project manager who will act as your primary contact throughout the project. You don't often hear the title "Webmaster" anymore because it's considered too vague.

Despite the fame and apparent expertise of high-profile shops, you must verify through diligent research, interviewing, and risk assessment that the firm you're considering is the best one for the job you've specified. Don't be dazzled by reputation or stunning portfolios; not all big, prestigious firms are easy to work with, and not all are brilliant every time with every client. Some have very distinct design styles, and some work only on certain kinds of projects or only with select clients. Again, be sure that any firm you consider offers what you need. Find the firm that's right for your project.

Small and mid-sized design firms

Smaller web shops, with perhaps 5 to 20 in-house employees, frequently offer a variety of styles and services, but sometimes focus more closely on a specific design style or a certain type of client. Like large firms, small and mid-sized shops usually assemble a team for each project that's tailored to the scope of the job. The team might include a producer or project manager, creative personnel, an information architect or usability engineer, a database developer, programmers, and HTML coders. Or it might be a much smaller workgroup.

Depending on who's on staff, who's available, and who has the right expertise for the tasks at hand, a small to mid-sized shop might assign only its own in-house staff to your job, or it might assemble a virtual team of in-house people working with subcontractors. It's common, for example, to subcontract the conversion of video and sound files to the appropriate web formats, or perhaps to job out programming and database development or even HTML coding.

Note

One advantage of using smaller shops is that they often take on only one big project at a time. You can usually get the full attention of whomever you hire from beginning to end. But a disadvantage is that if you accept a bid from a small shop while it's in the middle of another project, you might have to wait until that project is finished before yours can start.

Back-End Firms

As the Internet industry matures, more and more segmentation is occurring among web shops. Increasingly, the design of the front end is assigned to a specialized design firm while the development of the back end is placed in the hands of a company that specializes in databases, transactions systems, and so on. In fact, not all back-end firms handle all back-end systems; some offer deep expertise in specific applications (such as e-mail, chat, or broadband media). Others specialize in specific technologies or companies. Some back-end firms are Microsoft Certified Solution Providers, for example, and offer deep expertise in the use of Microsoft technologies.

Before you hire a back-end firm, you must, of course, perform the usual steps involved in researching and interviewing prospective vendors. In addition, you must find out:

- What sites they have built that have similar functionality and features to yours. (Investigate those sites to make sure they work smoothly and are usable in the ways you'd like your site to be.)

- Whether the sites they've built handle the level of traffic, the number of transactions, or the volume of interactivity you expect.

- How stable they are. This includes their fiscal health, the size of their staff (as compared to the number of freelancers they use), how long they have been in business, and so on.

**Tip**

In checking the references of back-end firms, talk to their clients, but also talk to front-end design firms they've worked with; design firms often have a different take on how projects went than clients do.

Integrators, Consultants, and Testing Labs

Integrators are companies that build back-end systems by combining existing software and that integrate back-end components to make them work well together. Integrators usually don't create a lot of original code; instead, they use tools and technologies created by other companies as the building blocks of entire systems. Often, an integrator builds the entire website by joining a design created by a front-end design firm with a number of back-end products (such as Microsoft .NET Enterprise Servers, Interwoven TeamSite, and more) along with some tools and coding that "glue" it all together. In hiring an integrator, you should address the same points raised in the previous section on back-end firms as well as in the upcoming section titled "Finding the Right Vendor."

Consultants range from individual people with expertise in some aspect of website creation to big consulting firms that offer a wide variety of services, including planning and execution of websites. Some consulting firms simply assess the opportunity, make recommendations, and leave the decision making and implementation to you. (You can then outsource those jobs to others as you like.) Some firms offer ongoing management services, including business planning, strategy, promotion, staffing, administration, and even procurement of office equipment and cubicles. Some also offer everything a back-end firm or integrator does. Generally speaking, a large consulting company has vast resources at its disposal and can make nearly anything a reality for its clients as long as the client is willing to pay the bill.

Testing labs focus on testing. They might test a focus group's responses to concepts or a design idea, they might analyze functionality by working with the site's specifications, or they might bang away at an alpha or beta version to see how it's shaping up. Sometimes a testing team puts the site through its paces, and sometimes the firm asks a group of users to test tasks, navigation, and overall usability. Not all testing labs offer all services; as always, find the one that suits your needs. Testing labs might be hired directly by a client company, or they might be hired by a design firm, back-end firm, integrator, or consulting firm.

To sort through how to approach, get bids from, select, and work with web shops and firms of any size or type, read on.

Independent Contractors

Very small, independent operators might specialize in one aspect of creating websites or they might be "shops" that consist of one person who does…well, everything. That person might sometimes dip into the same pool of freelancers that the mid-sized web shops do. If you're considering working with an independent contractor, keep in mind that the skills and abilities of the contractor will define what that person can do with your site. If you need only advice and that person offers a range of consulting services, that's fine. But (as an example) if your project requires the development of even a small-scale database, you must find someone who has those skills or has access to a proven subcontractor with those skills. If you need a designer but not much programming, hire someone with design skills but make sure that he or she has *web* design skills and that you've communicated about how production will take place. Also, figure out who, exactly, will do the HTML work. Will it be the designer or a subcontracted HTML coder? Who will manage that person—the designer or you? Investigate the relationship between the independent contractor and any freelancers, and be sure that everyone involved knows who is doing what and that they are qualified and can work as a team.

Using Multiple Vendors

Mixing and matching vendors offers the advantage of incorporating the expertise of various specialists. However, if the relationship among vendors is not set up carefully and managed well, working with many players can add to your managerial overhead. If two or more vendors haven't worked together before or don't have complementary work methods, for example, ironing out project details, communications paths, and potential problems can drive costs (and your blood pressure) through the roof.

In dealing with large or complex projects, many companies outsource the back-end development to a skilled back-end firm and assign front-end design to a specialized design firm. On very complex or big-budget projects, other specialists (such as branding consultants, usability engineers, and testing labs) might be called in as well. Again, the advantage in this strategy is that you can gain a lot of deep expertise. Even on smaller projects, a developer is sometimes called in to work on some specialized aspect of the back end.

Tip

If you find yourself working with multiple vendors, see to it that you've put in place a top-down understanding of roles and responsibilities. Have high-level people representing each vendor attend the early meetings, and make sure they understand the project's scope as well as who's who and how they'll work together. Someone has to be top dog or act as "general contractor." Decide up front who that will be, and make sure everyone knows.

In some cases, a front-end design firm will recommend a back-end firm (or vice versa) that it has worked with in the past. If the two companies know each other's processes and communication styles, that can help keep things smooth and quicken the pace of the project. However, if the two companies show signs of having more loyalty to each other than to you, the client, consider that a red flag. You might have to hire some other company to fulfill one of the roles so that all parties know you have the last word. Or you might be able to address the loyalty issue satisfactorily by bringing it up directly and simply talking it through.

Finding the Right Vendor

Word-of-mouth referral is often the best method for finding a contractor or vendor. If you can (sometimes competitive rivalries rule this out), contact the managers of e-commerce sites you admire and ask who created the sites. Alternatively, you can look online for potential contractors or vendors. Yahoo! (*www.yahoo.com*) provides listings of designers and other web shops, as does FirmList.com (*www.firmlist.com*). You can also find referrals through professional organizations such as the Association of Internet Professionals (*www.association.org*), Webgrrls (*www.webgrrls.com*), and San Francisco Women on the Web (SFWoW, *www.sfwow.org*). Or you can ask around for local listings; in the San Francisco area, for example, people seeking web shops or contractors are often referred to Craig's List (*www.craigslist.org*), a well-known website.

When you have a list of various vendors, take a look at their sites and the sites they list as those of their clients. Later in this chapter, you'll learn in more detail what to look for in assessing candidates; at this juncture, just get a sense of who's who and try to narrow the field to the vendors that are of real interest. To begin your assessment, you must focus next on what the project is and how to communicate that to potential vendors.

Define the Project

The one factor that most often leads to bloated budgets, missed deadlines, and disappointing results is the lack of clearly defined expectations. It's simple: Poorly defined or undefined expectations usually lead to poorly executed websites. Freelance project manager Gloria Keene relates one such experience: "I was asked to step in to complete a project when its manager left unexpectedly. A vendor had been hired to create the design and another to develop the back end. The outgoing project manager had little experience, and she started everyone out with specs that were vague and incomplete. We soon found ourselves in a meeting where the goal was to finalize details and get started with the actual production. At one point, one vendor turned to the other and said something about 'when you start coding,' and the other vendor said 'no, you're doing the coding.' It turned out none of the players had included doing the actual [HTML] coding in their bids."

To get the results you want in your website, whether you're jobbing it out to a shop, insourcing it, or outtasking parts of it, your first task (once you have developed your strategy) is to put in writing what you want. The more information you can provide, and the clearer it is, the more likely you are to get the result you want. A written request for a bid is known as a *request for proposal* (RFP). Providing potential vendors with an RFP ensures that when the bids come in they'll be similar enough in scope to allow you to make an apples-to-apples comparison.

As you discuss (in writing) your project with those who might execute your plan, be prepared to cover the following points:

- The general scope or nature of the project. Is it full-scale development and design of a new site? Revamping of an existing site? A relatively simple interface redesign? Simply the addition of new features or key areas of the site? Describe the project in general as well as the role you'd want the vendor to take in the project.

- The image or branding of your company, service, or product; also, any image or reputation you'd like to avoid. See Chapter 4 for a list of key questions to ask yourself in order to identify your audience and clarify the branding you plan to achieve. Include an abridged version of that information in your RFP.

- The deliverable product, described as clearly as possible. Use the specs you wrote based on the discussion in Chapter 7 as the basis of a summary. As you'll recall, your specs should communicate to those working on the site how it will look and function. Give vendor candidates an abridged version; then, before work actually begins, give the chosen vendor's contact person the full details. You must specify in your RFP, for example, whether you expect only front-end design or design plus implementation and whether implementation includes only coding the front end or developing the back-end systems as well. You can offer the particulars of your front-end and back-end requirements later.

- Any approval points or benchmarks required on your end (such as marketing approval, a legal review, and signoffs from executives or others).

- The timeline you anticipate. You set the deadline for launch; the vendor will describe its production process and tell you whether your dates can be met. An outline of the production process can translate into an overview of the project's schedule; both sides should understand whether these dates are simply goals or firm deadlines. You might want to establish consequences for missed deadlines for both sides; the consequence of a missed deadline on the part of the client might be simply a delay, while the consequence of a missed deadline on the vendor's side might be a reduction in payment (a penalty). Alternatively, and more positively, you can offer bonuses for meeting deadlines rather than penalties for missing them.

- Whether the vendor's services should include announcing and promoting the site (if it's a large, full-service vendor you're dealing with). Will you expect the vendor to submit your site's URL to search engines, indexes, and portals? Are there any specialty portals you want included? Will your public relations people make announcements to the media and appropriate discussion groups, or will the vendor? What other advertising, media placement, or promotion will be included? (See Chapter 12 for more on promoting a site.)

- What maintenance services you expect to be included, if any. Will you want the vendor to stay with the project after launch to provide bug fixes or other improvements based on user feedback? (You'll have to discuss with potential vendors whether that will involve a separate contract or will be included in a full-service contract.)

- Whether hosting should be included and, if so, what range of options and level of service you expect. (See Chapter 10.)

Refer again to the mission statement you created after reading Chapter 1. You might want to include some form of that information in your RFP. If you'd like a sample RFP to help you on your way, take a look at the example provided by the E-Commerce Management Center at *www.tauberkienan.com*. As you review the style, experience, skills, and references of various candidates, keep in mind your goals. Note, also, how closely the proposals you receive from candidates match up with what you defined in your RFP.

Assess Style and Approach

Although some design shops (and vendors of other sorts) can provide a wide range of looks and services, most work in a certain style or put a certain spin on what they do. Make sure that the style of any designer you select fits the project at hand. For example, if your mission is to provide customer support for your health care products for seniors, a shop that specializes in artsy, postmodern design and hip, leading-edge copy will not be appropriate.

Similarly, programmers and developers put their own spin on what they do. For example, some specialize in building custom transaction systems from the ground up (sort of like a fully-tailored suit that will fit only you perfectly), while others customize existing products to provide a transaction system (more like an off-the-rack suit with the cuffs and sleeves altered as needed).

The best way to assess the style of various shops is to look not just at their sites but also at their clients' sites. Try to find out exactly what role the shop had in each case, consider how closely it matches what you need, and evaluate how well the shop succeeded in situations that most closely match yours.

Evaluate Skill and Experience

Experience counts in all matters, but in the e-commerce world, just exactly what counts as experience and how much experience it is possible to have are big questions. To appropriately assess experience, research the backgrounds of the individuals who make up a shop's team. E-commerce is still

243

in its youth, so many people working in the field are either new to it or bring to it background from some other field. Some have rich experience from industries such as publishing, print design, marketing, and programming; others are fresh out of spanking-new certificate programs. Those who bring other experience with them need to fully understand the differences between their former industries and e-commerce; those straight out of school might not have the breadth of related experience you need. Consider carefully how much experience your project requires and what sort of experience is most appropriate.

Almost no one was working in web design, web development, and e-commerce before 1995. Anyone who tells you in 2002, for example, that he or she has 10 years of experience in e-commerce must have a unique twist on what that means. Ask that person exactly what he or she has been doing. Publishing content on gopher (a forerunner of the Web)? Designing electronic graphics for computer game developers and then for multimedia companies? That's certainly more relevant than having had an e-mail account or used newsgroups in 1993, but it still isn't 10 years of website experience. "Years of experience" can mean relevant, related experience, but you should closely question anyone who claims to have been directly involved in e-commerce or web design or development before 1995.

Also, while designers and artists in print and advertising media are required to have skill with color, layout, and visual balance, designers who work on websites also have to know how to convert graphics that include deeply saturated color into electronic files that are small enough to be transferred across the Internet quickly. Not just any designer can do web design. Unfortunately, many fine designers don't realize that the skills they've honed in designing for print don't prepare them for designing for the Web. It's unwise to hire a designer with no web experience to design your site, even if he or she is otherwise qualified in visual design and even if the site is to be implemented by someone else. A designer who has no web experience simply does not know the constraints and requirements of designing for the Web.

On the technical side, you might think that programming experience is programming experience, but it's not. Programming for the Web takes a variety of forms and some specific skills. Someone with experience developing spreadsheet applications or video games might not have the programming skills or mix of experience necessary for e-commerce programming. New technologies and techniques for developing e-commerce websites appear at lightning speed. Talent, diligence, and even passion are required to keep up and to distinguish hype from practical utility.

Ultimately, how many jobs a shop or an individual has handled is less revealing than what the shop or individual did on those projects and how those contributions led to the client site's success. Relevant experience is what counts. When a vendor offers examples of its experience, ask how success was defined in those projects. Also ask whether and when those success benchmarks were reached. If yours will be a sales site and the vendor is describing a successful endeavor that's similar, ask whether the shop followed up after launch to find out whether success had been achieved. If so, do they know what impact their input had? Did sales increase as much as or more than predicted? Did the customer base grow into previously untapped markets? Was the client satisfied with the process of delivering and handling those sales?

Note

You can interview candidates after you get bids, or you can interview them briefly as part of a screening process before you get bids and then follow up with a more detailed interview later.

Judge Quality of Interaction

How well vendors hear you as you communicate your plans and how they respond to feedback, changes, and guidance have a big impact on the success of your endeavor and on your stress level. As you interview vendor candidates, do you sense that you will get what you need and have a good experience working with these people? How can you tell? Consider not just how often a vendor communicates and how quickly you get responses to your questions, but also in what style the candidate communicates. Does the vendor respond appropriately to what you say or request? Do the vendor's people use jargon without regard for your understanding? Do they ask questions to clarify what you've explained? What are the vendor's office hours, and can you reach someone during off hours if necessary?

Ask specific questions. How many clients do they expect team members to maintain? (Will your project be put on hold for some other deadline?) Will the vendor work directly with your ISP, hosting company, or in-house technology group to coordinate installation and future updates of your new website? Does the vendor expect you to initiate or manage communications between its people and your ISP or hosting company? (If so, you need to know this up front; the vendor will have to provide you with the necessary information.) As you discuss details, note whether the vendor's people respond completely or with half comments or vague allusions. Ask how proactive the vendor will be in coordinating with your marketing or content development people, and whether the vendor expects you to deliver complete, final copy early in the project. Will the vendor be able to accept last-minute changes? Listen not only to what is said in the answers but also to tone and nuances of vocabulary. Avoid vendors whose communications reveal the possibility of arrogance, griping, or blaming; it's generally a lot more pleasant to work with people who are respectful, positive, and responsible.

Tip

If you'll be working with multiple vendors, try to get your final candidates together for a meeting before you sign everyone up. Note how they interact with each other as well as with you or your team. If, for example, one company is more responsive and communicative while the other is balking or suspicious of its new colleagues, the two are unlikely to work well together. It's better to know that and address it early on than to discover a conflict during the project.

Watch Out for These Red Flags

As you interview vendors, watch out for indicators of trouble. If you're trying to job out original site design and a designer presents you with only a menu of predefined templates, you're not being heard. If you've described two or three goals that your site should accomplish and the vendor comes back with a plan for addressing just one, you're not being heard. If you provide a potential vendor with a list of your competitors' sites and the vendor comes back with a plan mimicking one or more of them rather than presenting an original approach, you're not talking to a creative vendor. And if the vendor quotes a price or presents a proposal without first hearing in detail what you have in mind, you're probably dealing with an amateur. If red flags arise as you interview potential vendors, pause to investigate whatever makes you uncomfortable. Ask more questions. Clarify your intentions. And if you find that a certain shop has all the qualities you need but seems to communicate poorly, be especially diligent in getting details in writing.

Evaluating Quotes

In a best-case scenario, you'll get quotes from perhaps three potential vendors and those quotes will be similar enough in scope to allow you to compare them directly. Your best tool for getting such quotes is the specs list described briefly in Chapter 7 and detailed in the RFP (mentioned earlier in this chapter). Of course, you'll look at the bids to see which is lowest (an easy task if the quotes are based on similar specs); you'll probably also take into account the experience you've had in getting the quotes. The lowest bid is not always the best bid; sometimes the lowest bid is lowest because a lesser degree of service or commitment will be offered. If the lowest quote is from a vendor who has been slow in getting the quote to you, for example, you might consider that tardiness an indicator of the quality of service you'd get, which could counteract any potential savings indicated by the low quote.

Let's look briefly at what drives rates in website design and development. The scope of a project, how many staff-hours it will take to complete, and the expenses it might involve are clearly determining factors. A web shop's prices can also be affected by the shop's experience, level of service, and reputation. Some shops are so well known and have such prestige that they can afford to both charge more and select which clients they'll work with (based on their interest in a project or on the additional prestige a project might bring them). That's certainly understandable. But keep in mind that geographic location is also a factor. Web shops and developers in New York City or San Francisco charge more than those in Buffalo or Sacramento. Do these higher rates indicate more talent or ability? Maybe. It can be argued that bigger cities have a larger talent pool and that all those talented people teach each other new tricks daily, but your site might not require such cutting-edge skill.

If you have provided an RFP to your potential vendors and one comes back with a bid that is wildly different from the others, consider that a red flag. Look to see whether some piece of the project was dropped out of the bid or whether some cost-cutting shortcut was inserted. It's also possible that one shop charges more because it is in a different locale or simply because it can. An exceptionally high price might indicate an inflated opinion of worth or it might indicate better service. An exceptionally low price might indicate naïveté or suggest that the shop is in financial trouble and is hungry for business. Look for a shop whose fees are in an acceptable range as well as one that plans to provide exactly what you asked for. That vendor is your best bet.

Negotiating Fees

Just about everything in life is negotiable. Even in a field as competitive as website design and development, you can sometimes find room in an estimate to get a justifiable discount. If you decide to negotiate, a counteroffer of perhaps 10 to 20 percent less than the shop's bid might be reasonable, along with a rationale for the lower fee. Offering less, however, often starts things off on the wrong foot. To make negotiation easier, you can ask that estimates for your project be submitted in some modular form (so many dollars for this part, so many for that part, and so on) so you can scale back your plans if necessary. Also, if you get a bid that's beyond your budget but you want to work with that vendor for other reasons, you can ask for the vendor's assistance in reviewing the bid and determining where you can scale back to fit your budget. You might be able to scan your own art, for example, or rely on a two-step approval process instead of endless rounds of review by the heads of four departments.

Getting References That Count

Ask prospective vendors to supply you with three or more references that include current or recent clients whose projects were similar to yours in scope and purpose. You can do this either before you get bids or after you've narrowed the field to one or two final candidates. When you request references, ask for the name of a decision-making person who worked with the prospective vendor, that person's address and phone number, and a URL for the project involved. Start by looking at the websites. Then contact the reference and interview him or her, asking questions such as the following:

- Who managed your project at the vendor's end? What was that person's name and title? How was his or her professionalism demonstrated? How did he or she handle challenges or problems? Did you deal directly with anyone else? If so, who was it and how did that go?

- Did *deliverables* (specified items or portions of the project with set due dates) arrive on time and in the form you expected? How did the vendor manage the schedule? If the schedule slipped, why, and how was that addressed?

- Was the project completed within budget? What came up that affected the budget? Was feature creep a factor? Did the shop seem more concerned about staying within budget or pushing extra features and enhancements?

- In general, did the vendor perform as expected? Was the quality of work up to the level of the vendor's stated expertise?

- Would you hire this vendor for another project? Why or why not? How would you work differently with this vendor in the future?

Ask specific questions, take notes, and thank anyone you speak to for taking the time to help you.

Beware of Feature Creep

If you've ever remodeled your kitchen, you've probably experienced feature creep. *Feature creep* is the insidious accumulation of add-ons that were not part of the original plan. Let's say that in the course of the project, you change your mind (or give in to persuasion) and get higher quality sink fixtures, go with granite countertops instead of faux granite, and maybe get the fridge with the automatic ice maker instead of a simpler model. This type of gradual escalation will drive up the cost of any project in no time.

To avoid feature creep, set a budget for your site (see Chapter 2) and stick to it. Ask at every juncture and with each suggestion exactly what the financial implications of your decisions or ideas might be. Don't be pressured into features that aren't in the best interests of the website. Get individual estimates for additional features, and consider those estimates in the context of whether that bell or whistle will contribute to your site's real, long-term success. Look for less costly alternatives. Above all, remember that the quote you got at the outset of your website project was based on the specifications and RFP you provided. Most shops anticipate and account for a few minor changes in their estimates, but major changes and enhancements can bloat budgets in a jiffy. Bear in mind that you cannot expect vendors to monitor how changes will affect your budget. It's their job to run their business, and it's your job to keep your own costs in line.

Delivering Specs and Firming Up Details

Once you've sorted out the bids, talked to references, and selected a vendor, it's time to hand over detailed specs. You also need to settle a few more details. Clarify with the vendor the following issues:

- **The process for the project.** Every company has its own way of working, and you'll have to make sure you understand how this vendor does things. You might also want to ask for some adjustments in the procedures to accommodate how you do things. For example, if your site will be delivered as a beta version, find out how the site will be placed on the server. Can the shop do this for you? Or will your files be delivered to your tech people on a recordable CD or in some way uploaded to your hosting company? (See Chapter 10 for more on server and hosting options.)

- **How contingencies will be covered.** Things change, and things go wrong. That's just life. Of course, the more prepared you are, the less likely it is that unexpected developments will turn into real trouble. Part of being prepared is anticipating how you will cope if and when various potential problems crop up. You can't predict every contingency, but do give thought to what types of events are most likely to delay your project. Establish some guidelines for who will do what if and when the unexpected occurs.

- **On what basis payment will occur.** Payment is often tied closely to benchmarks such as the delivery of certain items. But negotiating for payment based on *acceptance* of deliverables provides you with more certainty that you'll be paying for what you asked for. It also provides you with the leverage you might need to get what you want. The agreement, then, is that when you get what you specified, you'll pay. Just remember that when payment is based on acceptance, you should also specify to the vendor in advance just whose approval is needed and what form it will take.

- **How payment will occur.** Most companies assume that payment will be within 30 days of invoicing. But if, for example, your company issues checks only once a month or every two weeks and that means payment might take as long as 45 days, tell the vendor up front. This will keep everyone's expectations in line with reality.

A Note on Nondisclosure Agreements

A *nondisclosure agreement* (NDA) is a document that protects confidentiality. It specifies an agreement between the signing parties that confidential information disclosed in the course of doing business will not be revealed to others. NDAs are standard in many modern contracts, but you might not find one in the contract of specific vendors. NDAs can also exist as stand-alone documents that are signed before a project is discussed in detail or when the contract is signed. If your website will include features, products, or services you do not want leaked to others before launch, you can ask your vendors to sign NDAs. An attorney can draw up an NDA for you.

Understanding the Contract

As the saying goes, a verbal contract isn't worth the paper it's printed on. Before the project begins, you need a written contract that's signed by both parties. A contract outlines what you expect from the vendor and what the vendor expects from you. It also spells out how and when payment will occur and what will happen if expectations aren't met. In a good contract, all the important questions one might ask about the business arrangement should be answered in writing. Remember that it's wise to have your attorney review contracts before you sign them and it's unwise to try to write a contract yourself. Attorneys see things in contracts that the rest of us don't see. As part of their job, they erase ambiguities and clarify language to avoid misunderstanding.

Note

Who owns what when a website is created is a deep and complex question. A single web page can contain many elements (writing, images composed of other images, code, and scripts) that might be licensed from others. For an introduction to the issues involved, review Chapter 3.

A contract is a document of mutual agreement. Until it's signed, its terms might be negotiable, but once it is signed it's binding. Before negotiations begin, have in mind which terms you consider negotiable and which could be deal breakers. (The vendor will have done the same.) You or your vendor might have a standard contract you can use as a starting point. Yours will be written with your interests at its core but might not address the vendor's business, processes, or specific interests. Theirs might be a better standard contract than yours for the type of work they do (and reading it might provide you with insight into their business practices) but is unlikely to address all of your key issues. Whether you use your standard contract as a starting point or use one drawn up by the vendor, you will almost certainly go several rounds of negotiation before reaching a firm agreement. If and when you get into any contract negotiations, consult your attorney. Sign the contract only after it matches your understanding of the job the vendor is being hired to do as you have defined it.

Addressing Maintenance After Launch

Your site will not take care of itself after launch. Like any business venture, it will need maintenance. You must clean up bad links, maintain and improve service, post new offerings, remove old products and pages, and change the site to adapt to an evolving market. You must also promote your e-commerce site to attract traffic and boost business. Who will do all this, and how?

It's easy to focus on launching the site and forget about what will happen the next day and thereafter. This is a common pitfall. You must consider now who will do necessary, routine, and special maintenance after launch. Will it be you, your staff, or the vendor? The web shop you hire might be interested only in producing your site and might plan to hand all subsequent concerns back to you. If you and your staff have the right skills and can deal with maintenance, that's fine. But you ought to require at least a warranty or time period during which the shop is required to fix any problems that occur. You can also request basic training in site maintenance for your staff; the web shop might agree, for example, to deliver the site and then train someone at your end to make changes and handle routine up-keep. The shop might provide templates, written instructions, or even on-site, hands-on training. This can be a great solution, but if you go with it, also agree on how your requests for assistance will be handled after basic training. That might require a separate maintenance contract.

In the most full-service scenarios, the web shop delivers and installs the site and then performs day-to-day maintenance after launch. The shop might implement daily updates to the content, upgrade the functionality, provide detailed performance analyses, and more. An ongoing relationship such as this requires a clear contract or retainer agreement that spells out the terms and the scope of the relationship as well as a procedure or process for ending the relationship if and when that becomes advisable.

Keep Overarching Management In-House

Never outsource the overarching, high-level management of your project. To ensure that your goals are met, someone in-house—either you or another team leader—must manage your project. Good in-house management is crucial. It can lead directly to satisfaction at your end and also to building positive relations with vendors. Better vendor relationships often result in mutual success, so to achieve the best possible outcome, do everything you can to find the right vendor and create a strong business partnership for the life of your project.

Ending a project on an upbeat note seals the business relationship and puts both parties in a position to extend or resume the relationship when other projects come up. A shop that has done its best work for you (and that now knows your site in detail) can be a time saver for you in the future. Such a vendor will be able to pick up future projects and run with them with little preparation and less supervision. You'll know you can trust them, and they'll know that you are a good client.

A positive relationship results when both the vendor and the client define responsibilities, keep promises, manage expectations, and keep communication clear. It's up to the vendor to deliver what it promised, but it's up to the client to specify the scope of the project, monitor delivery, and tend to the budget. It's also a client's responsibility to pay on time. Thirty days means 30 days, not 45 or 60. In order to maintain good vendor relations, keep your part of the bargain. If you do this and work with solid companies, you could find yourself with more than just a vendor. You might find that you have acquired a valuable partner who will see your success as a reflection of its own.

Chapter 10

Understanding the Back End and Hosting

You don't have to be a general contractor to own a house, and you don't have to be an automotive engineer to own and operate a car. Likewise, you don't have to be a programmer or a database developer to have an e-commerce website. Even so, you should know enough about the back end of a website to discuss the maintenance of your website intelligently and make smart business decisions. Just as being knowledgeable about construction enables you to buy a house with a sound structure and knowing the basics of mechanics enables you to see that your car is running smoothly, being at least conversant in back-end technologies helps you ensure that your e-commerce website remains in good working condition. You'll be far better qualified to make solid business choices about your site and troubleshoot some issues yourself if you understand the general technological underpinnings.

Note

This chapter is meant to help you make effective management decisions about the behind-the-scenes technology that drives your e-commerce website. It will make you more conversant with the technical issues, but it's not meant to make you into a developer.

Chapter 1 described the components that make up the back end of a website. To refresh your memory: The behind-the-scenes technical stuff that makes it possible for your e-commerce website to work includes the following components:

- The web server that delivers the web pages
- The database server that stores and delivers product information
- The mail server that sends out newsletters, as well as any other specialized servers that handle specific applications (streaming media, chat, and so on)
- The transaction systems—*scripts* (special, simple software programming), encryption systems, shopping cart software, and more—that enable your site to accept credit card payments

Let's start our exploration of the back end by looking at what a server is.

Note

If you create and run your e-commerce site using a packaged solution such as Microsoft bCentral Business Web, you don't have to deal with the issues of choosing and maintaining the platform, servers, and transaction systems; the packaged solution will have made those choices for you, and maintenance will be part of the package deal. However, if you're trying to decide whether to host the site yourself, host it elsewhere, or go with a more sophisticated packaged solution, you'll want to know what the issues are. Read on.

What Is a Server?

A server is essentially a computer that "serves" by providing files or data in response to requests from *client* computers (individual desktop computers). The tricky part, though, is that several servers can exist on one computer because what makes the computer a server is the *server soft-*

ware that runs on it. On a single computer, you can have a web server that serves your web pages, a database server that enables any databases (containing, for example, product information, content, or a dealer or outlet locator), and a mail server that handles your e-mail newsletters or discussion group. Alternatively, you can have just one type of server on one computer and another on another computer. For the purposes of this chapter, *server* will mean a computer that has server software running on it. When server software is discussed, it will be referred to as a specific type of server software.

Note

The decision about whether to run a database server and a web server on the same computer is often based on performance. Requiring a server to do double duty can make it run more slowly, and a user accessing the site might experience a slower response from the site.

A server has to be *hosted* somewhere. Hosting refers both to the storing of software and data on a server and to the operation and maintenance of a server in a given location. Your server (or servers, if you need more than one) can be hosted *onsite* (on your premises) or *offsite* (at an ISP or a dedicated hosting company that accepts responsibility for maintaining your server on its premises). ISPs and hosting companies often run *shared* servers, or servers that host many customers at once.

Tip

ISPs often offer economical website hosting among other services. This option can be appropriate if your site is only a small part of your overall business. But if you're operating a site that is mission-critical, you'll want to invest in the services of a dedicated website-hosting company. Such companies might charge more, but they often offer greater attentiveness to the proper functioning of your server, along with 24-hour support and service in case something goes wrong. (See the upcoming sections titled "Reliability Issues" and "Support Issues.") In this chapter, when we refer to a "hosting company," we mean either a dedicated hosting company or an ISP providing website-hosting services.

To some degree, the questions you address in deciding what server, platform, and hosting options to go with are chicken-or-egg questions. For example, whether you host your server onsite or offsite can have bearing on which server solution you choose, and that will influence which platform you use. If you have already chosen the platform, your choices in server software will be more narrow.

Note

The difference between a server and a website is that a *server* is a computer with *server software* running on it; the *website* also runs on the server and is the sum of the website's content and its supporting back-end systems.

Choosing a Platform

The platform your website runs on is simply the operating system used on the computer that serves your website. You cannot use a desktop operating system (such as Microsoft Windows Me or Windows 98) as the platform for your web server. While desktop operating systems are fine for your desktop computer or laptop, they're not designed for serving a website 24/7 (24 hours a day, seven days a week). A web server must be very robust to perform the varied tasks required for serving a website (especially when the website includes a database, mail server, or transaction system). The server also has to have powerful security features. So among Microsoft products, your best bet is an operating system such as one of the versions of Microsoft Windows 2000 created for hosting servers (Windows 2000 Server or Windows 2000 Advanced Server) or Microsoft Windows NT Server.

When choosing among all the possible platforms for your website, take into account the following factors:

- Any expertise you, your technical staff, your developer, or your web shop might already have. Tapping existing knowledge can save the time, trouble, and expense of retraining people on a new operating system.

- The platform your preferred tools (such as HTML editors and scripting tools) work with, the servers they support, and the platform those servers run on. The tools you use might also come down to the expertise your team already has. For example, websites created using Microsoft FrontPage work best when hosted on Windows 2000 or Windows NT because FrontPage takes advantage of certain features offered by those platforms.

- Your budget, obviously enough. Some operating systems cost more than others. However, don't forget to take into account the expense of training people and the cost of hardware, as well as the cost of down time if your platform isn't completely reliable.

Note

You definitely don't want to pay for your developer or web shop to tackle the learning curve associated with new software. If your preferred developer or shop is proficient in a certain platform, go with that. If your preferred platform is unfamiliar to a developer or shop and you feel strongly about your preferred platform, interview other candidates.

Choosing a Server

You can acquire a server through an outright purchase, a lease from the manufacturer, or a rental from an ISP or hosting company. If you host your site on a hosting company's server, you don't have to acquire a physical server at all; you share the hosting company's server with its other customers. The advantage of this approach is that you don't have to invest in your own server; the disadvantage (as developers will tell you) is that you might encounter limitations in your platform and server options as well as in what software you can run on the server. As you compare server options, pay special attention to performance, reliability, and support, as described in the upcoming sections.

Performance Issues

The level of performance a server offers is basically defined by the number of simultaneous users the server can handle. A more robust server machine with web server software on it can support more website users at any given time than a less capable server can. Performance is affected by many factors, the most important of which are the type and number of processors the server has, how much memory the computer has, and what type of hard disk it uses.

How processors affect performance

Your desktop computer most likely has a single processor, called the central processing unit (CPU). Servers, more often than desktop computers, have several processors. It's actually quite common for a server running web server software to have two or even four processors. Server performance is not a simple matter of a computer with two processors being twice as powerful as a computer with a single processor; however, the more processors a computer has, the more powerful it is.

The speed of the processors also affects performance. Speed is usually measured in megahertz (MHz), and the higher the number, the faster the processor. For example, a 650 MHz processor is faster than a 400 MHz processor. Higher speeds are measured in gigahertz (GHz); a 1 GHz processor is faster than a 650 MHz processor. The type of processor, in turn, affects the speed. More recent models generally provide greater speed and better overall performance. Pentium III processors are faster than Pentium II processors, for example.

How memory affects performance

A server must be capable of managing many tasks at once. These tasks can include responding to requests for web pages, querying a database for information, or running the transaction software required to process credit card transactions. Each task the server performs requires memory (random access memory, or RAM), and the more memory your server has, the more tasks it can perform simultaneously. It's common for servers to have at least 128 megabytes (MB) of RAM, but more RAM is preferable. As of this writing, 512 MB or even 1 GB (gigabyte, which equals 1024 MB) of RAM is common in robust servers.

How the hard disk affects performance

The server's hard disk influences its performance in a number of ways. The size of the hard disk determines how much can be stored on it, but it does not directly affect performance. Given that a website is made up of software, code, art, other graphics files, and scripts—all of which need storage space—the size of the hard disk dictates how large and complex the site can be. These days, the smallest hard disks are usually between 4 and 8 gigabytes (GB). To determine how much hard disk storage you'll need to host your website, add up these components:

- Space required by the operating system (from 100 MB to a few GBs or more, depending on the platform you use)

- Space needed for your website files (web pages, images, video, sound files, and so on)

- Space needed for files required by the operating system, such as log files (at least 10 percent of the total disk space)

- Space required for the web server and any other servers on the same machine, such as your database server or mail server

- A "cushion" of extra space that the operating system can use for its own purposes (estimate another 10 percent of the total disk space)

Tip

You can't estimate the 10 percent you need for the log files and the 10 percent you need for a cushion until you know how much total space you'll need, but there's a problem: That 20 percent will be part of the total space you need. What to do? Simply assume that you'll need 10 to 30 times the amount of hard disk space the operating system requires and then work up or down from there. Following along in the example, if the operating system needs 1 GB, assume that you need 30 GB plus 20 percent.

Although, as mentioned, disk size doesn't have a direct effect on performance, the type of hard disk does. Many desktop computers use Integrated Device Electronics (IDE) hard disks, which are optimized for accessing a single file at a time. On your server, a Small Computer System Interface (SCSI) hard disk will be more up to the task. SCSI (pronounced "scuzzy") hard disks are much faster than IDE hard disks and are optimized for accessing many files at once. This is crucial for multiprocessing and will make or break your website when it gets the traffic you hope it will attract.

Note

Server performance is also affected by the type of content your website delivers. Serving "static" HTML pages (made up of routine uses of HTML) puts very little demand on a web server. But if your site serves *dynamic* content (meaning that pages are generated from a database) and uses some form of middleware (discussed later in this chapter), much more server power is required, even to serve the same number of pages. Your developer can help you figure out the additional requirements, based on your middleware package and any dynamically served content you plan to include.

Reliability Issues

The importance of reliability boils down to this: If your server crashes, users cannot access your website. A crash can result in lost revenue, lost credibility and loyalty, and lost time as you troubleshoot the problem and correct it. This downtime is expensive and should definitely be avoided. To ensure reliability, you should buy, lease, rent, or use a computer specifically built to act as a server. You can also beef up the hard disk by specifying a *redundant array of independent disks* (commonly known as a RAID disk) instead of the plain SCSI disk mentioned earlier. RAID uses multiple SCSI hard disks and stores files on them in such a way that if one of the disks fails, the system will continue to function.

To ensure even greater reliability, ask your developer to build redundancy into your systems. *Redundancy* is simply a matter of using one or more additional components as backup systems so that if one component fails, another takes over automatically. An entire server can be added as a backup, ensuring that if the main server fails, the redundant server will take over some or all operations.

Redundancy is also often provided for *power supplies* (components in all computers that convert the electricity provided by the power company into the type the computer actually needs) and *network connections* (components that plug computers into local networks or a hosting company's network). When a redundant power supply is added to a server, the server can continue running even if its primary power supply fails. An acronym you might run across in discussions of redundancy and power supplies is *UPS*, which means uninterruptible power supply. A UPS provides a temporary backup to the electricity supplied by the power company.

Note

Providing for redundancy does require more hardware and software, so it can bump up the cost of your back end pretty quickly. Whether this is a wise investment depends on whether your e-commerce website can stand any downtime.

Support Issues

Most of the time, your server will hum along just fine, but even well-maintained servers have been known to crash and you must be prepared for that. A server might crash because it is overloaded, because its hard disk gives out, or because a power surge fries its power supply.

You (or your developer or tech staff) can prevent some crashes by monitoring your system. Servers track their own activities and generate *log files* to store this information over a given time period. (Log files are further described and an illustration of one is shown in Chapter 13.) Tech people also often monitor the system by using utilities that provide reports on usage. Some of these utilities convert the log files into reports, making them easier to read. Others monitor the server and create animated graphical charts showing current usage. If you or your tech people see that your server is running at 75 percent of its capacity, you are pushing its limits. Just as you don't want to run your car at its highest RPMs at all times (because that creates greater wear and tear and prevents you from having any capacity to accelerate when you need to), you don't want to max out your server. You need a cushion for when you get spikes in website traffic, for example.

Support for a server includes monitoring it, troubleshooting any problems that arise, and solving the problems you find. Support can be provided by the hardware manufacturer, the server software developer, your hosting company, or your tech staff; who is responsible for what depends on your agreements with these entities and on the nature of the problem. Your first line of defense is your tech staff or (if you have a server support agreement with your hosting company) your hosting company's tech staff.

Support contracts are sometimes sold separately from the server itself, so keep in mind that when you purchase, lease, or rent a server, the deal won't necessarily include support. Similarly, when you rent space on a server from a hosting company, the deal might or might not include support. But having a support contract with your server manufacturer or hosting company is a very good idea; this is not the time to skimp. You might need support only rarely, but when you need it, you *really* need it. Without a contract for ongoing support, you'll find yourself scouting around for someone or some place to do the job. With poor support, it can take as long as a week to fix a problem. That's a lot of downtime for even the least mission-critical websites.

Some server vendors will sell you two-hour or three-hour support contracts. That means they'll guarantee a technician at your site within two or three hours of a reported problem, regardless of the day or time you call. Other contracts guarantee same-day or next-day response and repair. When you select among service contract options, again, remember that downtime can cost you dearly. Compare the cost of the service contract to the cost of lost revenue and credibility.

Note

If your company has an information services (IS) or information technology (IT) department, a vendor, in-house technician, or outside consultant might already be available to provide support for your server. If those options are available and serve all of your needs, you don't necessarily have to purchase a support contract from your server manufacturer or hosting company.

What to Look for in Technical Support

Technical support for your e-commerce endeavor should encompass three general areas: the hardware, the software (including the web server software and the database), and the website itself (including the content, the transaction system, and so on). It's unusual to get support for all of these areas from the same person or team. Even if you have a technical staff, they'll sometimes need assistance from others who have even more expertise with the specific hardware, software, or coding in question. When you purchase or lease a server or when you rent space on one, clarify what the support agreements are for both the hardware and the software. Likewise, when you have a developer create a site, database, or transaction system for you, clarify what the support agreement is. Not all support is created equal. Prices and levels of service vary widely, and it's important to know what you're paying for as well as how diligently promises and guarantees are kept. Check references just as you would when hiring a web shop (as described in Chapter 9).

Considering Your Hosting Options

As mentioned previously, the server hosting your website can reside at your location or at a hosting company; it's also possible to rent a portion of shared space on your hosting company's server (at the hosting company's location) and host your website in that rented space. Each option has its pros and cons.

Hosting Your Website In-House

Until recently, it was quite common for mid-sized to large companies to host their websites on their own servers (yes, in their own office buildings). This only made sense; the skills and resources needed to maintain a server were similar enough to the skills and resources many companies already had available among their IS or IT staff. However, websites have gained in importance; they aren't the IT department's little darlings any more. They require specialized, sophisticated support, with people in segmented jobs dedicated to keeping them running and keeping them secure in website-specific ways. That's why hosting companies have come into being—to fulfill the need for housing and maintaining servers with 24/7 connectivity. As time passes, fewer and fewer companies host their own websites; more often, a company entrusts the care and feeding of its web server and other back-end systems to a hosting company, whose core competency lies exactly with those tasks.

If you do decide to host your own website, you'll have full control over it. You can use the software you prefer (within the limitations of the hardware) without having to consider what your hosting company prefers or can support. On the other hand, you (or your staff) will be responsible for keeping the server running around the clock. When something goes wrong at 4:00 in the morning, you or someone in your organization will have to leap from bed and get up and fix it. Depending on what the problem is, this might mean getting the phone company or cable company out (presumably the next morning) to address a connectivity issue, or it might mean having someone (you or your staff) deal with a server crash. If you have full-time, expert technical staff hosting your site at your location on your server, the latter solution might be an option, but for most companies, it isn't advisable.

Note

While many IS and IT departments have the technical skills required to run a web server, most are geared toward maintaining a corporate network. Also, most of them work on a vastly different timetable than that required for running websites. These days, most companies have their IT people handle the corporate network and internal computers and arrange to have their website "live" at a hosting company.

If you do host your own site, you'll want to install a firewall to protect your web server and the other computers on your local network from trespassers. A *firewall,* shown in Figure 10-1, is a system that simply puts up a selective roadblock. It allows outsiders to access sites on your web server but prevents them from accessing any of your other computers or tampering with any of your files. If your company already has a firewall in place, you might have to make changes to the way the firewall is set up in order to accommodate your web server. You might even have to provide a separate, second firewall especially for the web server.

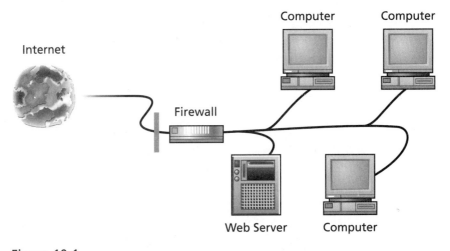

Figure 10-1

A firewall protects your internal systems from the outside world.

Keeping Your Server at a Hosting Company

If you keep your server (either your own server or a leased server) at a hosting company, you will gain access to the hosting company's generally high-speed Internet connectivity. (Placing your server at a hosting company is often called co-location or, in the vernacular, "co-lo.") Most hosting companies have multiple T1s or even higher-speed lines. You will also gain access to the hosting company's staff, which will be available (in varying degrees, depending on the level of service you purchase) to monitor and respond to problems. You might actually have to purchase a separate contract for full, round-the-clock support, but at a minimum any hosting company's staff will see to it that the connection between your server and the Internet is functioning. (Again, whether your server itself is functioning is often a separate issue. See the section titled "Support Issues" earlier in this chapter.)

Your hosting company might specify some limitations on what platform, server software, and other technologies you can use. If so, this is not an arbitrary set of rules. The hosting company is responsible for providing stable, secure, and fast connectivity to its clients; in order to do this, it can't allow anything to disrupt any aspect of its systems. Within any limitations imposed by the hosting company, if you keep your server at the hosting company, you can install and use your own software on the server.

Note

The cost of keeping your server at a hosting company can range from a few hundred dollars a month to thousands. The pricier options provide more service and usually guarantee that you'll experience less downtime. Hosting companies generally accomplish this level of service through reliable connections to the Internet and through hiring experienced staff to be on site around the clock. However, it's always wise to look carefully into any guarantees to be sure of both what is being promised and how the promise will be fulfilled.

Renting Space on a Hosting Company's Server

For smaller companies that don't need the power and sustenance of a fully staffed hosting operation with full-time support people, yet want more sophistication and control than is allowed by a prepackaged service such as those available from bCentral, renting space on a hosting company's server can be an economical and attractive option. (This option is referred to as using shared or *virtual server* space). You'll get space on a robust server without incurring the cost of buying, leasing, or renting a whole server. You'll also get the advantage of a professional staff that monitors and maintains the server all the time. (These people will not, however, monitor and maintain your website unless you sign a separate contract for that.) You—and everyone else who's using space on the server—can have your own domain name. You can run your own database transaction system (within whatever limitations the hosting company specifies), but the server software will be determined, provided, and maintained by the hosting company. The next section describes issues to address in choosing and dealing with a hosting company.

Choosing a Hosting Company

You don't have to limit your search for a hosting company to your immediate geographic region. Scout around for a good deal. (Microsoft Business, at *www.microsoft.com/business/*, provides information about specific hosting companies that you can consider.) Research whether the hosting companies you're considering provide and are proficient in the platform and server options you prefer. You should also consider the issues of redundancy and support described earlier in this chapter.

Hosting Companies, Connectivity, and Bandwidth

Hosting companies differ in their level of connectivity, which is as important a concern as redundancy and support. The issues you must consider have to do with how the hosting company is connected to the Internet. The Internet has several *backbones* (main arteries), which are interconnected. Some hosting companies are connected to the backbones; some are simply connected to other, larger hosting companies that are in turn connected to the backbone. The closer a hosting company's connection to the backbone, the better the connection is. Also, hosting companies that have multiple redundant connections are better able to provide continuous service.

Hosting companies also differ in the level of *bandwidth* (how much data can be transmitted through the available lines) they offer. A hosting company's bandwidth is affected by the type of lines it uses and the capacity of those lines. T3 lines have more capacity than T1 lines, for example, because they have more bandwidth. (The DSL or ISDN lines you might have in your office or home do not have as much capacity as T3s or T1s because they have less bandwidth.) The number of lines a hosting company has also affects the overall bandwidth it has. When you set up an account with a hosting company, you'll be allotted a certain amount of bandwidth. If you need more later, the hosting company might charge additional fees for the extra service.

Tip

Because Internet connectivity between countries is often unreliable, you should use a hosting company in the country in which you'll be doing business. And because you'll want technicians to be available to answer your questions during your business hours, you might even want to consider a company that's within your time zone.

A smooth relationship with your hosting company depends on clearly defined roles and responsibilities. Here are some questions that you can discuss with your hosting company in detail:

- Who will talk to whom when problems arise? Designate a single contact person within your company, and keep in mind that your hosting company will probably have several people on its end working various shifts.

- What types of changes on your site is the hosting company authorized to make, and what types do you expect them to make? You'll want them to address problems with the server immediately, but remember that it is your website: You'll want control of changes to content and functionality.

- Will they automatically notify you when they find a problem with your website? You certainly don't want to discover that the site is down at the very moment you're trying to show it off to associates or potential partners.

- How reliable is their service, and what level of uptime do they guarantee? Different hosting companies offer varying levels of connectivity, which affects how much uptime they can guarantee.

- How will they handle increases in site traffic? This is an issue regardless of how you've chosen to host your website. If you're hosting your site yourself, you'll need a plan for increasing the capacity of your connection to handle any increase in traffic. If your server is located at your hosting company or your site is on your hosting company's server, you'll need to know what they'll charge for additional bandwidth.

- If you're renting space on your hosting company's shared server, how much hard disk space will be allotted to you and what will be the charge for additional hard disk space? Hosting companies

269

usually start by assigning you 20 MB to 50 MB of hard disk space; if you need more, you have to pay for it. Find out the procedure for getting more space and what it will cost.

- Do they support the server technologies required to run your site (for example, Microsoft Active Server Pages [ASP] or a Microsoft SQL Server database)? Again, this is an issue only if you're hosting your site on your hosting company's shared server. The hosting company will probably be willing to support only certain technologies and won't want to install new technologies just because you want them.

- How proactive are they about security? What security measures are in place? What do they have in the way of firewalls and methods for making the building itself secure? Do they have a dedicated security team? Does the security team take responsibility for keeping only the hosting company's network secure, or do they also protect your server's security? How will they provide security for your server? Get specifics about these issues.

How these issues are handled will vary among hosting companies. As mentioned earlier, hosting companies often support only the actual Internet connection. They might not support the server unless the server in question is theirs and you are renting space on it. If the server is yours and something goes wrong with it, you'll have to address the problem yourself or call someone (not the hosting company) to troubleshoot. Some hosting companies provide basic support and will even back up your content on a regular basis. Others provide a higher level of support and will even go so far as to guarantee a certain level of uptime. Of course, you generally pay more for higher levels of support; which level of support is appropriate for you depends on how crucial it is that your site remain up and running at all times.

Tip

If you're using FrontPage to create a website that requires FrontPage Server Extensions in order to run properly, you'll have to verify that your hosting company supports the version of the FrontPage Server Extensions that corresponds to the version of FrontPage you're using. The FrontPage Server Extensions are special software that must be installed on the web server to enable some of the more advanced features of FrontPage.

The Power of Databases

A database is a system that makes organizing, storing, and accessing data easier. It is made up of *records*; each record is separated into a number of related elements called *fields*, which contain pieces of data. You can think of a phone book as a sort of metaphor for a database; each listing is a record, and the fields of the record, such as name, address, and phone number, contain data for that record. As another example, a typical record for a product catalog database has separate fields for the product name, price, and other distinct pieces of data related to the product. A collection of records in a database is known as a *table*. A database can be made up of a single table or many tables. All records within a table contain the same fields.

The following two basic types of databases are in common use today:

- Flat file databases, which have a single table in which all the data is stored

- Relational databases, which can accommodate multiple tables related through specific fields that they have in common

A good database is the bedrock of many an e-commerce website. Product catalogs, customer information, and inventory tracking are typically all stored in databases. When a database is created for a website's back end, scripts are written to call up the data in the database and present it on a web page to users of the website. When a user searches a website's database, he or she enters data into a web page form to submit a *query*, which is simply a question that is asked of the database.

That's the simple version of website databases. What you can do with a database-backed website is actually much more exciting than that.

Database-Backed Websites

Storing product data in a database allows you to update the information easily. The real power in having such a database, however, is that users can search the catalog of products in the database and the catalog can be coordinated with inventory, ordering, and tracking systems to automate purchase and fulfillment processes. Customers can search on any of the attributes of your products (size, color, price, weight, power, and so on), and they can also make a purchase in just a few steps (or even in one step, if their credit card data has been stored in a customer table in the database).

This is made possible via database-generated catalog pages linked to the transaction system. Website users can "customize" a product before purchase (selecting, for example, the color by viewing an image of the product and clicking a "color chooser" to change the product's color). They can find a local dealer or retailer by searching on city, ZIP code, or the specific products the dealer or retailer carries. When the catalog database is tied into inventory management systems, the customer can be notified immediately as to whether an item is out of stock or on back order. Notification can occur in the form of a message appearing automatically on the order form web page or in the form of an e-mail message generated and sent out automatically.

Databases can be applied to websites in other ways as well. For example, all of the data supplied by users or customers who register on your site, sign up for your mailing list, participate in your online survey, or complete an online transaction can be stored in a database. That data can then be sorted, indexed, or categorized to provide you with reports on who is visiting your site or buying from your catalog.

Databases can also be used to store text, images, and other media in fields. Your website team or developers can then write scripts to call forth that material and place it into web pages. This is known as *creating content dynamically*.

Note

When you view a website, you can tell when web pages are being generated dynamically simply by looking at the URL. If the URL doesn't end in a filename with an extension such as .html or .htm but instead looks like a line of programming code, it's likely that a script (represented by the code you see) is pulling data from a database to create the page.

Storing content in a database and creating pages dynamically makes maintenance of large and complex websites a lot easier. Making changes to the navigation bar, for example, is less complicated if you can do it once in the database and have the change appear on all pages on the site. That definitely beats making the change, say, 500 times! Also, content producers who don't know HTML can enter content into a form that automatically drops the content into the database. They simply type the text into a field, click a button on the form, and the new content becomes part of the web page—all without the need for HTML coding.

Note

It's quite common to include in an HTML document a *database call* (a query to the database) that dynamically pulls some content from the database. This allows you to store content that's repeated often on the site in the database. You can then make any change to that content (for example, raising the price of a product) just one time in the database, and the change will be automatically displayed wherever that content appears.

Often, large websites that are made up of thousands of pages use content-management systems that work in tandem with databases to store, track, update, and publish website content. Chapter 11 describes content management tools and how to choose among them.

Adding a Site Search to Your Web Site

A database can also be used to add site search functionality to your website. This functionality can have a dramatic effect on the site's usability. When users can search a complex site for content that interests them, they will find that material and get your e-commerce message more quickly. The following two types of site searches are possible:

- Full-text searches comb the text on the site's web pages (whether they are static HTML or content stored in a database) looking for words that match the search word or phrase the user specified.

- Keyword searches sift through either keyword fields in a database or keyword META tags (as described in Chapters 8 and 12), again looking for words that match those the user specified.

In a full-text search, generally the list of matching web pages that is provided to the user is ranked by *relevancy*; meaning that the web page at the top of the list (the one with, say 100 percent or 90 percent "relevancy") is the one on which the search term appears most often in comparison to other words. This might seem fine, but if a user searches for pages devoted to *Italian shoes* and the page that discusses Italian shoes has the terms *leather*, *sole*, or *hand-stitched* on it a lot more often than Italian shoes, that page might not rise to

(continued)

Adding a Site Search to Your Web Site (*continued*)

the top of the relevancy list. In a keyword search, the list provided to the user is likely to be shorter and more focused. It might again be ranked by relevancy, but this time, because the relevancy ranking will be based only on a comparison of keywords to other keywords, it's more likely that tangential phrases won't skew the results.

Implementing a full-text search system is much easier than implementing a keyword search system. In both cases, the developer will have to configure the search software to run properly, but in the case of the keyword search a lot of content identification work needs to be done—you have to set up and manage the keywords! You or your staff must standardize them, document them, and apply them to the content by entering them correctly into each web page's keyword META tag or keyword database field. Then, forever after that, you have to maintain the keyword list and prevent the introduction of too many variations on the keywords.

Realizing that managing keywords is a daunting task, you, as many others, might think that for simplicity's sake you'll go with a full-text search. You might even think that you'll launch with a full-text search and implement keywords later, when you have time. Trust me: You'll never have time. There will always be something more urgent (such as posting the new product information, creating the perfect strategic partnership, or migrating the site to a more powerful server) than going page by page through your website to assign keywords and set up a new site search. Whether a full-text search or keyword search is best for your site is one of the many strategic decisions you will make.

Microsoft Windows 2000 Indexing Service is a site search tool that can be set up to do full-text searches of HTML files, Microsoft Office documents, or content stored in SQL Server databases. It can also be set up to do keyword searches; however, as most site search products on the market, it will be most successfully implemented if you decide up front to favor one type of search or the other.

Relational Databases vs. Flat File Databases

Relational databases soar where flat file databases fall. A relational database allows you to store a lot of data in multiple tables. The tables within one database generally have certain fields in common, through which a relationship is established. The classic example is a database that contains one table for customers and another for orders. Each customer has a record in the customers table, and each order has a record in the orders table. Each order placed by a certain customer does not have to contain all the information regarding that customer; instead, a link from the order to the customer record (in the customers table) through a single field contained in both tables, such as *customerID*, calls forth the customer information.

A flat file database has only one table, so every order recorded in a flat file database has to include all of the customer information. That means that when Sally places an order on Tuesday and then again on Thursday, both orders have to include all of Sally's identifying data, including her address, credit card information, and so on. This gets really repetitive. What's more, having to manage all those big, bloated records puts a severe load on a database server.

Even a relatively small flat file database can undermine server performance; a fairly large and complex relational database, on the other hand, places a far lighter load on the server. The downside of using a relational database can be expense. It can cost thousands of dollars just to license the software. Depending on the complexity of the database, you might also need a database server on which to run the database software. Then you generally have to bring in a developer to build the database. A flat file database also has to be built by a developer, but it is built from the ground up using no licensed database products, and it requires no special server.

Note

Many businesses find Microsoft Access a good solution for harnessing the power of relational databases. Access is a relational database designed primarily for desktop computers. It allows multiple tables of information and allows you to create relationships among these tables just as you would using other, more powerful database software. While Access databases cannot support hundreds of users accessing millions of records (as SQL Server can), it can support a few users accessing thousands of records and it performs far better than a flat file database would. And if your web business soars, it is relatively easy to migrate from Access to SQL Server.

Choosing Middleware

Operating between the database and the web server is special software known as *middleware*, which does the job of transporting data. Various types of middleware take different approaches to the job. Some allow you to simply add special code (much like HMTL code) into the HTML that defines your web pages to call forth data from the database. Others require you to insert special scripts into the HTML that defines the web pages. Still others require that you use specific authoring tools to create the entire website (rather than creating it with HTML); you then have to always work within the environment of the authoring tool.

When you select middleware, look at compatibility with your database software. Consider, also, whether those who'll be using the middleware have the necessary programming expertise. Some middleware requires programming experience, and some doesn't. One approach to middleware is ASP, which allows you to insert scripts into HTML files.

Note

Middleware is not the only option for transferring data from the database to the web server. You can use standard programming languages (such as C++ or C#) to create programs that run on the server and manipulate your database. While this requires more expertise than using middleware, the result can be especially efficient and reliable. However, for most purposes, middleware is fine.

At the higher end, Microsoft .NET Enterprise Servers include development tools that act as middleware. These include Commerce Server, which allows programmers to create b2c and b2b transaction systems; and BizTalk Server, which allows programmers to create websites with b2b features and components. In fact, both products are often used along with other Microsoft .NET Enterprise Servers (such as SQL Server) to build very robust websites with complex functionality.

Maintaining a Database

Like nearly everything else on a website, the database must be maintained. Maintenance of the database content can be performed by even the most non-technically adept users via easy-to-use forms and other utilities. Some common maintenance tasks that fall into this category include:

- Adding and removing records as your data changes. For example, in the case of a product catalog database, you'll need to add new records as you add new merchandise and remove records as you discontinue items.

- Making changes to the data stored in the database. You might want to change the description of a product or some of the other information you keep in the database. (This is useful, for example, if you begin carrying a product in a new color.)

The developer who creates your database system should provide you with simple, password-protected forms that make adding and changing data easier. These forms might look like nothing more than HTML pages; you can use your web browser to work with them. While you cannot do backups via a web browser, your developer should identify the procedure for making backups and give you complete, easy-to-follow instructions.

Other database maintenance tasks include reviewing log files, monitoring server performance, and verifying that the hard disk is not overloaded. These tasks (similar to those necessary for maintaining a web server) are typically the responsibility of those more technically adept than the average manager. Do not wait until you have problems to find someone to handle such matters. Establish a maintenance agreement with your database developer when your system is first built. Regular maintenance will save you from unexpected downtime and poor performance.

Be sure that someone is creating a backup copy of your database regularly (as well as a backup copy of the rest of your site). Backing up your database is not necessarily included in the regular backup of your site that you, your developer, or your hosting company does. Because of the way that some databases work, special tools might be needed. Verify with your developer that those tools are in place and backups are occurring.

Also, don't wait until your database crashes to find out whether the backups are good. Have your developer test your backups occasionally by randomly selecting a file or a table from your database and restoring it from the backup.

Caution

When you restore a file to test your backup system, don't overwrite the live database. If it turns out that the backup data is bad, you will have caused the very situation you were trying to avoid. Instead, restore the data to your staging server and test it there. Seeing something restored from the backup is the only way to know for sure that your data is being protected.

The Basics of Transaction Systems

A transaction system is the behind-the-scenes combination of programming, databases, payment paths, and business rules that enables you to sell goods and accept payment from your customers. The elements that make up most e-commerce transaction systems include the following:

- A catalog (in the form of a database) that lists products available for sale along with data (such as the price, descriptive information, and perhaps a photo) describing those products.

- A database that stores customer information (at least temporarily), as well as the customer's choices about shipping and payment methods, and tracks purchases during the transaction process.

- A shopping cart (comprised of scripts or programming) that tracks what the customer selects for purchase while browsing the website. When a customer clicks a Buy button, the scripts that make up the shopping cart system add the selected items to a record in the database that deals with purchases.

- A purchase system (more scripts and programming) that pulls together the selections the customer made from the catalog (information from the shopping cart) and the payment and shipping information (from the customer database).

- A credit transaction processing system (usually consisting of licensed software) provided by a company such as CyberCash (*www.cybercash.com*) or CyberSource (*www.cybersource.com*) that facilitates online credit transactions.

- A connection or interface that triggers a fulfillment system that sends the order to a warehouse or otherwise sees to it that the ordered items will be shipped.

All of these elements work together behind the scenes when a user makes a purchase. In the best possible scenario, the user will be aware of only a few steps in the sales and transaction process: selecting the item or items of interest, viewing the order, entering credit card information, selecting a shipping method, and submitting the order. A confirmation web page or e-mail will signal that the order was successfully entered.

But in reality, a complex back-end system of programming, security-enforcing encryption, databases, credit and financial information transmission, and order fulfillment is at work. From a business perspective, it is important that you understand the need for a high level of security in that system and the nature of the relationships with the various financial institutions involved. So read on.

Security in E-Commerce Transaction Systems

Protecting the security of credit card data as it is stored and transmitted is crucial to the success of an e-commerce transaction system. Without assurance that their credit card data is safe, customers simply won't buy. And security breaches undermine the credibility of both the affected site and the e-commerce industry as a whole.

When security is effective, it goes unnoticed. Security in e-commerce is accomplished through a combination of *encryption* (data scrambling so that even trespassers cannot use it), barriers to intruders such as firewalls, and policies regarding who has what sort of access to the confidential data. When you set up an e-commerce transaction system, a certain amount of the system will be within your area of responsibility. For example, it will be up to you or your staff or developer to make secure your servers and any forms into which users will enter confidential data. (Your developer will know how to do this, but it is your job to provide a reminder.)

Any purchase system that accepts payment from a customer and authorizes a charge to the customer's credit card should use the industry standard security protocol, Secure Sockets Layer (SSL). SSL accomplishes security by encrypting data. When you view a web page, you can tell that this type of security is in place because the page's URL starts with *https:* instead of the more common *http:*. A special icon (in Microsoft Internet Explorer 5, it is a lock) might also appear on the status bar of the browser window.

For SSL to work, a *certificate* (a digital document that proves your identity) must be issued to you by a *certification authority* (an organization that is entrusted with vouching for others in this way). Again, your developer will take care of this. Note, however, that you must provide documentation to the developer to send to the certification authority. This might include bank references, a notarized statement or application, and other supporting documentation. Obviously, given that your developer is privy to your secure systems and confidential data, it's imperative that you select a knowledgeable, reputable developer and maintain a good working relationship with him or her; see Chapter 9 for pointers.

Note

A database of people's credit card numbers is a tempting target for unscrupulous, hacking thieves. Because of this, transaction systems normally store credit card numbers only temporarily. They are immediately passed to a third-party credit processing company, which sends back a transaction authorization number. It is that number that's actually stored in your database. This setup works because the number pertains only to one transaction and doesn't provide an electronic path the thief can follow to the credit card number itself.

Occasional security audits will turn up any holes in your systems. A security audit might take the form of a review of the code and systems, or it might include the additional tactic of approaching the site as a user would. In the latter case, an attempt is made to retrieve information a user shouldn't be able to access; for example, the test might involve acting as a user who is entering data into the system in a manner the scripts aren't set up to accept. In an improperly secured system, that action (which a perfectly innocent user might accidentally take) can trigger access to confidential data.

You can either hire a company that specializes in security audits to investigate your site, or you can ask a developer to do it. Hiring a specialized company is the more expensive option, but the company will probably provide a certain level of expertise in such audits. If you go the developer route, keep in mind that the developer who created the site might not be the most objective judge of the site's security system. On the other hand, a different developer who is on equal footing with yours might audit the site with an eye toward wrangling the job of beefing up your security and maintaining the site away from your developer. Get references, and scrutinize the experience and motivations of any developer you hire for an audit just as you would if you were hiring a developer to create your systems.

How Credit Card Transactions Work

From the customer's point of view, a credit card provides an easy way to make purchases and pay later. However, credit cards can be viewed from several other vantage points. From the viewpoint of your business when you are accepting payment, a credit card is both a convenient method for receiving payment and an assurance that the credit card user is creditworthy enough for you to assume that payment will actually occur. From your bank's point of view, a credit card is actually a short-term loan to your business. This is because your bank—the "acquiring" bank—makes payment to your business's merchant account days before it receives payment from the customer's bank. But the customer's bank—the "issuing" bank—actually pays the acquiring bank before it receives payment from the customer!

From the viewpoint of the banks involved, then, and despite the overall security of the credit card system, some risk is involved in handling credit card transactions. A customer might decline the charge or even default on payment, for example. And e-commerce adds an additional layer of risk for the banks. To understand why this is so, consider the steps involved in accepting a credit card in the physical world:

1. The customer presents the credit card to the merchant. The card is "swiped" through a reader or imprinted on hard copy. The card numbers are recorded directly from the card held in the customer's hand.

2. The merchant gets an authorization number for the purchase amount from the customer's bank over a terminal or a phone line.

3. The merchant gets the customer's signature on a credit slip, which creates a legally binding contract.

4. The merchant provides merchandise in exchange for the signed credit slip.

At the end of this process, payment is authorized and transferred. Everyone is fairly well assured that the entire transaction will proceed as expected. In an online setting, however, the customer is not physically present and cannot sign a credit slip. There is no signed "contract" that authorizes payment for an electronic sale. This makes banks nervous. (The merchant also can't verify the signature's validity, which removes one level of "security" from the whole process.) In their nervousness, banks want more assurance that e-commerce merchants are using secure systems; they also are inspired to charge online merchants higher fees.

As of this writing, new technologies are being developed to address these issues. E-signatures (described briefly in Chapter 3) might change the landscape of e-commerce payment systems. In the meantime, banks find the size of the e-commerce market and the level of security that is generally afforded by online systems persuasive enough to accept credit card transactions conducted over the Internet.

Note

In a traditional credit card transaction, the merchant gets an authorization number from the issuing bank the moment the customer signs the slip and before the customer receives the product. When you plan and build your e-commerce website, ask your developer to have your system get the authorization number and verify the billing address against bank records before the credit card is formally "accepted." Also have the developer make sure that payment will occur quickly (while the product is being shipped to the customer).

Getting Set Up for Credit Card Transactions

Because e-commerce credit card transactions are riskier for banks than face-to-face credit card transactions and because online payment systems have to be secure, the sign-up process for online merchants that want to accept credit cards is different than for brick-and-mortar merchants. First of all, the banks are a bit choosier. Also, the process involves different steps and some additional players. Not only do you have to deal with your bank and the credit card companies, but you also have to deal with companies that sell credit card processing software. Let's look at the process step by step.

Open a merchant account

The first step is to go to a bank and tell them you want to accept credit card payment over the Internet. You can start with the bank that handles your existing business accounts. If that bank doesn't offer e-commerce accounts, you might get referred to a bank that does or you can try to get references from other e-commerce merchants. Once you have a bank to work with, you will most likely open a separate account from the one you might already have for your business. The bank will also provide you with an application and contract for the credit card companies you'll be dealing with, which is distinct from your contract with the bank.

Note

The rules for taxing Internet sales are basically the same as the rules for taxing mail-order sales. For most small to mid-sized businesses, that means you must collect and pay sales tax according to your regional laws. Businesses with many locations must collect and pay taxes according to the regional laws of any place where they have a *nexus* (a business center).

Choose credit card processing software

In a brick-and-mortar store, a salesperson swipes a customer's card through a device that transmits information about the sale to the bank and credit card companies in an instant. In e-commerce, that role is played by credit card processing software companies (such as CyberCash and CyberSource). They provide software that resides on your server and transmits transaction data securely.

As you consider which credit card processing software to use, take into account which companies your developer has worked with before. As always, you don't want to pay for the learning curve and you do want to tap into your developer's expertise. Consider, also, which company's software your hosting company already has installed. (Your hosting company might not want to install new, unfamiliar software.) You'll also want to take costs into account. Companies that provide credit card processing software charge some combination of a setup fee and a per-transaction fee. Some also charge a monthly minimum fee when a merchant has not generated enough transactions to be a profitable client.

Integrate the credit card processing software with your transaction system.

Your developer will pull the account software and credit card processing software together with your databases and the scripts that make everything work. To ensure smooth integration, keep your developer in the loop, especially as you choose credit card processing software. Your developer should be able to advise you on the fine points of your options and how they fit with other choices you've made for your system.

Note

As you organize your transaction system, remember to deal with *fulfill-ment* (the process of shipping the product to the customer). A small e-commerce endeavor's fulfillment system might consist simply of generating an e-mail message that triggers shipment. In a more sophisticated system, scripts will run automatically when an order is placed. The order then appears along with other orders in the warehouse or shipping location's existing fulfillment system.

Fees and Charges for Credit Card Transactions

Banks charge your customers monthly fees as well as interest on any outstanding balances. They also charge you, the merchant, for every credit card transaction that occurs at your place of business. The specific mix of fees charged and their amounts vary from bank to bank, but you generally pay the following:

- Setup fees for opening an account.

- The discount rate, which is a percentage of each transaction that the bank keeps as part of its compensation. Discount rates vary drastically from bank to bank. They also vary based on the type of business you do. Generally, e-commerce companies pay a higher rate than brick-and-mortar businesses.

- Special charges for credits to the customer (when a transaction is canceled or a product is returned) or for special services such as providing printed statements rather than electronic statements or transferring funds between accounts.

Tip

Be sure that any credits to customers for returned products or canceled orders are processed quickly at your end. If you credit the purchase back to the customer, you'll pay a fee, but it might be only 15 cents. If, instead, the customer has to request a credit (because, for example, you took too long to process the return), the fee you pay can be $20 or even as much as $50, depending on the bank's policy.

Other Forms of E-Commerce Payment

Because credit cards are familiar to customers and easy to use, and because their underlying payment systems already exist, credit cards are the dominant method of payment in e-commerce. However, other methods of payment do exist:

- In a direct debit system, the customer enters his or her bank account number along with some identifying information and money is directly transferred from that account to a merchant account when a sale occurs. This method is not commonly used in e-commerce because it doesn't provide adequate security.

- A wallet system allows the customer to transfer funds from a bank account or credit card to an electronic "wallet." Once the funds are in the wallet, the customer can use that amount to make purchases. This option requires the customer to have a special account with the wallet company and requires the merchant to sign up with the wallet company so the customers can use the feature at the merchant's site. (Microsoft Passport provides this type of service and is available at *www.passport.com*. You'll find special instructions there for setting this up.) This technology is an alternative for companies that sell products priced so low that they don't warrant the expense (to the merchant) of credit card fees.

- Yet another system, offered by companies such as eCharge (*www.echarge.com*), bills the customer's telephone service account for e-commerce transactions. Essentially, the customer purchases a product or service through a website and the charge later appears on the customer's phone bill.

Armed with some understanding of transaction systems, payment methods, and other back-end issues, you're now in a position to consider just how your systems will be built.

Building Your Transaction System vs. Buying It

In Internet years gone by, the only option for creating a transaction system was to build it from scratch. That is still an option, but these days you might be better off customizing a transaction system built on top of purchased components or buying a complete, prepackaged transaction system (which you can then customize if only slightly). Each build-or-buy option has advantages and disadvantages, such as the following:

- Building from scratch involves hiring a developer (or team), specifying what you want the system to do, and paying for its development. The advantage is that your custom-built system can do virtually anything you want. The disadvantage is that this is an expensive and time-consuming way to go. Further, the end result (at least in its first iteration) is as likely to be as bug-ridden as the first version of any software. And finally, the system will not be familiar to those who must work on it after your developer does. For most companies (even large ones), building from scratch is not a good choice.

- Customizing based on purchased components involves licensing a product such as Microsoft Commerce Server and having a developer create custom programming to make it fit your needs. This method can net you almost the same level of customization you'd get if you built from scratch, but the economics are far better.

- Buying a fully functioning transaction system involves purchasing a complete system that you can customize, but only minimally. Such systems generally include all the components of a transaction system (catalog, databases, scripts, and so on). They can sometimes be customized with your own look and feel for the transaction and catalog pages, but they usually offer only limited functionality. For example, you might not be able to show two related products on a single web page (you can't easily cross-sell or upsell), as you would with a more powerful solution.

Note

Small and mid-sized businesses might consider using the Microsoft bCentral Business Web or Commerce Manager services to build and run a complete transaction system and sell products online or to offer online auctions or join and do business in other electronic marketplaces.

Of course, whether you decide to build a transaction system or buy one, you must still address the issue of support—keeping your site humming around the clock.

Keeping Your Site Running Night and Day

In the brick-and-mortar world, storefronts have posted hours. They open and close at specified times. But websites are expected to be up and running around the clock. A great advantage to doing business online is that your products and services are available to your customers when *they* want them, regardless of whether they're viewing your site from their desks at lunchtime in California, from home in the afternoon in France, or in the middle of the night in New York. When you commit to doing business on the Internet, you commit to having your site up and running at all times. Unfortunately, servers sometimes crash, and because they run day and night, they can crash at 3:00 in the morning, at dinnertime, or at any other inconvenient hour. Regardless of who is hosting your site, you must take this into account. You have to decide who will handle server emergencies.

As discussed earlier in this chapter, how seriously you take off-hours server failures will depend on how critical the constant operation of your site is to your business. How such failures will be handled depends on your hosting arrangement and support agreements. If you're hosting your site yourself, you (or someone you designate) will have to handle off-hours problems. If your site is hosted at a hosting company, the hosting company might provide 24-hour monitoring and (depending on your support agreement) might do basic emergency maintenance. In these cases, you might be in the enviable position of never knowing that anything went wrong until an error report arrives via e-mail the next day.

Note

Microsoft back-end and transaction products come with tools for maintenance and for monitoring usage. Also, third-party tools and reporting agencies can monitor uptime and report site crashes via either e-mail or pager (for a fee). One such system is Keynote Red Alert (*www.redalert.com*).

As is true of so much in life, preventing emergencies is far better than reacting to them. To prevent server emergencies—and website downtime—your best bet is to engage in a proactive program of server maintenance. Many managers don't fully comprehend the necessity of monitoring server logs, keeping an eye on usage, and preventing server overload by building redundancy into systems as needed. When your server is running smoothly, server maintenance might seem like an expendable concern. However, trust your developer and technical staff when they say it is necessary. Downtime leads to lost sales, which no manager or business owner likes to see. A very small investment in regular server maintenance can save you from experiencing inconvenient server emergencies and expensive downtime.

Part 4

Maintaining, Promoting, and Succeeding

Chapter 11

Keeping Content Usable, Manageable, and Fresh

Every e-commerce website has content. Content is, essentially, everything a site contains—whatever it offers the user as well as the text and images that enable the user to make the most of the site. Websites such as CNN.com, Salon.com, and BabyCenter.com, whose main offerings are timely or topical written material along with accompanying images, are considered *content driven*. Yet even sites that are not content driven have content. Many e-commerce websites, for example, provide data (such as product specifications, stock quotes, or weather information) or listings (such as a portal's list of links or an entertainment site's list of events). Such data and listings are content. Downloadable files (such as software, images, sounds, and so on) are also content, as is the text and images on a site that describe the downloadable files and how to get them. Whatever a website's content, how well the site delivers it can make or break a user's experience of the site.

Note

Websites generally include some *microcontent*—small pieces of content such as the page titles at the top of the browser window, the text of error messages, the subject lines of e-mail newsletters that lead users to visit the site, or even the bits of content that form the interface to the transaction system. The importance of microcontent to usability is too often overlooked. How understandable, friendly, and functional the microcontent and content are (along with how well they enhance the site's branding or identity) can make or break a website's usability.

Take a look at Figure 11-1, which shows the factors that drive repeat visits to websites (according to a Forrester Research survey of 8600 web-enabled households). Notice that 75 percent of the respondents said that high-quality content was a key factor that brought them back.

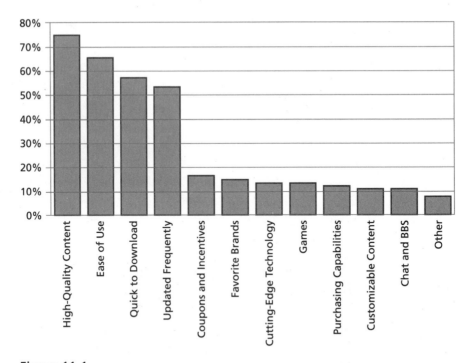

Figure 11-1

Factors that compel users to revisit websites.

The secret to maintaining fresh, compelling, credible content is to start with a clear understanding of your user and business goals as well as your branding, to organize your content and your site plan before production begins, and then to apply consistent quality assurance processes and strong content development to your site throughout its lifetime. Part 1 of this book covered the issues involved in setting strategic goals and establishing branding, Part 2 covered planning your site's structure and underpinnings, and this chapter introduces solutions to quality assurance (QA) and long-term content development issues.

Note

Technology is not the driving force that compels users to keep clicking. Multiple technologies can be used to support and provide a back end for user experience, and they contribute deeply to a website's functionality, but they are not the one, true answer to making a site usable. Just as a camera does not make fine photos, Internet technology does not make fine online content—people do.

Creating Strong Content

Content absolutely must fulfill the business goals you've set for your site. If your content doesn't further your site's business mission—whatever that might be—there's simply no reason to have a website. Content must also fulfill user goals—it must actually provide the user with the value the user expects based on the identity you've created for your website and its offerings.

Your content should also always express and further your branding. This might seem especially important in sites that are driven by marketing goals, sites that promote or distribute a product or service, and sites that sell. But all sites—even content-driven sites—can and should fulfill the brand identity. The publishers and editors who create and shape content for sites that inform or report strive deeply to create a recognizable identity for their work—for example, The New York Times website has a certain identity, as does BabyCenter.com. Branding your site's content means creating a recognizable identity and reputation that expresses and deepens the identity of your company, product, or service; it also means differentiating your content from that of your competitors and from any preconceived ideas your audience might have. (Refer back to Chapter 4 for more on branding.)

Well-developed content can integrate and fulfill user goals, business goals, and branding by

- Delivering a clear message
- Attracting a specific target audience
- Ensuring readability, usability, and quality of customer experience
- Expediting service and customer care (and lowering the costs of customer service)

What Is Stickiness?

Stickiness is a buzzword often heard at e-commerce conferences and seen in print. Everyone wants stickiness in his or her website, but what is it? Simply put, stickiness is what makes users stick around. It's also what keeps them coming back. What makes a website sticky is its relevance and appeal to the target market. It all goes back to who your audience is and what your site offers that they want and need. Not every site should inspire users to stay and browse—for example, a sales site, in order to fulfill its business goals, should allow users to quickly and conveniently make a purchase (which is likely to be the user's goal as well). But a sales site can be sticky *if the positive experience it offers inspires users to come back again and again.* That, also, is stickiness, and for many e-commerce sites it might be the best sort of stickiness to have.

In creating and developing strong content, you must consider the "four Cs" of the Internet: *content, community, commerce,* and *context* and how they affect each other. The concept of the "Cs" developed quickly during the first years of e-commerce; but for a while, Internet pros made reference to only the first three (content, community, and commerce). Much of the early chapters of this book were devoted to exploring aspects of each of those three concepts. Today it's generally agreed upon that in the most successful websites, content, community, and commerce converge to create a whole user experience. (A case study describing how Amazon.com does this was presented in Chapter 6.) When the term *context* was added to the lexicon as a fourth "C," it was in reference to the atmosphere or environment in which a person understands or experiences something. Context is a total picture that is influenced by and informs each piece of the picture, so how a site's mix of content, community, and commerce work together is a key issue in how the site is experienced by users.

Another key issue is how the site is created and developed—not only how its design and technology are shaped, but also how its language, linking, and so on fulfill and enhance the overall experience. Effective content development furthers the context and the user experience—it takes into account the site's overall strategy; its branding; and its mix of content, community, and commerce. Savvy content development creatively implements the site's text, art, media, and more to make the most of the context.

The bottom line: The context you create when you design and build a website affects the message you deliver. Again, the context should support and further the business goals and branding message you have defined. Each aspect of your site—what it contains; how it supports, serves, or creates community; and how it delivers on its e-commerce potential—has an effect on the other aspects of the site and on how the site is experienced as a whole by users.

Note

For many Internet users today, the novelty of surfing has worn off. Users want to find what they seek immediately. They also want what they find to be both useful and easy to use. As you develop your content, ask yourself again and again what your site and each page on it offers to its audience that is of *consequence* to them.

Simply delivering information, then, just isn't enough. If it were, you could provide users with raw data (for example, product information such as price, size, color, and so on) without any thought to how the data appears on the web page or how it might be interpreted. To effectively deliver content to advance all of your business and user goals, you must consider such factors as these:

- Writing style, word choice, tone, and other language devices
- Use of elements such as lists, tables, and charts to organize information
- Use of graphics, illustrations, and photos
- Use of animation, video, and sound
- Use of linking to optimize the message and to facilitate navigation

Note .

Remember that first impressions are lasting. When a user comes to your site, he or she has an immediate impression of its readability, ease of use, and overall identity. Establishing that impression the first time is far easier than reestablishing the correct impression after you've allowed a less than favorable one to take hold.

Writing for E-Commerce

All good writing starts with a compelling *lead*. A lead is the sentence that opens the main text. A good lead grabs the user's attention in an instant, and it propels his or her interest in reading on. Leads are often short, assertive, and sometimes even provocative. In e-commerce content, your lead should make the central point in that content; beyond the lead, you can expand or support your point while focusing on the goals you want to achieve.

In all of your text, the *editorial voice*—the tone and language you use—must match the look and feel of your site and appeal to your intended audience. (This is all part of branding, as mentioned earlier.) To get a sense of how voice works and how you can apply it to various topics, flip through the sections of your Sunday newspaper. In the food and travel sections, you'll find that the language is full of adjectives meant to evoke the senses. The goal there is to involve readers in the eating or traveling experience, so descriptive text is laced with imagery. Turn to the business section, and you'll find no lush descriptions or imagery; instead, the language will be more to the point, more clipped, laden with facts, and full of business jargon.

Tip

Avoid hackneyed phrasing. Use wording that differentiates your site from the millions that use worn-out clichés. On your website, ban the use of such phrases as *check out* (as in "check out our products"), which is vastly overused on the Web and can be replaced easily with *see, explore, take a look at,* or any of dozens of other phrases. Another overused (and not benefit-oriented) phrase is *click here.* For suggestions about phrasing links for best effect, see the section titled "Shaping Links to Highlight What's Compelling" later in this chapter. And finally, forget about "what's new" pages or areas—present what's new and fresh on the home page or in some other prominent location.

Providing Complete Information

When you're writing catalog copy or other information about your products or services, place all the information a customer might need in one place. It's extraordinary how many realtors who list vacation rentals on websites don't provide, for example, the rental price, the number of bedrooms and bathrooms, or other information a potential renter might need. To close a sale, you must give customers all the information they need, including the product data, reasons to buy, and a *call to action* (which in essence urges them to take a further step). A classic call to action is "Get yours today." Here are some other examples:

- Subscribe now
- Step into luxury
- Get free e-mail
- Win big

However, there might be a few exceptions to the rule about offering all information up front. If you're selling expensive capital equipment, of course customers will typically want to speak to a sales representative before making such a large purchase. Or if you deal in multimillion-dollar real estates, you might want to make sure the customer is qualified to make a purchase before you reveal key information such as the price. But even in those cases, you must provide information such as how to contact the seller's representative and include a call to action ("Call for details").

Tip

Word-processing software such as Microsoft Word offers features that can help you edit and polish your text. In Word, you can check spelling and use the electronic thesaurus to add variety to your phrasing. You can use other features in Word to track changes and record edits, keep a running word count, and so on. Microsoft FrontPage also offers a spell checker and thesaurus, but a word processor is specially designed to facilitate editing text in ways that HTML editors can't match, so it's best to refine your material using a word-processing program before you convert the text to HTML.

Making Online Text Easier to Read

Lengthy blocks of text are tough to read in any medium. On websites, big blocks of text are so daunting to readers that many simply skip that material. This has led to a common misconception that users don't read online. Not so! According to usability studies by experts such as Jakob Nielsen (*www.useit.com*) and a joint study by Stanford University and the Poynter Institute (*www.poynter.org*), users do read online—they simply read differently. Being aware of how users read online enables you to deliver the punchiest possible content on your website.

The typical website user "reads" the page by scanning it, looking for visual clues that indicate where to find what's of interest. A user's eyes will fall on graphics, headlines, links, and phrases that appear in brief lists; they will usually pass over (or "speed read") any large, uninterrupted blocks of text.

Note

In an online setting, paper size doesn't limit the length of the text, but it's best to keep the pages short. Users aren't fond of scrolling. One or two screens (and about 250-500 words) is about the limit for any web page.

Knowing this, you can shape the material on your web pages to lead users to what you want to convey. To do so, boil down the text to only your main points and, whenever possible, place your points in lists. Lists are easier to read than longer text.

Use a bulleted list when the items don't really have to be consecutively ordered.

- Apples
- Oranges
- Grapes

Use a numbered list when (because the listed items take place over time, for example) the items really must be in consecutive order.

1. Lather
2. Rinse
3. Repeat

When information is too complex to be presented in a bulleted or numbered list, you can use a table, which is also visually friendly.

Property	Bedrooms/ Baths	Features	Cost per Week
California condo	2/1	Near sunset beaches	$1,000
Kona Coast house	3/1½	Oceanfront lanai	$1,400
Maine cottage	1/1	Wood-burning stove	$800

Of course, some e-commerce content has to be presented in blocks of text—news stories, company information, or descriptions of services might all be more palatable to users in the familiar form of standard text. Still, you can use section headings, lists, new paragraphs, and occasional art to break up the text and make it more readable. For many fine examples of these principles in action, see the articles at *www.useit.com*.

When you have to break the general rule that pages should be very brief (when you're dealing with articles that are more than 1000 words long, for example), spread the content across several separate pages and at the bottom of each page, provide a link (with a description, if possible) leading to the subsequent page to pull readers along. You might also consider placing a short, linked table of contents at the top of each page or simply at the top of the first page.

Using Images, Video, Sound, and Other Media

When text is dense and you use a piece of art to break up the monotony (or to illustrate a point or depict a product), make sure the art you use truly serves the needs of your users. Gratuitous art is just that. To present product comparisons or instructions visually, you can organize complex information into charts or *infographics* (illustrations that pull together lots of information to make it easily understandable).

Similarly, make sure that any video, sound, or other media you use is on your site for some good reason. Here are some tips for what to use in which circumstances:

- Use animation when you must show change or transition, when it's truly necessary to present something in 3-D by showing all sides of it, or when it really enriches user experience. Don't use it as a tawdry attention getter.

- Use video and audio clips when they add to the user experience— for example, to promote entertainment events or to add some background sound to enhance a visual effect (such as dance). But bear in mind that video and audio are bandwidth-hungry and are actually unavailable to users with less than optimal connections or with low-end computers.

- Use 3-D effects (animated or otherwise) only when they enhance usability—for space planning, architecture, scientific modeling, engineering, and so on—or for sophisticated online games. But remember that the software necessary for navigating 3-D effects is not yet standardized, often has unusual conventions for navigation, and is particularly buggy.

- Use PDF (Adobe Acrobat) files when it's necessary to retain the print layout of a page or form so that users can print and fax the form, for example, or for text-only booklets. But when you're doing true repurposing of documents for your website, break up the text, make it easier to read, and shape links within the material as described in this chapter.

Tip

To meet the needs of users with hearing loss or visual impairments, don't rely on sound and graphics alone to deliver your message. Always make a text version available.

Shaping Links to Highlight What's Compelling

When a user accesses a web page, among the first items he or she sees on that page will be the highlighted, underlined phrases—the links! You can leverage these links as yet another opportunity to further your branding and compel users to click in the directions you want them to click. How? Make sure that the phrasing of each and every link conveys what a user will get if he or she follows the link. Give users a reason to bother clicking that link. Don't link on the generic and distinctly non-compelling "click here," and don't simply cast about in a sentence for the most convenient phrase to make into a link. Instead, rewrite or edit your text as needed to make the links telegraph both your branding identity and what the website offers.

Think about it—phrases such as "Back to" or "Go to" are not descriptive or compelling enough to be links. They don't describe to users what the benefit of clicking, going, or returning might be. "Go to Recipe Search" highlights the relevant part of a phrase, telling the user what to expect on arrival at the link's destination. "Get quick and easy recipes" is even better in the sense that it's more lively and describes the benefit of the recipes rather than just their existence. Take a look at these lines of customer service text:

How can I order this product?

Is it safe to purchase online?

What credit cards can I use?

How can I change my order?

Can I send this product as a gift?

Notice that the questions are short and that in each case the linked phrase highlights the most relevant part of the question. Users can scan the text quickly and find the answer they seek in a snap. In some cases, including an adjective in the link makes a stronger point than simply using a noun. For example, in a description of your credentials, which phrase makes the more compelling branding message, "background" or "rich background"?

Keeping Content Fresh

In television and other broadcast media, the term *evergreen* is used to describe material that retains its freshness over time. To achieve an evergreen quality, a TV show will avoid visual and verbal indicators of a specific time period. For example, instead of dressing the stars in the latest fashions, the costumers will stick to simple, classic looks. The script writers also reach for timelessness, often quite simply by avoiding hip terms and phrases or references to current events. Using these methods to make the show evergreen allows it to air in many countries and over the course of years without seeming dated or out of place.

Borrowing from the broadcast world, we can think of website content as *evergreen* (long lasting and thus requiring little maintenance) or *deciduous* (more changing and so requiring more maintenance). And you, in the course of planning and executing your web site, can determine which areas or pages on the site warrant less frequent maintenance and which will benefit the most from regular updates. Typically, news sites, online magazines, and e-commerce sites that feature seasonal product lines must maintain freshness in those areas, but even they can keep their About Us, Contact Us, and other "boilerplate" areas evergreen.

In general, the more specific and timely your content is, the more upkeep it will require. More upkeep means higher labor and infrastructure costs because updates usually require staff time and having staff do anything requires having the infrastructure to support having the staff. So think carefully about how much maintenance time you really want to invest in each area or page of your site.

To keep your website content evergreen and lessen your maintenance load (and in that way, keep labor costs down), follow these guidelines:

- Avoid using phrases that specify or imply dates (*now, soon, current catalog, next version, this summer*). And don't promise anything that's "coming soon," "under construction," or "launching February 13th" (or at any other time in the too-specific future).

- Name only the staff members you absolutely must name. People get promoted, change jobs, and sometimes leave the company. Other than key people such as executives (who are less likely to change jobs frequently) or press contacts (who simply must be directly available to the press), avoid naming specific staff members on your website.

- Provide only the company's main phone number, not the individual phone numbers of various staff members, which may change if those people move from office to office, for example. Again, an exception is that users must have access to your customer service phone number and if you have a press contact, the press must have access to that person's phone number as well.

- Keep your content reference-oriented rather than news-oriented.

Note that this is not to say you should avoid specifics altogether; obviously, you have to provide all the specifics about your products and services that customers will need in order to make a decision. But again, in every way that you can (without undermining the usefulness of the information), make the text evergreen. You can say, for example, that a certain product was launched "in the spring of 2001" rather than "last month." The former phrasing ("in the spring of 2001") will always be true, whereas the latter ("last month") is too rooted in the here and now and will go out of date quickly.

If delivering timely, more deciduous information is among your site's key goals, be prepared to devote staff time to managing update cycles (setting the update schedule, assigning tasks, managing a content calendar, and so on). Keep the content well organized, set up good quality assurance processes, and use technology tools (such as content management software or the website management features of Microsoft FrontPage to support your efforts.

Keeping Content Organized

Part of why you create a site plan, as discussed in Chapter 7, is to make maintenance easier. Just as keeping your kitchen pantry organized makes cooking easier (so you don't have to hunt around for tomatoes when you're making cioppino), organizing your website and keeping it that way makes content development and maintenance easier. Knowing where a specific piece of art or text is will save you time when you need to use that art or text or when you have to replace it with a fresher version.

Consider the worst-case example of a site that a court has ordered to remove certain content (perhaps because the proper permissions weren't granted, as described in Chapter 3). If the content in question is sprinkled throughout the site and is stored in various directories using filenames that are not associated with each other, and if no content management tools are in place, tracking down that content and destroying it will be extremely time-consuming.

As your site develops, don't add areas willy-nilly. It might be tempting to simply tack on a new area if you believe a new type of content will serve your site's users. Instead, try to tuck that new material into your existing structure. Imagine what would happen in your home if you simply added rooms without an overall plan. Disregarding architectural logic and navigation leads to dead-end paths, purposeless areas, and poor allocation of resources.

Tip

Make your site plan logical, and name files so that they can be easily identified. If you break a brochure into several sections and place each section on a separate web page, for example, put all of those pages in one directory or give them all filenames that indicate that they're associated, or both. (See Chapter 8 for tips on naming files.)

Where to Get Content

There are all kinds of ways to get content. Your staff can create content, or you can hire freelance researchers, compilers, writers, or editors to create it. You can repurpose existing material. You can also buy or license material. For example, information wholesalers sell raw content for a licensing fee; that fee might include a share of any ad revenue generated by the content. (They don't usually create the front end or the branding; that's up to you.) Or you can license content from syndication services such as iSyndicate (*www.isyndicate.com*) or ScreamingMedia (*www.screamingmedia.com*).

Other options include forming a strategic partnership with a content provider, in which case you can co-brand and even co-develop the content, extending both brands. Ad revenue sharing is again often part of the deal in that case, but even when ad revenues are shared one party might pay a fee to the other for the use of content, resources, or brand recognition.

In yet another scenario, you can act as an aggregator or portal by indexing content created by others. If you go this route, make sure that you're offering additional value of some sort; for example, you might offer a special search service, you might aggregate content that's hand-selected by topic experts, or you might offer other tools and services as adjunct to the content.

And finally, you can simply link to content. In that case, however, you absolutely must add some value to your listings of links; otherwise, users are more likely to seek the information at its source rather than at your website.

Wherever you get content, consider the business and legal wisdom of what you use and how you use it. See Chapter 3 for a discussion of who owns what content on your website as well as the legal ins and outs of linking.

Maintaining Quality and Credibility

You, like many other people, have probably had the experience of reading a book you were enjoying, falling into a reverie, and—oops!—stumbling across a little typo. In that brief moment, your experience was interrupted.

At least for one split second, you probably thought, "What's that doing here?" You were distracted. Because you don't want your customers distracted from the business at hand—perusing your website and getting from it what you want them to get—you and your website team must banish typos and other errors from your text. Details count: Spelling and punctuation are to a user's experience of online content as the condition of the coffee pot on an airplane is to a traveler's impression of the airline's safety equipment. (When the coffee pot is broken, travelers tend to think, "If they can't even get a coffee pot to work, how well does the rest of the plane work?")

Whatever your site's business goals, you want users to experience the site as you intended it. A stray typo, a broken link, a glitch in navigation, or inconsistencies in the use of language, fonts, or layout can distract visitors from your product or service. These mistakes can also damage your credibility. That's why it's important to have processes in place for ensuring the quality and accuracy of your content both during development and on an ongoing basis.

Tip

Validating links is a vital part of maintaining the integrity of your content. You must check links regularly to make sure they're still live and working. If you're running your site on Microsoft Internet Information Services (IIS), you can get and use Microsoft Commerce Server, a tool whose site analysis features include a way to quickly check links on your live site. Commerce Server also generates reports that will help you analyze traffic and determine which areas of your site get the most traffic. You can then decide how much effort to put into beefing up less popular areas and maintaining fresh material in more popular areas.

Ensuring the quality and credibility of your website content requires a two-part process: You must first create a style guide that describes your policies and procedures; then you must implement a workable quality assurance (QA) process. Some typical excuses for not carrying through on these tasks include:

- We have to get the site launched immediately; we don't have time to write a style guide.

- We have only one staff member available to review the pages, and that person knows all our policies.

- We aren't writers, so we can't write a style guide.

- We don't have a style guide, so we can't do QA.

But consider these reasons for taking the time to create a style guide and to implement QA processes:

- The hours spent creating a style guide will shave days off your QA cycle.

- Transmitting information as unwritten lore leaves you in a vulnerable position if the keeper of the lore becomes unavailable.

- Creating a style guide is a simple matter of compiling lists; no fancy writing skills are necessary.

- Conducting QA is a lot tougher and more time-consuming without a style guide.

What Does an Editor Do?

An editor's job is basically to be the reader's advocate. An editor smooths out the writing and considers issues of readability as affected by page layout, the use of art, charts, tables, and lists, and other factors. If the editor encounters anything that will act as a barrier to the reader's understanding or experience of the content, he or she will fix the problem or ask that the appropriate party fix it. In an online setting, an editor might also proofread, rewrite as needed, check links, and even make suggestions about navigational issues. For a terrific explanation of the roles editors fulfill, see the Bay Area Editors' Forum website at *www.editorsforum.org*.

Creating and Applying a Style Guide

A style guide documents your decisions about the look and feel of the site, its language and tone, and the conventions that will establish the site's personality to users and customers. Creating a style guide isn't difficult—you or your website team members can do it simply by keeping lists of the important decisions you make as you build a site. During the process of planning and building, just pop Word documents containing that information into a folder. As the project progresses, you can convert the Word documents to HTML, link among various topics in the sections of the newly created HTML style guide, and make the style guide into a small intranet site that your whole team can use.

The following list of style guide topics and what specific items of
information each should contain will get you going; you can modify it to
suit your needs.

- **Format and Structure**

    - A site map or index showing major areas of the site and
      major navigational paths

    - Notes about the site structure's overall logic

    - A diagram of the directory structure showing what types of
      files will be stored where

    - A record of what is stored in databases (perhaps generated
      by your database software's mapping and documenting
      feature)

    - A flowchart showing how transaction systems are organized

    - Notes about how to place content into the site's structure

    - A mission statement for the site (so that everyone knows
      what goals are to be achieved)

- **Visual Style**

    - Notes about how style choices were made and by whom

    - A record of who designed each element of the site (perhaps
      in a Word table or Microsoft Excel spreadsheet, which you
      can easily convert to HTML later)

- Guidelines on where and how to place page banners, navigational bars, buttons, company logos, advertising, or graphics.

- Guidelines on which colors to use (and which to avoid) for pages, backgrounds, logos, navigational bars, special elements, and so on

- Guidelines on which fonts or font families to use for page banners, navigational bars, body text, informational tables, forms, and so on; where those fonts are located; and in what sizes they can be used

- A record of where art is located

- Guidelines on how to implement basic page layouts and special effects

- **HTML and Page Layout**

  - Guidelines on how to handle the HTML for the fonts that are used (and on alternate fonts, if you're making them available to users who might not have on their computers the fonts you've specified for your site)

  - Guidelines on colors codes for backgrounds and special elements

  - Guidelines on headings (font, color, size, weight, and so on for each heading level)

  - Guidelines on whether to use the tags <B> and <I> or <STRONG> and <EM> for emphasis

  - Instructions for coding special characters such as ™,©, and ®

  - A list of META tags to be used for optimizing search engine rankings

  - Guidelines for creating page layout tables, such as preferred table and cell widths, cell padding, cell spacing, and where exceptions are allowable

  - Guidelines for creating frames, including naming conventions, targeting and default targets, and the directory structure for frame sets

- A list of characters (such as em and en dashes) that are not part of the standard HTML character set along with instructions for working around those limitations.

- **Graphics and Multimedia**

  - Guidelines on the maximum size (in bytes) for any page on the site

  - A list of file types that are allowable, and in what circumstances (for example, GIFs for simple graphics and JPEGs for photographic images), along with the maximum suggested file size

  - Guidelines on how and when to indicate the size of downloadable multimedia and graphics files (to help users decide whether their system can manage the files)

  - Guidelines on how and when to use ALT tags to describe images (for the benefit of users who've turned off graphics)

  - Suggestions on how to avoid dithering (which reduces image quality) and how to use interlaced files that load in several passes

  - Guidelines on the use of logos, company colors, and other company-identifying elements (or links to this information in the Visual Style, Editorial Style and Usage, and Legal Matters sections of your style guide)

  - Guidelines on placement and standard allowable dimensions of banner ads

  - A record of who designed and who approved various graphic elements so that in the future you can contact those people to make adjustments, create additional graphic elements, or approve new material

- **Editorial Style and Usage**

  - A list of reference books your site will follow for editorial style (*The Chicago Manual of Style* or *The Associated Press Stylebook and Libel Manual*? Which dictionary? Which edition of each?) as well as any online references (such as The Slot, at *www.theslot.com*, or the Poynter Institute's links for copy editors, at *www.poynter.org*)

- A list of conventions for capitalization, usage, spelling, and punctuation (such as how to handle capitalization in various heading levels; which acronyms to spell out and which ones you can assume are self-explanatory; whether to use *Web site*, *web site*, or *website*; whether to use *e-mail* or *email*; and so on)

- Formatting guidelines for special elements such as informational tables and the captions that appear with art

- Policies regarding the use of logos, linking, and legalese on your site

- **Linking and Cross-Linking**
  - Guidelines on the maximum number of links that should appear in a paragraph or story

  - Guidelines on what sorts of words to link on (such as avoiding the generic *click here* in favor of linking on the most pertinent and compelling phrases)

  - Guidelines on how to phrase links to downloadable files, graphics, and media

  - Guidelines on when to use buttons for links rather than text, and vice-versa

  - Guidelines on handling *jump links* (links that take the user to another part of the same page)

  - Guidelines on whether, when, and how it is acceptable to link outside the site

- **Legal Matters**
  - Guidelines on the wording and placement of copyright notices

  - Guidelines on indicating trademarks

  - Policies about obtaining permission for use of copyrighted material from elsewhere

  - Policies about granting others permission to use your material

  - A list of staff members who are authorized to grant permission to use your material

  - Any forms or permissions agreements that others will need to fill out in order to use your material

- Review and Approval Procedures
    - A list of review team members and what they are authorized to review (including who signals that the material has been fully approved and can be posted)
    - A clear description of the review and approval process, including how approvals should be recorded

Establishing an Approval Process

Ask your developer to provide you with a staging server on which you can place pages before they go live. This will allow you to test for navigability and usability without posting your unfinished site to the public. As part of your testing process, you might want to set up a review team that includes representatives from your company's marketing, legal, public relations, sales, editorial, production, and other departments. Alternatively, you can job out the testing of your site to a professional testing lab or, if your staffing budget allows, organize an in-house testing team.

It's also a good idea to have the site tested by some of your customers, but you'll probably want to do that only after the site is in pretty good shape. Start with an in-house review team or professional testing lab; you can then do a *soft launch* (an unannounced launch) and solicit feedback from your online customers. Once you've compiled their feedback and made the necessary fixes, you can launch with the official, public fanfare your site deserves.

Tip

Make sure that each member of your review team knows which aspects of the site he or she is supposed to review. You might want the legal representative to focus on legal issues, for example, and not on the choice of colors. Similarly, you might want the marketing people to concentrate on how the site's branding is coming across rather than on rewording the legalese. Let all members of the review team know the scope of their responsibilities. Let them know, also, what the deadlines are. (And make those deadlines a few days before your own "drop-dead" deadlines to give yourself some room to maneuver.) You can use an Excel spreadsheet to track who has submitted feedback, who has yet to do so, and where the files are in the production process. If you're using content management software, FrontPage, or Microsoft Project, you can use the features in those tools to track the workflow.

Reviewing and getting approval for each page on your site might seem like a headache now, but it will help you avoid the migraines that can be induced if you have to fix pages repeatedly after the site goes live. It might also save you from some embarrassing problems, such as those of the company that misspelled its own name three times in three different ways on its own website, and another company that accidentally posted a public announcement of a merger that hadn't been finalized (and ultimately fell through). Avoiding such blunders, along with maintaining the integrity of the site and upholding the credibility of the company, product, or service it represents, is the real value in creating and adhering to a good style guide. A style guide is among your best tools for building and maintaining a quality website that fulfills its intended purpose.

Managing Projects with the Right Tools

Ongoing site maintenance is a project like any other, with deadlines, priorities, and team members working on various aspects of the project. Good project management is paramount. Say you want to add some features and functionality to your site as a whole or just freshen up one area. Of course you'd like to know what the project will involve and whether it can be completed on time given the resources available. Using good project management software, such as Microsoft Project, you can predict how a project will play itself out and then manage resources and people throughout the course of a project. Microsoft Project allows you to juggle what-if scenarios and put together complex project plans, and it provides tools for following through by tracking who has done what and on what timeline. Project also lets you see how missed deadlines will affect the overall schedule. Project works smoothly with Microsoft Outlook; if you assign tasks using Project, the assignee will see the tasks appear in his or her Outlook task list. Project can also show you how resources are being used; for example, if your project plan is unbalanced or a delay is about to occur, you'll be able to see how much overtime certain people on your team will have to work in order to make up for it.

Similarly, FrontPage provides task management features that allow you to assign and watch the progress of various aspects of site creation and maintenance. For example, you can assign responsibility for various areas of the site to team members and list the tasks they must accomplish. Each team member can then update the task list as he or she completes tasks.

You can assign either general tasks (such as "Refresh product list") with priorities and deadline dates noted or more specific tasks (such as "Write home page headlines").

Another valuable tool is Microsoft Visual SourceSafe, which is version-control software that allows only one user at a time to work on a given file. Visual SourceSafe allows a user to "check out" a file, which prevents other people from making changes to separate copies of that file concurrently. (That would create version control problems because no one could be sure which version of the file or document was the correct one.) When the user has completed his or her changes to the file, he or she "checks in" the file, at which time Visual SourceSafe logs changes to the file and tracks the time and authorship of the changes. Visual SourceSafe stores a version of every set of changes to a file so that if you later want to restore a version, you can. Visual SourceSafe integrates into the menu structures of Word, FrontPage, Microsoft Visual Studio, and other Microsoft software.

Choosing Content Management Software

Content management software enables website teams to perform the varied, specialized tasks of creating and maintaining content with great efficiency. A good content management solution will provide tools for tracking who is doing what to the content as it is created, edited, reviewed, approved, posted, and even shared with licensees or partners. Content management software generally works in tandem with a database—the content is stored in the database and the content management software provides tools for enhanced workflow, version control, and site maintenance.

Content management software often provides distinct "workspaces" for various team members as well as a staging area where fresh and modified content can be tested. It should allow for testing with a variety of browsers. It should also make posting to the live server easy (after appropriate reviews and approvals).

Powerful content management solutions don't come cheap. But they can be as crucial to a complex site's success as a good transaction system is to a sales site. When you consider your content management options, note how each software solution establishes and maintains processes. How will producers, managers, editors, and other team members work with the content? What options does the software provide for scheduling workflow, tracking content through the review and approval channels, and creating appropriate links (both to and from the content)?

Also find out the following:

- Is the software used by other companies that are similar to yours?

- Does it meet the general industry standards for reliability, security, and robustness?

- Does it meet the specific standards your developer has set for reliability, security, and robustness as well as scalability, caching, and customization?

- Will it integrate smoothly with your other back-end systems?

- Can it handle your existing content and the content you anticipate adding during the time period you plan to use the software?

- Is the vendor stable and reliable?

- Does the software come with an acceptable level of technical support?

In addition, you might want to look into whether and how your team members can be trained in using the product. For a more comprehensive list of criteria to consider in choosing content management software, visit the E-Commerce Management Center at *www.tauberkienan.com*.

Archiving and Purging

Old web pages don't die, they languish—in public. When you remove a link from your website, that action doesn't remove the linked page. If you don't go to the effort of purging an outdated page by placing it in a separate directory or on a separate server from the live site, that old, molding content will continue to appear in search engines and user searches of your site. Links from other sites to that content will still be live as well; that content will, in fact, continue to be a live web page.

To purge web pages that you no longer want on your site, create an archive—a separate area on your server or, preferably, elsewhere—that is unavailable to the public or to any search engines that come trolling around. Keep your website as tidy as you wish the closets in your home were; otherwise, users who stumble into unkempt corners of your website will find pages that do not represent your e-commerce endeavor as you'd like it to be seen. This, again, is something that good content management software makes easier, but if you must work without content management software, set up a manual system for purging and archiving and make your system for keeping the site and the archive of old content known to all who work on the website.

Chapter 12

Promoting Your Website

The bottom line in building traffic is marketing, marketing, marketing. Promoting your e-commerce website, both online and offline, is crucial to success. Your content should soar, your design and technology should support your offerings, and your products must be backed up by service. But even with all that, if no one knows your terrific website exists, no one will visit it. Which marketing, advertising, and promotion techniques you choose and how you mix and match them will depend on your budget, and admittedly a bigger budget can buy more exposure. But using your budget wisely is most important. Even on a tight budget, you can implement numerous techniques for promoting your site and boosting traffic. Whatever your promotional funding, how you maximize the available opportunities through savvy targeting, creative messages, and consistent follow up is what really matters.

Tip

The techniques discussed in this chapter for building website traffic can also work for building newsletter or discussion group traffic. Newsletters and discussion groups can, in turn, be powerful tools for bringing traffic to your site. An investment in applying promotional techniques to newsletter initiatives, then, can pay back in an even greater boost in traffic.

Leveraging Permission Marketing

In traditional promotion, the modus operandi is *interruption*. Ads "interrupt" television, radio, print, and (in the form of billboards, taxi ads, and bus signs) the highways and byways we travel daily. On public television and radio, where commercial messages don't interrupt during the programming, sponsor messages still intrude between shows. Public relations efforts have as a goal placing a message in print or broadcast media. Again, this is an insertion of persuasive information into our experience.

But in Internet promotion, interruption is not always the most effective technique. Users despise unsolicited commercial e-mail, they resent intrusions into discussion groups, and they are jaded with advertising. Some sites have done well with *interstitial* advertising (particularly ads that interrupt the user experience in the form of pop-up windows), but many users find these ads annoying. To get your message across in most Internet venues, a combination of *attraction* and *permission* often works far more effectively than interruption. Permission marketing is the opposite of interruption. In permission marketing, instead of intruding on your audience's experience, you invite them to participate in whatever you're offering—you ask them to sign up for your e-mail newsletter mailing list, to visit your website, and so on.

Tip

Why reinvent the wheel? To find out what's working for others (and what isn't), join a discussion of marketing and promotion techniques. ClickZ (*www.clickz.com*) and ICONOCAST (*www.iconocast.com*) offer terrific online marketing insight via e-mail newsletters. An exchange of online advertising, promotion tips, and other information are archived and searchable at Microsoft bCentral Daily Digest (*digest.bcentral.com*). InterNT (*internt.com*) also offers advertising savvy. Search AltaVista, Yahoo!, and other venues for trade associations and discussion groups related to your industry.

Attracting Traffic with Your Site and Your Message

The foundation of your marketing plan should be a site that fulfills its promise, provides something of value to the customer, and establishes identity and credibility. (These were the subjects of earlier chapters.) Marketing is not just about selling; it's also about creating a need. It's about making people want something and making them want it as badly as possible. Marketing is part product, part packaging, part pricing, and part positioning (establishing the product in the perception of customers and in comparison to competitive products).

Setting Up Viral Marketing

The first goal of your marketing plan must be to create a site that not only compels customers to visit again, but also compels them to tell their friends what a terrific experience they had at your site and what value they received. The effect is somewhat like a virus—word-of-mouth spreads your URL, users suggest that other users sign up for your e-mail newsletters, people pass on to others information they've received at your site (along with enthusiastic endorsements), and so on.

Simply put, there's no better way to engineer word-of-mouth advertising (or *viral marketing*) than by offering a quality product. Your website should be this quality product. Your site can be a destination, a reference, a point of distribution, or a diversion. But it must first *attract* its customer base and then reward those whose visits are a result of your promotional efforts.

Targeting Based on Your Goals and Audience

As you focus your site's marketing strategy, build on what you know about your site's goals and target market (the audience you defined in Chapter 4). Your marketing strategy and the promotion plan it includes will target the same audience and be aimed at furthering the same goals.

Note

The Microsoft bCentral Traffic Builder service (at *www.bcentral.com*) offers tools for promoting your site, attracting repeat customers, and building user loyalty through effective promotion and advertising. Throughout this chapter, you'll find pointers to Traffic Builder tools you can use.

The graph in Figure 12-1 shows the results of a Forrester Research survey in which computer users from 8600 web-enabled households were asked how they typically find web pages. The most common avenues cited were search engines, e-mail, other websites, and word-of-mouth. Note that the numbers don't add up to 100 percent because a person might find web pages using a variety of methods. And *that*, my friends, means that you should use a variety of avenues for promoting a website. Let's take a look at the possibilities.

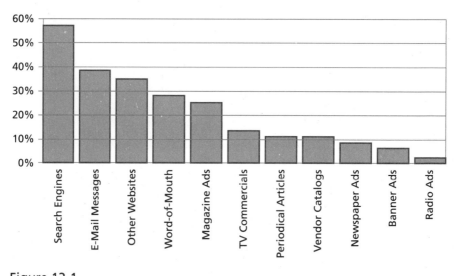

Figure 12-1

How users find websites.

Achieving Search Engine Ranking

How will people find you? Often through search engines, directories, and portals. It sounds simple, but it's not necessarily that easy. Not all sites are listed, and, more important, not all sites get high ranking. Let's examine what it means to get listed and then explore a few ways to do that *and* optimize your site to improve your chances of getting the best ranking possible.

What Are Search Engines, Directories, and Portals?

Search engines create the listings they contain more or less automatically. They're software-driven: The software crawls the Web and compiles a database that is searchable. You can submit your site to a search engine, but the search engine also finds sites on its own.

Directories, in contrast, are created by human beings. You submit your site to a directory, and then people, not software, decide whether it's appropriate to list. People manage the indexing of the list, also, by creating categories and subcategories. AltaVista is a classic example of a search engine, while Yahoo! is at its heart a directory. Hybrids of search engines and directories also exist. In fact, as time marches on, more and more search sites offer both a search engine and a directory (and sometimes two companies partner with each other to offer both options).

A *portal* is a site that provides entry to other sites; it's a jumping-off place. Portals often provide feature content and special services (such as discussion groups or free e-mail) in addition to a search engine, a directory, or listings and even reviews of sites. MSN (*www.msn.com*) is a portal; it includes value-added content and services as well as MSN Search and the MSN Yellow Pages, which lists businesses of all sorts. FindLaw (*www.findlaw.com*) is also a portal, although it addresses only legal resources and not the broad range of topics covered by MSN. In the discussion that follows, the focus will be on search engines and directories; note that the pointers also apply to the search engine aspects of directories and portals.

Tip

To get the latest scoop on search engines, directories, and portals, check into Search Engine Watch at *www.searchenginewatch.com*. Search Engine Watch also offers a newsletter that will keep you up to date on search engine happenings.

How Search Engines Work

The typical search engine, if you look behind the scenes, consists of the following three parts:

- A software program (called a *crawler*, *spider*, or *robot*) that "crawls" the Web, visits sites, scans them for key information, and follows their links. Crawlers crawl to and around a site because its URL was submitted to the search engine or because the crawler encountered the site on the Web. Once the crawler has identified a site, it returns periodically to look for changes, but how often it does that varies from search engine to search engine.

- A database (or an *index*) into which the crawler dumps what it finds (URLs and data related to the web pages that were crawled).

- The actual search engine software that allows users to search the database.

When you use a search engine, the search engine software performs its function by sifting through the data in the database. It then provides you with a list of web pages that it has ranked according to its interpretation of the pages' relevance to the terms you typed when you initiated the search.

Getting to the Top of the List

Your goal is for your site to appear among the first 10 to 20 sites listed when a user searches for sites such as yours. In other words, if your site sells western-style saddlery, you want a user searching on *saddle* to see your site as highly ranked as possible, preferably as the first site listed, but certainly among the top 20.

Note

In the case of directories, a good site is more likely to be listed or reviewed than a lousy one. Directories are created with human intervention, so the selection process can be subjective. Luck is also a factor, but building a site that's compelling and easy to navigate will attract attention and might make the difference between being indexed in a directory and not being indexed.

The following discussion can help you optimize your web pages to achieve better ranking in search engines (including those that are used by directories to allow their users to search their listings). Note that these techniques do not guarantee high ranking—getting good ranking is a complex process and the subject of some people's full-time jobs. How popular a site is (as indicated by how many links lead to it from other sites or how much attention it's getting in the press) often has great bearing on the ranking it gets. Some search engines even accept payment in exchange for listing your site or giving it better ranking. But if you don't optimize your site to enable good ranking, you're guaranteed to not get into the top 100, let alone the top 20. And even if you pony up the payment for ranking, if you haven't optimized your site for search engines, the site might appear at the top of the list, but with an entry that confuses and turns off users.

It's also important to remember that things change. Search engines, as other businesses, constantly improve their systems, and what achieves better ranking for you today might not work as well a few months from now. The companies that are most successful at getting top ranking employ someone to monitor their rankings at various search sites. Those people make modifications to the site, resubmit, monitor, and sometimes even conduct public relations campaigns with personal contacts at the search engine companies.

Tip

Achieving ranking at search sites should be part of an overall campaign for promoting your site. Each aspect of your campaign will work with and bolster the efforts of the other aspects. To formulate your campaign, read through this chapter and decide which promotional techniques to tackle and follow through on. One strategy, for example, might be to boost popularity by sending out a newsletter and actively campaigning for backlinks while also spiffing up the site and submitting it to targeted second-tier and third-tier search engines and portals. Once you achieve some popularity, submitting your site to the major search engines can lead to more success.

Tips to boost your site's ranking

Following a few simple guidelines as you plan and build your site can increase your chances of a high ranking in most search engines.

- In general, do not design your web pages using *frames* (panes within the larger window of the web page) or *image maps* (large graphics that contain within them the links that lead to interior pages of the site). Because of the technical structure of the HTML involved in creating framed pages or pages with image maps, many search engines cannot index those pages and will simply skip over them during the crawling process.

- Similarly, search engines have a hard time with pages created *dynamically* (that is, using content and images stored in databases).

Note

Workarounds for these issues do exist, and you can find out about those workarounds at Search Engine Watch (*www.searchenginewatch.com*). But if you don't want to invest in implementing the workarounds, just avoid using frames, image maps, or database-driven content.

- As you build your site, optimize its design, layout, writing, and HTML development to maximize your chances for a good ranking. (A technique for doing this is described in the next section, titled "Optimizing your pages.") A lot has been made of the use of META tags for this purpose; META tags are special HTML coding that lets you include, for example, a defined list of keywords and a description that many search engines use in their ranking processes. META tags are not the whole story—other factors you can control while you're building the site are also of concern. But using META tags wisely and well can be a key ingredient to search-engine-ranking success.

Note

You can use a few specialized HTML tags to "tag" your site's pages with words and phrases that will help the site to be categorized and indexed correctly. These include the TITLE tag, which defines the page's title (as it appears in the browser's title bar rather than on the page itself), and two META tags (one for a set of keywords and one for a description). But the page's title, its text, and even its popularity also count. More on this as we go along.

Crawlers, as mentioned, follow links. But different search engines work differently. They generally use algorithms or mathematical formulas to weigh various factors and determine relevancy ranking. Which factors have what weight and exactly how the algorithms are used at each search engine are closely guarded secrets. For the most part, however, search engines compare how often certain words appear—as opposed to other, presumably less significant words—in the web page's title (as it appears in the title bar at the top of your web browser window), its text (including any titles on the page itself), the keyword and description META tags, and sometimes even the URL.

Here's a simplistic example: Among a group of websites devoted to 1966 Mustangs, the site that has the words "1966 Mustang" appearing most often in its URL, title, text, and META tags should theoretically come to the top of the list in a search on *1966 Mustang*. However, rankings are actually generally based on the frequency and location of keywords in comparison to other words on the page. Search engines usually check for repeated words (assumed to be keywords) that appear near the top of the page, in the headline, and in the first few paragraphs. They also check how often those words appear compared to other words. But search engines aren't so bright; they take things quite literally. A search engine won't know, for example, that *car*, *auto*, *automobile*, *vehicle*, and *Mustang* all refer to essentially the same thing.

Optimizing your pages

Knowing all this about how the major search engines work, you can leverage a few simple tactics to maximize your ranking. Note that it's best to do this as you build the site. That's far easier, less daunting, and certainly less time consuming than going back through your site page by page and making the necessary modifications. Making modifications after you build the site might involve rewriting text, altering page titles, or even reworking URLs; and the more you tinker after you build, the more you'll have to check for the unexpected effects of that tinkering. You might find, for example, that a change to the text necessitates rewriting links within that text, or you might find that other seemingly minor changes affect linking or even navigation.

Search engine ranking is important enough to be a key part of your site building process. But if you find that you've neglected it, daunting as going back and making modifications might be, search engine ranking is also important enough to justify that expenditure of time. Optimize for search engine ranking as you build if possible, but do it after you build if that is your only option.

To get started, take these preliminary steps:

1. Jot down two to five words that match the topic of your page. (You can use one such list for the whole site or customized lists for each page on the site.) These words usually should not be close variations on each other. (*Car* and *cars* are not good together, but *car* and *auto* might be.) If your content is yet to be written, see to it that these words are communicated to whomever's doing the writing and that they are included in the page's text. If your content is already written, one way to come up with the most important words is to keep crossing out irrelevant words on your web page until you're left with just a few words.

2. In a separate list, expand on the "keywords" you've specified by brainstorming variations, synonyms, and closely related words. Come up with perhaps 15 of these. Avoid plurals (again, *car* and *cars* aren't the best option) unless the plural takes a different form (as with *goose* and *geese*).

3.   Write a very short sentence that describes your page clearly and simply, and include in that sentence a few of the words from the original list of most relevant keywords.

Once you've completed these preparatory steps, do the following:

1.   Open the page using an HTML editor.

2.   Incorporate a few of the keywords you identified into the "title" portion of the HTML code. (They don't have to be the only words in the title section, but they must appear there.) Here's an example for a site that sells adventure camping equipment:

```
<TITLE>Adventure Camping Outfitters: Equipment for camping,
backpacking, climbing, hiking, canoeing, kayaking;
everything for camping and adventure camps</TITLE>
```

3.   Incorporate the most important words (adventure, equipment, camp, and perhaps a few variations, such as camping and camper in this example) in the page's text, near the top of the page, and scatter them throughout the page's text as well.

Note

Again, ideally, you build the keywords into the page's text when you create the site. (See Chapter 7 for pointers.) If you're working with an existing site, you can rewrite the text as necessary to include the keywords. Also, if your site design uses tables as a formatting technique, the table layout can sometimes push the text that appears at the top of the page down in the HTML file. See Search Engine Watch for tips on dealing with this and other dilemmas.

4.   In the "head" portion of your code, enter a META tag for the keywords you identified. For example, this META tag could be used for the adventure camping site:

```
<META NAME="keywords" VALUE="camp,adventure,equipment,camping,
backpack,camper,hike,climb,kayak,canoe,adventure
camping,backpacking,adventure camp,hiking,equipment
for camping,climbing,sport camping,kayaking,canoeing,
camping equipment,adventure sport">
```

Place the most important words or phrases at the beginning of the keywords META tag list. Use only lowercase letters in the keywords, even for titles and proper nouns. Make everything singular (again, *sport*, not *sports*). Use synonyms liberally, and include occasional synonyms in the page's text. However, do not simply repeat words (*camp, camp, camp*) because the search engines are onto that trick and might penalize you by lowering your ranking or by even kicking out your site altogether.

5. Enter a description META tag using the descriptive sentence you wrote. (Note again that the sentence must include some of your keywords.) Here is an example:

```
<META NAME="description" VALUE="Equipment for adventure
camping, backpacking, climbing, hiking, canoeing, kayaking;
get everything you need for camping and adventure camps.">
```

Use third-person references instead of first-person references ("I") because they're more descriptive and let you fit in another keyword (as in "camping equipment for adventure campers"). Also, avoid phrases such as "Welcome to." The goal here is to use specific, descriptive keywords that will get your site indexed properly.

Caution

Don't think you can place your competitors' names and their product names into your META tags to lure potential customers your way. Not only is that unethical, but it might be grounds for a lawsuit.

Remember that some search engines also take into account the popularity of the web page; in other words, among groups of sites about 1966 Mustangs or about adventure camping, those with the largest number of *backlinks* (links leading to it from other sites) or with listings in other search engines or directories will get an extra edge in the rankings.

One two-pronged strategy for leveraging the importance of popularity in search engine rankings is to develop a lot of backlinks *and* get your site listed in some specialized directories (travel, health, personal finance, or whatever is appropriate to your topic and audience). That will have the dual effect of driving traffic and boosting your rankings.

Note

Search engine ranking is not permanent. Search engines change their algorithms all the time, and more and more sites are indexed every day. Even if you achieve a good ranking, it pays to monitor your ranking and refine your techniques. Traffic Builder's Position Agent provides convenient features for testing and monitoring your ranking; you can also use Traffic Builder's Submit It! service to submit your site to multiple search engines and directories quickly and easily.

As of this writing, at least one search engine accepts payment for higher ranking. It remains to be seen whether others will follow the lead. However, it seems unlikely that payment for ranking will become common; to many people, paid listings have less credibility and, after all, the search engine and directory industry runs essentially as a service to people.

Tip

To find out what works for others, view the source. Do a search on a term that closely matches your own site, go to the sites that show up at the top of the search results list, and use your web browser's View Source feature to see what META tags and other tricks that site used to get its ranking.

Making Some Pages Off-Limits to Search Engines

You might not want certain sections of your site indexed by search engines. Some pages need to be entered through other pages in order for their content to make sense, for example. You also might not want transaction system pages and other pages that have specific functionality to be indexed. A trick for preventing most search engines from trolling around where they aren't wanted is to include a specially formatted file called robots.txt in the root directory of the website's files. This file designates which pages are to be accessible or off limits to search engines. To find out more about robots.txt files and how to implement them, ask your developer, check with the major search engines, or look into Search Engine Watch.

There's an easier but less effective method for preventing the indexing of specific pages. You can simply embed this line among the page's META tags:

```
<META NAME="ROBOTS" CONTENT="NOINDEX">
```

Note that fewer search engines recognize and respect this method than the robots.txt method, so using the robots.txt file is preferred.

Submitting Your Site to Search Engines and Directories

Once your pages are optimized for the best possible ranking, you have two basic options for submitting them to search engines as well as directories, and portals: You can go to each one and use the form on its submissions page, or you can use an automated service (such as Traffic Builder's Submit It! service) that allows you to fill out just one form (which often includes a checklist for selecting the search services you want to target) and send your submission to many search engines and directories at once.

Tip

One strategy that has worked well for some companies is to start by submitting the most important pages of the site (perhaps two or three of them) to second-tier and third-tier search services and to appropriate niche search engines and directories. This can establish the site's "popularity" and make it more appealing to the major search engines and directories. Once your site has been listed in the smaller venues, you can then go for the big leagues with more oomph in your submission.

While submission services that allow you to fill out a form and submit your site to dozens or hundreds of search engines and directories at once are a tremendous time saver, the pros generally think it best to submit to the major search engines manually, one at a time. This allows you to tailor each submission precisely. There are only a few major search engines and directories, so the time investment is pretty minimal. If you're going to use an automated submission service, it's probably best to use it for the second-tier and third-tier search services.

Remember that it can take as long as a month or more for your submission to be processed. Don't spam the search engines; that only clogs the pipeline for everyone and is likely to hurt your chances. Do keep in mind that establishing and improving your search engine ranking is a project that might take months. It is, however, a worthwhile endeavor because your traffic will improve dramatically if you do get a top-20 ranking in the major search engines.

This really can't be stressed enough: Before you submit your site to search engines, optimize it for ranking. It's always best to get the correct information in place first. While many of the search engines' crawlers do come around to check for changes, the Web is large and complex and they don't come by terribly often.

Persuading Others to Link to You

You want your site to have many entry points, offer content and service that inspires customers to stick around, and then provide as few exits as possible. Let's focus now on *entry points,* or ways in to your site. How do you develop a lot of entry points? To create them, you must persuade as many other sites as possible to link to yours. Getting these backlinks is the direct result of providing something of value to others, but it also involves persuasion, negotiation, and sometimes trading.

Getting Backlinks and Trading Links

Getting backlinks is easiest for sites that offer strong content or a unique service. Obviously, other sites will be more inclined to link to yours if your site's offerings deepen, add interest to, or complement theirs. To launch a backlink campaign, first identify sites that are likely backlinking candidates. You might do well to get links (either reciprocal or nonreciprocal links) with vendors, suppliers, sister companies, trade associations, professional groups, or your college alumni association. If you link to others (say, in a directory of related resources), let them know and ask them to link to you as well.

Tip

Trade at the rate of real value. If, for example, your site gets five times the traffic of the site you're swapping with, you should get five times as much exposure on that site in exchange for what you're providing them. That might mean better placement for you (on the home page rather than on a little-trafficked interior page), or it might mean more placements or placement for a longer period of time.

Take a look at bCentral's Banner Network (formerly known as LinkExchange), a service that allows you to swap ads with an enormous range of other sites, target ads based on content or other criteria, and track your ads based on customized statistics.

If you offer something for free on your site—a screensaver, software demos, postcards, or a nice interactive tool—directories that index sites offering free stuff, such as *www.thefreesite.com,* can list your site.

If you have a logo you can provide to others as a linkable button, it will stand out on their pages more than a simple link. However, if you ask someone to use your logo as a link without giving them a compelling reason to use it, they might rightfully be reluctant because your logo will merely interrupt or dilute the branding on their site. If you offer something of value such as useful or entertaining software to download from your site, you can make a logo for that software available as a button that links directly to the download page.

Checking Your Backlinks

You can use online search engines such as AltaVista and HotBot to quickly check how many backlinks you enjoy (and who has provided them). For example, to use AltaVista to check your backlinks, follow these steps:

1. Open your web browser, and navigate to the AltaVista site (*www.altavista.com*).

2. In the search box (where you'd normally enter a word or phrase to start a search of websites), type the following (in all lowercase):

   link:http://www.yourdomainname.com/ –host: yourdomainname.com

   Note that the - is a minus sign, and be sure to replace each instance of *yourdomainname* with your own domain name.

3. Click the Search button. A list will appear showing the URLs of all the web pages indexed by AltaVista that link to your site. (The list will show only backlinks to the page whose URL you supplied. To find out about links to interior pages, you have to run a separate search. Simply include a page's entire URL in the search rather than just your domain name.)

   You can check your backlinks using HotBot by following these steps:

1. With your web browser, open HotBot (*hotbot.lycos.com*).

2. In the search box (where you'd normally enter a word or phrase to start a search of websites), type your URL.

3. In the menu box labeled Look For, select Links To This URL.

4. Click the Search button. A list will appear showing the URLs of all the web pages indexed by HotBot that link to your site. (Again, this list will show only backlinks to the page you specified. To find out about links to other pages, search again and specify the page's URL in the search box.)

Forming Partnerships and Joining Alliances

Partnerships and alliances can take many forms, ranging from simple trading of ads or even links to full-fledged affiliate programs and sponsorships (both discussed in an upcoming section) to co-branding relationships (where two companies together release a product branded with both their identities). Because search engines often consider a site's popularity in the rankings and because publicity and prestige seem to beget more publicity and prestige, making your site prominent by joining forces with others is vital to your promotional campaign.

Develop relationships with sites that complement or are related to yours (but not with competitors, obviously). As you visit other sites that cater to the same market, contact their managers and request a link or offer to trade a link. If you join a professional or trade association, have it list your website address and other contact information. Sister companies, business partners, and other associates are all candidates for trading ads or otherwise leveraging alliances.

Entering Competitions and Offering Awards

Consider entering your site into competitions for design awards, content and presentation awards, "Best of the Web" awards, and general awards for notable sites. Examples range from the Webby Awards (*www.webbyawards.com*) to Cool Site of the Day (*www.cool.infi.net*) to an individual site's "best resources" awards. As always, don't just spam the awards sites. Make sure your site is actually qualified for the award, and polish it up before you enter. Enter only competitions you are ready for and have a shot at; otherwise, you'll get the wrong sort of reputation.

Similarly, if you're in a position to legitimately offer an award, you can provide an attractive button that award winners can place on their sites and that links back to your site. For example, if your organization is a nonprofit association of professional editors, you might offer an award each month to a website that is particularly well edited; or if your company sells pet supplies, you might offer an award to especially clever personal websites featuring pets. Awards appear legitimate and prestigious if they are offered by organizations or companies that have real standing. They can look cheap if they're handled poorly, so be sure that you've set things up fairly and that you're recognizing real value in making the award.

Creating Affiliates

Affiliates (also known as *associates* or, less commonly, *resellers*) place prominent links on their sites leading to your site in exchange for a reward or commission. The types of rewards or commissions can include outright payment, finder's fees, bounties, or even barters such as ad placement or products in exchange for click-throughs (explained in an upcoming section) or sales.

You can think of your affiliates as a kind of commissioned sales force. When you organize an affiliate program, plan a compensation package that provides a good base and allows affiliates to earn big bonuses. Some e-commerce sites report that their affiliates earn between 3 and 30 percent (!) of the revenue from each sale generated. These figures vary according to the cost of the product involved and the level of competition for affiliates in that target market. Because an affiliate program has almost no up-front cost (you only have to design a little logo and announce your program), your affiliate program can seem infinitely scalable. You can have hundreds or thousands of affiliates if your product and program are attractive. Participation in this kind of affiliate program packs the triple advantage of getting you backlinks, extending your branding, and selling your product or site.

Tip

It's time consuming to manage and optimize affiliate programs because you have to do a certain amount of tracking and accounting. Joining an affiliate service such as that provided by Microsoft Revenue Avenue (available through bCentral) can relieve you of the burden of finding potential affiliates and make tracking and accounting for commissions easier, allowing you to concentrate on other important endeavors.

Setting compensation rates for your affiliate program is tricky. You have to decide how much a customer or sale will be worth and how much you can afford to pay. First remember to figure in processing fees and other customer acquisition costs. Then set the commission or payout as high as you can; that will get the quick attention of those who might opt in to your affiliate program. Also keep in mind that credibility is an issue. As always, having a good name or attaching yourself to one will persuade potential affiliates that you'll actually make payment and do it on time.

> ### *Tip*
>
> Encourage your affiliates to add value. If your site sells fresh lobster, your affiliates, like you, can add recipes and information to their sites to support the lobster program. Also, asking affiliates to place buttons throughout their sites rather than in one spot three levels down will help generate more visibility and more return for both the affiliates and you. Provide tips to your potential affiliates along with links to other sites that have successfully implemented your affiliate program.

Gaining Recognition with Banner Ads

Advertising is typically an expensive venture. For premium, national ad space on respected, highly trafficked websites and the creation of ads to go in the space, a budget in excess of $40,000 per month is typical. Obviously, the bigger your budget, the higher profile your ad campaign can be. However, there are ways to advertise no matter what your budget. You can advertise through banner ads on targeted niche sites and even on high-profile sites such as Yahoo!, Excite, and Microsoft.com. Before we get into how to use banner ads and how to advertise on big-name sites without a big budget, let's take a look at what banner ads are.

The Basics of Banner Ads

A banner ad is simply a message delivered in the form of a piece of art, usually a GIF image, that appears on a website and is linked to another website. The typical banner ad measures 468 pixels wide by 60 pixels high and appears at the top of a web page. Vertically oriented banners and smaller ads (often known as postage stamp, thumbnail, or button ads) are usually placed elsewhere on a page.

Ad rates are set by the sellers of the ad space and are based on how much traffic the site gets and how targeted the market is. For example, Yahoo! reaches a broad market (one that includes a broad range of people) and Golf.com reaches a targeted or vertical market (a market that is narrowly focused). For the purposes of selling ad space, traffic is discussed not in terms of *hits* (the number of files accessed when a user visits a page) but in *impressions*, or *page views*. (Note that both terms refer to the same thing—an impression or page view occurs when a browser displays the page as a whole. For a full discussion of these terms, see the section titled "Understanding Measurements of Traffic" in Chapter 13.) The price of ad space is described in *cost per thousand* (CPM), meaning what the ad space costs per thousand impressions or page views. CPMs vary widely; more highly trafficked sites get higher CPMs, but smaller sites with highly targeted and much-sought-after markets can, also.

Do They Work?

There's an old saying in advertising that half of your advertising works, but you never know which half. This, of course, refers to traditional media, where the size of the audience an ad space seller claims to be reaching can be measured according to agreed upon standards and even verified via a trusted third-party auditing company (Nielsen Media Research for TV, Arbitron for radio, and Mediamark Research Inc. [MRI] for print.) But it's impossible to determine exactly how many of those reached by a specific ad appearing in a specific venue at a specific time actually bought the product as a result of that ad.

Online media has turned that whole business on its ear. For a long time, there was no third-party auditing system to verify claims of high traffic; even today, while there are companies engaged in verifying traffic numbers (ACNielsen, Engage, and Media Metrix, for example), standards comparable to those used in traditional media aren't fully set. (Again, see Chapter 13 for more information about this.) Early on, measuring advertising success in terms of *click-throughs* or the *click rate* came into vogue because it was easy to count how many users clicked on an ad to visit the site it led to. (These days, banner ad rates tend to be based on CPM.) But users have clicked through fewer and fewer ads each year, leading many to believe that the online public is suffering from banner ad overkill. By the year 2000, overall banner ad click-through rates had dropped to a fraction of 1 percent, and many interpreted that to mean that the banner ad was doomed.

However, measurement of the click rate does not take into account the level of brand awareness achieved or supported via the banner ads. A seminal study by Stanford University and the Poynter Institute (*www.poynter.org*) showed that users perusing a web page do see banner ads. They focus on an ad for perhaps one second, which is long enough (according to the study) to deliver a marketing message. This sounds similar to the function of ads that appear in print publications. And, in fact, a report by Engage AdKnowledge (*www.engage.com/uk/adknowledge*) concluded that more consumers visit a specific site and make a purchase there as a result of viewing a banner ad than as a result of a direct and immediate click-through on an ad. Another study by Ipsos-ASI (*www.asiresearch.com*) determined that banner ads were as effective as television ads in boosting brand awareness among consumers.

We all know advertising works because with it business increases and without it business goes down. But isolating which specific advertising is working for your company and which isn't is still a tricky matter. In a sense, we're back at square one: Probably half of your advertising works, but you might not know which half. It's crucial to target your ads and carefully track the results of your ad campaign.

Achieving Real Results

As a result of the banner ad dilemma, many marketers have put more emphasis on affiliate programs and e-mail campaigns, but banner advertising remains an avenue for supporting brand awareness and is an important component in the mix of most big e-commerce promotion campaigns. To make the most of a banner ad campaign, you must first set realistic expectations. A banner ad campaign probably won't drive traffic through the roof; it isn't a direct response medium. But it can further brand awareness, and if you plan your campaign well, you might also achieve a reasonable level of cost-effective click-throughs.

Creating targeted ads with a call to action

Your first step in building an effective banner ad campaign is to create effective ads. Hire a professional designer, or use a good service. A designer who is savvy about banner ad design will probably ask you whether the ad is meant to drive click-throughs or further brand awareness, so be prepared to describe your goals.

The text in your ad must include a call to action. "Click here" is thought by many to be a call to action, but luring the user to click by clearly communicating the benefit of doing so ("Unleash the power of…") is a better call to action. A time-limited offer can work, but be sure when the user arrives at your site by clicking the ad that the benefit offered is actually there. Scour the Web looking at banner ads, and note those that intrigue you and study their messages. Generally, you'll want to shape ads to appeal to different demographics on different sites; you'll also do well to rotate ads. People get tired of an ad after seeing it even a few times, and they tune it out. Brand names in banner ads might draw in the loyal customer and the curious clicker, but the brand name should be secondary to the branding message. (See Chapter 4.)

The typical banner ad's on-screen size is 468 x 60 pixels, although variations also occur, as mentioned earlier. These variations make it possible for websites to sell ad space at a range of prices; they also make it possible for designers to lay out pages with a little more latitude than is allowed when a 468 x 60 banner ad simply has to appear at the top of the page and there are no other options. Standard dimensions for banner ads, vertically oriented banner ads, and assorted button ads are shown in Figure 12-2.

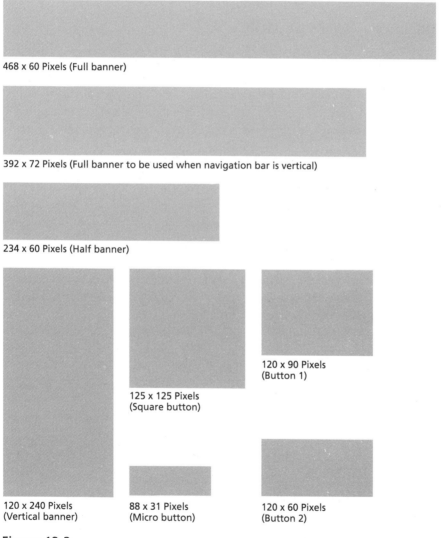

468 x 60 Pixels (Full banner)

392 x 72 Pixels (Full banner to be used when navigation bar is vertical)

234 x 60 Pixels (Half banner)

120 x 90 Pixels
(Button 1)

125 x 125 Pixels
(Square button)

120 x 240 Pixels
(Vertical banner)

88 x 31 Pixels
(Micro button)

120 x 60 Pixels
(Button 2)

Figure 12-2

Standard dimensions for banner ads and button ads.

Whatever an ad's dimensions or orientation, its file size (including all panels and animations and everything) should be less than 10 KB. That's because you want it to load very, very quickly. You want it to pop into view before the user clicks away. To keep the file size under 10 KB, a designer will make the ad visually simple and will generally use web-safe colors. Animation is popular, but as always, use it judiciously. Using two or three panels with some simple animation is fine, but you don't want your ad to look like a circus—unless your company is a circus.

Buying the right ad space

Websites sell ad space in various forms. You'll pay differently depending on which of the many possible options you choose, for example:

- **"Run of the site."** This means that the ad might appear anywhere on the site, "in the rotation." It will be rotated among the other ads that have been sold on a run-of-the-site basis.

- **Placement on a designated page.** This puts your ad on a page whose content is intriguing to your target audience. For example, you might place an ad for gourmet dog treats on a page devoted to dog health on a site that deals more generally with pets.

Tip

It can be more effective to place your ad on a page *leading* to the page that's more closely aligned with your target audience. Why? Because you might capture your target audience by luring them away with your offerings as they're seeking what interests them.

- **"Buying a word."** In this case, you purchase the privilege of popping your ad in front of anyone who searches on a certain keyword. If the word you select is *anniversary*, for example, every time a user searches that site for *anniversary*, your ad for fresh flowers will appear.

- **A targeted category of users.** Your ad is served to individual users based on criteria such as the browser or operating system they use, the domain name suffix that appears in their e-mail address (such as .org or .edu), or even the geographic location of their ISP. You can even target users based on certain preferences if they've provided that information via a site registration system or if you've tracked it via cookies (as described in Chapter 13).

To reach new customers, aim for a broad reach when you buy ad space. This might mean run-of-the-site on a general interest site, a search engine, or a site devoted to a topic that is generally of interest to your target market. (Notice that in the print world, cars are advertised in magazines as varied as *People*, *Esquire*, and *Time*, depending on which topics are of interest to the buyers of specific cars.) To reach more targeted audiences, buy strategically—for example, buy keywords on a big site or run-of-the-site ads on niche or vertical market sites. And to reach the most closely, individually targeted people, use preferences, cookies, or other electronic methods of reaching exactly who you want to reach.

Remember that in the ad space market, rates are set with the expectation of being negotiated down. You can offer less than the going rate—as much as 30 percent less as a starting point is not unreasonable.

Tip

Special bargains can be had during slow times in the industry. One such time is mid-winter; ad sales are slow for the weeks following the winter holidays, and you can get some nice deals for January.

You can also find good bargains through the bCentral AdStore, where you can purchase ad space in big sites (even the major search engines and directories) as well as targeted sites in a variety of industries. Using AdStore, you can purchase ad space for as little as $50 or as much as $2,000. You can also tailor your campaign by viewing demographics and other data, and you can log in to see the results of your campaign or to modify your ad.

Trading ads

Trading ads can be as simple as trading ad space on one site for space on another, as described earlier. You can also be wonderfully creative. One e-commerce manager reports that he barters ad space on his site for discount hotel club memberships, which he then offers as prizes to his e-mail newsletter subscribers and as incentives to affiliates. Another company describes approaching trade show producers within the target market and trading banner ads on the company's site for print ads in the trade show directory. You can trade ads with many of the same types of sites you trade links with: sister companies, vendors, clients, and sites that offer complementary services or products. Yet another good option for trading banner ads is to get involved with Banner Network, a service offered by Microsoft via bCentral. Banner Network offers its members the opportunity to trade banner ads, target the sites on which the ads will appear, and track and measure results.

Sponsoring Other Websites

Chapter 2 described sponsorship as a revenue source. If you turn it around so that you are the sponsor rather than the one being sponsored, it's a way to promote your site. In this scenario, you pay to "sponsor" someone else's site; in return, you get prominent placement on the site, usually with links back to your site. The relationship here is a deeper partnership than occurs when you buy banner ad space. A sponsorship deal can include the sponsor having a say in the content, for example. It can also include a combination of banners and buttons to indicate the sponsorship, and it can include distribution of co-branded content or interactive tools (such as financial planning tools). In a sponsorship arrangement, you can leverage content and a target audience without having to create the content or build the audience yourself.

When you consider a specific sponsorship arrangement, ask yourself whether the site you'd be sponsoring is an appropriate venue for you. Appropriate questions to consider are:

- Does the site's content, design, and functionality reflect well on your brand?

- Does the site reach the target audience you seek?

- Does the site attract a large enough audience to achieve your goals?

- Is the site's content updated frequently?

In a best-case scenario, you'd do well to survey the site's users to find out how effective they feel the site is. At the very least, ask the site's producers for some indication of that; perhaps the producers have conducted user surveys and have results available for you to see.

As mentioned, one of the differences between buying ad space and entering a sponsorship arrangement is that as a sponsor, you can have some input into the site's content. You can, for example, object to content that might offend or undermine your appeal to your target audience. If such an objection is not addressed to your satisfaction, you can withdraw your sponsorship. But beware of actually controlling the content. To maintain audience loyalty and credibility, a site must usually keep its content free from interference. And you chose a site to sponsor presumably because the content was popular and well done. As a sponsor, your job is really to pay for—not to develop—content.

Becoming a sponsor can allow you to ride the crest of a wave of popularity without having to generate the attraction. The downside is that the up-front deal-making can be time consuming. Be honest with yourself as you evaluate this option. Will sponsoring a site help you achieve your promotional objectives as well as or better than another method of promoting your site?

Leveraging Newsletters and Community Forums

E-mail newsletters are among the most effective methods for boosting traffic. For example, one e-commerce venture reports that it has achieved a 25 percent click-through rate from its newsletter and a 6 to 7 percent conversion-to-sales rate. E-mail is an especially good way to drive traffic because it's effective and it's inexpensive to implement, but you must respect the universal resentment of junk e-mail. Content has to be of value and interest, and to avoid the stigma of spam, it's best to allow people to opt in to your e-mail newsletters and announcement lists. As you develop your e-mail program, apply traditional direct marketing techniques by testing to find out what combination of content, offer, copy, and recipient list really works for you.

If you host a discussion group on your site, you can subtly or not so subtly evangelize your site, product, or service. (Chapter 6 discusses in detail the ins and outs of using e-mail newsletters and discussion groups to drive traffic.) Alternatively, you can participate in other online or e-mail discussion groups and offer advice, counsel, tips, and, incidentally, pointers to your website. You do not, however, want to do this willy-nilly. Because you don't want to waste your own time and because you don't want the effort to backfire, you must target appropriate venues and behave appropriately within them. To find discussion groups that fit your target, start with the bCentral List Builder groups and the directory called Liszt (*www.liszt.com*). You can also check sites that specialize in hosting frequent chats (such as Talk City, at *www.talkcity.com*) and sites that offer calendars of scheduled chats.

Before you start actively evangelizing in an electronic discussion, be sure to find out about the group's ground rules. Some groups allow outright advertising and promotion, whereas others do not. You can still be an authoritative presence to those groups that do not, and the combination of your signature file (showing your URL) and the wisdom of your commentary will, presumably, do the job as well as or better than a more blatant ad or announcement.

Publicizing Your URL

It probably goes without saying these days that you should make your URL obvious on every piece of print and every e-mail message that goes out of your office. Add it to your stationery, business cards, brochures, sales sheets, and product packaging. Include it in a signature file that appears automatically at the end of every e-mail message from everyone in your company. (A signature file of no more than half a dozen lines of text is just about right; longer ones start to look tacky.)

Also include your URL in your yellow pages ads and in any advertising you do on taxicabs, billboards, TV, radio, and matchbook covers. Paint it on your trucks. If you don't have trucks, you can rent them. Some dot-com companies pay for the privilege of splashing their branding across other companies' trucks, cars, or even city buses. It's believed in some quarters that such moving ads attract extra attention. But it's also possible that seeing a company's branding on something as tangible as a truck inspires a perception of solidity (and credibility) in consumers.

Tip

In creating your offline promotion campaign, focus on value to the consumer, include a call to action, and consider including a human face to give consumers someone to identify with easily. These are the same guidelines you'd adhere to in any branding message. (See Chapter 4.)

Whenever possible, go beyond just showing your URL in promotional pieces. Showing the URL during an entire TV ad as well as working it into the ad's script increased results by 25 percent for one company. Even in print, on billboards, and elsewhere, a branding message that tells customers what your site offers can improve results. A quick tagline that identifies your site, telegraphs its benefit or value proposition, and attracts attention will get more notice than a generic URL. Tauber Kienan Associates along with the

URL *www.tauberkienan.com* doesn't say much about the company; the tagline "Internet business, technical, and content solutions" says more.

Getting Coverage in Print Media

You should get your name out there, favorably and inexpensively and as often as possible, using traditional public relations (PR) techniques in nontraditional ways. PR does not require the capital an ad campaign does; instead, it takes time and energy. Remember that public relations involves *relations*. You have to build a relationship with the press, nurture it, and leverage it. Successful PR professionals hone their interpersonal and organizational skills to a fine edge. They know who's who, what their media contacts care about, and how to approach them. They also know how to set priorities, plan and manage time, and control torrents of paper and endless rounds of telephone calls and e-mails. They know when to trumpet successes and how to put the right spin on trouble to perform damage control. You can learn and use professional PR techniques to inexpensively promote your e-commerce venture.

Your goal is positive exposure in business journals, trade magazines, newspapers, other local and regional publications, and on the Web. Getting your website's address into print or broadcast has the extra benefit (in addition to valuable exposure) of being similar to a third-party endorsement. You can do a lot with no budget and just an investment of your time. With a small budget, you're even better off. While a $20,000 budget for promoting a website over the course of a year buys nothing but stale peanuts in the advertising world, in the PR world it can land coverage in major news media, garnering both exposure and credibility. For far less than that, you can launch a successful local or regional campaign. Let's take a look at how to launch a PR campaign.

Gathering Materials

Your first order of business is to pull together materials. You need to identify a few phrases that describe your company, product, and site. Like the words and phrases you developed earlier in this chapter (for your site's title and META tags), these phrases should be precise and descriptive. Create a very short description (just a few words), a mid-sized description (perhaps 15 words), and a longer description (perhaps 25 words) of your company, product, and site.

Tip

Esther Schindler, along with members of the Internet Press Guild, has written a wonderful piece on establishing and maintaining press relations, which you can find at *www.netpress.org/careandfeeding.html*. Kirk Hallahan at Colorado State University provides a great Publicity Primer (*lamar.colostate.edu/~hallahan/hpubty.htm*) that includes checklists of materials.

You should also pull together the following resources:

- A professional photograph (slide, 8 x 10 glossy, or TIFF for traditional media; a JPEG or, if necessary, a GIF for online media) of your store, website, product, or your own face, whichever seems most appropriate to your campaign

- A list of key information (specs, data, dates, timelines, graphs, charts, awards) that relates to whatever you're publicizing

- A few testimonials, endorsements, or quotes you can use (with permission)

Writing Press Releases

Armed with the materials discussed above, when you have news to publicize, you can write a press release. To get noticed, your press release must be, above all, newsworthy. What makes news? That's a big question, and the answer depends on the size and focus of the publication, on how your story compares to others received on the same day, and, frankly, on which way the wind is blowing. Here are a few possibilities:

- New products, services, locations, distributors, or personnel
- Sponsored events, rallies, awards, or seminars
- Receipt of awards, grants, honors, or designations
- Offerings of awards, grants, honors, or designations
- Formation of strategic partnerships, alliances, or co-branding ventures

As you write your press release, follow the standard format. Many books and websites describe this in detail, and Microsoft Office includes templates for use in PR and media campaigns. Here is a press release primer to get you started:

- At the top, provide the date as well as complete information about who can be contacted for further information.

- Provide a concise headline that telegraphs your message.

- Place your most important message in the first paragraph.

- As you write the follow-up text, focus on the topic you're presenting, making clear what makes it unique and worth covering. Keep the press release short and to the point; it should never be more than one page long.

- In the text, use the active voice; avoid verbs that end in *ing*, for example. Eliminate unnecessary words or phrases, and avoid corporate-speak or industry jargon. "Leveraging our core competency, Fabrikam Incorporated's value proposition is a unique offering to our e-commerce partners" says just about nothing and takes a long time to do it. "Fabrikam Incorporated offers business support services to e-commerce companies" is more immediate and clear.

- In the final paragraph, provide company information and a brief paragraph of background. Include a URL that goes directly to a page on your site that provides more information.

Launching Your Press Campaign

Send your press release to every appropriate person, avoiding those who are not appropriate. You can find out who's who via services or publications that list editors and honchos at major media outlets and portals (MediaMap at *www.mediamap.com* lists technology and computer editors, for example) or by checking the mastheads (listings of personnel and information) in print publications you've targeted. Alternatively, you can use distribution services such as those available at InternetNewsBureau.com (*www.newsbureau.com*), PR Web (*www.prweb.com*), or Xpress Press (*www.xpresspress.com*). Remember, however, that the cost of these services varies and results are not guaranteed. You might find that keeping your own media list is ultimately more efficient and effective.

When you send out your press release, address it to individuals, not "the news desk." And please, spell people's names correctly. You want to show them respect and demonstrate your competence.

When preparing press releases for delivery via e-mail, make the header informative; don't make it look like spam. Avoid the phrases "press release," "demo," or "e-commerce solution" in your header; instead, use one of the headers you came up with for this occasion. Place your full contact information (name, phone number, address, e-mail address, and URL) in your signature file. And while you'll probably send the press release to a number of contacts, don't include your entire press contact list in the To line. Instead, send out your press release individually if you must, or put the list in the Bcc (blind courtesy copy) line available with most e-mail applications. Keep your electronic press release short, and follow standard pointers for writing press releases such as those described earlier.

Tip

To reach new customers, focus your press efforts on consumer and news media. For the deepest penetration into an existing market, reach into narrowly focused media; for example, if you sell pet supplies and are trying to reach deeply into a market of dog owners, go for highly targeted dog magazines.

Posting Press Releases to Your Online Press Room

Of course, if you send out frequent press releases, you'll want to post your press release to an online press room on your website. When you do, follow these guidelines:

- Make the contact information obvious. Ideally, your online press room should include a list of all the PR people you have on staff (as well as any PR agency staff assigned to your account), along with their e-mail addresses, surface mail addresses, and phone numbers. If your company offers more than one product or service and various people act as PR representatives for those products or services, list each person's area of responsibility.

- Link to a page listing your company's executives with photos, titles, and correctly spelled names.

- Provide a link to a product page with information and perhaps another link to actual product specs.

- Use minimal graphics in your press room area—time is of the essence to the press. A downloadable photo of your product or some other art the media can use is fine, but only if the download is quick. Gratuitous graphics, heavy visual branding, animations, and trendy adornments that slow down access to your press room pages are only barriers to meeting deadlines and will drive the press away.

Under no circumstances should you make press people register for access to your press room. These are deadline-driven people who work at a high clip; they are disinclined to be inconvenienced. And your goal is _relations_, remember? You want to make things as easy for these folks as possible so you can set up a long-term, productive relationship with them.

After you've sent out a press release, don't follow up by calling and saying, "Did you get my press release?" It's extraordinary how many editors despise being intruded upon, especially with that hackneyed line. In addition, don't attach digital demos or photographs to your e-mail. Don't assume that editors will automatically look at any demos you include; again, they are busy people and will ask for a demo if they want to follow up with you.

PR can be a very effective and inexpensive (though labor-intensive) technique for promoting your site. The downside, of course, is that it takes a while to build press relations and you must constantly be generating buzz. But especially for sites with strong content or newsworthiness, the results of a PR campaign will build over time and can certainly pay off.

Integrating Online and Offline Promotional Efforts

While some methods of promoting your e-commerce venture will suit your needs better than others, it should be clear by now that an integrated campaign is the way to go. Traditional, offline advertising focuses on awareness—repeating a branding message with frequency to a mass audience. An online campaign using mixed, interlocked media can leverage messages tailored to targeted groups of customers. Offline media (print, broadcast, and so on) seem to reach a broader audience, while online media (links, search engine listings, and e-mail) reach a more targeted audience.

But how do you know exactly what's working? As mentioned earlier, there is no great method at this juncture for tracking overall response to specific promotional activities, especially in the short term. Often, you'll see a spike in traffic but not know exactly what caused it. You can match traffic data as closely as possible to advertising schedules or watch for jumps after a PR success. You can compare the zip codes of those who buy to the locations of your current regional ads or PR campaigns. You can also try giving customers a discount that's tied to use of a unique code, or you can push them to a unique URL to see whether they're taking the bait.

Note

A promotional effort that employs a number of techniques, both offline and online, certainly nets you more than the sum of its parts. A diligent backlink campaign creates popularity, boosting your search engine ranking, which in turn makes the site more popular and attractive to the media. This makes your site more interesting to prestigious sites that might backlink and further boost your search engine ranking. The overall result is a dynamic interweaving of promotional wizardry.

To best measure the progress of individual aspects of your promotional efforts, change one thing at a time and watch closely to isolate what works. As you get a feel for what's working, you can cut back on efforts that show marginal returns and focus on what's apparently successful. Don't look exclusively at what drives traffic; focus instead on what drives sales and what is cost-effective. If you get most of your customers from full-color advertising in a niche magazine but the advertising costs a pretty penny and you also have to mail out brochures to provide more information and close the sale, that represents a lot of expense and legwork. If you get fewer sales from your website but the costs are comparatively minimal, your dollar might be better spent on website promotion.

Keep in mind that the business of promoting online ventures is evolving. In one Forrester Research study, 47 marketing managers reported that an average of 44 percent of their marketing budgets went to offline efforts and the rest to online efforts. None of the respondents reported conclusive results from their efforts, however. Your best bet, then, is to monitor success stories as reported by ClickZ, ICONOCAST, and other venues and promote your site using as wide a variety of techniques as you can envision. As you market and promote your site, track what works and focus your efforts there. You'll need to know how to measure success for areas of your site as well as the site as a whole, how to set up metrics that logically follow the goals you've set, and what modifications to make to your site based on what you discover. Those are the subjects of the next chapter.

Chapter 13

Assessing Your Success

To many business people, the key measurement of success is dollars earned. That is as it should be—profitability drives most businesses. And for many websites, traffic has been cited as the benchmark of success. But for some ventures, benchmarks other than revenue, profit, and traffic are actually more appropriate. The goals you've set for your website will define the terms of its success. For a site that promotes a product or service, for example, certainly the overall success of the product or service is the ultimate achievement. But the amount of media presence that's generated, the acceptance of the product by its potential customer base, and many other factors will tell the story of the website's success even before the company's annual financial reports are written.

Depending on the business and user goals that have been set for them, various types of websites might strive for success that's defined by a certain level of community involvement, by a reduction in customer service inquiries, or by the number of sales leads generated. In the case of a research site, the quality of the data acquired in the site's surveys and the credibility that the site's reports achieve are likely to be measures of success. In print publications, circulation is often used to measure a company's success both before and after the company achieves profitability.

Whatever the nature of your website, in order to satisfy potential advertisers, investors, any media that take an interest in your venture, and your own basic business interests, you must have methods for quantifying the website's success. Measuring traffic, although it's again not the only metric that's of interest, is one such method. In addition to quantifying your success, measuring traffic can also support your efforts to focus your business development and marketing plans, to buy and sell advertising, and to allocate resources effectively. Measuring traffic is, in fact, equally important to sites that have nonprofit, profit, cost savings, media presence, purchase support, or other goals. Measuring traffic and getting a complete picture of who uses your site and how they use it will help you direct your e-commerce endeavor regardless of its goals. While measuring traffic is seldom the whole story, statistics about the who, what, why, and when of your website's audience will help you refine your strategies, develop better tactical solutions, and apply your resources in the right direction.

This chapter addresses establishing appropriate metrics for assessing how successful your e-commerce website has been at accomplishing defined business goals. It also explains how traffic measurement works, how site statistics are compiled, how audits of traffic levels are conducted, and how you can use surveys to get user feedback. Once you get a grip on analyzing statistical data and user feedback, you'll want to improve your site. At the end of this chapter, you'll get insight into what modifications you might make based on what you've discovered. But first, let's look into how you can set the right benchmarks.

What Does Success Mean to You?

The measurements you use as you assess your success must conform with the goals you set when you planned your site. For a retail sales site, some obvious measures of success are traffic, how many users are making purchases, how few returns occur, how few customer service events are experienced, how much revenue is produced, and, ultimately, how much profit is generated. In business-to-business settings, the best measurements might be those that account for getting and keeping customers. In a case where the product is capital equipment (for example, expensive biotechnical devices), the number of calls received and the number of sales generated by website leads and closed later by sales reps can be the milestones.

Depending on your site's mission, you can evaluate its overall success from a number of angles. For example, if your goal is to promote something (a company, product, service, person, or viewpoint), you can assess your success in terms of:

- Media presence (print, broadcast, online), as measured in the quantity or frequency of appearances but also in the quality and prestige of appearances
- Number of registrants at the site or for your newsletters
- Growth in traffic (which indicates that your message is being received by an increasing number of people)
- Growth in overall acceptance of the object of the company, product, service, person, or viewpoint being promoted

If your goal is to inform, you can measure your success in terms of:

- Growth in subscriber base or traffic levels
- Level of penetration into the target audience
- Increased credibility with audience and other media (as shown by how the product or service is described or referenced by others, for example)
- Growth in ad sales and the ability to charge higher rates

If your goal is to educate, you can measure your success in terms of:

- Number of registrations
- Number of graduates from courses or programs
- Number of repeat students
- Level of market penetration
- Higher scores on tests or evaluations
- Increased recognition as a learning center

If your goal is to distribute, you can measure your success in terms of:

- Number of visitors who download the product or files
- Level of penetration into the potential audience
- Decrease in number of support events (which indicates how usable your systems and site actually are)

If your goal is to sell, you can measure your success in terms of:

- Number of customers and repeat customers
- Number of sales
- Number of sales compared to number of site visitors (conversion rate)
- Level of market penetration

- Revenue generated
- Profit produced
- Decrease in number of support events
- Decrease in cost of acquiring and retaining customers

If your goal is to conduct research, you can measure your success in terms of:

- Quality of data gathered
- Credibility with the target audience
- Media presence
- Number of participants in online surveys and the quality of their participation
- Number of potential qualified participants who are actually participating

If your goal is to provide customer service or technical support, you can measure your success in terms of:

- Decreased costs
- Quicker resolution of problems
- Fewer events requiring staff response

If your goal is to facilitate workflow or collaboration, you can measure your success in terms of:

- Increased productivity
- Expedited time to market
- Higher morale (and lower turnover) among employees

Note

Both standards and methods differ depending on what you're assessing; to analyze an online community or an intranet, for example, you need an approach that varies from those described in this chapter. For more information about other approaches to analyzing information, see "Conduct Surveys" in Chapter 5, "Measuring Community Success" in Chapter 6, and "Measuring Success" in the Appendix.

Evaluating Performance Related to Reaching Customers

In analyzing the overall performance of your e-commerce venture, you can benefit from understanding the following concepts related to reaching, providing service to, and retaining customers:

- **Market penetration**   Market penetration is a measurement that's expressed as a percentage; it describes how much of the potential audience or market is actually being reached, making purchases, or otherwise engaged with the business activity. For example, if you're promoting a chain of fitness clubs, you'll want to know how many people you've succeeded in reaching among the vast number you could be reaching. That might include not only those interested in fitness and motivated to seek out fitness centers but also the less motivated, less fit people who could become customers under the right circumstances.

- **Customer relationship management (CRM)**   CRM is a business strategy that involves anticipating, understanding, and responding to a business venture's current and potential customers' needs and wants. CRM, then, uses measurement rather than being a measurement. An overall CRM solution involves capturing accurate, complete customer data; consolidating and storing that data; analyzing it; and distributing the resulting information to whomever deals with the customer in person or electronically. The goals of such an endeavor are to offer better customer care and to support a long-term, profitable relationship.

- **Lifetime customer value (LCV)**   The concept of LCV is founded on the principle that profitability comes not just from acquiring new customers but from repeat business from a pool of loyal customers. Many traditional companies have long been interested in calculating the costs of acquiring new customers, retaining them, and converting product interest into product purchases—getting adequate data to describe such long-term cost is difficult. E-commerce

(continued)

Evaluating Performance Related to Reaching Customers (continued)

technologies provide an unprecedented opportunity to track and understand customers, but the tools and standards for calculating LCV precisely are not yet mature.

- **Customer acquisition and customer retention** You can quite reasonably look at the cost of acquiring customers along with the amount each customer spends. You can also track the cost of keeping the customer and converting that customer into a repeat buyer. Technology for doing this is readily available.

To get such measurements, you must start with technology that can glean data, analyze it, and generate accessible reports. At the high end, customizations of Microsoft technologies can help. For example, developers can use Microsoft SQL Server Analysis (OLAP) Services (a component of SQL Server) to quickly and efficiently perform analysis on large volumes of data. In the midrange, developers can use SQL Server and Microsoft Excel to produce less finely tailored reports or use the Microsoft Commerce Server Business Analytics System to produce reports based on data stored in a database. For more modest budgets, Microsoft bCentral offers customer management tools along with options for analyzing data and generating reports.

The Benefits of Measurement

The benefits of setting the right standards for measuring success are many. With the right kind of measurement, you can:

- Maximize ad revenue by quantifying and verifying traffic to advertisers, make informed decisions about buying and selling ad space, and set your ad rates accurately

- Time your promotions to leverage what you know about traffic and your audience's habits

- Increase the response rate for promotions, surveys, registrations, and other ventures

- Demonstrate return on investment (ROI) to yourself, your company's executives, and your investors

- Monitor and forecast trends so that you can provide the best possible service when it's actually needed

- Tune your site's performance and make better technology decisions

- Structure and enhance your site's content, navigation, and usability based on user feedback and observations about how the site is actually used

- Allocate resources wisely to improve efficiency and optimize content and design when needed

- Know your customers better, meet their needs, expand what you offer them, and extend your brand and your business reach to meet the right target audience

Consider the case of one research and information site that launched with strong expectations of achieving its intended goals. Within a few months, close monitoring of the site's traffic and usage patterns along with analyzing a survey of site users revealed that unexpected areas of the site were getting attention. But one area, which had been planned as a real traffic-getter, was languishing with low numbers. The company quickly decided to spend time and attention on the more popular areas and jettison the loser. In another example, the management of a casino found through monitoring its website that Wednesday night was the most active night for booking weekend reservations. The company was then able to plan its promotions and staffing accordingly. At an education site, managers discovered many users taking an interest in a web page that described a certain course, but few people were registering for it. What was the problem? A little tinkering with the wording of the course description resulted in a spike in registrations.

Getting to Know Your Audience

Long before you launch your site, you will have defined your intended audience. As an entrepreneur or manager, that's part of the basic planning you must do to assure yourself (and potential investors) that your endeavor is a viable business venture. Defining your audience allows you to focus strategy for your offerings, branding, and overall marketing plan. It also allows you to predict your expected ROI.

As time goes on, however, your initial speculation might need some adjusting. As you monitor your site, glean reliable statistics, and watch trends in user feedback, you can gain increasingly accurate knowledge of the audience you're actually reaching. In e-commerce, you have a more direct connection with your customers than is possible in many business environments. E-mail, online surveys, and other direct feedback loops give your customers the opportunity to communicate more directly. Those avenues, along with other methods of tracking customer activities and responses, provide you with valuable knowledge. The more you know about what your audience is doing at your site and when and how they are visiting, the more closely you can align your business with their needs. And that, most assuredly, spells success.

Note

Your online audience might differ dramatically from that of your brick-and-mortar store. For example, your online audience might be more concerned with convenient, quick delivery than with product merchandising. Or they might be more technically savvy—for example, online book buyers buy more Internet books per capita than book buyers at brick-and-mortar stores do. Don't assume that you know your e-commerce customers based on your knowledge of your "3-D" customers. Get to know your market as it exists rather than as you believe it exists.

What Objective Data Can You Gather?

Just a few years ago, Internet professionals had to rely on their judgment and overall intuition for a sense of what worked. Of course, user feedback could be immediately received via e-mail or online surveys, but objective data was scarce, and what there was of it came from detailed *log files* (long lists of electronic events as recorded by the server). Log files—such as the one shown in Figure 13-1—are hard to read and harder to interpret. (Log files are further explained later in this chapter.)

Log files serve a fine purpose for server administrators and other tech types—they aid those people in monitoring and maintaining servers. But executives and managers want reports. They want readable facts about their site's visitors and what the visitors are doing at the site. Unfortunately, tracking website statistics such as these is a science that's still in its infancy. Detailed, accurate website statistics are hard to come by. The whole question of what should be counted and how it should be counted is, in fact, much more complex than it might seem at first glance. Consider, for example, these technical variables:

- One server can host multiple websites (as described in Chapter 10).

- One website can be hosted by multiple servers (either because it is mirrored on another server or because pieces of a single site are stored on several servers).

- Any URL can be redirected to another URL. Identifying which URL is the true URL when one is redirected to another is tricky. In order to compile statistics, you'd have to segment and combine data for both URLs.

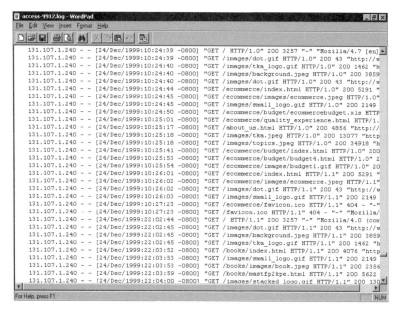

Figure 13-1
Log files aren't especially user-friendly.

Further, the very question of how to identify and count a seemingly obvious and agreed-upon statistic—the *unique users* that visit in a certain time period—is a real problem. The issue, which illustrates an area of general confusion, is that you can determine which computers are accessing the site and how many of them there are, but several people might use the same computer. There is simply no way to know how many users are truly using the site compared to how many computers are accessing it. You could force everyone to register and log in each time they use the site, and perhaps that seems like a solution. But individual users would still be able to register under different names, two users would be able to log in using the same name, and the numbers could easily be skewed. What's more, many people find registering and logging in daunting or annoying enough to be utterly off-putting, so you'd actually be driving away a lot of users in the name of counting users.

Another problem is that it's difficult to take accurate measurements and compare them to each other in an industry where overall, agreed-upon standards of measurement have yet to be defined. Many tools exist for measuring impressions (which we'll discuss shortly) and other information, but no two tools base their measurements on precisely the same set of criteria. For instance, different tools make different assumptions about how (from a technical perspective) a user session is defined. This can be a real mind boggler for many site managers: You can use two perfectly respected tools to measure one site's traffic for a specific time period and actually come up with two different sets of numbers! Using even the most sophisticated tools and packages, you can know what is going on with your website's traffic and audience with, at best, only a high degree of probability. But at this juncture, you cannot know exact numbers—at least not numbers precise enough for business statisticians to be happy. If this is of any comfort, however, note that your competitors are in the same boat. Also, many smart people are working feverishly to solve this problem, and it's of such importance that we can all expect real solutions to become available in the not-too-distant future.

In the meanwhile, because no single data source can provide everything you need to know to run your site effectively and no single tool or technology exists to bring data together into perfectly meaningful information you can use, you'll get the most complete, accurate information by using tools that analyze and cross-analyze information found in the following sources:

- Server, network, and operating system log files
- User registration databases
- Transaction system databases
- Reports from third-party services that compile and verify data

Most of the site statistic tools, packages, and techniques currently available rely on some combination of log files, registration databases, and transaction system databases to provide data that's compiled into readable reports. High-end products such as Microsoft Commerce Server, for example, pull data from log files and generate that data into very understandable and even customizable statistical reports. You can also glean information from surveys that encourage users to "tell us about yourself," from site registration systems, and from how many views and clicks your online ads receive. (If you store such information in a database, you can use Microsoft Access or Excel to analyze the data.) Coding print ads or coupons or providing in them a special URL for accessing your site can also help you track information; again, you can use Access or Excel to compile or index the results.

Those products and tools are a great boon to anyone tracking and analyzing site statistics. Bear in mind, though, that even without sophisticated feedback systems, high-powered technology, or pointed surveys, you can learn or infer quite a bit about your site's users. Using the most fundamental data sources and tools, for example, you can learn such basic information as:

- How many users or customers are visiting the site or a specific area of it.

- How many users are new and how many are return users. (This is possible only in cases where users are required to provide a username and password or where some similar method is used to track user identities.)

- What customers do at your site, including what areas or pages they visit, how long they stick around, whether they make a purchase, or how they otherwise partake of your site's offerings. You can also learn:

- The most requested pages (the top 5 to 10 on a weekly basis), the most frequently used entry and exit pages, and the files most often downloaded.

- The amount of activity experienced by the site as a whole and by main pages, as measured by day of the week and by hour of the day.

- Which browsers and platforms are most often used (by both name and version number).

- Which sites, URLs, and search engines are sending traffic your way, as well as which phrases and keywords users are using to find you.

Note

To some extent, you can identify the countries or states users are in when they visit your site. Log files track which ISPs or domain names are sending visitors your way, and most site statistic software can pinpoint where those ISPs or domains are located. But that information can be skewed. If you note that a disproportionate number of visitors appear to be in the same state, take a look at the domain name involved. If it's aol.com, for example, that traffic is America Online (AOL) traffic, and AOL is located in Virginia. Notoriously, all AOL traffic appears in everyone's site statistics to be coming from Virginia, which can easily throw off any assessment of the geographic location of users.

You can also identify visits by the crawlers or spiders that search engines send out to troll the Internet and index websites. And from the sort of data tracked in error log files, you can know which pages are not found when requested by users, which pages load most slowly, and what other server errors are occurring. Error information is invaluable in that it identifies the ways your website is not working and allows you to make the appropriate corrections.

Note

You can also infer some information about your site's users. If people are accessing your site or a specific page between 8 AM and 5 PM, for example, you can assume they're using a fast business connection. If they're primarily visiting in the evening or on weekends, they're probably at home, which often means they're using a 56K modem at best.

Having as much information as possible (and understanding it) allows you to focus your efforts. It enables you to create one-to-one custom communications, build strong and lasting business relationships, further your existing goals, and develop new goals. For example, if you do know you're getting a lot of traffic from a specific geographic region—again, generally a matter of deducing this from listings in log files—you can target that region as a new market or one worth expanding. If you run a radio ad that provides both a phone number and a URL, you can track the number of calls and any spike in traffic you receive immediately after the ad airs. Then if calls go up 10 percent and traffic 23 percent, you can demonstrate that the target audience has an interest in the website.

By using a few tricks of the trade, conducting some clever online surveying (discussed later in this chapter), and understanding how traffic measurements and user profiling work, you can go much deeper in your analysis of what's working for you.

Measurements of Traffic

Let's start with that old standby, hits. Every time a user accesses a web page using a browser, the user's computer is actually requesting from a server the electronic files that make up the page. Each request is known as a "hit" on the server. (The measurement of traffic widely known as a *hit*, then, occurs every time a user's computer requests a file from a server.) But remember that a single web page can be made up of many files or of just a few. Also, pages that look utterly alike can be created using different methods. This means that (at least hypothetically) three web pages that appear to be identical can generate very different numbers of hits. One web page might generate 4 hits, for example, another might generate 20, and a third might generate 35. This alone makes counting hits a poor measurement of traffic.

Caching (the temporary storage of frequently accessed files) further complicates matters. Cached files—such as logos, backgrounds, or navigation buttons, for example—are served once and then stored (either by the web browser or by a special caching server). They can thus be used repeatedly without the need for additional requests for the files; the upshot of this is that one hit might result in the caching of a file that then appears many times on many pages. Counting the appearances of cached files on individual pages is very complex. Basically, it's an impossible task. And that makes calculating how many hits make up a web page a real nightmare.

So comparing the number of hits that one site or web page gets to the number that another gets is a crude system that leads to inaccurate comparisons. A better and more common method of comparison is to count *impressions*. An impression occurs every time a page appears. Actually, from a technical perspective, it's the number of times a page (rather than a file) is requested from the server. But, as mentioned earlier, while impressions represent a more accurate method of counting traffic, what really constitutes an impression (what combination of electronic data gleaned from the log files) has not been established within the industry. So again the whole business of measuring traffic accurately is a bit thwarted.

Note

When advertising space sales representatives talk about *guaranteed impressions*, they're describing the number of impressions the buyer is promised (regardless of any dips in traffic during the specified time period).

How many unique users a site or page gets is also of great interest. While most executives and managers asking about unique users would like to know how many individual people are using the site, the reality is that only unique computers can be counted. If half a dozen people are using the same computer, that computer will still register as only one unique user.

Clicks are very measurable. The clickthrough rate, also known as the response rate, is a measure of how many times a link, button, or banner ad is clicked.

Note

Many people consider viewing to be a passive response; in e-commerce, you want a more active response from users. You generally want them to click through, buy, or otherwise act on what you've presented. The rate at which passive viewing becomes active response is known as the *conversion rate*.

Tracking Preferences and Profiles with Cookies

Cookies are a feature of most web browsers that allow the storage of a kind of a "note" among the browser's files on the user's computer. A cookie is placed there when the browser requests a web page from a server that uses cookies; the note is from the server to itself but is stored on the user's computer.

Most cookies are used for harmless tasks such as identifying users' preferences (which allows for personalization of content, for example) and storing users' passwords (which avoids the necessity of users remembering and entering their passwords from one session to the next) Cookies can be very handy for following traffic patterns and tracking trends as well. Because a cookie can actually identify an individual user, cookies offer a way to measure unique users. They enable the gathering of aggregate data that shows how users click

> ***Tracking Preferences and Profiles with Cookies*** *(continued)*
>
> around the site and in what paths traffic flows. Cookies also provide developers with options for tying surveys to transaction histories and accomplishing other sophisticated feats of correlation.
>
> Cookies get a bad rap, however, because some users worry about someone else placing a file on their computer. They also worry that cookies will allow for increasingly intrusive marketing and perhaps even manipulation by commercial ventures. As you develop your website and its systems, keep in mind that how you use cookies is of as much concern to users as other privacy issues.

Analyzing Website Statistics

Considering the limitations and capabilities of website measurement, how can you know what sort of traffic you're actually getting? Most of the data used to analyze traffic comes from log files. Even many third-party auditors base their reports on your log files. Other data can be obtained from surveys, registrations, and reports offered by banner exchanges and other programs, but because log files are so prevalent as a basis for reports, let's start there.

Looking into Log Files

If your site is hosted at an ISP or hosting company on its server, you'll usually be given access to weekly or monthly log files for your review. In most cases, you must retrieve the log files right away; they won't be available forever. If your site is on your own server (either at your location or elsewhere), retrieving and reviewing log files is again your job (or your technical staff's job) but the log files in this case will sit there until you delete them. (The files can really pile up, so it's best to delete or archive them regularly.)

Server log files record the following for each hit:

- The date and time of the hit

- The name of the host from which the request that resulted in the hit came

- The visitor's login name (if the user is authenticated)

- The referrer

- The visitor's IP address and host

- The number of bytes that were transferred

- The path (name and location) of the file that was served (which file, in other words, and exactly where the file was located on the server)

- A listing of messages that indicates whether the file was actually served or an error occurred; if an error occurred, an error code will be provided

From this data, other data can be deduced; for example, log file analysis software can generate lists of the log file data. In those lists, the top-most item in the "path of the file that was served" list is the most popular page, while the bottom-most item in that list is the least popular page. An impression occurs (very roughly speaking) when a request is made to the server for an HTML file (as opposed to an image file or some other sort). A unique user is counted based on a combination of data, including the date and time, the name of the host, and the IP address.

Selecting Analysis Tools

You must use some type of analysis software to measure and analyze traffic as it's recorded in the log files. In selecting the tool to use, consider the following criteria:

- **Price**   The price range starts at free or cheap for basic software and ranges up to $300,000 or more for custom solutions.

- **Capacity**   Some software is better at crunching big numbers and large files than other software. Compare the software's capabilities to the volume of traffic you have or anticipate.

- **Customization**   Some software offers only a predefined set of reports, while other software enables you to write your own queries and specify what to include in the reports.

- **Platform**   You'll probably run the software on your desktop computer rather than on the server; choose software that runs on the operating system used by the computer you'll use.

- **Service**   Everything said in Chapter 10 about service-level agreements and how to assess them applies here.

- **The vendor's stability and growth potential**   If you rely heavily on your website and need reliable reporting, choose software from a known, reputable source that is likely to continue to service the software for the length of time you plan to use it.

Microsoft Commerce Server includes website traffic analysis software that translates log files into useful information about requests to the server as well as the users and organizations that interact with a website. It provides reports in an HTML format or in formats that can be used in Microsoft Office applications such as Word or Excel. You can find out more about Commerce Server at *www.microsoft.com/servers*.

Note

To work within a constrained budget but get the best analysis tools, you can barter for traffic analysis reports by running a company's ad, for example, in exchange for their premium reports package. Another option is to sign up with beta programs to minimize costs by using prerelease software that perhaps offers more complete statistics and tracking reports than any currently released software.

Auditing Your Data

If you plan to sell ad space, you'll quickly find that potential advertisers want independent confirmation of your website's reported traffic (as discussed in Chapter 12). They'll also want to know key information about the audience your site reaches. However, as mentioned earlier, industry standards for exactly what to measure and how to measure it are still lacking. For example, different software and different companies use a different technical definition of impressions. This leaves the entire system of counting impressions deeply flawed (although as a basis for comparison, it's not as wildly inaccurate as counting hits). Despite all of these issues, media buyers want third-party confirmation, so you must provide it.

Various companies are in the audit game, including Media Metrix (*www.mediametrix.com*), AC Nielsen Media Research (*www.eratings.com*), ABC Interactive (*www.abcinteractiveaudits.com*), Engage (*www.engage.com*), and I/PRO (*www.engage.com/ipro*). Each does the job in its own way, but in general you can expect to find variations on these themes:

- **Site popularity estimates based on consumer sampling** Consumer sampling generally works by providing groups of users with software to install on their computers. As the users go about their online routines, the software tracks what they do (what they click on, how long they stay, and so on). The sampling company retrieves this information and compiles it into reports.

- **Software you can run on your server to generate reports** The reports include those that media buyers appreciate: information about the most frequently accessed fields and directories, geographic distribution of the site's audience, which organizations are visiting the site, and so on. In some cases, custom reports can also be generated.

- **Traffic auditing based on your log files and the verified monitoring of a selected group of users** This is a "hybrid" system that incorporates elements of the two approaches just mentioned. The reports generated are based on both log file and consumer sampling data and are provided in formats familiar to media buyers.

Note

Developments in third-party auditing are emerging quickly. Check the websites of the audit companies mentioned earlier as well as ClickZ (*www.clickz.com*) to find out what's new in the world of site traffic verification and audience profiling.

Soliciting and Analyzing User Feedback

Part of the beauty of doing business on the Web is that you can get input directly from the user or customer with fairly minimal effort. Offering an online survey and using automated tools to store, retrieve, report on, and analyze the data is a dream compared to sending out printed surveys, getting people to return them, and then compiling the data to make usable reports. (Chapter 5, in its discussion of staying close to the customer and providing top-notch customer care, discusses techniques and tools in detail, including how to leverage e-mail for better communication with customers.) You can, of course, outsource the creation, execution, and analysis of surveys to third-party firms that specialize in such endeavors. Even if you do that, you'll be better prepared to manage the survey process if you first understand how surveys work.

As you organize and write your surveys, follow these guidelines:

- **Use interception or incentives to encourage participation.** You can intercept every 10th or 20th visitor with a request to fill out a quick survey (this will also facilitate a more random sampling), or you can offer those who participate an incentive such as a chance to enter a drawing for a prize. (Keep in mind, however, that this will encourage participation by people who want the prize and will not represent a random group.)

- **Make the survey and the questions short.** Specific questions with a few multiple-choice responses tend to get the best results. Keep the questions brief and offer between two and five possible responses. (A site geared toward education might ask users to identify themselves using a question such as "I am a: student/ alumnus/potential student/parent of a student.") Include one or more open-ended questions as needed, but remember that few people enjoyed essay questions in high school and your users might find a survey full of open-ended questions off-putting, too.

- **Ask the most personal questions last.** Structure the survey so the less personal questions build to the more personal ones. If you must ask about income level, for example, place that toward the end of the survey so that participants will have warmed up to responding and be more likely to answer. Place questions about your product or services earlier in the lineup.

Note

Keep in mind that the Internet is a public place. If you ask for highly personal data, protect the privacy of survey respondents by using a secure server. And as you create your survey, don't ask questions that will reveal your confidential strategies to your competitors.

In your analysis, separate first-time users' responses from those of return visitors—they'll have differing viewpoints. (You can include a question in the survey to ask whether the respondent is new to your site.)

What to Do with the Data You Gather

All too often, companies gather statistics and reports and then stack that valuable data in a closet to gather dust. Someday, they tell themselves, they'll take all that information into account when they rebuild the website. Often, they simply aren't sure what the information suggests about what they ought to do. Think back to your site's goals and the methods of measuring traffic discussed throughout this chapter as you look at Table 13.1. It will help you determine what data to analyze most closely and which areas of site development might need attention.

If Your Goal Is	Analyze This	And Improve This
To promote (a company, person, or viewpoint)	Media presence, registrants, impressions	Branding message; price; promotion; how the site's product, service, offerings, content, and design fulfill the branding
To inform	Number of subscribers, impressions, media presence, ad sales	Content, navigation, usability
To educate	Number of registrations, graduates, repeat students; scores on tests or evaluations; recognition	Course content, pricing, promotion, and branding; site content, navigation, usability
To distribute	Number of visitors and downloads, number of support events	Placement and descriptions of product, navigation, speed of download, customer service FAQ
To sell	Number of customers and repeat customers, number of leads and sales, conversion of traffic to sales, revenue generated, profit produced	Call to action, value proposition, presentation of product information, promotion, ease of use, navigation and usability of transaction system
To conduct research	Quality of data, credibility, media presence, number of participants in surveys and quality of participation, number of highly qualified participants	Call to action, method of generating random or targeted sampling, ease of participation, method of targeting or selecting participants
To provide customer service or technical support	Cost per event, time to resolution, number of events requiring staff response	Customer self-service tools (FAQ and other methods), writing for the target audience, ease of use

Table 13-1

Basing Improvements on Appropriate Data.

Table 13-1 *(continued)*

If Your Goal Is	Analyze This	And Improve This
To foster community	Number of participants, quality and frequency of participation, loyalty to the group or sponsor	On-topic interaction, quality of moderating, recognition of leaders, spin-off topics, call to participate
To facilitate workflow or collaboration	Increased productivity, expedited time to market, higher morale and lower turnover among team members	Selection of tools provided for communication, collaboration, and project management; speed and ease of use of those tools; the site's overall usability

Is the Customer Always Right?

Your job, as an e-commerce entrepreneur or manager, is to assess trends and make changes to your site, your products, and your services as needed. Businesses that don't adapt to changing markets rarely stay in business. Whatever your business, you have to take user feedback into account and give customers what they want and need. The customer is not just always right; the customer is your reason for being.

You must always reply to user input and make changes based on trends, but it's important to recall that you don't have to do what every individual user demands. You cannot be all things to all people, and by trying to do so you'll leave your company, site, product, or service undifferentiated in the eyes of the public. How can you know when to implement a user's suggestion and when not to? The answer will be different for each business, but it is usually based on clear understanding of your target market and how your product or service meets the market's needs.

E-commerce management is all a loop: Know what your audience needs, build a site, launch and promote it; build up business and garner customer support and feedback; modify your product, service, and site based on your new understanding of your audience and their needs; and then rebuild, relaunch, and so on.

Buzzwords come and go. Trends swell and recede. You can ride the crest or fall behind. The real promise in e-commerce is that those who stay close to their customers can compete and succeed. To win in e-commerce, you must put in place a keenly strategic, practical business plan but be flexible in the face of change. You must be able to identify opportunity, be first to market, and be the best at what you do. You must harness the technology you need to support smart business solutions. And you must create a website that's of deep and lasting consequence to those who use it.

Appendix

Supporting Your Business with an Intranet or Extranet

You can use many of the same technologies that are used to create publicly accessible websites to create an _intranet_ (an internal website for communication and collaboration among employees) or an _extranet_ (a secure external website for communicating with vendors, buyers, or partners). Increasingly, intranets are becoming integral to the infrastructure of many companies; they are much less expensive to build than private networks and can help streamline processes, procedures, and the dissemination of information. Intranets and extranets often result in a fast and astonishingly high return on investment (ROI). CMPnet (_www.cmpnet.com_) has reported that leveraging existing web development infrastructure (to create an intranet or extranet, for example) can result in an initial ROI of 1000 percent or more! This sort of result has been widely reported; in fact, according to a Computer Economics (_www.computereconomics.com_) study, 78 percent of surveyed companies that had launched extranets experienced returns equal to or in excess of their investments.

Among the many benefits companies report when they implement intranets and extranets are the following:

- Better communication between users and the individuals and organizations they regularly interact with

- Reduction in paperwork

- Streamlining of processes and procedures

- Better use of human resources (HR) and other personnel through employee self-service

- Increase in loyalty of customers and business associates

Underlying the key advantage here is that you can establish a *knowledge base* (a collection of experience and information about processes and initiatives that are of significance to a company). The intranet or extranet will then allow the appropriate people access to that knowledge base.

An intranet empowers employees in much the same way that a FAQ empowers customers: An intranet provides a tool for keeping employees informed and allows them to quickly locate information without having to call on others. For example, many HR "events" are routine inquiries that eat up valuable HR staff time; each event costs a company roughly the same as a customer service event. If an answer is provided electronically rather than face-to-face, costs are dramatically lowered. As a comparison, an interaction that costs one dollar face-to-face might cost 10 cents by phone and less than 3 cents via website-based or intranet-based employee self-service. Further, an intranet allows information such as the employee handbook to be updated quickly and easily without requiring the reprinting and redistribution of the information to all employees.

Note

If your organization is small and the employees are all based in the same place, you probably don't need an intranet. A simple network will allow you to share resources, and you'll probably communicate effectively via e-mail and face-to-face conversation. However, if you work with virtual teams or have a decentralized organization or if your company has expanded beyond 50 employees, you might find an intranet invaluable. Similarly, an extranet is of more value to larger companies with a broad base of associates that require frequent interaction.

What Are Intranets and Extranets?

An intranet is simply a website created for the internal use of an organization. It uses the same general technologies as the public Internet but is accessible only to employees or authorized agents of the organization. The language used on the intranet might differ from the language used to communicate to the public, and sometimes the visual branding on the company's public website isn't carried through as extensively on the intranet. Users access the site with a web browser just as they would a public website. An intranet is "protected" from the outside world by a firewall. (For more information about firewalls, see Chapter 10.)

An extranet, by contrast, is accessible to authorized off-site users, including people and organizations with whom the company does business. Only users who have been given a valid username and password can use the extranet. Even then, some users might have their access limited to specific sections of the extranet. For example, buyers might have access only to their own account information, sales representatives working in the field might have access to their accounts, and receptionists logging in from home to check e-mail probably won't have access to financial information.

Typical Uses of Intranets and Extranets

The basic goal of intranets and extranets is to facilitate communication and workflow. In a typical scenario, HR information is placed on an intranet so that employees can look up information in a snap. For example, an employee who wants information about benefits can access it without going to an HR professional and can access it 24 hours a day. Reports, white papers, software manuals, and website style guides can be placed online as well. All employees can benefit from this legacy of wisdom, which can help them focus more of their time and energy on the productive aspects of their jobs. Other examples of shareable information include training schedules, newsletters, vendor information, and internal job postings.

Consider the following examples of the material various departments can place on an intranet:

- **Human resources** Procedures and policies related to hiring and firing, orientation and training, benefits (medical and dental plans, vacation, pension, 401K, and stock options), grievances, and drug and alcohol use; employee records (which can be made available only to a select group or to each employee individually to update his or her own record, such as when a change of address occurs); and downloadable forms for insurance enrollment, vacation requests, and changes to tax status or pension plans.

- **Sales and marketing** Product information (prices, specs, and manufacturing or delivery schedules), information on new marketing initiatives, advertising schedules, press releases, "best practices" sales advice, and customer leads. (You can also link authorized business associates to internal systems.)

- **Product development** Documents and charts relating to research, planning, and project status; schedules and timelines maintained via group and individual calendars; contact information for team members working on a project; and discussion groups or message boards for direct communication. An electronic whiteboard or other collaborative software can allow a group to work together despite being separated geographically; this software can be available for download via the intranet.

- **Customer service** Reports of issues, problems, or customer service events; problem-tracking information; price and product information; policies about returns and exchanges or service agreements; scripts and training materials for customer service representatives; and links to a knowledge base.

- **Management** "Managers' Tool Kit" applications that offer a system for processing new employees, conducting reviews, granting raises and promotions, and processing terminations. Some companies use the intranet for electronic employee pay stubs, dispensing with paper pay stubs entirely.

- **Information Services (IS), also known as Information Technology (IT)** Internal technical support via online documentation, FAQs, and e-mail; lists of company-approved software that employees can download from the intranet; and computer-based training (CBT) systems that allow for self-paced study of new software.

- **General** Job postings and procedures for applying for in-company transfers; employee directories (with a search engine); organizational charts for the company or department; and company or department newsletters.

An intranet can facilitate the exchange of information and sharing of resources within and between departments. Employees, team members, or business associates can be encouraged to post their Microsoft Word documents, Microsoft Excel spreadsheets, Microsoft Visio drawings (such as organization charts), Microsoft PowerPoint presentations, or Microsoft Project timelines to the intranet. In a more innovative example, a product group might post a dozen different packaging proposals to the intranet so that employees can vote for their favorite.

Former intranet site manager Maureen Nelson reports that where she worked, webmasters responsible for a wide range of sites met weekly to discuss issues and share strategies. Because the group was geographically scattered, the meetings were conducted by conference call and any material presented at the meeting was later posted to the intranet for those who missed the meeting. Maureen says, "All attendees were required to 'sign in' over the intranet so meeting leaders could tell who had attended. As people signed in, their e-mail addresses were made available so everyone could contact each other after the meeting to discuss things further."

The examples are endless. As your company grows, you can place a company "library" on the intranet where designated employees can conduct research or download PDF files or electronic books that the company has licensed for use. A company store can offer employees special discounts; a company travel center can facilitate travel planning for executives, sales representatives, or other frequent travelers; a company directory can offer maps and directions to various locations or campuses; and an online registration system can offer employees the opportunity to sign up for training sessions that are then conducted either online or offline.

As with intranets, the uses and applications of an extranet can range from A to Z and back again. For example, a temporary employment agency that has outgrown the capacity of its paper-based payroll system can build an extranet using Microsoft systems and technologies including Microsoft Internet Information Services (IIS), Microsoft SQL Server, and Microsoft Internet Explorer. Employees and client companies can then use these technologies to log in time sheets and other information, enabling the agency to handle its growth while cutting costs and payroll processing time dramatically.

Note

According to industry projections, by 2002 all mobile and wireless devices will be able to access the Web. As wireless access becomes more widely adopted, you might want to provide much of your intranet or extranet content via cell phone, PDA (Personal Digital Assistant), and other mobile devices.

Assessing Costs and Return on Investment

The cost of creating an intranet or extranet can vary widely depending on the site's purpose, the technologies used, and whether you have to build it from the ground up. If you can piggyback on existing systems built for your public website and if the intranet or extranet is simple, the costs can be negligible. The process can be as simple as converting some company documents to HTML and posting them on a password-protected portion of your web server. Using the design templates created for your public website will also keep costs to a minimum.

If your intranet or extranet endeavor is more complex or if you have to build it from the ground up (meaning that a back end and a design have to be generated), the development and implementation costs will be comparable to those of a public website of the same size and complexity. To find out more about the range of possibilities, see the discussion in Chapter 2 about the expenses involved in building a website.

As you consider ROI, ask yourself how the intranet or extranet will genuinely support or enhance your business. It should provide you with some combination of the following benefits:

- Improved competitive edge, perhaps through shared knowledge
- Increased sales resulting from faster access to information required to support and close a sale
- Reduction in labor, production, or distribution costs resulting from the automation of everyday functions
- Increased productivity through access to information, resources, or tools or through online access to data traditionally available in another form
- Faster time to market
- Ability to share more information with vendors or partners
- More effective customer support
- New and more practical support for collaboration among virtual or decentralized teams

Quantifying the potential returns on your investment based on objective data can be challenging. (See the sidebar "Getting Support from Upper Management" later in this chapter.) However, many companies report that they see evidence of return very quickly after the intranet or extranet is launched. Still, keep in mind that an intranet or extranet, once launched, is likely to require as much care and upkeep as a public website.

Note

The immediate cost savings as a result of launching an intranet or extranet can be dramatic, but in the months and years that follow, those savings might no longer be seen as savings because they'll be absorbed into the company's day-to-day operations. At that point, managers of intranets or extranets must document and evangelize their contributions to the company's success, as described later in this chapter.

Management Considerations

As with the building and management of a public website, preproduction planning is vital to the success of an intranet or extranet. In this case, a great deal of the planning will concern internal management of the intranet or extranet site. To begin with, you must specify a vision and purpose for the endeavor because, as with other company efforts, the intranet or extranet will be subject to the varying agendas of departments and individuals. You must also determine who will be responsible for (who will "own") the day-to-day management of the site. How will the site be focused in its early phases? How will it grow? And of all the groups that might be served by the site, which must be served first? You simply cannot serve all groups at once; it's best to choose one or two to participate in a pilot program as you develop your plan. Then you can expand your efforts later. HR and perhaps product development are generally good candidates for a fledgling intranet. Once your initial efforts are in place and the kinks are ironed out, you can expand to include other groups. But even then, you cannot be everything to all groups; in most cases, you must focus on doing as much good for as many beneficiaries as possible within the parameters of your budget, of the available technologies, and of the company's overall business priorities.

Note

To boost intranet or extranet use and maximize results, you must constantly evangelize. Let employees know that the intranet or extranet is there. Add its URL to print and e-mail documents wherever appropriate. If employees or associates hear a different on-hold message than consumers do when they call within the company, add the URL to that message. Send out a monthly e-mail newsletter telling employees what's new on the intranet or describing to business associates (who have opted in to the newsletter) what's new on the extranet. Include links to new or featured pages.

> ## *Getting Support from Upper Management*
>
> In order to get adequate funding for an intranet or extranet endeavor, you must have the support of upper management. Management's first concern will rightfully be ROI, which can be difficult to measure. For example, savings related to no longer distributing printed information might be evident, but the savings in employee time is less immediately quantifiable. Good indicators of the success of an intranet or extranet can include the site's traffic and the volume of e-mail the site receives. (See the section titled "Measuring Success" later in this chapter as well as the discussion in Chapter 13 about assessing the success of a public website.)
>
> Always tie your effort into the business. If the site doesn't support the people who support the business, it will be seen as a cost center (an unprofitable drain on revenue). Place high-level executives on the planning committee to make sure the intranet or extranet's business relevance is addressed. This will avoid the uncomfortable necessity of "making up" a business justification later. And make sure that management is leading the intranet or extranet movement, not following it. An "underground" effort might be viewed with suspicion or seen as a hobby by the company owners or executives.

Site Planning Considerations

Information on an intranet can be organized by department, by professional interest, by function, or by extracurricular interest. All the HR information can go in an HR area or site; an internal publication of interest to all the IS people can be posted in an IS area; a newsletter for managers can be placed in a cross-departmental Management area; and information about the softball team, the safety group, the diversity group, or the company branch of Toastmasters can go in an Extracurricular area. On an extranet, information can similarly be divided according to the needs of the business associates the extranet serves.

You must determine who the content providers will be. Will all departments post to the intranet at will in a decentralized approach? Will one central, authorized person or team be assigned to act as site manager? Once you make these decisions, you must also specify standards for publishing or posting to the site. (See Chapter 11.) Is a standard look and feel or editorial tone called for? In the case of multiple-site intranets or extranets, will each site be allowed to have its own look? Will all users have the same browser (freeing you from the multitude of design decisions required if you serve an audience that has several versions or a variety of browsers)? Research from IDC (*www.idc.com*) has found that most companies rely on internal expertise in building their intranet and most impose a corporate standard for web browsers used. Most companies are also moving away from a top-down, hierarchical approach to intranet management in favor of a more horizontal, collaborative approach. However, what works for others might not work for your company; make your strategic decisions based on your business goals and your own company culture.

Many of the decisions you'll have to make in setting up your intranet or extranet will revolve around how information is managed. It's been said, in fact, that building an intranet or extranet is 80 percent process and 20 percent technology.

Tip

If you have more than one website on your intranet (in order to serve the needs of various internal groups), you might want to establish one portal or home page that serves as an entry point to the other sites. The portal will make it easier for staff to navigate around a group of sites and will provide room for the overall intranet effort to expand through the addition of more sites.

Creating Consistent, Clear Policies

Rules might be made to be broken, but they do provide people with a set of parameters to work within. In that sense, rules help keep the peace. Providing your staff with written policies about key aspects of your intranet or extranet will keep everyone on track. It will also help to avert challenges from individuals and groups within the company who have special agendas. At times, you might want to grant privileges or bend the rules for special circumstances, but in general, applying guidelines consistently will help everyone avoid unpleasant surprises.

(continued)

Creating Consistent, Clear Policies *(continued)*

Here are examples of policies that will clarify roles and procedures:

- **Access policy**   This states who (among the employees or business associates served by the intranet or extranet) gets access to which information or areas of information. You might have to implement a certain amount of training and orientation to ensure that those who have access know how to use the applications.

- **Publishing policy**   This defines the strategic purpose and vision for the intranet or extranet. Without a publishing policy, your intranet or extranet can become a chaotic jumble of information that slows rather than facilitates communication. Navigation will be awkward, and you'll give an impression of weak credibility. The publishing policy should also address who can publish and what can be published. (Not everything that *can* be published should be—you might not want your quarterly profit and loss statements posted for all employees to see.) Appoint an "editor-in-chief" or site manager to make sure the publishing policy is followed.

- **Content policies**   These prevent content from quickly becoming redundant, conflicting, and outdated. You can empower departments within your company to publish their own information on the intranet or extranet. Indeed, they can each have their own sites, if that is advisable. Remember, however, that you must provide parameters. Should they use the standard look-and-feel or editorial guidelines? Should they use only certain technologies? Should they post only certain types of content? What is the review and approval process? Ultimately, someone will have to watch over the efforts of the various departments or offer technical support. At the very least, communication will be required to ensure that the same information is not posted and updated by different teams and at different times. A single portal to common information and to the various departmental sites, along with clear publishing policies, can be key to avoiding such problems.

Creating Consistent, Clear Policies (*continued*)

- **Security policy**   This will put employees, business associates, and your network administrator at ease. Some employees might worry, for example, that an intranet that asks them to enter their social security numbers in an online form is not adequately secure; someone must maintain security and notify employees that security measures are in place. On an extranet, make sure that those accessing password-protected areas are able to reach only the servers they're authorized to reach.

As with all guidelines, policies about access, publishing, content, and security will evolve with time, but thinking them through at the outset will keep you from scrambling to address problems (and force compliance) later.

Note that you'll also need to make clear who is in charge of creating and enforcing the policies. You might appoint one person to be accountable, or you might go with a cross-functional or cross-departmental team whose members all have a stake in the site and who will therefore develop an appreciation of its potential.

Caution

As always, it's important to manage expectations. Do this both up and down the ladder. It's typical for people new to online media to first dismiss its potential and then, when they see what's possible, to expect the world. At first, HR might see only the benefit of posting job openings, but when they get a whiff of what others are doing, they might request a pie-in-the-sky list ranging from online job application processing to video interviewing over the intranet! In such a case, a little communication is necessary; the limitations of available technologies, the company's overall agenda, and the current priorities must be explained clearly to the newly enthusiastic supporters of the intranet or extranet.

Technology Considerations

The technology issues involved in building an intranet or extranet are similar to those for building a public website; again, what differs is mainly the level of security and the method of restricting access. An intranet or extranet comprises a back end and perhaps middleware. (See Chapter 10.) It has a front end that can look like a public website and is accessed via a browser. The design of its pages is usually bound by the same general limitations of HTML and graphics as a public website. But if you require all employees to use the same web browser, or if you create your intranet using the Microsoft Office workgroup website features, you can avoid basing the design of your intranet pages on these limitations.

Tip

The Microsoft Office 60-Minute Intranet Kit makes creating a workgroup website easy. See the upcoming section titled "Boosting Productivity with a Workgroup Website" to find out more.

To work effectively with intranet or extranet developers, you need a basic understanding of servers, databases, ISPs, and security. Your developer will talk about intranet-specific and extranet-specific concepts such as authorization, authentication, encryption, and firewalls. These concepts are described in Chapter 10. As a manager, you don't need a developer's level of knowledge but you do need to address some basic strategic questions, which will be similar to those introduced in Chapter 1. Here are some strategic issues you'll want to consider:

- What you want the site to do—for the employees it serves if it's an intranet or for the business associates it serves if it's an extranet.

- How you'll measure success; in other words, how will you know if the intranet or extranet is succeeding? What will it have to accomplish for your company?

- Who will "own" the intranet or extranet? In a small company, the intranet, extranet, and public websites will probably all be managed by the same individual or group. In a mid-sized company, a specific team might be responsible for the intranet or extranet, perhaps within the department that's most directly associated with the site's goals or purpose. A larger company might have multiple departmental intranet or extranet sites, with each department managing its own site. In that case, overall strategy will be set at the corporate level, with a group or committee consisting of representatives from the various departments assigned to develop overarching policies for the sites.

Note

Extranet sites are usually owned by the person or department that interacts most with the business associates who use the extranet. For example, an extranet site devoted to supporting sales will be managed by the sales department, while an extranet site supporting product development might be managed by the research and development team.

Your choice of hardware and technologies will be integral to security as well as to the overall effort. Standard questions in this area include: Who will make regular backups of the site and its information? How will scalability (the ability of the site to grow as needed) be ensured? Who will monitor usage and the server's load capacity? And who will decide when it's time to upgrade or add servers? You or your technology staff must determine what software and hardware to use, as well as what staff will be needed. Will you train existing technology staff or hire new people? If you train existing staff, remember not to spread them too thin. Unless your company is very small, your main IT person simply can't also be your intranet or extranet webmaster. Each of those jobs can easily be a full-time responsibility.

Note

Whether you hire new people or use employees you already have, remember that they'll have to be trained and retrained as tools and technologies evolve. Sending them to a class or a conference will allow them to buff up their skills and network with their peers, from whom they can pick up time-saving tips. Buying them more sophisticated software allows them to work faster with better tools and produce a more professional-looking site. The Web changes quickly, so be prepared to invest in this group continuously.

You'll also have to address how people will access the intranet or extranet. You need to know whether your business associates—not to mention your staff—actually have computers, browsers, and Internet access. If not, how will those people be served? If yours is a company that's not well served by providing all employees with computers and Internet access, you might instead provide one or more general-use computers that staff members can use on their lunch hour or during key times of the year, such as open enrollment periods for insurance. One manufacturing company was so convinced of the long-term cost savings of an intranet that they bought PCs for every employee. Even factory workers could access the intranet from home—all they needed was a password. Another manufacturing company placed a single computer in a kiosk on its plant floor for workers to use.

You must also consider how the intranet or extranet will be connected to legacy (already existing) systems, including databases and order-fulfillment systems that supported your core, brick-and-mortar business. On the HR intranet, will employees be able to access their own records? Will they only be able to look at them, or will they be able to update them and see their changes reflected in the records in the legacy system? Think about integrating the extranet with the customer service call center, if you have one. Some companies require their business associates to use the company extranet to conduct business. For example, a printing company might require its clients to upload print-ready files to the company's extranet, or a car parts dealer providing parts to smaller auto supply retailers might require that all orders be placed via the extranet. In either case, the status of the project or order can also be tracked via the extranet.

Tip

Using technology such as Microsoft Active Server Pages, developers can create web page front ends on some legacy systems. Whether your legacy system can be converted in this way will depend on its age, what type of database it uses, and other factors. Ask a qualified developer for advice.

Security Considerations

Security is of enormous concern for a site whose content is private employee material or confidential company information. As the executive or manager who oversees management of the site, you'll want to ensure that appropriate security policies and systems are in place. Enabling and implementing security measures is the responsibility of developers or technology staff, but making key decisions about the levels of security that are necessary should be a joint management/technology process.

You will have to specify, for example, who has access to what information on the site. Will there be different levels of security for various types of information? In one case, a company determined that three levels of access were necessary just for the HR site. The broadest access was for all employees, allowing them access to the same policies and procedures found in the employee handbook; medium-restriction access was provided to HR specialists, allowing them to access information on how to handle employee issues such as hiring and termination as well as how to communicate about a recent merger; and the most restricted access was for staffing specialists, allowing them to access information about which departments were cutting back on staff and which were recruiting. Security policies must be documented, communicated, and enforced in order for the intranet or extranet to succeed.

Tip

If you're using IIS as your web server software and users of the intranet are using Internet Explorer as their web browser, security can be both simple to implement and powerful. Users can log in to the intranet and the network in one step, and the security established for your network will carry over to your intranet without much additional effort.

Boosting Productivity with a Workgroup Website

Using the Microsoft Office web collaboration features, you can build a workgroup website that will be a key asset in improving team performance. Microsoft provides a kit on the Microsoft Office Update website called the 60-Minute Intranet Kit that makes this task easy. You start by using the Microsoft FrontPage wizards to walk you through setting up the site—once it's running, your team will be able to share documents, communicate ideas, collaborate on projects, and synthesize information much as they would with a higher-priced custom-built intranet. With Office and the Intranet Kit, your team will be able to accomplish the following:

- Publish documents and presentations (created with Word, Excel, or PowerPoint, for example) directly to the workgroup site
- Work with live data to accomplish such tasks as timesheet tracking, issue resolution, inventory, and sales analysis

- Collaborate in team discussions or meetings
- Receive e-mail notification when a document has been updated or modified
- Track team news, project milestones, and company or department events

The kit includes templates for sales and marketing, information systems (IS), human resources, product development, and other departments. The interface is also customizable. You will need the right back-end systems in place, but tutorials are available to guide you in setting up, running, and maintaining the site.

Measuring Success

Like any other online venture—and indeed any business venture—the intranet or extranet will be expected to meet goals. These goals are likely to be set in a business or project plan; they might be "soft" goals (such as improved internal communications, improved processes, quicker time-to-market, or a boost in customer loyalty) or "hard goals" (such as revenue produced from new customers).

Assessing success based on soft goals is not the easiest task. To address this, you can survey employees or business associates to find out whether the site meets their needs. Ask them whether they have access to the intranet or extranet, whether they use it and how often, what other sites they visit most in the course of their work, and what kind of information or applications they would like to see on the intranet or extranet. One large company originally had a "company store" in the form of a print catalog, but when employees said that they'd prefer to buy over the intranet, the company added an e-commerce sales component to the internal site.

Soft benefits also won't win the day when budget time rolls around. A measurement of hard benefits, such as reduced costs, increased revenue, or growth in the customer base, is more convincing. Traffic measurements can suggest an intranet or extranet's usefulness, in that a highly trafficked intranet or extranet is clearly one that is meeting the needs of its users. (See Chapter 13 for a discussion of measuring traffic.)

In the end, in order to be seen as a business asset rather than as a cost center, an intranet or extranet (just like a public website) must achieve specific, attainable goals. Over the years that follow the launch of the intranet or extranet, it (again like the public website) must be maintained and refocused as necessary to align and realign with the company's objectives.

Glossary

acquiring bank   A bank that handles merchant accounts, allowing companies to receive payments (from customers) made via credit cards. *See also* issuing bank; merchant account.

affiliate program   A system in which website owners display an ad, link, logo, or template to direct traffic or sales to another website in return for compensation, which can be fee-based, commission-based (with payment per clickthrough or per order), barter-based, or some combination of the above.

American Standard Code for Information Interchange (ASCII)   Simple text that includes no formatting. ASCII text looks essentially the same on most computers.

anchor   An HTML tag that defines a text or image link. Also known as HREF because the <A> (anchor tag) demands an HREF (hypertext reference) attribute.

anonymous FTP   A feature of File Transfer Protocol (FTP) that allows users to transfer files between a server and a local computer without a unique user name and password. *See also* File Transfer Protocol (FTP).

applet   A "small" application (or program) created to exist and work within a web page or another program. Applets can add extra functionality to web pages; for example, an interactive calendar or puzzle might be created as an applet.

application service provider (ASP)   A third-party company that provides services and software to client companies from a central location. ASPs allow companies to outsource their technology needs, ranging from business services to website services to high-end IT solutions.

ASCII   *See* American Standard Code for Information Interchange (ASCII).

audience penetration   The percentage of a potential audience that a site, service, or product is reaching.

authentication   The process of identifying a user to a secure system, usually by requiring the user to provide a valid, known user name and password.

backbone   Any of several high-speed networks that are the main arteries of the Internet.

back end   For a website, the database, the transaction system, and the scripts that work together to provide website functionality.

bandwidth 1. The capacity of a communications channel such as a network or a modem, measured by the amount of data that can be sent through at one time. 2. (slang) The capacity of a person or company to get something done based on available resources.

bitmap An image file in which the image is made up of dots.

branding Establishing an immediately recognizable identity for a company, product, service, or website.

brick-and-mortar (slang) Describes a "real-world" business with a physical location as opposed to an online (or digital) business. An e-commerce site might have a brick-and-mortar component, however, as Barnes & Noble does; in that case, it might be called a *click-and-mortar* business. *See also* click-and-mortar; dot com.

broadband Describes very high-bandwidth access to the Internet. This sort of access enables users to experience high-speed Internet access and high-quality, seamless streaming media.

broad market A general target audience for a site, product, or service. *See also* vertical market.

business-to-business (b2b) Describes a business whose clients or customers are other businesses rather than consumers.

business-to-business-and-consumer (b2bc) Describes a business whose clients or customers are other businesses as well as consumers.

business-to-consumer (b2c) Describes a business whose clients or customers are consumers.

cable modem A device that uses television cable (the same cable that carries cable TV service to homes and businesses) to connect to the Internet. The use of television cable allows for more bandwidth than is possible with the ordinary telephone lines a dial-up modem uses. *See also* bandwidth.

cache 1. To temporarily store data such as image files or web pages. 2. A place (a portion of a computer's memory, for example) where such storage occurs.

certificate Data that cannot be forged and that uniquely identifies a user to a server or vice versa. Certificates are provided by certification authorities. *See also* certification authority; secure transaction.

certification authority An organization that issues certificates and ensures their authenticity. *See also* certificate.

channel In content, thematically related material grouped by topic (travel, news, finance, and so forth) and presented on a website or sometimes via push technology. In marketing and sales, the company's various sales outlets. *See also* push technology.

chat To communicate via typed messages that are received and can be responded to in real time (meaning almost immediately).

click-and-mortar Describes a company that has both a brick-and-mortar presence and an online presence. *See also* brick-and-mortar; dot com.

click rate A measurement of how often users click on a given link. Also called *click-through rate*.

click-through The act of clicking a link in a website. A click-through occurs when a user clicks a link or a banner ad, for example, and is transported to the site it represents. *See also* click rate.

client In technology, a computer that receives data via its connection to a server. *See also* server.

community 1. A feeling of identification and bonding with a group based on shared affinities and a common purpose. 2. A group of people who gather to exchange ideas and information about shared interests frequently enough to identify and feel a bond with the group.

compressed Describes data that has been condensed, packed, or "zipped." WinZip and other utilities allow users to compress files to conserve storage space and enable faster transfer of files. In addition, compression is often part of the process of preparing audio and video files for use on the Web.

configure 1. To set up programs, applications, or computer systems. 2. To make programs, applications, or computer systems work together.

consumer-to-consumer (c2c) Describes a website that enables consumers to interact with each other directly. An auction website is an example. *See also* business-to-consumer (b2c); business-to-business (b2b); business-to-business-and-consumer (b2bc).

content Everything a website contains, including, but not limited to, its text and images. All the offerings of a website as well as the material that enables users to use the website are part of the site's content. *See also* macrocontent; microcontent.

content assets The items of material (text, images, and so on) that are contained in a website. *See also* content.

conversion-to-sales rate Describes the number of actual purchases that result from contacts (electronic or otherwise) with customers.

cookie An electronic "note" stored on a user's computer to hold information specific to a website such as the user's passwords or preferences.

copyright The right of ownership to a Work (such as a document, art, or music) and the right to make copies and profit from the Work. *See also* public domain; Work.

cost per thousand (CPM) A pricing method applied to advertising space on a website. For example, if a website is selling ad space at a CPM of $8, the ad space buyer is promised 1000 impressions for $8. *See also* impression.

CPM *See* cost per thousand (CPM).

crawler A software program that travels the Internet, following links and gathering data about websites to be compiled into a database that will form the basis of a search engine. Also known as a *spider*, *wanderer*, or *robot*.

cross-platform Describes a computer program that works on more than one operating system.

cross-sell The offering or promotion of a product or service that's related to the main product or service requested by or shown to a customer. *See also* upsell.

customer acquisition cost A calculation that describes the expense of getting a new customer. This number is especially meaningful when compared to the amount that customer spends. *See also* customer relationship management (CRM); customer retention cost; lifetime customer value (LCV).

customer relationship management (CRM) A business strategy that involves anticipating, understanding, and responding to a business venture's current and potential customers' needs and wants. CRM software solutions provide companies with the technological means to implement this business strategy.

customer retention cost A calculation that describes the expense of converting a new customer into a repeat customer or keeping the new customer's business through a service cycle. *See also* customer acquisition cost; customer relationship management (CRM); lifetime customer value (LCV).

data Distinct facts or pieces of numerical or textual particulars that when combined in a meaningful way become information. For example, a first name and a last name are both data. When they are combined and applied to an actual person, they become information that identifies the person.

database An organized, searchable set of records containing data. In terms of e-commerce, a database might contain records of all your customers, their contact information, and their latest purchases. *See also* data; flat-file database; relational database.

database call A script (coding) that retrieves data, text, an image, or some other element from a database for some specific use (for example, as an element to be displayed on a web page).

dedicated Describes a line, server, or other piece of computer-associated equipment that has only one purpose. A dedicated line, for example, might be a phone line that leads only to your PC (or modem).

deliverable The item to be provided to a client by a vendor. For example, when a client commissions the design of a website, the deliverable might be just a design or it might be the fully functional website.

development server *See* staging server.

DHTML *See* Dynamic HTML (DHTML).

dial-up The type of connection that occurs when a modem dials a phone number to access the Internet.

Digital Subscriber Line (DSL)   A technology that provides fast online access via existing telephone lines. DSL is faster than ISDN (which also runs on existing telephone lines) but not as fast as T1 access, which requires special cabling. *See also* Integrated Services Digital Network (ISDN).

directory   1. A portion of an organizational system roughly similar to a folder in a filing cabinet. Sometimes a directory is known as a *folder*. 2. An organized index or listing of websites or other resources that is always browsable and sometimes searchable (meaning that a search feature is provided, enabling you to find what you seek with more immediacy). *See also* index.

discount rate   The percentage of each credit card transaction that's kept by the bank as a service fee.

discussion group   A forum for interaction among multiple users via e-mail. Discussion groups can be centered around a single theme or group of topics. They might be small (half a dozen participants) or large (hundreds or thousands of participants).

disintermediation   The process of cutting out the middle person. This occurs when a company (a manufacturer, for example) sells directly to its end customers via a website and no longer needs the distributors and retailers that once acted as vital links in getting the product to consumers.

dithering   A technique used to create the illusion of shades of color by varying a pattern of dots that make up the color. Dithered images look blurrier and load more slowly than nondithered images. *See also* Joint Photographic Experts Group (JPEG); graphics interchange format (GIF).

DNS   *See* Domain Name System (DNS).

domain name   A unique name that identifies a computer or a set of computers on the Internet. Examples of domain names include *microsoft.com* and *tauberkienan.com*. *See also* Domain Name System (DNS).

Domain Name System (DNS)   The system through which domain names are assigned.

dot com   (slang) Describes a business that is online and has no traditional or brick-and-mortar counterpart—for example, Amazon.com. *See also* brick-and-mortar; click-and-mortar.

download   To transfer files from another computer to your computer.

down time   An interval during which a computer, network, database, or other system is not functioning. *See also* lag time.

DSL   *See* Digital Subscriber Line (DSL).

dynamic content   Content that appears on a web page as the result of database calls or scripts pulling the content from the database in which it is stored and assembling it for display on the page. Also called *dynamically generated content*.

Dynamic HTML (DHTML)   A specialized type of HTML coding that enables items on a web page to change their look or behavior in response to a user's actions. *See* Hypertext Markup Language (HTML).

encryption   A method of disguising or protecting a message or any other data (such as credit card numbers or the specifics of a transaction) to prevent the unauthorized reading or use of it.

extended partnership   A sales model in which businesses form strategic partnerships to leverage their assets and add value and functionality for customers.

Extensible Markup Language (XML)   A technology that allows developers to create their own markup tags so they are not limited to the tags available in HTML and to the functionality HTML allows. Content that is marked up in XML can be displayed in a variety of media; for example, it can be published in print, online, and on CD-ROM, all without the necessity of recoding the content for each type of media.

extranet   A secured website (or portion of a website) that is available only to authorized people outside a company's firewall. Extranets can be used, for example, by a company's business partners or vendors, or by salespeople on the road who need to access confidential information. *See also* firewall; intranet.

fair use   The privilege (not the right) to use a small portion of a copyrighted Work for the purpose of reviewing that Work, teaching, reporting events, or creating a parody. *See also* Work.

FAQ   *See* frequently asked questions (FAQ).

field   In a database or on a form, the space provided for entering data.

file transfer   The movement of a file from one computer to another over a network or via a modem.

File Transfer Protocol (FTP)   A standard, agreed-upon way for files to be transferred quickly from one computer to another over the Internet. *See also* anonymous FTP.

firewall   A security system that creates an electronic barrier to protect part or all of an organization's network and its computers from access by outsiders.

flame   An unfriendly written attack against someone in an electronic discussion group. (A *flame war* occurs when both parties engage in and continue such an exchange, perhaps even inspiring others in the newsgroup or message area to take sides.)

flat-file database   A simple database with only one table; usually that is a plain text file. *See also* relational database.

footer   The text or links that appear at the bottom of a web page (usually containing the copyright notice, for example). The same footer is often repeated on every page in the website.

frames Panes within the larger window of a web page. Each frame is actually a distinct web page and can have its own scroll bar and other navigational features; each can also contain text, images, and other media as well as links.

freeware Programs that are distributed free of charge by those who developed them. *See also* shareware.

frequently asked questions (FAQ) A list of questions and answers intended to help people help themselves. A well-constructed and easily accessible FAQ can be a powerful customer service tool.

front end 1. The interface of a web page or program; the part the user sees and interacts with directly. 2. The software that provides an interface to a back end. For example, a web browser acts as the front end to a website or a transaction system.

FTP *See* File Transfer Protocol (FTP).

fulfillment The last part of processing an online order, including the logistics of distributing, warehousing, and shipping.

GIF *See* graphics interchange format (GIF).

GIF89 A method of saving a GIF file to allow a transparent background in the image. The advantage of using a transparent background in the image is that the background does not have to match the background of the web page on which it's placed. GIF89s can be stacked to create animations. Another term for GIF89 is GIF89a. *See also* graphics interchange format (GIF).

graphics interchange format (GIF) A file format used for computer graphics. GIFs (pronounced *jifs*), like JPEGs, can be saved at various qualities; however, the higher the quality (the more colors they include), the slower they will appear on a web page. GIFs can also be animated. Inside an animated GIF, several images are stacked in what amounts to a flipbook so that they appear to be one animation. If you look at animated GIFs with a plain graphics viewer, the animation is not apparent. *See also* GIF89; Joint Photographic Experts Group (JPEG).

hack To manipulate a program or system "behind the scenes," presumably to make improvements or to find out how it works. Hacking is not necessarily malicious, although malicious hacking is of great concern and should be prevented.

hard-deliverable A product that must be shipped, such as food or a computer, as opposed to a product that can be downloaded, such as music or software.

hit A request to a web server for data, a file, or an object. Because each web page might comprise dozens of files (text, graphics, animations, and so on), and what looks like a single piece of art might comprise several image files, counting hits does not indicate the number of visitors to a website. *See also* impression.

home page The front page or main page of a website; also known as a *default page* or *index page*. Note that a visit to a website doesn't have to start at the home page but can actually start anywhere in any site.

host To house a server or store a website. *See also* server.

HTML *See* Hypertext Markup Language (HTML).

HTTP *See* Hypertext Transfer Protocol (HTTP).

HTTPS *See* Secure HTTP (HTTPS).

Hypertext Markup Language (HTML) The coding used to create web pages.

Hypertext Transfer Protocol (HTTP) The agreed-upon, standard way for web documents to be transferred across the Internet.

ICE *See* Information & Content Exchange (ICE).

IIS *See* Internet Information Services (IIS).

image map A complex image, sometimes large enough to fill one whole screen of a web page, that includes several areas of clickable links. The first image maps actually were maps; they offered links to information about the places on the map.

impression One look at a web page or banner ad by a user. The number of impressions indicates how many times the page, ad, or website appeared. Also referred to as a *page view*. *See also* hit; unique user.

index 1. A data file that lists the information to be found in a specific directory. 2. To organize data according to specified criteria. 3. A website (also known as a directory) that lists in categories other websites and perhaps other Internet resources. Indexes are usually searchable as well as browsable. *See also* directory.

Information & Content Exchange (ICE) A protocol developed to enable the syndication of content. ICE is based on XML. *See also* Extensible Markup Language (XML).

inline Describes an item that appears directly on a web page. Graphics (or video or animation) that must be downloaded manually are not inline. *See also* inline image.

inline image A graphic in a web page that does not have to be downloaded manually to be viewed.

insourcing Jobbing out portions of a project to other departments within the same company or borrowing employees from other departments.

Integrated Services Digital Network (ISDN) A type of communications access that allows transmission of voice, data (such as the code that makes up web pages), and video via the ordinary telephone cables (digital or otherwise) that already lead into homes and businesses. With ISDN, you can have one line for voice and one or two lines for data; this is because ISDN allows two lines to operate over a single cable. ISDN is faster than a standard dial-up connection but not as fast as DSL or a cable modem.

intellectual property   A piece of work (code, art, a trademarked image, or product specifications, for example) that is intangible until it is fixed or made tangible through printing or some other method of recording. Intellectual property is owned by its creator unless ownership is transferred; it is also a business asset. *See also* copyright; trademark.

interface   The "face" a piece of software or website shows a user; the *front end* with which the user interacts. *See also* front end.

Internet Information Services (IIS) Microsoft web server software that runs on Microsoft Windows 2000 and Microsoft Windows NT.

Internet presence provider (IPP)   A company that provides hosting as well as some combination of content and design. *See also* Internet service provider (ISP).

Internet Protocol (IP)   An agreed-upon set of standards that allows computers to exchange data over telecommunications lines. IP is somewhat like the postal system in that a direct connection between sender and recipient is not required. Instead, when a file is requested from a server by a web browser, for example, the file is dropped into the system for delivery to the addressee (the requesting web browser). The system finds the correct addressee based on the addressee's IP address. *See also* IP address.

Internet service provider (ISP)   A company that provides access to the Internet but does not necessarily provide site design or content. *See also* Internet presence provider (IPP).

interstitial advertisement   An ad that appears in a separate browser window; often the appearance occurs between the time a user requests access to a web page and the moment the web page is actually displayed.

intranet   One or more connected websites contained wholly inside a company's firewall and made available only to authorized users whose computers are usually also within the firewall. Intranets can facilitate interdepartmental exchange and streamline human resources tasks by providing self-service for employees or team members. *See also* firewall; extranet.

IP   *See* Internet Protocol (IP).

IP address   A unique number assigned to a single computer on the Internet as an address. No two computers can share the same IP address at the same time, but Internet servers can rotate the IP address assigned to a set of computers.

IPP   *See* Internet presence provider (IPP).

ISDN   *See* Integrated Services Digital Network (ISDN).

ISP   *See* Internet service provider (ISP).

issuing bank   A bank that offers credit cards to consumers. *See also* acquiring bank.

Joint Photographic Experts Group (JPEG) A type of file format used for graphics. JPEGs (pronounced *jay-pegs*) can be very high resolution, can use many different colors, and compress very well. JPEGs are the file format of choice for photographs online. *See also* graphics interchange format (GIF).

JPEG *See* Joint Photographic Experts Group (JPEG).

knowledge base A collection of information or wisdom about a particular subject or technology.

lag time The interval that occurs between the time data is requested and the time it arrives; for example, the time between when you click a link and when the page that it is linked to appears.

LAN *See* local area network (LAN).

legacy system A computer, network, database, or other system that already exists or that an administrator "inherits" from an outgoing administrator.

liability Accountability—for example, to customers, co-owners, business affiliates, the government, and the public. False advertising, for instance, incurs liability that might result in legal repercussions.

libel Negative or false information about someone or something that is damaging. To be libelous, that information must be written or publicly broadcast. *See also* slander.

licensing The act of obtaining (usually for a fee) permission to use a Work, generally within specific guidelines such as length of time, types of use, and geographic location of the use. *See also* Work.

lifetime customer value (LCV) A calculation that refers to the cost of acquiring new customers, retaining them, and converting product interest into product purchases. *See also* customer acquisition cost; customer retention cost; customer relationship management (CRM).

local Describes something that is near you. The computer on your desk, for example, is local, as compared to a remote computer, such as a server, that is elsewhere. *See also* remote.

local area network (LAN) A number of computers (as few as two or as many as thousands) that are connected by cables, normally within a small geographical area. LANs enable the sharing of resources such as printers and software. *See also* network; wide area network (WAN).

log A data file on a server that lists events such as every instance of users accessing a web page.

look and feel The tone and style of a site, which is determined by the colors, fonts, graphics, and language used in it as well as the navigation and overall user experience.

lurker   Someone who only observes the conversations in a discussion group without contributing. It can be seen as courteous to lurk before joining a discussion group; this allows you to learn the group culture and avoid transgressions.

macrocontent   Large pieces of content, such as the blocks of text on a web page that contain the main message. *See also* content; microcontent.

mailing list   A compilation of e-mail addresses. An electronic discussion group that broadcasts e-mail messages to all of its participants can also be called a mailing list.

mail server   A computer that sends and receives e-mail for a group of users.

merchant account   A business bank account that accepts credit card payments from consumers.

microcontent   Small pieces of text and other content, such as error messages, the footer on a web page, the subject lines in e-mail messages, and so on. *See also* content; macrocontent.

middleware   Software that connects two distinct software programs, enabling them to work together.

moderated discussion   A discussion in which a specific person ensures that the conversation sticks to the stated topic, that administrative issues are handled, and even that disputes are resolved. In an unmoderated discussion, members regulate themselves. *See also* discussion group.

mouseover   An effect that occurs on a web page when the curser controlled by the mouse rolls over an item and the item changes its appearance. Mouseovers, also called *rollovers*, often occur in navigation bars or pop-up boxes, often to indicate a link.

multimedia   Describes the use of a variety of media (graphics, audio, video, and text) in combination within a document or a presentation.

NDA   *See* nondisclosure agreement (NDA).

network   A system in which a number of computers are cabled together to share software, printers, and other resources. *See also* local area network (LAN); wide area network (WAN).

network administrator   Someone who organizes, maintains, troubleshoots, and manages a network.

newbie   (slang) A user who is new to the Internet or to a specific part of the Internet. The term by itself is not usually derogatory.

nondisclosure agreement (NDA)   An agreement between signing parties specifying that confidential information disclosed in the course of doing business will not be revealed to others.

opt in   A method of gaining subscribers to a mailing list that allows potential subscribers to sign up. *See also* opt out.

opt out   A presumptuous and unpopular method for gaining subscribers to a mailing list that automatically signs up everyone whose e-mail address is known to the mailing list's owner or is provided during online interactions (such as transactions or requests for customer service). Those who are automatically subscribed must then take action to unsubscribe (opt out) if they are not interested in participating. *See also* opt in.

outsourcing   The act of hiring a job out to another company.

outtasking   The act of contracting out part of a job to another company.

packet   A piece of data that carries a destination address with it as it's transmitted over a network such as the Internet. On its arrival at its destination, the packet is reassembled (according to instructions that it also carries with it) with other pieces to form a message or a web page.

page elements   The items that appear on a web page, including, but not limited to, the blocks of text, headlines, buttons, and graphics.

page view   *See* impression.

path   The complete description of the location of a file on a specific computer.

permission marketing   A method of marketing that relies on eliciting interest and consent from people before an attempt is made to deliver the marketing message or promotional material to them. The "permission" approach is the opposite of the "interruption" model traditionally used for broadcast advertising; in that approach, a customer's experience of content (a TV show, for example) is interrupted in order to deliver a marketing message or advertisement.

ping   1. To contact a computer to find out whether it's active. 2. (slang) To contact a person to check in about something.

port   1. To rewrite a program so it runs on another platform. 2. A number that identifies a particular Internet server. 3. One of a computer's input/output plugs.

portal   A site that serves as a gateway to many other sites. A portal might be theme-based (such as FindLaw), general, or customizable (such as those offered by MSN and Excite). *See also* directory; vortal.

post   To make public—for example, by publishing as a message in a discussion group or as a web page. You post a message to a discussion group by sending e-mail; you post a web page to a web server by sending an HTML document.

posting ratio   In an online community (such as an e-mail discussion group), the number of times participants post compared to the number of impressions (or page views). *See also* impression.

project plan   A plan that describes what you want your website to accomplish and how you're going to get there.

public domain   A Work that is available to the public at large without the necessity of getting permission to use it or paying a licensing fee is said to be *in the public domain. See also* copyright; intellectual property; Work.

push technology   A method for sending (or "pushing") content to users. In a client/server scenario—for example, when a web page is viewed—the client (the web browser) requests that the web page be served. In a push scenario, the content is served (perhaps at regular intervals) without request. For example, push can be used to deliver updated news or stock quotes; a news site might push new headlines to people without requiring them to reload the news site's home page.

record   In a database, a set of data that forms complete information. A record contains fields, which contain data; in a relational database, a record exists within a table of records.

redirect page   A page that automatically loads another page—that is, it redirects traffic from the variations of a domain name to the domain name that is the actual location of the website. For instance, people who enter the incorrectly spelled *www.hewlittpackard.com* are taken to the same page as those who enter *www.hp.com*.

redundancy   The intentional repetition of elements within a back-end technology system; redundancy in servers, for example, ensures that if one server goes down another can take over the task of serving the site to users.

relational database   A database in which data is stored in several related tables. Tables contain fields, and each table is linked to other tables through the data stored in one or more fields that the tables have in common.

remote   Describes an entity that exists elsewhere. For example, a remote computer is not near you; it is somewhere else. *See also* local.

request for proposal (RFP)   A written request for a bid from outside sources or vendors you're considering using.

return on investment (ROI)   The proceeds or results garnered from the money paid for a project or venture. The ROI for websites is sometimes intangible (such as greater name recognition) or not easily tied to the website (such as increased purchases at the brick-and-mortar store), but it can also be measured in revenue.

revenue model   The plan for generating income for a business. Examples of revenue models include product sales, ad sales, sponsorship, paid placement, subscription, fee for services, licensing, affiliate programs, and cost savings.

RFP   *See* request for proposal (RFP).

robot   *See* crawler.

ROI   *See* return on investment (ROI).

rollover   *See* mouseover.

router   A computer that transfers packets of data between networks.

scalability   The ability of a site or system to grow as needed.

script   A simple computer program that adds functionality (to a website) that cannot be accomplished using HTML alone. For example, a script is required to make a form on a web page function.

Secure HTTP (HTTPS)   A form of HTTP that allows secure transactions to take place over the Internet. *See also* Hypertext Transfer Protocol (HTTP).

Secure Sockets Layer (SSL)   The protocol used for Secure HTTP. *See also* Secure HTTP (HTTPS).

secure transaction   An interaction (which might involve a monetary exchange) over the Internet that is always encrypted to protect against harm or loss. *See also* encryption; Secure HTTP (HTTPS).

server   1. A computer that provides files or data to clients who request them. 2. A computer that manages files and resources on a network such as a local area network. *See also* client; network.

service-level agreement (SLA)   An agreement between your company and another company detailing the maintenance or technical infrastructure they will provide for your website for a fee.

shareware   Software that is offered by its developer to others for trial use. Those who want to continue to use shareware are generally required to register it and pay a fee. *See also* freeware.

shopping cart   Software that creates the interface between a company's website and its catalog database, allowing customers to choose products to buy, review the items they've chosen, add to or delete items from their order, and make their purchases.

signature file   A file that you can create to be automatically added to the end of every e-mail message you send. This file (sometimes called a *sig file*) can include your company's name, motto, and contact information.

SLA   *See* service-level agreement (SLA).

slander   A spoken message that reflects negatively or falsely on someone or something. *See also* libel.

specifications (specs) Written documentation that describes the precise details of a project such as a website or a back-end system. Specs can also define the content or design elements on a single web page.

spider *See* crawler.

sponsorship A revenue model in which another company supports your company financially in exchange for a prominent mention on your website and perhaps other considerations.

SSL *See* Secure Sockets Layer (SSL).

staging server A computer that mirrors the content and functionality of a live server, allowing web pages to be tested before they become available to the public. Also known as a *development server*. *See also* server.

storyboard A set of sketches or notes that, when combined with other sketches or notes in the same format, illustrates the planned continuity of a website, film or TV program, animation, or multimedia production.

strategic partnership A formal relationship between two or more companies aligning their resources or assets. A strategic partnership can be used to provide greater service or a co-branded product, for example. Also known as a *strategic alliance*.

style guide A document establishing guidelines that ensure a consistent look, tone, and style on your website; an essential element of quality control. Style guides can discuss page specs, graphics, linking, review processes, and editorial and legal matters.

support 1. To provide assistance, as in offering the necessary information to a customer to enable his or her choice of one product over another (purchase support) or as in delivering aid in using a product or service after it has been acquired (product support or technical support). 2. To enable the use of, as when a web browser enables users to experience the functionality of forms (form support) or when a network supports multiple users of a single server.

system administrator A person who organizes, maintains, troubleshoots, and generally manages a computer system such as a server or network. Also called *sysadmin* or *sysop*. *See also* network administrator.

table 1. A compilation of data or information organized into columns and rows on a printed page. 2. A method in HTML for controlling page layout by creating a (usually invisible) grid on a web page into which text and graphics can be placed. 3. A set of records in a database. *See also* relational database.

tags   HTML or XML code, which tells a web browser how to interpret a web page.

target market   The audience you intend to reach regarding your site, product, or service.

template   A prototypical page or document with no data or content in it. On a website, a template shows the layout of the page, into which content can be entered without each page having to be separately designed. In spreadsheets and databases, a template shows the cells or fields and defines the data that can be placed there.

template-driven   Describes a site that uses templates as the basis for laying out content rather than requiring each page to be freshly designed.

thread   A chain of messages on a single topic, written by different people posting to one discussion group.

trademark   A symbol, word, or name that identifies a business or product and is the intellectual property of a company, organization, or individual.

traffic-analysis software   Software that reads a server's log files and massages the data into meaningful information, such as number of pages served or number of site visitors in a given time period. Some traffic-analysis software also provides insight into "clickpaths" or traffic patterns through a site.

transaction system   An automated system for taking orders, accepting payment, and triggering fulfillment of an order. The system might be a secure server and a custom-built payment system or a complete payment system built by a third party.

Uniform Resource Locator (URL)   An address or a location of a document on the World Wide Web. URL is pronounced *you-are-ell*.

unique user   An individual user as identified to traffic-tracking software. It's difficult to track individual users accurately because only individual computers can be counted and several people might use the same computer.

upsell   The offering of an upgraded service or product to customers when they've shown an interest in a lesser service or product. *See also* cross-sell.

URL   *See* Uniform Resource Locator (URL).

usability   Describes a site's ease of use; usability is the sum of feature and content selection, organization, navigation, readability, interface design, page layout, and other factors.

vertical market   A focused, narrow audience with a deep interest in a single topic or a very narrow range of closely related topics. *See also* broad market.

viral marketing   A method of generating excitement and inspiring users to spread the word about a website, product, service, or company.

vortal   A portal-type site that acts as a gateway to other sites that are focused on a specific, vertical-market topic or interest. *See also* portal; vertical market.

WAN   *See* wide area network (WAN).

wanderer   *See* crawler.

web crawler   *See* crawler.

web-safe palette   A palette of 216 colors that will appear in web browsers without dithering and without substantial distortion. *See also* dithering.

wide area network (WAN)   Computers networked together over long distances (across a city or across the nation, for example). A general rule is that if data travels over cables that you don't own (such as the phone company's), the network is a WAN. *See also* local area network (LAN); network.

wireless   Describes access to the Internet via mobile devices such as personal digital assistants (PDAs), cell phones, and other handheld devices that (unlike a desktop PC) are not connected via phone wires at the time the user views online content.

Work   A creation that is intellectual property. Examples include art, writing, code, maps, and music. A Work is owned by its creator unless the creator transfers or assigns ownership. *See also* copyright; trademark.

work for hire   A legal term in copyright matters that refers to work prepared by an employee or contractor within the scope of his or her employment or a work specially commissioned for use as a contribution to a larger work. For a Work to be considered work for hire, both parties must agree to the arrangement in writing.

XML   *See* Extensible Markup Language (XML).

zipped   *See* compressed.

Index

Symbols and Numbers

I

ICONOCAST, 86
ideas, expression of, use of the term, 65,
66–67
illustrations, 295, 299. *See also* graphics
image maps, 210. *See also* graphics
images. *See* graphics
<IMG> tag, 195, 210
impressions, number of, 159, 359–61
income statements, 30
independent contractors, 239. *See also*
contractors
indexes, registering with, 242. *See also* search
engines
index page, 183. *See also* home pages
infographics, 299–300
information
architects, 235, 236
services (IS) departments, 264, 265
technology (IT) departments, 264, 265
innovation, 24
insourcing, 229–31
Integrated Services Digital Network (ISDN),
207, 268
integrators, 238–39
integrity, 16–17, 85, 101–2, 107
intellectual property, 60–61. *See also* legal
issues
IntelliQuest, 101
interaction, with candidates, judging the
quality of, 245–46
interactivity, adding to websites, 221–22
International Data Corporation (IDC), 3,
22–23
international markets, 22–23, 25, 71–72, 92
Internet
"four Cs" of, 294–95
history of, 135–36
Internet Corporation for Assigned Names and
Numbers (ICANN), 92–94
Internet Explorer browser. *See* Microsoft
Internet Explorer browser
Internet News Bureau, 148
Internet presence providers (IPPs), 233
Internet Protocol (IP) addresses, 93, 94

Internet service providers (ISPs), 206, 219,
232–33, 358. *See also* hosting services
backup systems offered by, 118
guest book features offered by, 142
legal issues and, 70
log files provided by, 361–62
managing communications with, 245
servers run by, 257
Internet Wire, 148
interviewing candidates, 245–46
intranets, 230, 231, 306
inventory tracking, 271
investors, 25
invoicing, 250
IPPs (Internet presence providers). *See*
Internet presence providers (IPPs)
ISDN (Integrated Services Digital Network).
See Integrated Services Digital Network
(ISDN)
ISPs (Internet service providers). *See* Internet
service providers (ISPs)
iSyndicate, 304
<I> tag, 200
IvanHoffman.com, 67

J

Japan, 92
Java, 5
JavaScript, 205, 222
job titles, 236
JPEG (Joint Photographics Expert Group)
files. *See* Joint Photographics Expert
Group (JPEG) files
Joint Photographics Expert Group (JPEG)
files, 207, 209. *See also* graphics
Jupiter Communications, 107

K

Keene, Gloria, 241
Keynote Red Alert, 287
keyword searches, 273, 274

411

Index

The manuscript for this book was prepared and submitted to Microsoft Press in electronic form. Text files were prepared using Microsoft Word 97. Pages were composed by Microsoft Press using Adobe PageMaker 6.52 for Windows, with text in Berkely and display type in Frutiger. Composed pages were delivered to the printer as electronic prepress files.

Cover Graphic Designer
Tom Draper

Interior Designer
James D. Kramer

Interior Graphic Artist
Joel Panchot

Principal Compositor
Dan Latimer

Principal Copy Editor
Holly M. Viola

Indexer
Liz Cunningham

Proof of Purchase

0-7356-1275-7

Do not send this card with your registration.
Use this card as proof of purchase if participating in a promotion or
rebate offer on *Managing Your E-Commerce Business, Second Edition*.
Card must be used in conjunction with other proof(s) of payment
such as your dated sales receipt—see offer details.

Managing Your E-Commerce Business, Second Edition

WHERE DID YOU PURCHASE THIS PRODUCT?

CUSTOMER NAME

Microsoft®
mspress.microsoft.com

Microsoft Press, PO Box 97017, Redmond, WA 98073-9830

OWNER REGISTRATION CARD

Register Today!

0-7356-1275-7

Return the bottom portion of this card to register today.

Managing Your E-Commerce Business, Second Edition

FIRST NAME   **MIDDLE INITIAL**   **LAST NAME**

INSTITUTION OR COMPANY NAME

ADDRESS

CITY   **STATE**   **ZIP**

(   )

E-MAIL ADDRESS   **PHONE NUMBER**

U.S. and Canada addresses only. Fill in information above and mail postage-free.
Please mail only the bottom half of this page.

For information about Microsoft Press® products, visit our Web site at

mspress.microsoft.com

Microsoft®